Applied Afro-Communitarian Ethics and Foreign Armed Intervention

"Danny Singh's exploration of just war theory through the lens of Afro-communitarianism is a groundbreaking contribution to military ethics and international law. His detailed analyses of interventions in Rwanda, Sierra Leone, Kosovo, and Iraq offer a refreshing perspective that emphasises communal values and global peace. This book is essential for anyone interested in decolonising the ethics of war and understanding the impact of Afro-communitarian ethics on global conflict resolution."

—Haian Dukhan, Lecturer in Politics and International Relations at Teesside University and a Fellow of the Centre for Syrian Studies at the University of St Andrews, UK

"The book, *Applied Afro-Communitarian Ethics and Foreign Armed Intervention*, duly represents a high-quality original contribution to the field of ethics of foreign military intervention (EFMI). Specifically, the book qualitatively advances an African dimension, which was hitherto largely absent in this area of scholarship. Generally, the new book will strongly resonate within the field of *Ethics of War and Peace*. Thus, I am very pleased to recommend the book to my undergraduates and (post)graduates."

—Badru Ronald Olufemi, Professor of Political Philosophy and Development Ethics, Lead City University, Nigeria

"For several decades, the ethics and legality of war and foreign intervention have been studied from a Western perspective without a thorough analysis of the African agency. This book presents an excellent dimension of understanding these narratives through the lens of Afro-communitarianism. I am delighted with this addition to literature."

—Olayinka Ajala, Reader in Politics and International Relations, Leeds Beckett University, UK

Danny Singh

Applied Afro-Communitarian Ethics and Foreign Armed Intervention

palgrave
macmillan

Danny Singh
Criminology and Policing Faculty
The University of Law
Leeds Campus, UK

ISBN 978-3-031-64109-1   ISBN 978-3-031-64110-7 (eBook)
https://doi.org/10.1007/978-3-031-64110-7

This Palgrave Macmillan imprint is published by the registered company Springer Nature Switzerland AG.
The registered company address is: Gewerbestrasse 11, 6330 Cham, Switzerland

Preface

The purpose of this book takes the normative ethics of war further by examining an approach that is distant to many Western scholars. Just war theory has received prevalent debate since the end of the Cold War era, which is largely due to the increase of intra-state strife and civil wars. Within these conflicts, there have been a variety of foreign armed interventions that have been endorsed by the United Nations, regional organizations such as the African Union, Economic Community of West African States or the North Atlantic Treaty Organization (NATO) and unilateral incursions that are allied with a coalition of willing states. The rules of just war theory focus on ethics to consider when initiating war (*jus ad bellum*), rules of conduct within an armed conflict (*jus in bello*), and justice in the aftermath (*jus post bellum*).

Even with these rules, the geopolitical realities of powerful states cement their influence to assert their national security interests and foreign policy agenda and thus, from a realist or cynical perspective, a just war is merely a war that engages with rules to sell a strategic liberal narrative to populations. To support this postulation, there have been a range of incursions that have not consulted a legitimate authority, which today is notably the United Nations Security Council. This includes NATO's bombing over the former Yugoslavia in 1999, America's invasion of Iraq in 2003, and Russia's incursion of Ukraine in 2022. The military strikes have also marred the credibility of combat operations due to high civilian casualties and thus the *ad bellum* and *in bello* criteria have been violated.

Due to these and many more criticisms of just war theory and international law, this book engages with an alternative non-Western approach when considering permissible forms of violence as a last resort. Afro-communitarianism focuses on retaining and/or repairing communal relations and thus attempts to sway away from geopolitical agenda and instead exercise shared solidarity, compassion, friendliness, benevolence, and forgiveness. This African moral philosophy has been tested with internal struggles of liberation in South Africa and anticolonial movements from European imperialism. However, many contemporary armed conflicts comprise a foreign armed intervention and therefore this book applies Afro-communitarianism with such interventions around the globe. It offers an alternative insight concerning when diplomacy and a settlement fails or would prove fruitless, which can result in permissible violence to rebut violence and form a more harmonious, and less discordant, state of affairs. Once a settlement has been reached, violence should be aborted and processes of reconciliation can commence.

I would like to thank my very supportive and loving family while spending a lot of time writing this book. This includes my beautiful wife (Sonali), and lovely children (Ishaan and Shanaya). My academic career has also been fortified by my father (Gurmit), mother (Palbinder) and brother (Paul), so I also thank you all. On a professional note, I would like to thank Professor Luís Cordeiro-Rodrigues for introducing me to Afro-communitarianism and Amy Invernizzi at Palgrave USA for taking an interest in this book.

The University of Law
Leeds Campus, UK

Danny Singh

CONTENTS

About the Author

Danny Singh is Senior Lecturer at The University of Law. His previous role was Senior Lecturer in Politics and International Relations at Teesside University, where he was Course Leader for MA in International Relations / MA International Relations Applied. Singh holds a PhD in Politics and Criminology. His research interests include police corruption and anti-corruption in war-torn environments, just war and military ethics, international relations theory, and conflict studies. He is author of *The Tripartite Realist War: Analysing Russia's Invasion of Ukraine* (Palgrave), *Investigating Corruption in the Afghan Police Force: Instability and Insecurity in Post-Conflict Societies* (Policy Press), and co-editor of *Comparative Just War Theory: An Introduction to International Perspectives* (Rowman & Littlefield).

List of Abbreviations

ADT	Atrocities Documentation Team
AFISMA	African-led International Support Mission to Mali
AFRC	Armed Forces Revolutionary Council
AMIB	African Mission in Burundi
AMIS	African Mission in Sudan
AMISOM	African Union Mission to Somalia
ANC	African National Congress
APC	All People's Congress
ASF	African Standby Force
AU	African Union
BBC	British Broadcasting Corporation
CDF	Civil Defense Forces
CDR	Coalition for the Defense of the Republic
CIA	Central Intelligence Agency
CJTF	Civilian Joint Task Force
CNDD	National Council for the Defense of Democracy
CNN	Cable Network News
CPA	Coalition Provisional Authority
DDR	Disarmament, Demobilization, and Reintegration
DPKO	Department of Peacekeeping Operations
DRC	Democratic Republic of Congo
ECOMOG	Economic Community of West African States Monitoring Group
ECOWAS	Economic Community of West African States
FAR	Forces Armées Rwandaises [Rwandan Armed Forces]
FDD	Forces for the Defense of Democracy
FNL	National Forces of Liberation

FRELIMO	Liberation Front of Mozambique
FRODEBU	Front for Democracy in Burundi
G8	Group of Eight
GDP	Gross Domestic Product
HDI	Human Development Index
HSRA	Hindustan Socialist Republican Association
ICC	International Criminal Court
ICG	International Crisis Group
ICISS	International Commission on Intervention and State Sovereignty
ICRC	International Committee of the Red Cross
ICTR	International Criminal Tribunal for Rwanda
ICTY	International Criminal Tribunal for the former Yugoslavia
IDPs	Internally Displaced Persons
IGAD	Intergovernmental Authority on Development
IHL	International Humanitarian Law
IMF	International Monetary Fund
ISIS	Islamic State of Iraq and the Levant/Syria
IS-K	Islamic State Khorasan
KDF	Kenya Defense Forces
KFOR	Kosovo Force
KLA	Kosovo Liberation Army
LOAC	Law of Armed Conflict
MENA	Middle East and North Africa
MEND	Movement for the Emancipation of the Niger Delta
MICEMA	Economic Community of West African States Mission in Mali
MK	uMkhonto we Sizwe (Spear of the Nation)
MOCKY	Movement of Concerned Kono Youth
MPLA	People's Movement for the Liberation of Angola
MRND	National Revolutionary Movement for Development
NATO	North Atlantic Treaty Organization
NCDDR	National Committee for DDR
NDDC	Niger Delta Development Commission
NDPVF	Niger Delta People's Volunteer Force
NGO	Non-governmental organization
NIAC	Non-international armed conflict
NMLA	National Movement for the Liberation of Azawad
NPFL	National Patriotic Front of Liberia
NPRC	National Provisional Ruling Council
OAU	Organization of African Unity
OIF	Operation Iraqi Freedom
ONUB	United Nations Operation in Burundi
ORHA	Office for Reconstruction and Humanitarian Affairs

OSC	Operation Safe Corridor
OSCE	Organization for Security and Co-operation in Europe
P–5	Permanent Members of the United Nations Security Council
PAIGC	African Party for the Independence of Guinea and Cape Verde
PAP	Post-Amnesty Program
PARMEHUTU	Party of the Movement and Hutu Emancipation
PDD	Presidential Decision Directive
PMCs	Private Military Companies
PMF	Popular Mobilization Forces
PoWs	Prisoners of War
R2P	Responsibility to Protect
RGF	Rwandan Government Forces
RPF	Rwandan Patriotic Front
RTLM	Radio Télévision Libre des Mille Collines
RTS	Radio Television Serbia
RUF	Revolutionary United Front
RwF	Rwandan Franc
SAP	Structural Adjustment Program
SAPSD	South African Protection Support Detachment
SDF	Syrian Defense Forces
SFRY	Socialist Federal Republic of Yugoslavia
SHIRBRIG	Standby High Readiness Brigade
SLM/A	Sudan Liberation Movement / Army
SLPP	Sierra Leone People's Party
SNA	USC/Somali National Alliance
SNM	Somali National Movement
SSA	USC/Somali Salvation Alliance
SSR	Security Sector Reform
TRAFIPRO	Work–Fidelity–Progress in Rwanda
TRC	Truth and Reconciliation Commission
UK	United Kingdom
UN	United Nations
UNAMIR	United Nations Assistance Mission for Rwanda
UNAMSIL	United Nations Mission in Sierra Leone
UNITAF	United Task Force
UNMIK	United Nations Mission in Kosovo
UNMIS	United Nations Mission in South Sudan
UNOMSIL	United Nations Observer Mission in Sierra Leone
UNOMUR	United Nations Observer Mission Uganda–Rwanda
UNOSOM	United Nations Operation in Somali

UNPROFOR	United Nations Protection Force
UNTS	United Nations Treaty Series
UPRONA	Union for National Progress
US	United States
USC	United Somali Congress
WMD	Weapons of Mass Destruction
WSB	West Side Boys

CHAPTER 1

Introduction

Introduction

This introductory chapter will cover the main themes of contemporary just war theory. Christian concepts of this theory were debatably derived from the theological notions of Aquinas who revised Augustine's earlier interpretation.[1] Thomas Aquinas contended that a just war can be permitted from an institutional authority and it must be waged for just means, namely, self-defense and a restoration of peace, rather than self-gains or targeting innocent civilians to qualify as a just cause, with peace being the primary and right military intention.[2] Subsequently, contemporary notions of engaging in warfare (*jus ad bellum*), conduct within a conflict (*jus in bello*), and justice in the aftermath (*jus post bellum*) will be applied to international law, namely, the United Nations (UN) Charter and Geneva

[1] Rory Cox, "The Ethics of War up to Thomas Aquinas," in *The Oxford Handbook of Ethics of War*, edited by Seth Lazar and Helen Frowe (Oxford: Oxford University Press, 2018), p. 114.

[2] Scott Sheeran and Catherine Kent, "Protection of Civilians, Responsibility to Protect, and Humanitarian Intervention," in *Protection of Civilians*, edited by Haidi Willmot, Ralph Mamiya, Scott Sheeran and Marc Weller (Oxford: Oxford University Press, 2016), p. 31.

D. Singh, *Applied Afro-Communitarian Ethics and Foreign Armed Intervention*, https://doi.org/10.1007/978-3-031-64110-7_1

Conventions.[3] With this historical outlook, I will demonstrate that war theory and legal conventions reflect Global North values, and I make a case for decolonizing the ethics of war with a different approach: Afro-communitarian ethics. The final part will provide a summary of the chapters contained within the manuscript.

Just War Theory

Just war theory concerns the morality of engaging in warfare, the conduct in war, and justice—including democratization and reconstruction—in the aftermath to terminate war.[4] The rules of initiating war, known as *jus ad bellum*, from a traditionalist just war perspective rest on the initiator of war presenting a just cause, the right intention, and demonstrating a reasonable chance of victory, conducting violence as a last resort, a legitimate authority authorizing force, and proportionality to avoid the unintended consequences of war.[5] The initiation of warfare can be separated from rules of conduct within armed conflict (*jus in bello*) and justice after a conflict has ceased (*jus post bellum*).

Traditionalists of just war theory tend to respect contemporary international law and argue that the laws of armed conflict must apply.[6] Under this thought, states can wage war to secure their national defense, with purposes to defend other states, or intervene to stop shocking heinous crimes to humanity.[7] Walzer's comprehension of the legalistic paradigm conforms with the Charter of the United Nations, namely, Article 2 (4), and an international society of independent states to contend that all sovereign states are equal and are united by laws and rules.[8] Only aggression can permit a war as a pre-emptive retort when any imminent threat or the use of force is presented by one state against another to authorize

[3] Danny Singh, "Undertaking Critical Legal Theory to Examine Just War Intervention: A Smokescreen for Political Ambitions," in *Comparative Just War Theory: An Introduction to International Perspectives*, edited by Luís Cordeiro-Rodrigues and Danny Singh (Lanham, MD: Roman & Littlefield, 2020), pp. 61–79.

[4] Helen Frowe, *The Ethics of War and Peace: An Introduction*, 2nd ed. (Oxon: Routledge, 2016), pp. 25, 75, 99, 239.

[5] Amy E. Eckert, *Outsourcing War: The Just War Tradition in the Age of Military Privatization* (Ithaca, NY: Cornell University Press, 2016), pp. 36–38.

[6] Michael Walzer, *Just and Unjust Wars: A Moral Argument with Historical Illustrations* (New York: Basic Books, 1977).

[7] Michael Walzer, *Just and Unjust Wars: A Moral Argument with Historical Illustrations*, 5th ed. (New York: Basic Books, 2006), 107.

[8] Walzer, *Just and Unjust Wars*, 1977.

self-defense by the victim state and other members of the international society.[9] This centers on the role of the United Nations (UN) Security Council to authorize sanctions, the use of force, and individual or collective self-defense.[10] A regional arrangement can be sought to conduct sanctions and the legitimate use of force, but it must seek permission from the United Nations Security Council.[11] In other words, under contemporary international law, the United Nations Security Council is the legitimate authority—as Aquinas spoke of—to sanction the initiation of war *jus ad bellum*. The traditionalist school of just war theory shares traits with the theory of liberalism to advance transborder laws, protection, rules, and freedoms.

Once a war has been sanctioned, the conduct within it must comply with the principles of the laws of armed conflict *jus in bello*. These include military necessity, chivalry, distinction, and proportionality. Military necessity permits a national armed force to attack oppositional combatants with targeted attacks for the purpose of significantly weakening that side for a quick surrender—so thus "*lawfully* kill," injure soldiers, and "destroy property."[12] Justified military targets include belligerent forces, military barracks, weapons storage cache or center, military logistics, and communications that present a clear military advantage.[13] Chivalry is associated with honor regarding the declaration of battle and the means of which it is fought that is based on a reciprocal risk of soldier's lives from both sides of a conflict.[14] Distinction is based on distinguishing between active combatants and noncombatants (civilians and service workers) so that the

[9] Walzer, *Just and Unjust Wars*, 1977, pp. 61–62.

[10] See Articles 41, 42, and 51 of the Charter of the United Nations respectively. The literal rule of international law prohibits the use of force as per Article 2 (4) of the Charter of the United Nations, and the only exception rests on self-defense (Article 51). Yet, humanitarian intervention that involves the encroachment of a state's territory without their permission (to allegedly save lives) clearly violates the literal rule on the use of force in international law. Humanitarian intervention would violate Article 2 (4) of the Charter of the United Nations, and this term is not mentioned in the Charter. Therefore, traditionalist's interpretation of the legalistic paradigm also considers these rules.

[11] See Article 53 (1) of the Charter of the United Nations.

[12] Ian Henderson, *Law of Targeting: Military Objectives, Proportionality and Precautions in Attack under Additional Protocol I* (Leiden: Martinus Nijhoff Publishers, 2009), p. 44.

[13] Protocol Additional to the Geneva Conventions of 12 August 1949, and Relating to the Protection of Victims of International Armed Conflicts (Protocol I), *Additional Protocol I*, Chapter I, Article 52 (2), June 8, 1977.

[14] Jens David Ohlin, "Sharp Wars Are Brief," in *Weighing Lives in War*, edited by Jens David Ohlin, Larry May and Claire Finkelstein (Oxford: Oxford University Press, 2017), p. 71, pp. 58–76.

latter are not targeted in warfare.[15] Proportionality shares a complementary relationship with military necessity because it permits the destruction of oppositional military infrastructure, but it prohibits the targeting, and "unreasonable" excess, of civilians and private property.[16] These principles guide the ethics and legality of warfare. International humanitarian law has sheltered the laws of armed conflict with the Four Geneva Conventions by protecting inactive combatants on land and sea, prisoners of war, and civilians and private property from armed conflict.[17]

In relation to *jus in bello*, the work of Walzer contends that there is moral equality between combatants, and fighting for a purported wrong side does not involve wrongdoing.[18] To put in another way, traditionalists concentrate on the moral equality of all combatants, irrespective of they are fighting for just or unjust reasons. When required, intervention is acceptable to rebut an immoral combatant and is worth the risk.[19] In contrast, revisionists argue that noncombatants can be tolerably targeted if they are considered liable. This would mean that Walzer's perspective on the moral equality of all combatants is flawed because innocent combatants, which contain a military force who justly participate in a war, cannot be permitted targets.[20]

Justice in the aftermath of war (*jus post bellum*) can include post-conflict reconstruction, statebuilding, Security Sector Reform (SSR), and post-war justice. The former components rest on international actors attempting to rebuild vital state infrastructure and engage with the reform of a new civil service, police, and judicial staff for state functionality that can avert a relapse into conflict as part of a "no exit without strategy" approach.[21] Within such a structure, elections and economic liberalization form part of liberal peacebuilding. The latter concerns the promotion of accountability either with retributive or restorative forms of justice. For example,

[15] International Committee of the Red Cross, "Rule 1. The Principle of Distinction between Civilians and Combatants."

[16] Jeroen van den Boogaard, *Proportionality in International Humanitarian Law: Refocusing the Balance in Practice* (Cambridge: Cambridge University Press, 2023), pp. 267–268. However, it has viably been argued that the calculation of military necessity and "likely civilian casualties" is "ambiguous" (Neta C. Crawford, *Accountability for Killing: Moral Responsibility for Collateral Damage in America's Post-9/11 Wars* (Oxford, Oxford University Press, 2013), p. 170.

[17] International Committee of the Red Cross, *Four Geneva Conventions*, August 12, 1949.

[18] Michael Walzer, *Just and Unjust Wars* (Harmondsworth: Penguin, 1977), p. 21.

[19] Walzer, *Just and Unjust Wars*, 1977.

[20] Cécile Fabre, *Cosmopolitan War* (Oxford: Oxford University Press, 2012).

[21] Roland Paris, "Saving Liberal Peacebuilding," *Review of International Studies*, Vol. 36, No. 2 (April 2010), p. 342, pp. 337–365.

territorial *ad hoc* criminal tribunals were established to deal with war crimes, crimes against humanity, and genocide in the former Yugoslavia, Rwanda, and Sierra Leone in the mid-1990s and early 2000s as part of retributive justice;[22] and an amnesty for perpetrators during the apartheid era in South Africa was applied in exchange for truth, reconciliation, and forgiveness in 1995 as part of restorative justice.[23]

The three forms of *ad bellum*, *in bello*, and *post bellum* as the morality of war can be measured from a variety of military and philosophical ethics that include theological, consequentialist, and realist schools of thought.[24] Various military interventions, such as Bosnia, Afghanistan, and Iraq, have been analyzed and evaluated and criticized from a Western and, especially, liberal perspective.[25]

The Way of *Ubuntu*: Afro-communitarian Ethics

In this book, I analyze foreign armed interventions from another perspective. The approach is Afro-communitarianism that contains a segment of *Ubuntu* used in sub-Saharan Africa. In southern Africa, *Ubuntu* can be translated to constitute humanness and covers the coexistence and interdependence of human beings, solidarity, and communalism that is embedded in African indigenous cultures.[26] Although *Ubuntu* has been associated with southern parts of Africa, Metz has argued that these communal ethics grounded on humanness and belonging is "universally" applicable.[27] For *Ubuntu*, the quality of human beings is based on their interconnectivity with fellow people, meaning that children are not solely raised by their parents, but by the entire community because "each hand washes the

[22] William A. Schabas, *The UN International Criminal Tribunals: The Former Yugoslavia, Rwanda and Sierra Leone* (Cambridge: Cambridge University Press, 2006).

[23] Promotion of National Unity and Reconciliation, Act 34, December 1, 1995; Kimberly Spiers, *Restorative Justice in South Africa's Truth and Reconciliation Commission* (Winnipeg: University of Manitoba, 2008).

[24] Brian Orend, *The Morality of War* (Peterborough, ON: Broadview Press, 2006); Valerie Morkevičius, *Realist Ethics: Just War Traditions as Power Politics* (Cambridge: Cambridge University Press, 2018).

[25] Roland Paris, *At War's End: Building Peace after Conflict* (Cambridge: Cambridge University Press, 2004).

[26] Joseph Mukuni and Josiah Tlou, *Understanding Ubuntu for Enhancing Intercultural Communications* (Hershey, PA: IGI Global, 2021), p. 161.

[27] Thaddeus Metz, "A Life of Struggle as Ubuntu," in *Nelson Rolihlahla Mandela: Decolonial Ethics of Liberation and Servant Leadership* (Trenton, NJ: Africa World Press, 2015), p. 3.

other."[28] Community ideals are steered by values that the community embrace, which augments "social solidarity."[29] These values are learned in the community. As part of this normative moral philosophy, the utmost good is positive community relations via shared solidarity, identity, caring, and goodwill that result in social harmony and friendship.[30] Based on these ethics grounded on communal values, the moral theory of Afro-communitarianism focuses on community and peaceful relationships. Therefore, friendly-like relations must be prioritized to exhaust friendly alternatives rather than resorting to violence. Afro-communitarianism promotes dialogue to avert national violence and military conflict.[31] This is the deontological perspective of Afro-communitarianism.

However, under Afro-communitarianism, violence is only permissible from an initiator of fighting as a last resort if there are no longer friendly alternatives to accomplish a less discordant situation and more harmonious state of affairs. If undertaking violence after friendly measures do not resolve violence, for example, peaceful demonstrations, negotiations, and/or diplomacy, then an initiator of violence that intends to rebut enmity violence must seek the desired ends of a harmonious and less discordant state of affairs.[32] This is the consequentialist version of Afro-communitarianism. It can permit stages of hierarchized violence (sabotage, guerrilla warfare, terrorism, and open revolution) if friendly alternatives fail to rebut violence.

For example, Nelson Rolihlahla Mandela applied *Ubuntu* ethics with peaceful protests, but it failed to rebut white-government discrimination and violence of the National Party's apartheid policy. After the March 21, 1960, Sharpeville Massacre of police officers shooting and killing 69 unarmed protestors against oppressive laws in a black township,[33] the

[28] Vuyisile Mslia, *Ubuntu: Shaping the Current Workplace with (African) Wisdom* (Randburg: Knowres Publishing, 2015), p. 4.

[29] Ndjodi Ndeunyema, *Re-Invigorating Ubuntu through Water: A Human Right to Water under the Namibian Constitution* (Pretoria: Pretoria University Law Press, 2021), p. 79.

[30] Thaddeus Metz, "Toward an African Moral Theory," *Journal of Political Philosophy*, 15, no. 3 (2007): 321–341.

[31] Kwasi Wiredu, *Cultural Universals and Particulars: An African Perspective* (Bloomington, IN: Indiana University Press, 1997).

[32] Thaddeus Metz, "Ubuntu as a Moral Theory and Human Rights in South Africa," *African Human Rights Law Journal*, 11, no. 2 (2011): 532–559.

[33] United Nations South Africa, "The Blood we Sacrificed was Worth it – Sharpeville Massacre," *United Nations South Africa*, July 17, 2021. https://southafrica.un.org/en/135812-%E2%80%9C-blood-we-sacrificed-was-worth-it%E2%80%9D-sharpeville-massacre.

African National Congress (ANC) was banned by the Unlawful Organizations Act. However, Mandela established the uMkhonto we Sizwe (Spear of the Nation (MK)) paramilitary wing of the African National Congress in 1961 to move to violence, namely, "symbolic sabotage," and fight against the white South African government.[34] Subsequently, MK combatants targeted government infrastructure with sabotage and then entered the next stages of violence: guerilla warfare and debatably terrorism.[35] From a consequentialist position, the violence initiated by Mandela was justified because peaceful protests had failed, and an oppressive government had to be rebutted to form a better harmonious and less discordant state of affairs.[36] The deontological perspective of Afro-communitarianism would be against violence in all circumstances—but this is not the approach used to assess foreign armed intervention in this book because such an incursion usually involves violence, for example, humanitarian intervention, international aggression, self and collective defense, collective security, and peacekeeping operation.

In foreign armed intervention like Iraq, Rwanda, or Sierra Leone, there is no real Afro-communitarian consequentialist analysis, which is what gap this book fills. Perspectives from the Global North merely provide a limited perspective on traditional and revisionist perspectives on just war theory and humanitarian intervention in incursions involving a variety of foreign actors—and what should have been done, for example, with Iraq. Non-Western perspectives to analyze wars continually study global politics.[37] The book will analyze a range of interventions, involving foreign actors to provide a non-Western discussion on the morality and ethics of war and its efforts to establish a more harmonious, and less discordant, state of affairs between the belligerents fighting in the conflict and communal relations in the aftermath.

By looking at these interventions with this non-Western perspective, I contribute with new academic arguments to assess it. I also introduce new concepts for political discussion based on the morality of warfare and efforts to formulate a less discordant, and more harmonious, state of

[34] Janet Cherry, *Umkhonto weSizwe: A Jacana Pocket History* (Auckland Park: Jacana Media, 2011), pp. 13–15.

[35] Metz, "A Life of Struggle as Ubuntu," pp. 1–20.

[36] The same can be argued from a range of anti-colonial movements.

[37] Boaventura de Sousa Santos, *The End of the Cognitive Empire: The Coming of Age of Epistemologies of the South* (Durham, NC: Duke University Press, 2018).

affairs between belligerents. In this way, *Ubuntu* as part of Afro-communitarian moral philosophy will be applied to a variety of foreign armed interventions to test whether they resulted in (1) a more harmonious state of affairs, (2) a less discordant situation, and/or (3) both 1 and 2.

The purpose of the book will serve an alternative, and non-Western, approach to the morality of war and efforts to promote sustainable peace in the aftermath of conflict between warring belligerent parties. Statebuilders can also learn from the application of Afro-communitarianism. During interventions, statebuilders can better strategize longer peaceful relations rather than engaging in short-term political bargaining in exchange for an immediate cessation of hostilities or fighting an international enemy.

Contents and Summary of Chapters

Chapter 1: Introduction

The introductory chapter has covered some definitional terminology of just war theory and Afro-communitarianism. This will be followed by a list of the forthcoming chapters and a summary of what each chapter entails.

Chapter 2: Principles of Afro-communitarianism and Permissible Violence

The theoretical chapter will cover the just war tradition and relates it to community values, mutual friendships, shared solidarity, goodwill, identity, and social harmony that frame the ideals of Afro-communitarian ethics. The opening part will focus on the reason for the applied project to pursue an analysis of foreign armed intervention and its relationship with Afro-communitarian moral philosophy. I will explain *Ubuntu* ethics and the African dialogical perspective to conflict. Subsequently, I will exhibit when violence is morally justifiable from the consequentialist Afro-communitarian perspective. Several sub-Saharan African settings address three principal consequentialist points regarding the ethics on warfare and scenarios of permissible violence to rebut enmity-based behavior with acceptable violence. Under this approach, violence is only morally permissible if it leads to a less disharmonious situation or a more harmonious state of affairs that may involve temporary interests that become dominant ones later. When friendly alternatives are exhausted and/or absent, the objectives from the responder(s) to violence must outweigh the outcome of actions (in consequentialist terms) and principally envisage to promote a better state of affairs (that is less discordant and more harmonious).[38] When the resort to violence becomes a necessary condition to rebut violence and bring a more harmonious and less disputatious condition, there are four types of hierarchized acceptable forms of violence that can be initiated, which includes sabotage, guerrilla warfare, terrorism, and open revolution.[39]

Following this discussion on consequentialist Afro-communitarian ethics, this moral philosophy is applied to several comparative instances of acceptable indiscriminate violence against soldiers and civilians. The context of the African National Congress and its MK military wing in South Africa eventually initiating peaceful negotiations after almost four decades of apartheid rule will illustrate the four types and stages of permissible violence. This is followed by several anti-colonial rebellions. The emancipatory movements include the artido Africano para a Independência de Guiné e Cabo Verde [African Party for the Independence of Guinea and Cape Verde] (PAIGC) fighters in Guinea-Bissau that captured Portuguese soldiers, Movimento Popular de Libertação de Angola [People's Movement for the Liberation of Angola] (MPLA) forces in Angola that led the War of Independence against the occupation of Portuguese armed forces during the War of Independence, the Frente de Libertação de Moçambique [Liberation Front of Mozambique] (FRELIMO) combatants in Mozambique also fighting against oppressive Portuguese colonial rule, and the Mau Mau rebellion uprising comprising guerilla warfare in Kenya against British colonial rule. Moreover, the context of peaceful protests against British colonial rule in India that resulted in aggressive retaliation from the British Indian Army and violent reprisal from Hindustan Socialist Republican Association (HSRA) revolutionary organization will be covered.

The failed attempt of the Maji Maji rebellion of tribal former Tanganyika against German East African occupation in Ruanda-Urundi will also be covered. These contexts on the struggle for liberation and anti-colonialization intend to generate the principles of Afro-communitarianism

[38] Bernard Matolino, *Afro-Communitarian Democracy* (Lanham, MD: Lexington Books, 2019), p. 63.

[39] Allison Drew, "Visions of Liberation: The Algerian War of Independence and Its South African Reverberations," *Review of African Political Economy*, 42, no. 143 (2015): 22–43.

when responding to foreign interventions, which include the motives of belligerents (involving insurgencies and open revolution), for the theoretical application of Afro-communitarian consequentialist ethics to the subsequent chapters. It must be noted that these contexts cover internal opposition and forms of violence against an oppressive and discriminate white-government in South Africa and colonialization in the other settings that were met with justified violence against the apartheid-based racial institutionalized segregation and foreign occupational armed forces (regarding colonialism). These contexts have been assessed before with similar ethics, but this book takes this non-Western, and specifically African, ethical debate further by applying and testing Afro-communitarian consequentialist ethics to foreign armed intervention (rather than internal struggles or colonialism). Finally, I will underline some potential objections to the consequentialist principles defended in this chapter from the deontological position (that does not warrant violence in any circumstances because it will have to contain or further a discordant state of affairs—even for the short term) and respond to them.

Chapter 3: Rwanda, the United Nations, France, and Weak Intervention

This chapter will initially, and briefly, provide the longer-term causes of ethnic conflict and salience between Hutu and Tutsi groups from colonial influences and Hutu governance fighting with Tutsi refugees (the Rwandan Patriotic Front (RPF)).[40] Subsequently, the intervention from the 1993 United Nations Assistance Mission for Rwanda (UNAMIR) is covered. This is followed by the shorter-term causes of the genocide in the summer of 1994, namely, the assassination of the Rwandan and Burundi Hutu presidents (Juvénal Habyarimana and Cyprien Ntaryamira) with both sides blaming one another, and weak mandate of the UN peacekeeping force without authorization to defend civilians in danger.[41] The main part will apply the principles of Afro-communitarianism to demonstrate the failed attempts of peaceful negotiations with the Arusha Accord to end the

[40] Tom Streissguth, *Rwanda in Pictures* (Minneapolis, MN: Lerner Publishing Group, 2008), p. 28.

[41] Linda Melvern, "United Nations Observer Mission Uganda – Rwanda (UNOMUR) and United Nations Assistance Mission for Rwanda I (UNAMIR I)," in *The Oxford Handbook of United Nations Peacekeeping Operations*, edited by Joachim A. Koops, Norrie MacQueen, Thierry Tardy and Paul D. Williams (Oxford: Oxford University Press, 2015), p. 468.

civil war, the failed call of UNAMIR's commander (Roméo Dallaire) for more troops and the RPF's permissibility conducting violence to rebut enmity-behavior from the Hutu government and backed *Interahamwe*. The application of these African consequentialist ethics is applied to the RPF and the United Nations. It will be argued that the militia attempted to create a less discordant state of affairs but a more harmonious state of affairs did not initially commence when Paul Kagame seized power. This is because victor's justice was debatably exercised to, namely, punish Hutu *genocidaires* over RPF crimes.[42] Moreover, the UN peacekeeping force failed to conduct permissible force due to weak mandates and the lack of political will from major powers resulted in the removal of international troops from the country.[43]

Chapter 4: ECOMOG, PMCs, the United Nations, and Britain in Sierra Leone

This chapter commences with coverage of the diamond trade in West Africa and the mobilization of Charles Taylor's National Patriotic Front of Liberia to control Sierra Leone's southern diamond mines and support of the rebel army, the Revolutionary United Front (RUF).[44] Foday Saybana Sankoh headed the RUF that protested against the government by ordering killings, systematic rapes, forced abduction and labor for further recruits, diamond mining (for funding), and the amputation of civilians.[45] The Sierra Leonean government comprised of single-party elections. Moreover, unemployment was high, the economy was stagnated, and jobless youths were prey to corrupt political elites to work as thugs during political campaigns in exchange for drugs.[46] It will be argued that the

[42] Victor Peskin, "Beyond Victor's Justice? The Challenge of Prosecuting the Winners at the International Criminal Tribunals for the Former Yugoslavia and Rwanda," *Journal of Human Rights*, Vol. 4, No. 2 (2005), pp. 225–226.

[43] Tamar Gutner, *International Organizations in World Politics* (Thousand Oaks, CA: Sage, 2017), p. 73.

[44] Chukwunyere Kamalu, *The Little African History Book: Black Africa from the Origins of Humanity to the Assassination of Lumumba and the Turn of the 20th Century* (London: Orisa Press, 2007), p. 159.

[45] Chetan Bhatt, "Contemporary Geopolitics and 'Alterity' Research," in *Researching Race and Racism*, edited by Martin Bulmer and John Solomos (London: Routledge, 2004), p. 24.

[46] Elizabeth Lavallie, "Gender Equality in Political and Public Decision-making," in *Women and Men in Partnership for Post-Conflict Reconstruction: Report of the Sierra Leone National Consultation Freetown, Sierra Leone, 21–24 May 2001*, edited by Rawwida Baksh-Soodeen and Linda Etchart (London: Commonwealth Secretariat, 2002), p. 39.

forms of violence conducted by the RUF were not permissible, under Afro-communitarianism, to rebut a corrupt and failing government because the attacks mainly harmed civilians with violence that falls outside of the four permitted forms of violence. In addition, most RUF activity was debatably for socioeconomic, rather than ideological or political, reasons. Subsequently, the chapter provides coverage of the United Nations intervention in 1999 and attempts with a ceasefire from the Lomé Peace Accord, disarmament, and later support from Britain (a former colony) with Operation Palliser ending the civil war.[47] The attempts from the United Nations were predominantly peaceful and warranted a more harmonious state of affairs, and Britain's involvement was more forceful with permissible violence to rebut RUF enmity-behavior—even if for the main motive of rescuing British forces held hostage from the West Side Boys—and bring about a less harmonious state of affairs.

Chapter 5: NATO's Intervention for Kosovo

This chapter commences with coverage on the horrors that occurred during the Bosnian civil war that alarmed European powers and the United States. These states did not want another massacre to occur in the former Yugoslavia. The central focus engages with the conflict between the non-violent Kosovo League and subsequent armed Kosovo Liberation Army (KLA) (weapons obtained from Albania and fighting for independence) and the Serbian security forces within the autonomous province that was still claimed under Serbian state territorial sovereignty. The Serbian President, Slobodan Milošević, wanted to focus on conflicts to avoid internal problems and appeal to rural elder nationalists. The Organization for Security and Co-operation in Europe (OSCE) implemented an observer mission that reduced the violence, but the Rambouillet negotiations advocating potential Kosovo independence collapsed. Fighting reignited between KLA and the Serbian police forces within Kosovo. The North Atlantic Treaty Organization (NATO) did not want another Bosnia situation so decided to conduct a short bombing campaign—without UN Security Council approval—that would force Milošević to sign the

[47] Larry J. Woods and Timothy R. Reese, "Military Interventions in Sierra Leone: Lessons from a Failed State," *The Long War Series Occasional Paper 28* (Fort Leavenworth, KS: Combat Studies Institute Press, 2008), pp. 60, 73.

Rambouillet Agreement, but Serbian-based ethnic cleansing of Kosovar Albanians exacerbated. Milošević did not sign and NATO continued the aerial bombing of Serbia and Kosovo for 78 days until Milošević ceded.

After the dynamics of the conflict is discussed, it will be argued that the initial non-violence from the Kosovo League attempted to build parallel state systems as a response to Serbian discrimination, but KLA belligerents engaged in the sabotage of Serbian forces and civilians were also killed. The chapter will exhibit those diplomatic efforts with OSCE observers and later force from NATO followed *Ubuntu* stages of violence from a political settlement to sabotage targeting Serbian military and communication constellations. However, civilian workers were also killed from NATO airstrikes, and the independent Kosovo still contains a disharmonious state of affairs between Kosovar Albanians and Kosovar Serbs.

Chapter 6: United States and Allied Unilateral Intervention in Iraq

This chapter covers an international intervention that was part of foreign policy aligned to the war on terror. However, the intervention in Iraq differed from Afghanistan because the United States failed to attain direct authorization from the UN Security Council. The United States had no permission from a legitimate authority, namely, the UN, but formed a coalition of willing states to support the war on terror.[48] In March 2003, the intervention commenced to topple the Saddam Hussein government on the premise of acquiring weapons of mass destruction (WMD).[49] Despite "joint Coalition and Iraqi military operations," the aftermath of the intervention and efforts of promoting de-Ba'athification into a new Iraq political system failed to avert increasing sectarian violence, killings, and kidnapping.[50] Therefore, when assessed with Afro-communitarian consequentialist ethics, the intervention from the US and Coalition Forces did not attempt to foster better friendship relations, and it resulted in a

[48] Matt Peterson, "Did Iraq Ever Become a Just War? As Contours Evolved, the Morality of Fighting Did Too," *The Atlantic*, March 24, 2018.

[49] Paul Taylor and Devon Curtis, "The United Nations," in *The Globalization of World Politics: An Introduction to International Relations*, 6th ed., edited by John Bayliss, Steve Smith and Patricia Owens (Oxford: Oxford University Press, 2014), p. 314.

[50] Anthony H. Cordesman with Emma R. Davies, *Iraq's Insurgency and the Road to Civil Conflict – Volume I* (Westport, CT: Praeger Security International, 2008), p. 355.

less harmonious state of affairs. UN weapons inspectors did not find any functional WMD in Iraq,[51] and violence intensified.

Peaceful relations and diplomacy were not fully compliant because geopolitical interests triggered the robust intervention, which is non-compliant with Afro-communitarian ethics. In addition, the social identity of the US intervention and means of violence undermined Afro-communitarianism. This was because geopolitical interests of overthrowing a despot and forming a democracy for better oil relations within the Middle East were debatably the main objectives of major Western powers,[52] rather than bringing a less discordant state of affairs. The intervention in Iraq has exacerbated transnational terrorism with the rise of Islamic State and the 2006 "Surge" attempted to defeat terrorist groups that resulted in an immediate 43 percent increase in violence.[53] Several splinters of Islamic State have emerged, functioning in the Middle East and Asia. This includes the Khorasan Chapter that has been active since 2015 in Iran, Afghanistan, Pakistan, and India.[54] Hence, the foreign armed intervention in Iraq has resulted in a heightened dissonant state of affairs that is at odds with Afro-communitarian ethics.

Chapter 7: African-Led Military Interventions

The previous contexts focus on the role of foreign armed intervention from Western actors in a variety of settings, including African (Rwanda and Sierra Leone) that are analyzed with applied Afro-communitarian ethics. The purpose of this chapter is to evaluate the role of Afro-communitarian ethics in a selection of African countries without robust Western intervention. This will cover the roles of the African Union (AU) and the Economic Community of West African States (ECOWAS). The AU has the legitimate authority to endorse, and engage in, military intervention on behalf of member states as per Article 4 (h) of its Constitutive Act of the AU and ECOWAS functions as a regional security organization that can attain authorization from the UN Security Council as per Article 53 (1) of the

[51] United Nations Security Council Resolution 1441, "A Final Opportunity to Comply with its Disarmament Obligations," UN Doc. S/RES/1441, November 8, 2002, adopted 4644th meeting.

[52] Singh, "Undertaking Critical Legal Theory", p. 74.

[53] Hall Gardner, *Averting Global War: Regional Challenges, Overextension, and Options for American Strategy* (New York: Palgrave Macmillan, 2007), p. 73.

[54] Center for Strategic and International Studies, "Islamic State Khorasan (IS-K)," 2018.

UN Charter. Several AU military interventions within Africa will be analyzed to consider the implications of whether Afro-communitarian ethics or Western legal and political theories drive such interventions. The contexts evaluated comprise the AU in Burundi, Darfur, and Somalia and ECOWAS in Mali and Liberia.

In 2003, in Burundi, the AU Mission in Burundi was deployed as a regional peacekeeping mission at the closing stages of the Burundian Civil War. A total of 2,870 troops located from South Africa, Ethiopia, and Mozambique entered Burundi for one year, with South Africa remaining once a UN operation succeeded the African Union mission.[55] The Civil War (1993–2005) comprised protracted ethnic animosity between Hutus and Tutsis, resulting in an estimated 300,000 deaths and the displacement of 1.2 million people.[56] Like this succession by a UN peacekeeping operation, in 2004, the AU deployed a regional peacekeeping force in Darfur to assist the UN Mission in Sudan. The troop size increased from 150 to an estimated 7,000 troops that included Nigerian, Rwandan, and Senegalese personnel.[57] In late December 2007, the AU mission was replaced by the United Nations.

From March 2007 to March 2022, the African Union deployed a large regional peacekeeping operation, consisting of over 20,000 troops, in Somalia.[58] This was approved by the UN Security Council to help the Somali administration fight the al-Qaeda-supported al-Shabaab insurgency attempting to overthrow the weak government.[59] In addition, the mandate included initiating a National Security Plan, training the national security forces, and allowing a safe passage for humanitarian aid in, namely, central and southern Somalia. It was replaced by another AU mission, rather than the United Nations, to transition and support the Somali National Armed Forces, and the mission will dissolve late 2024.[60]

[55] Isiaka Alani Badmus, "The African Mission in Burundi (AMIB)," *India Quarterly*, 73, no. 1 (2017): 1–20.

[56] Eric Demers, "The Burundian Civil War – 10 Years On," *Norwegian Refugee Council*, May 2, 2003.

[57] United Nations Security Council Resolution 1564, "Report of the Secretary-General on the Sudan," UN Doc. S/RES/1564, September 18, 2004, adopted 5,040th meeting.

[58] Malte Brosig, *Cooperative Peacekeeping in Africa: Exploring Regime Complexity* (London: Routledge, 2015), p. 73.

[59] United Nations, "UN Security Council Votes for New Somalia Peacekeeping Force," *France 24*, March 31, 2022.

[60] Meressa K. Dessu, "Is the AU Mission in Somalia Changing in Name Only?" *Institute for Security Studies*, March 29, 2022.

In Northern Mali, on December 20, 2012, the United Nations Security Council authorized an organized ECOWAS mission to support Mali to combat Islamist extremists.[61] In this conflict, the Mouvement National de Libération de l'Azawad (MNLA) [National Movement for the Liberation of Azawad] had taken control of the area in April 2012 that declared an independent homeland for the Tuareg ethnic group from Mali.[62] However, Islamist groups (Ansar Dine, al-Qaeda in the Islamic Maghreb, the Movement for Oneness and Jihad in West Africa, and Boko Haram) became more active than the NMLA in Northern Mali and imposed Shari'a Law in the area.[63] As a result, in January 2013, French military forces intervened with Operation Serval and ECOWAS rapidly deployed aerial and ground forces to Mali.[64] The African-led, and UN-mandated, African-led International Support Mission to Mali (AFISMA) comprised almost 7,500 troops from 21 African countries, including 1,800 personnel from Chad and 1,200 from Nigeria. Most of the Northern Mali was retaken by the Malian armed forces, and in mid-2013, a ceasefire was signed between the government and Tuareg rebels, and the UN-led Multidimensional Integrated Stabilization Mission in Mali succeeded AFISMA with French troops remaining.[65] Yet, the peace agreement ended when Malian soldiers shot unarmed protestors.

In February 2015, another ceasefire was signed between the Azawad movements and Malian government, but Malian leaders refused their autonomy while agreeing on their local devolution powers. This is now deemed as a low-level conflict. It will be argued that the efforts to bridge

[61] United Nations Security Council Resolution 2085, "The Situation in Mali," S/RES/2085, December 20, 2012, adopted 6,898th meeting.

[62] Tchioffo Kodjo, *Mali Conflict of 2012–2013: A Critical Assessment – Patterns of Local, Regional and Global Conflict and Resolution Dynamics in Post-colonial and Post-cold war Africa* (Chisinau: Lambert, 2015), p. 52; Lyal S. Sunga, "Has the ICC Unfairly Targeted or Has Africa Unfairly Targeted the ICC?" in *The International Criminal Court in Search of its Purpose and Identity*, edited by Triestino Marinello (London: Routledge, 2015), p. 170.

[63] Catherine Gegout, *Why Europe Intervenes in Africa: Security, Prestige and the Legacy of Colonialism* (Oxford: Oxford University Press, 2017), p. 185.

[64] United Nations Security Council Resolution 2085, "Concerning the Deployment of the African-led International Support Mission to Mali," UN Doc. S/RES/2085 (December 20, 2012); Yinka Olomojobi, *Frontiers of Jihad: Radical Islam in Africa* (Ibadan: Safari Books, 2015), p. 218.

[65] Matteo Tondini, "Coalitions of the Willing," in *The Practice of Shared Responsibility in International Law*, edited by André Nollkaemper and Ilias Plakokefalos (Cambridge: Cambridge University Press, 2017), p. 702.

peace were commendable to form a more harmonious state of affairs between NMLA belligerents and Malian government, but shooting protestors and excluding Islamist groups (that have now either disbanded, moved, or joined another insurgency) from all peace processes have not necessarily achieved a less discordant state of affairs. Democracy has failed in neighboring Burkina Faso with two military coups commencing between January and September 2022 that have left insecurity in the state, and Mali, fighting Azawad- and al-Qaeda-related insurgencies.[66] Therefore, Mali is in a less discordant state of affairs, especially in the north and south of the country.

In Liberia, ECOWAS provided a peacekeeping force between 1990 and 1997 to resolve the intra-state conflict and efforts to broker peace for an interim government and democratic elections. In 1990, ECOWAS initially met to form a ceasefire, install a transitional government, and establish a monitoring group consisting of "3,000 troops from Nigeria, Ghana, Guinea," Sierra Leone and Mali joined a year later.[67] After, the National Patriotic Front of Liberia (NPFL) besieged Monrovia, the interim government crumbled.[68] The United Nations and Organization of African Unity (OAU) later attempted to bring the war to an end, but factions continued fighting until a democratic process was sought. An estimated 250,000 were killed—out of Liberia's 2.5 million population—and over 1,000 peacekeepers were slain.[69] Eventually, Charles Taylor's party, the NPFL, one of the main warring factions, won the presidential election in July 1997 by a landscape margin.[70] It will be contended that ECOWAS and regional efforts intended to seek a more harmonious state of affairs, but even when the United Nations assisted, a second civil war and spillover in neighboring Sierra Leone commenced.

[66] Aminata Diaby and Nicolas Klingelschmitt, "De Facto Sovereignty and Multilateral Sanctions for a Return to Constitutional Order in a Context of Regional Armed Conflict: The Case of Mali," in *War, State and Sovereignty: Interdisciplinary Challenges and Perspectives for the Social Sciences*, edited by Grégory Daho and Yann Richard (Cham: Palgrave Macmillan, 2023), p. 189.

[67] Alex J. Bellamy and Paul D. Williams, *Understanding Peacekeeping*, 2nd ed. (Cambridge: Polity Press, 2010), p. 313.

[68] Bellamy and Williams, *Understanding Peacekeeping*, pp. 313–314.

[69] Patricia Levy, Michael Spilling and Brett Griffin, *Cultures of the World: Liberia* (New York: Cavendish Square, 2018), p. 29.

[70] Thomas Jayne, "ECOWAS and Liberia: Implications for Regional Intervention in Intra-State Conflicts," in *Africa at the Millennium: An Agenda for Mature Development*, edited by Bakut tswah Bakut and Sagarika Dutt (London: Palgrave Macmillan), pp. 155–176.

Chapter 8: Implications of Non-interventions in Nigeria, the Niger Delta, Niger, and Syria

The penultimate chapter considers the implications of African communitarian ethics for the lack of foreign armed interventions. This is of importance because internationally led interventions may be driven by utilitarian purposes (or at least in rhetoric). There has also been a selectivity of Western nations failing to intervene in African conflicts if they do not benefit from the process and intervening when they do.[71] Koskiennieni argued that "selectivity is unavoidable" because a reaction to aggression will result in "some members" receiving "more protection than others."[72] This was evident with the Rwandan genocide and diamond exploitation by the West in Sierra Leone respectively.

This chapter focuses on scenarios that, for humanitarian reasons, could constitute foreign armed intervention from an Afro-communitarian perspective. The contexts covered are northern Nigeria, neighboring Niger, and Syria. The situation in Nigeria covers prolonged banditry, terrorism from Boko Haram in the northeast attempting to Islamize the region, and militancy in the Niger Delta area to challenge environmental dilapidation and an unfit dispersal of oil revenues from the Nigerian federal government. National efforts to refute foes (Boko Haram and militias in Niger Delta) with initial enmity-like violence and subsequent amnesty and deradicalization programs to attain a harmonious situation are weakening. The disharmonious state of affairs bears excessive insecurity and high civilian casualties, widespread destruction of property, and economic repercussions that merit foreign military intervention to achieve a less disharmonious state of affairs.

Niger has experienced a coup in July 2023, and a military junta has succeeded office. This has left the Economic Community of West African States (ECOWAS) to consider whether to deploy regional armed intervention to reinstate democracy. ECOWAS is also cautious of close by military regimes in Burkina Faso and Mali and the Community is losing members and these states backed by Russia and the Wagner Group as part of a patron-client relationship with Russian illiberalism. It will be interesting to see whether the Nigerien military junta continues with civilian support or if ECOWAS promotes further sanctions and a possible incursion to

[71] Singh, "Undertaking Critical Legal Theory", pp. 75–76.

[72] Martti Koskiennieni, "The Place of Law in Collective Security," *Michigan Journal of International Law*, Vol. 17, No. 2 (1996), p. 464.

restore friendly-like relations to the ethos of the democracy that ECOWAS promotes within the West African area.

Finally, Syria in the Middle East discusses the atrocities that have occurred during the ongoing civil war. President Bashar Hafez al-Assad is Russia's military and diplomatic ally. The Syrian authoritarian regime has conducted several chemical weapons attacks against civilians in rebellion-held regions. Members States of the United Nations have presented draft Security Council resolutions proposing a political settlement of an interim government to uphold elections and install an observer and/or potential peacekeeping operation, but the Moscow and Beijing vetoes tarnish action. In April 2018, the United States, France, and the United Kingdom reacted with military airstrikes on the Syrian regime's military and weapons composites. Despite NATO conducting the use of force in Libya to retort to atrocity crimes committed by Colonel Muammar Muhammad Abu Minyar al-Gaddafi and the Libyan military against oppositional rebels and civilians to fulfill the Responsibility to Protect (R2P) doctrine, the Alliance was criticized for regime change and thus has not been contemplated for armed intervention in Syria.

Chapter 9: Conclusions

The conclusion will reflect on the main principles and permissible modes of violence related to Afro-communitarianism. This will be followed by an overview on the applicability to the main cases covered by focusing on the role of the United Nations in foreign armed intervention that often endorses multidimensional peacekeeping operations to monitor a ceasefire agreement and secure areas for a transitional government, other political settlement, and disarmament process. American-based unilateralism and support from democratic allies have been utilized in Western-based foreign armed interventions that will be demonstrated with the repercussions of the protracted Iraq invasion that failed the ethics of Afro-communitarianism because a more discordant state of affairs was the outcome with a rise on sectarian violence and growth of terrorism once American forces left in late 2011. Subsequently, the role of the African Union and ECOWAS is provided to assess Africa's regional role to peace and security by dealing with ethnic conflict, grievances, and terrorism to restore better communal relations.

The next part will infer what contribution the applicability of Afro-communitarianism can bring when analyzing the role of foreign armed intervention in conflicts to provide an alternative mode of ethics for better peaceful relations, even when resorting to justified violence. This will be done by comparing Afro-communitarianism with all-inclusive conflict resolution and just war theory. A pragmatic argument will also be brought out in the final section to illustrate that compliance with Afro-communitarianism can be attained with temporary interests based on external geopolitical pursuit. By arguing in this manner, Afro-communitarianism can gain more interest in the West and be considered by ethicists and politicians in the Global North when deciding to engage in a foreign armed intervention.

References

Badmus, Isiaka Alani. "The African Mission in Burundi (AMIB): A Study of the African Union's Peacekeeping Success and 'Triangular Area of Tension in African Peacekeeping'." *India Quarterly: A Journal of International Affairs*, Vol. 73, No. 1 (March 2017), pp. 1–20. https://doi.org/10.1177/0974928416683038.

Bellamy, Alex J., and Paul D. Williams. *Understanding Peacekeeping*, 2nd ed. Cambridge: Polity Press, 2010.

Bhatt, Chetan. "Contemporary Geopolitics and 'Alterity' Research." In *Researching Race and Racism*, edited by Martin Bulmer and John Solomos, pp. 16–36. London: Routledge, 2004.

Boogaard, Jeroen van den. *Proportionality in International Humanitarian Law: Refocusing the Balance in Practice*. Cambridge: Cambridge University Press, 2023.

Brosig, Malte. *Cooperative Peacekeeping in Africa: Exploring Regime Complexity*. London: Routledge, 2015.

Center for Strategic and International Studies. "Islamic State Khorasan (IS-K)." 2018, https://www.csis.org/programs/transnational-threats-project/terrorism-backgrounders/islamic-state-khorasan-k.

Cherry, Janet. *Umkhonto weSizwe: A Jacana Pocket History*. Auckland Park: Jacana Media, 2011.

Cordesman Anthony H., with Emma R. Davies. *Iraq's Insurgency and the Road to Civil Conflict – Volume I*. Westport, CT: Praeger Security International, 2008.

Cox, Rory. "The Ethics of War up to Thomas Aquinas." In *The Oxford Handbook of Ethics of War*, edited by Seth Lazar and Helen Frowe, pp. 99–121. Oxford: Oxford University Press, 2018.

Crawford, Neta C. *Accountability for Killing: Moral Responsibility for Collateral Damage in America's Post-9/11 Wars*. Oxford, Oxford University Press, 2013.

Demers, Eric. "The Burundian Civil War – 10 Years On." *Norwegian Refugee Council*, May 2, 2003. https://reliefweb.int/report/burundi/burundian-civil-war-10-years.

Dessu, Meressa K. "Is the AU Mission in Somalia Changing in Name Only?" *Institute for Security Studies*, March 29, 2022, https://issafrica.org/iss-today/is-the-au-mission-in-somalia-changing-in-name-only.

Diaby, Aminata, and Nicolas Klingelschmitt. "De Facto Sovereignty and Multilateral Sanctions for a Return to Constitutional Order in a Context of Regional Armed Conflict: The Case of Mali." In *War, State and Sovereignty: Interdisciplinary Challenges and Perspectives for the Social Sciences*, edited by Grégory Daho and Yann Richard, pp. 185–208. Cham: Palgrave Macmillan, 2023.

Drew, Allison. "Visions of Liberation: The Algerian War of Independence and Its South African Reverberations." *Review of African Political Economy*, Vol. 42, No. 143 (February 2015), pp. 22–43. https://doi.org/10.1080/03056244.2014.1000288.

Eckert, Amy E. *Outsourcing War: The Just War Tradition in the Age of Military Privatization*. Ithaca, NY: Cornell University Press, 2016.

Fabre, Cécile. *Cosmopolitan War*. Oxford: Oxford University Press, 2012.

Frowe, Helen. *The Ethics of War and Peace: An Introduction*, 2nd ed. Oxon: Routledge, 2016.

Gardner, Hall. *Averting Global War: Regional Challenges, Overextension, and Options for American Strategy*. New York: Palgrave Macmillan, 2007.

Gegout, Catherine. *Why Europe Intervenes in Africa: Security, Prestige and the Legacy of Colonialism*. Oxford: Oxford University Press, 2017.

Gutner, Tamar. *International Organizations in World Politics*. Thousand Oaks, CA: Sage, 2017.

Hawley, Michael C. "Can Just Wars Be Fought Proportionately? A Critique of *In Bello* Proportionality." *Journal of Military Ethics*, Vol. 22, No. 2 (September 2023), pp. 89–102. https://doi.org/10.1080/15027570.2023.2257916.

Henderson, Ian. *Law of Targeting: Military Objectives, Proportionality and Precautions in Attack under Additional Protocol I*. Leiden: Martinus Nijhoff Publishers, 2009.

International Committee of the Red Cross. *Four Geneva Conventions*, August 12, 1949. https://www.icrc.org/en/war-and-law/treaties-customary-law/geneva-conventions.

International Committee of the Red Cross. "Rule 1. The Principle of Distinction between Civilians and Combatants." https://ihl-databases.icrc.org/en/customary-ihl/v1/rule1#Fn_3E28356C_00003.

Jayne, Thomas. "ECOWAS and Liberia: Implications for Regional Intervention in Intra-State Conflicts." In *Africa at the Millennium: An Agenda for Mature Development*, edited by Bakut tswah Bakut and Sagarika Dutt, pp. 155–176. London: Palgrave Macmillan.

Kamalu, Chukwunyere. *The Little African History Book: Black Africa from the Origins of Humanity to the Assassination of Lumumba and the Turn of the 20th Century*. London: Orisa Press, 2007.

Kodjo, Tchioffo. *Mali Conflict of 2012–2013: A Critical Assessment – Patterns of Local, Regional and Global Conflict and Resolution Dynamics in Post-colonial and Post-cold war Africa.* Chisinau: Lambert, 2015.

Koskiennieni, Martti. "The Place of Law in Collective Security." *Michigan Journal of International Law*, Vol. 17, No. 2 (1996), pp. 455–490. https://repository.law.umich.edu/cgi/viewcontent.cgi?article=1497&context=mjil.

Lavallie, Elizabeth. "Gender Equality in Political and Public Decision-making." In *Women and Men in Partnership for Post-Conflict Reconstruction: Report of the Sierra Leone National Consultation Freetown, Sierra Leone, 21–24 May 2001*, edited by Rawwida Baksh-Soodeen and Linda Etchart, pp. 39–46. London: Commonwealth Secretariat, 2002.

Levy, Patricia, Michael Spilling, and Brett Griffin. *Cultures of the World: Liberia.* New York: Cavendish Square, 2018.

Matolino, Bernard. *Afro-Communitarian Democracy.* Lanham, MD: Lexington Books, 2019.

McCarthy, James P. "Ethical Implications of Kosovo Operations." In *The Sacred and the Sovereign: Religion and International Politics*, edited by John D. Carlson and Erik C. Owens, pp. 66–76. Georgetown, Washington, DC: Georgetown University Press, 2003.

Melvern, Linda. "United Nations Observer Mission Uganda – Rwanda (UNOMUR) and United Nations Assistance Mission for Rwanda I (UNAMIR I)." in *The Oxford Handbook of United Nations Peacekeeping Operations*, edited by Joachim A. Koops, Norrie MacQueen, Thierry Tardy and Paul D. Williams, pp. 462–472. Oxford: Oxford University Press, 2015.

Metz, Thaddeus. "Toward an African Moral Theory." *Journal of Political Philosophy*, Vol. 15, No. 3 (May 2007), pp. 321–341. https://doi.org/10.1111/j.1467-9760.2007.00280.x.

Metz, Thaddeus. "Ubuntu as a Moral Theory and Human Rights in South Africa." *African Human Rights Law Journal*, Vol. 11, No. 2 (2011), pp. 532–559. https://scielo.org.za/pdf/ahrlj/v11n2/11.pdf.

Metz, Thaddeus. "A Life of Struggle as Ubuntu." In *Nelson Rolihlahla Mandela: Decolonial Ethics of Liberation and Servant Leadership.* Trenton, NJ: Africa World Press, 2015, pp. 1–20. https://philarchive.org/archive/METMAUv1.

Morkevičius, Valerie. *Realist Ethics: Just War Traditions as Power Politics.* Cambridge: Cambridge University Press, 2018.

Mslia, Vuyisile. *Ubuntu: Shaping the Current Workplace with (African) Wisdom.* Randburg: Knowres Publishing, 2015.

Mukuni, Joseph, and Josiah Tlou. *Understanding Ubuntu for Enhancing Intercultural Communications.* Hershey, PA: IGI Global, 2021.

Ndeunyema, Ndjodi. *Re-Invigorating Ubuntu through Water: A Human Right to Water under the Namibian Constitution.* Pretoria: Pretoria University Law Press, 2021.

Ohlin, Jens David. "Sharp Wars Are Brief." In *Weighing Lives in War*, edited by Jens David Ohlin, Larry May and Claire Finkelstein, pp. 58–76. Oxford: Oxford University Press, 2017.

Olomojobi, Yinka. *Frontiers of Jihad: Radical Islam in Africa*. Ibadan: Safari Books, 2015.

Orend, Brian. *The Morality of War*. Peterborough, ON: Broadview Press, 2006.

Paris, Roland. *At War's End: Building Peace after Conflict*. Cambridge: Cambridge University Press, 2004.

Paris, Roland. "Saving Liberal Peacebuilding." *Review of International Studies*, Vol. 36, No. 2 (April 2010), pp. 337–365. https://doi.org/10.1017/S0260210510000057.

Peskin, Victor. "Beyond Victor's Justice? The Challenge of Prosecuting the Winners at the International Criminal Tribunals for the Former Yugoslavia and Rwanda." *Journal of Human Rights*, Vol. 4, No. 2 (2005), pp. 213–231. https://doi.org/10.1080/14754830590952152.

Peterson, Matt. "Did Iraq Ever Become a Just War? As Contours Evolved, the Morality of Fighting Did Too." *The Atlantic*, March 24, 2018. https://www.theatlantic.com/international/archive/2018/03/iraq-war-ethics/556448/.

Promotion of National Unity and Reconciliation, Act 34, December 1, 1995. https://www.justice.gov.za/legislation/acts/1995-034.pdf.

Protocol Additional to the Geneva Conventions of 12 August 1949, and Relating to the Protection of Victims of International Armed Conflicts (Protocol I). *Additional Protocol I*, Chapter I, Article 52 (2), June 8, 1977.

Santos, Boaventura de Sousa. *The End of the Cognitive Empire: The Coming of Age of Epistemologies of the South*. Durham, NC: Duke University Press, 2018.

Schabas, William A. *The UN International Criminal Tribunals: The Former Yugoslavia, Rwanda and Sierra Leone*. Cambridge: Cambridge University Press, 2006.

Sheeran, Scott, and Catherine Kent. "Protection of Civilians, Responsibility to Protect, and Humanitarian Intervention." In *Protection of Civilians*, edited by Haidi Willmot, Ralph Mamiya, Scott Sheeran and Marc Weller, pp. 29–62. Oxford: Oxford University Press, 2016.

Singh, Danny. "Undertaking Critical Legal Theory to Examine Just War Intervention: A Smokescreen for Political Ambitions." In *Comparative Just War Theory: An Introduction to International Perspectives*, edited by Luís Cordeiro-Rodrigues and Danny Singh, pp. 61–79. Lanham, MD: Roman & Littlefield, 2020.

Spiers, Kimberly. *Restorative Justice in South Africa's Truth and Reconciliation Commission*. Winnipeg: University of Manitoba, 2008.

Streissguth, Tom. *Rwanda in Pictures*. Minneapolis, MN: Lerner Publishing Group, 2008.

Sunga, Lyal S. "Has the ICC Unfairly Targeted or Has Africa Unfairly Targeted the ICC?" In *The International Criminal Court in Search of its Purpose and Identity*, edited by Triestino Marinello, pp. 147–173. London: Routledge, 2015.

Taylor, Paul, and Devon Curtis. "The United Nations." In *The Globalization of World Politics: An Introduction to International Relations*, 6th ed., edited by John Bayliss, Steve Smith and Patricia Owens, pp. 334–348. Oxford: Oxford University Press, 2014.

Tondini, Matteo. "Coalitions of the Willing." In *The Practice of Shared Responsibility in International Law*, edited by André Nollkaemper and Ilias Plakokefalos, pp. 701–732. Cambridge: Cambridge University Press, 2017.

United Nations. *Charter of the United Nations.* 1 United Nations Treaty Series XVI, October 24, 1945.

United Nations. "UN Security Council Votes for New Somalia Peacekeeping Force." *France 24*, March 31, 2022, https://www.france24.com/en/live-news/20220331-un-security-council-votes-for-new-somalia-peacekeeping-force.

United Nations Security Council Resolution 1441. "A Final Opportunity to Comply with its Disarmament Obligations." UN Doc S/RES/1441, November 8, 2002, adopted 4644th meeting.

United Nations Security Council Resolution 1564. "Report of the Secretary-General on the Sudan." UN Doc. S/RES/1564, September 18, 2004, adopted 5,040th meeting.

United Nations Security Council Resolution 2085. "The Situation in Mali." S/RES/2085, December 20, 2012, adopted 6,898th meeting.

United Nations South Africa. "The Blood we Sacrificed was Worth it – Sharpeville Massacre." *United Nations South Africa*, July 17, 2021. https://southafrica.un.org/en/135812-%E2%80%9C-blood-we-sacrificed-was-worth-it%E2%80%9D-sharpeville-massacre.

Walzer, Michael. *Just and Unjust Wars: A Moral Argument with Historical Illustrations.* New York: Basic Books, 1977.

Walzer, Michael. *Just and Unjust Wars: A Moral Argument with Historical Illustrations*, 5th ed. New York: Basic Books, 2006.

Wiredu, Kwasi. *Cultural Universals and Particulars: An African Perspective.* Bloomington, IN: Indiana University Press, 1997.

Woods, Larry J., and Timothy R. Reese. "Military Interventions in Sierra Leone: Lessons from a Failed State." *The Long War Series Occasional Paper 28.* Fort Leavenworth, KS: Combat Studies Institute Press, 2008. https://www.armyupress.army.mil/Portals/7/combat-studies-institute/csi-books/OP28.pdf.

CHAPTER 2

Principles of Afro-communitarianism and Permissible Violence

Introduction

This theoretical chapter initially engages with just war theory and principally the traditionalist version that respects international law when considering the justification of waging war, the rules within an armed conflict (including the principles of the law or armed conflict), and justice in the aftermath. Subsequently, the relationship of just war theory to communal values will be applied with Afro-communitarian ideals on shared solidarity, identity, goodwill, mutual friendships, social harmony, and community values. A justification will also be provided on the motive for the application of Afro-communitarian ethics to analyze foreign armed intervention.

The main section of the chapter explains *Ubuntu* ethics that are based on placing the community as the utmost good. This will aid an explanation on the deontological perspective of Afro-communitarian ethics that focuses on friendly alternatives to violence because violence is not permissible. I will then move to the consequentialist Afro-communitarian perspective to exhibit when violence is morally permissible and the scenarios and hierarchized stages of justifiable violence with the objective to rebut enmity-based behavior for the accomplishment of a less discordant situation or a more harmonious state of affairs. It will be clearly displayed that when friendly alternatives have been exhausted, are absent or fruitless, then the intentions from the responder must overshadow the result of the

D. Singh, *Applied Afro-Communitarian Ethics and Foreign Armed Intervention*, https://doi.org/10.1007/978-3-031-64110-7_2

actions (hence, consequentialism) and mainly foresee the promotion of a better state of affairs (that is more harmonious and less disputatious).[1] When opting for the use of violence, it may become a necessary condition to challenge violence and convey a more harmonious and less hostile condition; there are four types of hierarchized permissible arrangements of violence, comprising sabotage, guerrilla warfare, terrorism, and open revolution.[2]

After the discussion on consequentialist Afro-communitarian ethics, this African moral philosophy is applied to several comparative examples of permissible indiscriminate violence against both soldiers and civilians. One main context covers the role of Nelson Rolihlahla Mandela advancing the African National Congress (ANC) after its paramilitary wing was suspended. Mandela's leadership finally initiated a peaceful negotiation after decades of apartheid domination and brought an immediate end to its violence. After an analysis of this internal struggle, several anti-colonial emancipatory movements against Portugal are covered. This includes liberation groups in Guinea-Bissau, Angola, and Mozambique. Subsequently, rebellion groups against British colonial rule in Kenya and India are presented. The final context is the unsuccessful attempt of an Islam and animist rebellion against German East African occupation in Ruanda-Urundi. It will be argued that these contexts warranted Afro-communitarian consequentialist moral philosophy to permit stages of violence due to exhausted and/or fruitless friendly alternatives, such as unarmed peaceful protests, for internal liberation and anti-colonialism. This provides the rationale for examining these ethics in a novel way for foreign armed interventions across the globe.

The penultimate part will provide some counterarguments to the consequentialist points of Afro-communitarianism from the deontological approach that does not permit violence in any circumstances. This is due to the argument that the violence will always form enmity-relations—at least in the short-term even if the longer-term objective of peace is reached. Finally, just war theory will be compared with Afro-communitarianism.

[1] Bernard Matolino, *Afro-Communitarian Democracy* (Lanham, MD: Lexington Books, 2019), p. 63.

[2] Allison Drew, "Visions of Liberation: The Algerian War of Independence and Its South African Reverberations," *Review of African Political Economy*, Vol. 42, No. 143 (2015), pp. 22–43.

Just War Theory

Just war theory idealistically attempts to demand justice, morality, and ethics during the horrors of war.[3] Although just war ethics can be traced to Confucian perspectives and earlier civilizations,[4] Western approaches from the Global-North tend to reflect on military ethics that derives from Christian thinking. In the thirteenth century, Saint Thomas Aquinas asserted that war is a sin against charity, but it was permissible for human beings to resort to proportionate violence, even if it involved killing, to defend others and to defend themselves.[5] If protecting human rights is morally confirmed as a precondition to be part of a war, then Aquinas' conditions can explain how war may be initiated. There are three principles of just war theory. This is based on the ethics of initiating war (*jus ad bellum*), the rules of conduct within war (*jus in bello*), and justice in the aftermath (*jus post bellum*).

In relation to *jus ad bellum*, Aquinas contended that war can only be morally justifiable if three provisions are convened: (1) authorization by a proper (legitimate) authority, (2) contain a just cause, and (3) have the right intent.[6]

First, for a war to be deemed legitimate, it requires the authorization of a proper, or higher, authority to satisfy the decision to wage war.[7] At that time, a proper authority could include a head of state, such as a prince, or other sovereign figure that could command the war and have the power to use force within the state against criminals, but also use violence against outsiders that caused a threat or harm to the polity. In contemporary global politics, the legitimate authority exists in the United Nations (UN)—and edifices in its Security Council—to serve a "common good"

[3] Michael Walzer, *Just and Unjust Wars: A Moral Argument with Historical Illustrations*, 4th ed. (New York: Basic Books, 2006), p. 20.

[4] See Luís Cordeiro-Rodrigues and Danny Singh, *Comparative Just War Theory: An Introduction to International Perspectives* (Lanham, MD: Roman & Littlefield, 2020) for a range of examples.

[5] Thomas Aquinas, *Summa Theologiae*, II-II (London: R & T Washbourne, 1911); Gregory M. Reichberg, *Thomas Aquinas on War and Peace* (Cambridge: Cambridge University Press, 2017), pp. 173–174.

[6] Aquinas, *Summa Theologiae.*

[7] Reichberg, *Thomas Aquinas on War and Peace*, pp. 114–115.

and sanction unilateral or collective self-defense against an act of aggression.[8]

Second, war must be waged for a just cause. According to this second principle of just war theory, a war cannot be justified if a country or coalition of willing allied states invade the sovereign territory of another state for national or collective gain. Aquinas stressed that a group of people must be defended, and protected, which means that war cannot be initiated to destroy a governmental enemy, and killing innocent civilians is morally impermissible. For Aquinas, the just cause serves peace to consent to any action for a good reason that may occur from misconduct by outsiders or a disciplinary response required for an opponent to be attacked because of the wrongful acts they committed.[9] Saint Augustine of Hippo previously contended that secular punishment is only permissible if it is conducted in a justified way and deters retaliating to wrongs by discarding revenge and retribution, and encourage repentance, so that wrongdoers can acquire virtue and be spared "divine punishment."[10] To put simply, state leaders have the moral right to defend their country from acts of aggression, but do not have the moral duty to punish such aggressors.[11]

Third, a just cause can only be morally justifiable if it contains the right intention. To qualify as the right intention, the initiation of war must be presented by state leaders. A legitimate authority that acts with the right intention (a just cause) can wage war.[12] The proper authority must be a sovereign and a minor authority must consult a senior authority for dispute resolution before initiating war.[13] A more harmonious state of affairs

[8] Joseph Boyle, "Traditional Just War Theory and Humanitarian Intervention," *Nomos – American Society for Political and Legal Philosophy*, Vol. 47 (2006), pp. 36–37.

[9] Aquinas, *Summa Theologiae*.

[10] Deidre Golash, *The Case Against Punishment: Retribution, Crime Prevention, and the Law* (New York: New York University Press, 2005), p. 11.

[11] This rule can be upheld in contemporary international law. The United Nations Security Council is the legitimate authority that is against the use of force, but there is an exception to the rule if a state is not the receiving end of aggression and thus can act in individual or collective self-defense (Articles 2 (4) and 51 of the Charter of the United Nations, 1945).

[12] It has also been argued that a legitimate authority must also "supervise" a war (Lawrence Ogbo Ugwuanyi, "Towards an African Theory of Just War," *Revista de Estudios Africanos* [Journal of African Studies], Vol. 1 (November 2020), p. 54.

[13] Austin Fagothey, *Right and Reason: Ethics in Theory and Practice*, 3rd edition (Saint Louis, MO: The C.V. Mosby Company, 1963), p. 653; Charles A. Jones, *More than Just War: Narratives of the Just War Tradition and Military Life* (London: Routledge, 2013), p. 68.

can be sought by defending a victim of an unjust attack—as the objective of the war—to qualify as a just war if authorized by a proper authority and other aims are unjustified.[14]

Three further conditions on war were subsequently exhibited in the sixteenth century by theologians Francisco de Vitoria and Francisco Suárez. This included proportionality to contend that civilian casualties are the evils of war that must be deterred or eradicated by war. The objectives of initiating war must not be disproportionate that results in the expected harms of war. It is important to note that under the rule of *jus ad bellum*, it is morally justifiable to avert actions with the use of force. For example, Vitoria illustrated that responding to sins committed against one's neighbors can be commenced by "any Christian prince" to counter such harmful actions, which in his example includes Caribbean Indians engaging in cannibalism and euthanasia, "even if it means shedding blood."[15] Hence, limited moralism can protect the rights of innocent civilians that justified the intervention of Spaniards. Moreover, alternatives to measures to war that attempt peace and diplomacy regarding injustice must be exhausted, ensuring that war is only waged as a last resort. Furthermore, the initiator of war must have a reasonable chance of success. If these six criteria—with three presented from Aquinas and the remainder exhibited from Vitoria and Suárez—of the just war tradition are failed, then the use of force *jus ad bellum* is unjustified.[16] Hence, the rules of *jus ad bellum* incorporate the legitimacy of a proper authority, contain a just cause, maintain the right intention, war be fought proportionately to the means, war must be waged as a last resort, and war should have a high chance of success.

In relation to *jus in bello*, the law of armed conflict (LOAC) provides five main principles for international humanitarian law that is applicable in armed conflicts that many states have recognized and accepted in older civilizations and contemporary international treaties.[17] LOAC establishes the rules and protections for combatants to avert the "horrors that accompany total warfare" and to promote the protection of noncombatants,

[14] Boyle, "Traditional Just War Theory and Humanitarian Intervention," p. 42.

[15] Francisco de Vitoria, "On the Evangelization of Unbelievers," (1534–1535) in *Colonial Latin America: A Documentary History*, edited by Kenneth Mills, William B. Taylor and Sandra Lauderdale Graham (Denver, CO: Rowman & Littlefield, 2002), p. 70.

[16] David Luban, "Will Syria Redefine the Just War?" *Just Security*, September 24, 2013.

[17] Jonathan O. Chimakonam and Victor C.A. Nweke, "An Examination of Nigerian, Sri Lankan, and Guatemalan Civil Wars in Light of the Law of Armed Conflict" in *Comparative Just War Theory: An Introduction to International Perspectives*, ed. Luís Cordeiro Rodrigues and Danny Singh (Lanham, MD: Rowman & Littlefield, 2020), p. 87.

mainly civilians, private property, and injured, wounded, and sick *inactive* combatants.[18]

There are five main segments of war that rule armed conflict constitute LOAC. These include unnecessary suffering (humanity), military necessity, distinction (discrimination), proportionality, and chivalry (honor). These concepts will be immediately discussed in turn.

Unnecessary suffering limits the horrors of warfare by prohibiting and controlling weapons to ensure that they kill combatants when executed without producing further suffering.[19] Certain arms, projectiles, or hazardous substances that cause additional suffering or other injury must not be utilized or else usage would contravene the proportionality of military advantage, or military objectives, and thus weapons should only be utilized for legitimate military objectives.[20]

The principle of military necessity assesses whether a pre-emptive target is segment of a valid military objective that also balances the "requirements of humanity."[21] A military target can be defined as an object that facilitates military action and thus its destruction or seizure provides an evident military advantage.[22] This military strategy attempts to secure a quick submission of the opposition. For instance, military barracks, military communications, a weapons cache, and military electricity supply would qualify as a valid military target and thus its destruction or capture would contribute to effective military action. However, if civilian

[18] Robert Kolb and Richard Hyde, *An Introduction to the International Law of Armed Conflicts* (Oxford: Hart Publishing, 2008), p. 49.

[19] Robin M. Coupland, "The SIrUS Project: Towards a Determination of which Weapons Cause 'Superfluous Injury or Unnecessary Suffering,'" in *The Changing Face of Conflict and the Efficacy of International Humanitarian Law*, eds. Helen Durham and Timothy L.H. McCormack (The Hague: Kluwer Law International, 1999), p. 99.

[20] Jean-Marie Henckaerts and Louise Doswald-Beck, *Customary International Humanitarian Law – Volume II: Practice, Part 1* (Cambridge: Cambridge University Press, 2005), p. 1512. The Hague Conventions of 1899 and 1907 are examples of such prohibitions and controls on the use of illegal weapons, substances and hazardous gases.

[21] Jan Römer, *Killing in a Gray Area Between Humanitarian Law and Human Rights: How Can the National Police of Colombia Overcome the Uncertainty of Which Branch of International Law to Apply?* (Berlin: Springer, 2010), p. 68.

[22] International Committee of the Red Cross (ICRC), *Protocol Additional to the Geneva Conventions of 12 August 1949, and relating to the Protection of Victims of International Armed Conflicts (Protocol I)*, 8 June 1977, 1125 United Nations Treaty Series (UNTS) 3–4, Article 52.

infrastructure such as private property or an entertainment radio or television station were targeted, then it would not qualify as military necessary.

The rule of distinction applies to the identification of a belligerent actor, ensuring that combatants and noncombatants have been distinguished. Moreover, military purposes and places or protected property must also be detected. Under customary international law, this distinction confirms that no indiscriminate attacks beyond the parameters of military objectives are initiated.[23] Examples of an indiscriminate attack include aerial bombardment, besieging a residential area due to suspected opposition forces, and disdain of jurisdictional military objectives or combatants. Belligerents are permitted to engage in hostilities if they are distinctively uniformed, contain a military command structure, carry weapons, and conduct military operations that comply with the customs and laws of war.[24] Deceitful fighting in an enemy's uniform and the taking of hostages are forbidden practices of conduct in warfare.

The rule of proportionality concerns the consideration of the advantages of targeting a facility or compound for a military advantage (as part of military necessity) whilst bearing in mind civilian casualties and private property damage.[25] If there are anticipated civilian deaths and collateral damage to property, then proportionality is applied to calculate whether the military action is permissible.[26] Civilian casualties and property damage must not be excessive to accomplish the military advantage acquired from hitting a particular target.[27] For instance, in 1999, it would have been morally unjustifiable for NATO to conduct airstrikes with nuclear devices over Belgrade to destroy the military infrastructure and

[23] Dražan Djukić and Niccolò Pons, "Entries: Distinction," in *The Companion to International Humanitarian Law*, eds. Dražan Djukić and Niccolò Pons (Leiden: Brill Nijhoff, 2018), p. 307.

[24] Kleffner, Jann K. "Scope of Application of International Humanitarian Law," in *The Handbook of International Humanitarian Law*, 3rd ed., ed. Dieter Fleck (Oxford: Oxford University Press, 2013), p. 225.

[25] Terry D. Gill, "Trapped: Three Dilemmas in the Law of Proportionality and Asymmetric Warfare," in *Yearbook of International Humanitarian Law 2015*, ed. Terry D. Gill (The Hague: Asser Press, 2016), 178.

[26] Walzer, *Just and Unjust Wars*, 2006, p. 153.

[27] Martin, Francisco Forrest, Stephen J. Schnably, Richard J. Wilson, Jonathan S. Simon and Mark V. Tushnet, *International Human Rights and Humanitarian Law: Treaties, Cases and Analysis* (Cambridge: Cambridge University Press, 2006), p. 536.

intelligence of the Yugoslav armed forces.[28] The regulation of proportionality is clearly outlined to inhibit attacks against a civilian population and private property that exceed predicted military gain.[29] However, the rule of proportionality is subjective to military necessity because Protocol I to the Geneva Conventions does not clearly outline what constitutes 'excessive.'[30] It has also been argued that a just war cannot truly exercise the pillar of proportionality because destruction and the deaths of innocent civilians (the harms) cannot be truly outweighed by the military necessity/gain (goods) achieved.[31] To put another way, proportionality is abused when the goods sought (from military necessity) do not exceed the harms. However, it is difficult to apply and calculate proportionality because the actions of active combatants cause some degree of harm and destruction *in bello*.

The rule of chivalry (honor) considers fairness and the retention of trust with oppositional armed forces and thus the procedures of injuring the enemy must not be unrestricted.[32] Combatants represent their states and must fight within a professional conduct and within the parameters of legal controls, regulations, and protections that the state has ratified.[33] By way of illustration, Section 3 (a) of the US military training manual infers that active belligerents must not exercise violence beyond its military purpose to conform to chivalry and humanity.[34]

These five principles of LOAC derive from various international treaties that control the conduct of war *jus in bello*. Most famously, the Four Geneva Conventions of 1949 were enacted to protect inactive combatants (namely, wounded and sick) armed forces in the battlefield and the sea; to

[28] John Janzekovic, *The Use of Force in Humanitarian Intervention: Morality and Practicalities* (Aldershot, Hamps: Ashgate, 2006), pp. 52–53.

[29] ICRC, *Protocol Additional I to the Geneva Conventions*, Article 5 (b).

[30] ICRC, *Protocol Additional I to the Geneva Conventions*, Article 51.

[31] Michael C. Hawley, "Can Just Wars Be Fought Proportionately? A Critique of *In Bello* Proportionality," *Journal of Military Ethics*, Vol. 22, No. 2 (September 2023), pp. 89–90.

[32] Katharine Fortin, "Armed Groups and the DoD Manual: Shining a Light on Overlooked Issues," in *The United States Department of Defence Law of War Manual: Commentary and Critique*, ed. Michael A. Newton (Cambridge: Cambridge University Press, 2018), pp. 389–390.

[33] Helen M. Kinsella, *The Image Before the Weapon: A Critical History of the Distinction Between Combatant and Civilian* (Ithaca, NY: Cornell University Press, 2011), p. 27.

[34] United States Army Field Manual, *The Law of Land Warfare*. Department of the Army Field Manual, FM 27–10, July 1956.

uphold the fair treatment prisoners of war (POWs) that no longer undertake activity during hostilities;[35] and to protect civilians during war.[36]

These rules, controls, and protections contained in the Four Geneva Conventions apply in war that involves more than one armed force and was then applied to the legality of international armed conflict with its Additional Protocol I to the Four Geneva Conventions in 1977. Additional Protocol II widened the jurisdiction from international armed conflict to the protection of victims and relinquished soldiers in non-international armed conflicts (NIAC).[37] The extension of the Geneva Conventions now considers civil wars and intra-state conflicts *jus in bello*.

In relation to *jus post bellum*, the phases of terminating a war and the responsibility to engage in rebuilding are based on six principles. This includes rights vindication, publicity and proportionality, discrimination assessed between senior military and political leaders, soldiers and civilians, punishment and accountability, compensation and reparations, and rehabilitation. The regime of human rights and international humanitarian law has dominated the initial principles of *jus post bellum*, and international *ad hoc* criminal tribunals have supported post-war justice in the aftermath of atrocities and termination of war, and the final facet rests on statebuilding and post-conflict reconstruction in the aftermath of war. In relation to the latter, after the Cold War era signaled the defeat of communism in Europe, liberalism was to be maintained by the American global hegemon.[38]

As part of liberalism, the United Nations has engaged in statebuilding missions for war-torn countries or provinces vying for independence that advocated foreign militaries assisting in Western-based reforms of the political, security, and judicial sectors so the intervened territories can "govern themselves."[39] For example, the United Nations transitional

[35] ICRC, Geneva Convention Relative to the Treatment of Prisoners of War (Third Geneva Convention), 12 August 1949, 75 UNTS 135, Article 3.

[36] Gasser, Hans-Peter, "Geneva Conventions I–IV (1949)," in *The Law of Armed Conflict and the Use of Force: The Max Planck Encyclopedia of Public International Law* – Thematic Series Volume 2, ed. Frauke Lachenmann and Rüdiger Wolfrum (Oxford: Oxford University Press, 2017), p. 397.

[37] ICRC, Protocol Additional to the Geneva Conventions of 12 August 1949, and relating to the Protection of Victims of Non-International Armed Conflicts (Protocol II), 8 June 1977, 1125 UNTS 609–610.

[38] Francis Fukuyama, *The End of History and the Last Man* (New York: Free Press, 1992).

[39] David M. Edelstein, "Foreign Militaries, Sustainable Institutions, and Postwar Statebuilding," in *The Dilemmas of Statebuilding: Confronting the Contradictions of Postwar*

administrations in Kosovo and Timor-Leste in 1999 provided extraordinary law-making powers provided to the appointed United Nations Special Representatives of the Secretary-General.[40] As part of newly independent states fighting for the right to self-determination, they have confronted military dictatorships, military annexation or occupation that now needed the configuration of rules and a system related to establish democratic order.[41] These contexts, such as Kosovo and Timor-Leste escaping Serbian and Indonesian military occupation respectively, promoted the liberal peace that endorsed rapid democratization and economic liberalization.[42] The democratic peace thesis postulates that democratic states do not initiate war with each other due to their attempt to promote amicable political, economic, and trade relations.[43] These aspects are affiliated with the respect for international law, requiring the United Nations to promote transitional administrations or robust institutional reforms, with the help of international military forces, so that states will not relapse into conflict.

Traditionalist and Revisionist Approaches

There are several schools of contemporary just war theory. This includes traditionalists that attempt to improve, with careful consideration, the moral foundations of war that integrates international law and the law of armed conflict.[44] Under the traditionalist approach, states can initiate war (*jus ad bellum*) for their national defense, to defend other states, or to inhibit shocking atrocious crimes to humanity.[45] At the same time, Walzer complies with the legalistic paradigm to respect the basic rules of the Charter of the United Nations, principally Article 2 (4), and an international

Peace Operations, edited by Roland Paris and Timothy D. Sisk (London: Routledge, 2009), pp. 81–89.

[40] Hansjörg Strohmeyer, "Collapse and Reconstruction of a Judicial System: The United Nations Missions in Kosovo and East Timor," *American Journal of International Law*, Vol. 95, No. 1 (2001), pp. 46–63.

[41] Michael Doyle, "International Ethics and the Responsibility to Protect," *International Studies Review*, Vol. 13, No. 1 (2011), p. 78.

[42] Roland Paris, *At War's End: Building Peace After Civil Conflict* (Cambridge: Cambridge University Press, 2004).

[43] Michael Doyle, "Kant, Liberal Legacies, and Foreign Affairs," *Philosophy and Public Affairs*, Vol. 12, No. 3 (1983), pp. 205–235.

[44] Michael Walzer, *Just and Unjust Wars: A Moral Argument with Historical Illustrations* (New York: Basic Books, 1977).

[45] Walzer, *Just and Unjust Wars*, 2006, p. 107.

society of independent states to postulate that there is an equality of all sovereign states that are bound by rules and laws.[46] The exception to the respect of a state's territorial integrity is when a pre-emptive response to any imminent threat or use of force posed by one state against another warrants self-defense by the victim state and others members of the international society (that generally responds to aggression).[47] Therefore, traditionalism concentrates on collectivism.[48] Global redistributive ethicists have attempted to expand approving military intervention by widening the justification of humanitarian intervention that would undermine sovereignty in the event of a state failing to save their civilian's lives.[49] A humanitarian intervention involves the incursion of a third party and its armed forces into another territory without its consent to save lives. It has famously been defined as:

> [T]he threat or use of force across state borders by a state (or group of states) aimed at preventing or ending widespread and grave violations of the fundamental human rights of individuals other than its own citizens, without the permission of the state within whose territory force is applied.[50]

Therefore, the scope of a humanitarian intervention can challenge state sovereignty that would in turn violate mainstream international law. There is the danger of humanitarian interventions defying the logic of fighting wars to protect national self-defense.[51] In addition, "military superiority" is not sufficient to result in clear victory because the population of the

[46] Walzer, *Just and Unjust Wars*, 1977.

[47] Walzer, *Just and Unjust Wars*, 1977, pp. 61–62; Article 51 of the Charter of the United Nations, 1945; David Luban, "Just War and Human Rights," *Philosophy and Public Affairs*, Vol. 9, No. 2 (Winter 1980), pp. 163–165. Yet, the United Nations often fails to cover the moral realities of war because human rights are frequently flouted and basic human rights that are subject to proportionality for self-defense is an alleged just war (Luban, "Just War and Human Rights, pp. 175–176).

[48] James Pattison, "The Case for the Nonideal Morality of War: Beyond Revisionism versus Traditionalism in Just War Theory," *Political Theory*, Vol. 46, No. 2 (2018), p. 243.

[49] Henry Shue, "Eroding Sovereignty: The Advance of Principles," in *The Morality of Nationalism*, 3rd ed., ed. Robert McKim and Jeff McMahan (Oxford: Oxford University Press, 1997), pp. 340–359.

[50] J.L. Holzgrefe, "The Humanitarian Intervention Debate," in *Humanitarian Intervention: Ethics, Legal, and Political Dilemmas*, eds. J.L. Holzgrefe and Robert. O. Keohane (Cambridge: Cambridge University Press, 2003), p. 18.

[51] Hawley, "Can Just Wars Be Fought Proportionately?", p. 96.

intervening state may, overtime, become cynical and influence the withdrawal of supporting the war.[52]

It is debatable whether *jus ad bellum* should be separate to *jus in bello*.[53] The aims and justification of the war are debatably distinct from how a war is fought.[54] Based on this traditionalist approach of just war theory, it is possible to fight a war that is not justified, but the use of violence and targeting is done in correct way.

In relation to *jus in bello*, Walzer claims that moral equality between combatants exists and fighting for a perceived wrong, or evil, side does not involve wrongdoing.[55] To put another way, traditionalists focus on the moral equality of all combatants, whether they are just or unjust. Intervention is justifiable, when needed, to disavow an immoral combatant, which is worth the risk and part of a reciprocal risk of soldiers on both sides dying when fighting.[56] When soldiers are fighting in a war, they no longer keep their right to life and the protection of liberty.[57] These basic civil and political rights are lost because soldiers threaten other people's lives and become a "dangerous man" when assigned on a mission, which results in soldiers surrendering their right to life.[58]

Conversely, noncombatants are not dangerous and therefore do not threaten the lives of others, so they must retain their basic rights to life and liberty and should not be attacked. This idea on combatant equality emanates with the postulation that even if combatants fighting for an unjust cause are not guilty when killing just combatants due to the reciprocal moral equality of combatants. The traditionalist equality of combatant debate concerning unjust combatants fighting for unjust causes cannot

[52] Hawley, "Can Just Wars Be Fought Proportionately?", p. 97. This was certainly the case in the wars in Iraq. The Powell doctrine of using brute and extreme force was supported in the First Gulf War but was criticized as overly disproportionate (E. Thomas Sullivan and Richard S. Frase, *Proportionality Principles in American Law: Controlling Excessive Government Actions* (Oxford: Oxford University Press, 2009), p. 25). The United States and Britain attained initial support for the Second Iraq War, but civilian popularity faded as the incursion went on that resulted in the departure of American and coalition forces in late 2011.

[53] Ugwuanyi, "Towards an African Theory of Just War," p. 55.

[54] Walzer, *Just and Unjust Wars*, 1977.

[55] Michael Walzer, *Just and Unjust Wars* (Harmondsworth: Penguin, 1977), p. 21.

[56] Walzer, *Just and Unjust Wars*, 1977.

[57] Walzer, *Just and Unjust Wars*, 2006, p. 136.

[58] Walzer, *Just and Unjust Wars*, 2006, pp. 142, 145.

compensate for abuses and fatalities perpetrated against their targeted victims has been opposed by revisionists.[59]

Revisionists contend that just combatants maintain the right to life and unlike the traditionalist approach, *jus ad bellum* and *jus in bello* are inseparable because the cause(s) for the initiation of war are bound with the activities within war.[60] Soldiers may fight in a war that they may deem as just, even if unjust and noncompliant with international law, but their actions *in bello* must be judged instead of *ad bellum* because the latter is political.[61] From this revisionist perspective, all soldiers or some soldiers should not be protected by the right to life that is crucial to considerations on proportionality. The work of McMahan clearly argues that war does not create new moral standards, insofar that conduct in war can be regarded just or unjust.[62] Killing people outside of war holds the same ethics, such as killing in individual self-defense or defending others.[63] It is morally incorrect for unjust combatants to strike just fighters and their civilian population.[64] Noncombatants can be justifiably targeted if they are believed liable that contradicts Walzer's moral equality of all combatants because innocent combatants (an army that justly participates in a war) cannot be admissible targets.[65]

In addition, Ranganathan stresses that "moral parasites" corrupt "conventional morality" to assist their hostility to transform morality as a weapon for "the unjust," which presents the *tactics* used by an unjust side that Walzer ignores.[66] Based on this revisionist argument, unjust combatants are recommended to surrender their arms. When considering this revisionist critique on the moral status of combatants with contextualization, many manifestations of Westerners state that the causes of war from

[59] David Rodin, *War and Self-Defence* (Oxford: Clarendon, 2002); Thomas Hurka, "Proportionality in the Morality of War," *Philosophy & Public Affairs*, Vol. 33, No. 1 (2005), pp. 34–66.

[60] Jeff McMahan, *Killing in War* (Oxford: Oxford University Press, 2009).

[61] Hawley, "Can Just Wars Be Fought Proportionately?", p. 99.

[62] McMahan, *Killing in War*.

[63] Rodin, *War and Self-Defence*; Jeff McMahan, "War as Self-Defence," *Ethics & International Affairs*, Vol. 18, No. 1 (2004), pp. 75–80.

[64] McMahan, *Killing in War*.

[65] Cécile Fabre, *Cosmopolitan War* (Oxford: Oxford University Press, 2012).

[66] Shyam Ranganathan, "Just War and the Indian Tradition: Arguments from the Battlefield," in *Comparative Just War Theory: An Introduction to International Perspectives*, edited by Luís Cordeiro Rodrigues and Danny Singh (Lanham, MD: Rowman & Littlefield, 2020), p. 189.

Islamic State are unjust and their objectives of targeting towns leading to unintended harm to civilians (noncombatants) in Iraq, Syria, and Afghanistan are morally unjustified. Therefore, rather than focus on collectivism like traditionalists do, revisionists prefer concentrating on individuals and a reductionist perspective to an immersed morality of conflict to articulate ethics related to individual self-defense.[67]

Communitarianism and the Way of *Ubuntu*

Now that an understanding of famous Western perspectives on just war theory has been discussed, *Ubuntu* and Afro-communitarian ethics are covered. Despite most conflicts within the African continent, there is not much literature on the morality of war in Africa.[68] From *Ubuntu* and Afro-communitarian moral philosophy, the morality of war and particularly outlining when violence is permissible can be explained.

Communitarianism can be broken down into four rays of analysis: methodological, ontological, epistemological, and axiological. The methodological form of communitarianism explains the relations of people in a shared community. The ontological segment of communitarianism provides the reciprocal expectation of how humans relate with other people as part of living in a community. The epistemological version of communitarianism shares the collectivity of knowledge that is created, and respected, by elders that constitute the knowledge and wisdom of that given community. The axiological form focuses on the values of the community that structure the behavior of people in society.[69] Afro-communitarianism is part of African moral philosophy and shares commonality with Western perspectives of communitarianism. For instance, American sociologist Amitai Etzioni claims that society must articulate what is deemed as good and that such articulation is required and legitimate.[70] Therefore, Etzioni is arguing that communitarians analyze how the good—which have their

[67] Jeff McMahan, "The Ethics of Killing in War," *Ethics*, Vol. 114, No. 4 (July 2004), pp. 693–733.

[68] Uchenna Okeja, "War by Agreement: A Reflection on the Nature of Just War," *Journal of Military Ethics*, Vol.18, No. 3 (November 2019), pp. 189–203.

[69] Olúfẹ́mi Táíwò, "Against African Communalism," *Journal of French and Francophone Philosophy*, Vol. 24, No. 1 (October 2016), pp. 81–100.

[70] Amitai Etzioni, "Communitarianism," in *Encyclopedia of Community: From the Village to the Virtual World*, edited by Karen Christensen and David Levinson (Thousand Oaks, CA: Sage, 2003), pp. 224–228.

values established—is justified, conveyed, and enforced. This means that values are historically transmitted and units of the community (or society) convey and enforce these rules. The values may range from schools to the family, churches, and social clubs that are all the social fabric of communities.

Like Western forms of communitarianism, as presented by Etzioni, Africans focus on the relationship between individuals and their communities within a regular African-based society. Metz convincingly argues that African values are communitarian and relational, so harmonious communal relationships are highly valued by a group, which is contrasted with Western individual, and alleged rational, autonomy.[71] Unlike classical liberalists that focus on individualism that result in individual rights, freedom, and liberties (deriving from notably John Locke), the values of the community and the norms that are created, justified, and even enforced are placed at higher importance than individual characteristics. Yet, Afro-communitarianism is not entirely against the interests of individuals and human progress as classical liberalism worked so hard for. Instead, Afro-communitarianism ambitiously attempts to consider the interests of individuals within a community. It is of communal interests to seriously consider the needs of its peoples because individual interests constitute the collectivity of individuals.[72] It is thus the community that incorporates individuals rather than individuals making up a community.

Social harmony is part of *Ubuntu*. Since 1846, *Ubuntu* was written about that which covered the moral quality of person(s).[73] *Ubuntu* once meant manhood that was used interchangeably with virtue, moral goodness, and common humanity, and from the 1950s, it moved beyond its

[71] The relational aspect rests on people relating to one another harmoniously, or communally, with mutual respect Thaddeus Metz, "An African Theory of Just Causes for War," in *Comparative Just War Theory: An Introduction to International Perspectives*, edited by Luís Cordeiro-Rodrigues and Danny Singh (Lanham, MD: Roman & Littlefield, 2020), pp. 131–132.

[72] Jonathan O. Chimakonam and L. Uchenna Ogbonnaya, "Can Afro-Communitarianism Be Useful in Combating the Challenge of Human Interaction Posed by the COVID-19 Pandemic?" *International Journal of Environmental Research and Public Health*, Vol. 19, Issue 21, 14255 (October 2022), p. 3.

[73] Christian B. N. Gade, "The Historical Development of the Written Discourses on *Ubuntu*," *South African Journal of Philosophy*, Vol. 30, No. 3 (2011), pp. 306–309.

male-based morality to human nature, humanness, and humanity.[74] There are notable differences to *Ubuntu* and its applicability for all human beings universally,[75] distinct for Africa,[76] or for the Bantu-speaking people.[77] Despite the debate on the applicability of *Ubuntu*, it is an African moral philosophy promoting positive community and friendly relations, goodwill, generosity, caring, and benevolence.[78]

Ubuntu can more simply be explained by relational ethics and communality, which are the main central facets of Afro-communitarianism. For relational ethics, individualism is not associated with moral perspectives, but it is the relationship of people considering moral values with the community that matter most. As part of relational ethics, *Ubuntu* requires *palaver*[79] to embrace the historical collectivity of human beings as one sharing solidarity and hospitality to others that can never be abandoned.[80] From an African moral perspective of *Ubuntu*, a person is validated as a person through other people that can be compared with Jesus acting as "the man for others."[81] If someone is benevolent, kind, hospitable, or compassionate, then they can be said to "have *Ubuntu*" by acting good toward others.[82] When someone is praised, they have *Ubuntu* and are "hospitable," generous, caring, and friendly with social harmony of the community being "the greatest good" (*summum bonum*).[83] Conversely, Africans would argue that if a person relates to others negatively, then that

[74] Luís Cordeiro-Rodrigues, "Towards a Tutuist Ethics of War: *Ubuntu*, Forgiveness and Reconciliation," *Politikon: South African Journal of Political Studies*, Vol. 45, No. 3 (June 2018), p. 429.

[75] G. H. Calpin. *The South African Way of Life: Values and Ideals of a Multi-racial Society* (New York: Columbia University Press, 1953).

[76] Noni Jabavu, *Drawn in Color: African Contrasts* (London: John Murray, 1961).

[77] Edwin William Smith, *The Blessed Missionaries: Being the Phelps-Stokes Lectures Delivered in Cape Town in 1949 (with Foreword by Sir Herbert Stanley* (Oxford: Oxford University Press, 1950).

[78] Tutu, *No Future Without Forgiveness*, p. 35.

[79] *Palaver* can loosely be defined as a customary meeting and the establishment or preservation of social links and harmony that is instituted in a village with a traditional house, tree, or hut to settle disputes amicably.

[80] Bénézet Bujo, *Foundations of an African Ethic: Beyond the Universal Claims of Western Morality* (Spring Valley, NY: Crossroad Publishing, 2001).

[81] Colin Tinei Chasi, "Tutuist Ubuntu and Just War," *Politikon: South African Journal of Political Studies*, Vol. 45, No. 2 (2018), p. 234.

[82] Kwame Gyeke, "African Ethics," in *The Stanford Encyclopedia of Philosophy*, edited by Edward N. Zalta (Fall 2011 Edition), https://plato.stanford.edu/entries/african-ethics/.

[83] Tutu, *No Future without Forgiveness*, pp. 31, 35.

person lacks *Ubuntu*.[84] Rightness and doing the right thing bind people with togetherness, and those who engage in wrongdoing are separated.[85] People exhibit solidarity to mutually benefit one another that is acted repetitively over time, and failing solidarity would involve displaying "ill will in the form of hostility and cruelty."[86] Honoring relationships with sharing and caring is crucial for *Ubuntu*, thus aiding a person to respect amicable relationships and avert entering enmity ones.[87] *Ubuntu* and Afro-communitarianism, thus, is against enmity-like relations, social disharmony, and discordant state of affairs.

Ubuntu represents a well-known African ethic, and it explains what actions are made right and wrong. Deceit, theft, lying, abuse, and cheating are unfriendly insofar that these actions contravene friendship. The actor is more concerned with one's own or another's interest rather than the mutual social harmony and togetherness with the recipient. *Ubuntu* shares characteristics with religion, but it is a secular, relational, and communitarian moral ethic.

Despite the principles of *Ubuntu* being notably secular, *Ubuntu* also has traits based on religion, namely Christianity. Harmonious communal relations and "human conciliation" are the foundation of *Ubuntu* that is similar to Christianity.[88] Tutu contended that religion influences peace, justice, togetherness, righteousness, and reconciliation within political, social, and economic spheres because all humans belong to God's Kingdom and humans act as his agents.[89] Based on this relational, communal, and religious assertion, lying, disloyalty, breaking promises, and/or kidnapping is morally impermissible, and 'wrong,' because outside, or innocent parties, parties are treated discordantly that contravenes their capacity to harmonize or be harmonized and thus would not qualify as a person.[90] This is different to rights based on violating the autonomy of individuals,

[84] Thaddeus Metz, "Human Dignity, Capital Punishment, and an African Moral Theory: Toward a New Philosophy of Human Rights," *Journal of Human Rights*, Vol. 9, No. 1 (February 2010), p. 83.

[85] Heidi Verhoef and Claudine Michel, "Studying Morality within the African Context," *The Journal of Moral Education*, Vol. 26, No. 4 (1997), p. 397.

[86] Metz, "Human Dignity, Capital Punishment, and an African Moral Theory," p. 84.

[87] Metz, "Human Dignity, Capital Punishment, and an African Moral Theory," p. 84.

[88] Chasi, "Tutuist Ubuntu and Just War," p. 234.

[89] Tutu, *The Rainbow People of God*, pp. 71–72.

[90] Thaddeus Metz and Joseph B. R. Gaie, "The African Ethic of *Ubuntu*/Botho: Implications for Research on Morality," *The Journal of Moral Education*, Vol. 39, No. 3 (August 2010), pp. 275, 277; Metz, "An African Theory of Just Causes for War," p. 136.

which is generally the Western-based liberal benchmark on protecting rights, liberties, and fundamental freedoms.

Communitarianism, unlike individualism, places emphasis on community values rather than individual features. It has that African cultural unity can be compared to Asian and Western regions to describe the totality of life, work, thinking, and philosophy within "a given society."[91] It can therefore clearly be argued that communitarianism is applicable in Africa.[92] African culture, as a type of communitarianism, focuses on solidarity, caring, sharing, "complementarity," and "mutual independence."[93] This is African communitarianism, and Afro-communitarianism is used in its shorter form.

African cultural traits determine who an African is and is part of a community that shares a likeliness toward "cultural arts and symbols" with the "worship of ancestors," "religion" permeating "total life" and a "thorough cultural upbringing," meaning "the African is not individualistic."[94] A form of African-based communitarianism is thus established with the notion of an extended family where "everybody is linked with all the other members, living or dead, through a complex network of spiritual relationship into a kind of mystical body."[95] Sacredness (humans containing spirit) is highly regarded in African moral theory that can be accompanied with sense of hospitality, community, identity, and good human values and relations.[96] In relation to the former segment, religion is part of *Ubuntu* and there are links made to the Bible.[97] When respecting the Bible and the

[91] Jacques Jérôme Pierre Maquet, *Africanity: The Cultural Unity of Black Africa*, translated by Joan K. Rayfield (New York: Oxford University Press, 1973), pp. 4, 8–9.

[92] However, communitarianism is not only applicable for African civilians and cultures. In Asia, community values, religion, the importance of neighbors and benevolence are common practice.

[93] Chimakonam and Ogbonnaya, "Can Afro-Communitarianism Be Useful in Combating the Challenge of Human Interaction Posed by the COVID-19 Pandemic?" p. 1.

[94] Chukwudum Barnabas Okolo, "The African Person: A Cultural Definition," *Indian Philosophical Quarterly*, Vol. 16, No. 1 (January 1989), pp. 70–72.

[95] E. A. Ruch and K. Chukwulozie Anyanwu, *African Philosophy: An Introduction to the Main Philosophical Trends in Contemporary Africa* (Rome: Catholic Book Agency, 1981), p. 328.

[96] Ugwuanyi suggests that these combined principles present the African conceptions of just war theory (Ugwuanyi, "Towards an African Theory of Just War," p. 56).

[97] I will discuss some religious points of *ubuntu* in brief here, but my intention rests on extracting the reciprocal principles of mutual solidarity, a shared identity, caring, kindness, love, hospitality for strangers, equality and social justice that can also be applied with Afro-communitarian ethics to test in the remainder of the chapters on foreign armed intervention.

opening book of Genesis, God shares a relationship with people that is attached with mutual love and social justice in reciprocity.[98]

The African concept of *Ubuntu* has like-mindedness with the teachings of the Bible concerning mutual caring for each other and justice.[99] *Ubuntu* claims that God made humans in his image with the characteristics to dispense equality, kindness, charity, love for neighbors, and social justice to humans as fellow beings.[100] From this postulation and deriving from the Nguni language, *Ubuntu* implies the humanness of human beings as people containing intrinsic relationships to other human beings on how to live life and perform actions that is innate from God's creation.[101] *Ubuntu* promotes biblical relationships of social justice to establish communal relations to embrace justice and equality.

The Nguni term, *Ubuntu*, is embedded in, and derives from, "African indigenous cultures."[102] *Ubuntu* covers the global interdependence of human rights, "communalism," and "solidarity" that is traceable to "pre-colonial Africa" and is part of all "indigenous" African cultures.[103] African moral philosophy, and notably *Ubuntu*, stands for the sub-Saharan African ethics of "living harmoniously" with other human beings and supporting

This is not to say that the theological aspects of *ubuntu* cannot be applied to such armed conflicts, but this is beyond the scope of this book.

[98] Social justice concerns the justifiable relationships between social classes and groups for the equitable distribution of state and private benefits and goods linked to domestic and economic growth (David Miller, *Principles of Social Justice* (Cambridge, MA: Harvard University Press, 1999)). Therefore, acts of corruption, nepotism, ill-will and cronyism would violate equitable social justice and the social contract of fairness, including basic human rights and civil liberties, which only permits inequality of wealth, but not poverty (John Bordley Rawls, *A Theory of Justice* (Cambridge, MA: Harvard University Press, 2001, p. xi)).

[99] Christians are to help disadvantaged people in need irrespective of their relationship or race (Jacques Walter Beukes and Laurika Elouise Beukes, "Proposing a Social Justice Approach to Diaconia for a South African Context," *Religions*, Vol. 14, No. 668 (May 2023), p. 6).

[100] Selaelo T. Kgatla, "Relationships Are Building Blocks to Social Justice: Cases of Biblical Justice and African Ubuntu." *HTS Teologiese Studies/Theological Studies*, Vol. 72, No. 1, a3239 (October 2016), pp. 1, 4.

[101] Tutu, *No Future without Forgiveness*, p. 35.

[102] Christian B. N. Gade, "What is *Ubuntu*? Different Interpretations Among South Africans of African Descent," *South African Journal of Philosophy*, Vol. 31, No. 3 (2012), p. 486.

[103] Christopher J. Roedder and Darren Moellendorf, *Jurisprudence* (Lansdowne: Juta, 2004), p. 441.

"communal relationships."[104] Afro-communitarianism is based on the morality of sub-Saharan Africans and *Ubuntu* of people being connected to one another by virtue of being human, so people adapt humanness, an identity, and strive to become a "full," real, or "genuine" human.[105] *Ubuntu* has different terms in sub-Saharan Africa that mean roughly the same thing, *e.g.*, *umuntu* and *umundu* in Kimeru and Kiknya (Kenyan), and *bomoto* and *gimuntu* in Bobangi and KiKongo (Democratic Republic of Congo), respectively.[106] Thus, African *Ubuntu* proposes that all human beings have humanness, and people of African descent emphasize it more. Gade takes this debate forward on *Ubuntu* identifying the possession of the moral qualities of "African humanism" and interconnectivity of people, exclusive to "South Africans of African descent" who are black and accept these moral values or "persons."[107] Metz disagrees by further arguing that *Ubuntu*, as an African moral philosophy, is "universally" applicable.[108] Behaviors and actions are based on relational communal harmony, and these characteristics of *Ubuntu* can be studied by non-Africans also.

Ubuntu promotes mutual love and connectedness to foster better human relations. Pure experience forms the in between that relates human beings to other humans on a mutual basis. The betweenness constitutes love regarding human experience and relationships. This can be explained with an I-Thou analogy insofar that active experience overcomes ego to create relationships with other human beings.[109] Under *Ubuntu*, human beings hold I-Thou relationships that makes humans inclusive of each other to also help and consider disadvantaged groups. In attaining togetherness, the principles of fairness and justice are based on the belief that God desires the perseveration of mutual friendly relationships with neighbors, irrespective of race or color. The teachings of Jesus contend that a neighbor, who is also a stranger from a blood relation, should be given social justice.[110] Equality constitutes the even/fair distribution of capacities to lead a normal life, which is the most crucial component of social

[104] Metz and Gaie, "The African Ethic of *Ubuntu*/Botho," p. 273.

[105] Metz and Gaie, "The African Ethic of *Ubuntu*/Botho," pp. 274–275.

[106] Gade, "What is *Ubuntu*? p. 486.

[107] Gade, "What is *Ubuntu*? p. 492.

[108] Metz, "A Life of Struggle as Ubuntu," in *Nelson Rolihlahla Mandela: Decolonial Ethics of Liberation and Servant Leadership* (Trenton, NJ: Africa World Press, 2015), p. 3.

[109] Martin Buber, *I and Thou*, 2nd edition (New York: Charles Scribner's Sons, 1958), p. 62.

[110] David E. Lanier, "Who Is my Neighbor?" *Biblical Illustrator Magazine*, April 9, 2013, p. 1.

justice.[111] If a person neglects these ideals, then they lack rationality as a non-person, which—according to Aristotle—makes a human being absurd.[112]

Afro-communitarianism does have links with African moral philosophy. As discussed in the former part of this chapter, *Ubuntu* concerns an individual who represents a person via other people. Other African moral philosophy, which is not exhaustive, can be brought to our attention. The 1930s Francophone inspired surreal literary studies on Négritude raised and cultivated black consciousness throughout Africa and diaspora groups to disavow colonialism, Eurocentrism, and racism by underlining that an individual asserts their self, identity, ideas, and belonging to relate with others.[113]

According to *Ibuanyidanda* ontology, questioning the reality of oneself rests on belonging that is collective and not being or acting alone to fulfil a reciprocally complementary bond of "consciousness, which integrates all modes of self-expression of being into one framework of mutual interrelated units."[114] When an understanding of social relations is reached, all community members then strive toward accomplishing the common benefit of everyone.[115] According to the late Bujo, African theology reflects the social reality and historical experiences of African people that are needed for African consciousness, the "mystical body" of both living and dead members, mutual obligations to each other, and an understanding of humans, not God, being responsible for sins.[116] In this way, resembling *ujamaa* (a type of rural Tanzanian socialism), humans act in "mutual respect by each member of the kinship group" that obligates all members to work without economic differentiation "to contribute to the collective

[111] Rawls, *A Theory of Justice*, pp. 18–19.

[112] Mogobe B. Ramose, "An African Perspective on Justice and Race," *Polylog: Forum for Intercultural Philosophy*, 2001, para 11. https://them.polylog.org/3/frm-en.htm. To maintain social justice, political, economic, and environmental injustices, including powers that exploit ordinary people, should be confronted.

[113] Sylvia Washington Bâ, *The Concept of Négritude in the Poetry of Léopold Sédar Senghor* (Princeton, NJ: Princeton University Press, 1973).

[114] Innocent I. Asouzu, *Ibuanyidanda: New Complementary Ontology: Beyond World-immanentism, Ethnocentric Reduction and Impositions* (Zürich: LIT Verlag, 2007), pp. 56–57.

[115] Kwame Gyekye, *Beyond Cultures: Perceiving a Common Humanity* (Washington, DC: The Council for Research in Values and Philosophy, 2004), p. 16.

[116] Bénézet Bujo, *African Theology in Its Social Context* (Eugene, OR: Wipf & Stock, 1992), pp. 22, 32.

welfare of the group."[117] To exist as a person, one must belong with members of a community (*Uwa*), which creates peace in society. The late Ghanian philosopher, Gyekye, defended that the maintenance of socialism adopted by African kings and liberation armies for independence favoring the public, rather than private entities, owning the means of production was an inherent part of traditional African communal values.[118] Like Karl Marx's conception of commodity fetishism, Gyekye did not favor capitalist profit-making purchasing labor and selling goods and services to the liberal consumer market without their input. Social harmony can be intertwined with consciousness (*palaver*) and respecting traditional beliefs to preserve harmony and sharing values in a community (*Ubuntu*).[119]

Under this African moral philosophy, humans should engage with the synchronicity of a community to bolster the relationship of their identity to achieve harmonious solidarity and mutual coexistence.[120] In contemporary capitalist societies, many governments and the organic solidarity of societies—as suggested by Émile Durkheim—attract individuals to leave their communities to enter the private sphere. Yet, under Afro-communitarianism, such individuals can never realize their identity due to the detachment from the original community.[121] The integration of a person is more beneficial than being alone.[122] Humans are species that always lust for interaction, so individuals need to coexist within a community to truly discover and enjoy their identity. These aspects of African moral philosophy present the thesis that Afro-communitarianism attempts to

[117] David Feldman, "The Economics of Ideology: Some Problems of Achieving Rural Socialism in Tanzania," in *Politics and Change in Developing Countries: Studies in the Theory and Practice of Development*, edited by Colin Leys (Cambridge: Cambridge University Press, 1969), pp. 87–88. With this point, I am merely emphasizing the principles of working together and the collectivism of a community rather than advocating that the means of production should be owned by individuals and earn similar wages (socialism).

[118] Kwame Gyekye, *Tradition and Modernity* (New York, NY: Oxford University Press, 1997), pp. 149–157.

[119] Simonmary Asese Aihiokhai, "Remembering Bénézet Bujo, who Offered a Vision of African Theological Imagination," *National Catholic Reporter*, November 21, 2023.

[120] Thaddeus Metz and Sarah Clark Miller, "Relational Ethics," in *The International Encyclopedia of Ethics*, edited by Hugh LaFollette (Hoboken, NJ: Wiley-Blackwell, 2016), pp. 1–10.

[121] Thaddeus Metz, "An Overview of African Ethics," in *Themes, Issues and Problems in African Philosophy*, edited by I. Upokolo (Cham: Palgrave Macmillan, 2017), pp. 61–76.

[122] G.O. Ozumba and Jonathan O. Chimakonam, *Njikoka Amaka: Further Discussion on the Philosophy of Integrative Humanism* (Calabar: 3rd Logic Option, 2014).

promote and enhance the values of solidarity, complementarity, and coexistence that should be exercised and practiced by the collectiveness of people within a given community. This African moral philosophy is based on communitarianism, which is the bedrock of the methodological aspect of Afro-communitarianism.

The values of Afro-communitarianism from the axiological segment rest on the values of integration, human actions seeking to respect others as humans, promote equality, and be aware of human limitations that can be joyful—as part of complementarity and interdependent interaction and mutual benefits of respecting these principles. As part of the process of integration, an individual realizes their being via their community,[123] by exercising moral actions. The communal belonging encourages the person to act morally with behavior and actions. These values can reach social harmony, which is the ultimate and desirable good to form social harmony, and the interests rest on every individual to share the same community as everyone else.[124] In sum, the promotion of identity and solidarity are to be preserved for peaceful relations and is thus preferred for the bolstering of humanness and respect of each other. Africans emphasize a completeness of the person who respects these amiable traits.

Based on African moral philosophy, the upmost good for Afro-communitarianism is constructive communal associations. Positive community relations are part of *Ubuntu* that have been traditionally exercised from Bantu-speaking people in the region of southern Africa. *Ubuntu* portrays individuals as human beings that are so by virtue of the existence of other human beings. With interconnectedness, *Ubuntu* clusters the morality of human beings and their acceptable multifaceted ethical behavior to respect friendliness, compassion, hospitality, and generosity for the community to fulfil the moral quality of people.[125] *Ubuntu* considers the upmost commitment for the benefit of the community that frames and binds identity, compassion, respect for others, and life experiences.[126] For instance, if someone is lost in another village, a villager will accommodate

[123] Chimakonam and Ogbonnaya, "Can Afro-Communitarianism Be Useful in Combating the Challenge of Human Interaction Posed by the COVID-19 Pandemic?" p. 8.

[124] K. Gyekye, *Tradition and Modernity: Philosophical Reflections on the African Experience* (New York, NY: Oxford University Press, 1997).

[125] Gade, "What is *Ubuntu*? pp. 484–503.

[126] Gessler Muxe Nkondo, "Ubuntu as a Public Policy in South Africa," *International Journal of African Renaissance Studies*, Vol. 2, No. 1 (September 2007), p. 91, pp. 88–100. https://doi.org/10.1080/18186870701384202.

that person and arrange secure transport so that the person can comfortably reach their destination. If the villager cannot personally help, they will go out of their way to ensure the person is taken care of.[127] Therefore, all human beings are bound with an interconnected relationship, and all have the duty to act in good faith with fellow human beings within a community. This demonstrates mutual solidarity, sharing and caring with others in the community.

Forgiveness is more important than retaliation, so violence is avoided when possible, for *Ubuntu*.[128] Alongside forgiveness (and not forgetting), *Ubuntu* prescribes reconciliation, truth-telling, and humane treatment to renew or release the broken relationship and alleviate anger.[129] Under African morality, reconciliation is sought with wrongdoers, for relational purposes, to restore tarnished relationships.[130] This approach is preferred over victims wanting retribution (punishment) and examples are provided from historical African acts of reconciliation.[131] For Africans, the community is valued and they are against retribution as a form of punishment and vengeance because, under the ethos of *Ubuntu*, punishing someone needs to improve the lives involved to be justified.[132] Instead, the African ethic prefers reconciliation between the parties involved: perpetrator, victim, their families, and the wider community with the purpose of providing an explanation and resolution between the parties.[133] Therefore, when applying *Ubuntu* to justice, it differs from Kantian or Durkheimian justifications of retributive justice (proportionate punishment and conspicuous imprisonment based on the severity of the crime). The moral deliberation

[127] Gade, "What is *Ubuntu*?" p. 490.

[128] Forgiveness was adopted by South Africa with its Truth and Reconciliation Commission.

[129] A. Okechukwu Ogbonnaya, *On Communitarian Divinity: An African Interpretation of the Trinity* (New York: Paragon House, 1994), p. 2.

[130] Thaddeus Metz, "A Theory of National Reconciliation: Some Insights from Africa," in *Theorizing Transitional Justice*, edited by Claudio Corradetti, Nir Eisikovits and Jack Rotondi (Surrey: Ashgate, 2015), pp. 119–135.

[131] As one example, when King Moshoeshoe I of Lesotho (enclaved by South Africa) accomplished the defense of his territory of the mountain by night (*Thaba-Bosia*) and peoples from unjustified force, he issued cattle as a gift to the defeated sides (the Mzilikazi and British Commander Sir George Cathcart) (Khali Victor Mofuoa, "The Exemplary Ethical Leadership of King Moshoeshoe of Basotho of Lesotho in the Nineteenth Century Southern Africa," *Journal of Public Administration and Governance*, Vol. 5, No. 3 (2015), p. 28.)

[132] Metz, "Human Dignity, Capital Punishment, and an African Moral Theory," p. 86.

[133] Metz and Joseph B. R. Gaie, "The African Ethic of *Ubuntu*/Botho," p. 278; Metz, "Human Dignity, Capital Punishment, and an African Moral Theory," p. 86.

of wrongdoing is the driver of utilitarianism and Western criminal justice consequentialism that allegedly deters future offending, but *Ubuntu* focuses on rebuilding friendly relations—as a process of social harmony—with reconciliation and notably, restorative justice.

For conflict mediation, the concept of togetherness can result in a democratic consensus and cooperation to meet everyone's needs to resolve political conflicts.[134] *Ubuntu* is the fundamental foundation of African moral philosophy that is based on the notion of "being" as "a oneness and an indivisible whole-ness."[135] When analyzing war from the perspective of *Ubuntu*, all sides are human beings (e.g., whether Russia or Ukraine in relation to their contemporary war) and all persons and people.[136] Hence, the relations of mutuality toward others are part of *Ubuntu* compassion, kindness, respect, solidarity, and benevolence for others.

It is important to justify why *Ubuntu* has been framed as the bedrock of Afro-communitarianism for the purpose of this book. Contrary to this theoretical imposition, it could be contended that African moral theory as a looser term constitutes Afro-communitarianism because the principles of *Ubuntu* are part of many other African philosophies and locations. To provide a few examples, in Ghana, for Akan people, moral and ideal virtues—like *Ubuntu*—include kindness, benevolence, compassion, respect, and courtesy for others.[137] As part of Akan maxims, recognizing the worthiness of human beings as equal to oneself by virtue of humanity is more significant than gold and comparable to a "universal human brotherhood."[138] For the Igbo Nsukka and Iso-Uzo people in northern Nigeria, those who possess the qualities of integrity and "love for truth" on communal interests, need, and mediation are *Akumugha*.[139] Based on these varieties of African moral theory, solidarity, sharing, caring, compassion, helpfulness, kindness, unselfishness, respect, dignity, trust, and

[134] Thaddeus Metz, "Developing African Political Philosophy: Moral-Theoretic Strategies," *Philosophia Africana*, Vol. 14, No. 1 (September 2012), pp. 68–70, pp. 61–83. https://doi.org/10.5840/philafricana20121419.

[135] Ramose, "An African Perspective on Justice and Race," para. 3.

[136] Moeketsi Letseka, "How Would *Ubuntu* Respond to the Crises in the World Today?" *London School of Economics and Political Science*, November 15, 2023.

[137] Kwame Gyeke, "Traditional Political Ideas: Their Relevance to Development in Contemporary Africa," in *Person and Community: Ghanian Philosophical Studies, I* (Washington, DC: Council for Research in Values and Philosophy, 1992), pp. 243–255.

[138] Gyeke, "African Ethics."

[139] Ugwuanyi, "Towards an African Theory of Just War," p. 59.

sacrifice to do good are components of African theological social harmony and principally *Ubuntu* ethical values.[140] When engaging with these *Ubuntu* principles, people enter and engage more deeply into their community with other people that exclude selfishness and include sharing with others like with a family in Africa.[141] Therefore, people can possess these indigenous cultivating virtues, such as *Ubuntu*, which maintains a harmonious communal state of affairs. These traits are highly valuable to society and communities that resound with a considerable part of sub-Saharan people.[142]

Afro-communitarian Deontological and Consequential Ethics

From the way of *Ubuntu*, Afro-communitarianism considers the integration between social harmonious and positive communal relationships as the greatest good.[143] Tutu identified that social harmony (*summum bonum*) is the greatest good and undermining it must be averted because the consequence is comparable to the plague.[144] Tutu was a Christian liberation theologian, who promoted peace, harmony, and reconciliation with his references to *Ubuntu* (aligned with his Christian beliefs). Tutu intertwined Christian and African indigenous belief systems by advocating that the Bible promoted one humanity bound by unity, harmony, friendliness, and fellowship.[145] Communitarianism, and its African version, rests on social organization to formulate human relationships, behavior, interaction, and conduct in society. The given community shares these values that inform mutual friendship, goodwill, caring, solidarity, a shared identity, and reciprocal benevolence to form social harmony.[146] These

[140] Mluleki Mnyaka and Mokgethi Motlhabi, "The African Concept of *Ubuntu/Botho* and its Social-Moral Significance," *Black Theology*, Vol. 3, No. 2 (April 2005), p. 227.

[141] Augustine Shutte, *Ubuntu: An Ethic for the New South African* (Cape Town: Cluster Publications, 2001), pp. 29–30.

[142] Luís Cordeiro-Rodrigues, "Afro-Communitarianism and the Role of Traditional African Healers in the COVID-19 Pandemic," *Public Health Ethics*, Vol. 14, No. 1 (March 2021), p. 62.

[143] Cordeiro-Rodrigues, "Afro-Communitarianism," p. 61.

[144] Tutu, *No Future without Forgiveness*, p. 35.

[145] Desmond Mpilo Tutu, *The Rainbow People of God: The Making of a Peaceful Revolution* (New York: Doubleday, 1994), p. 61.

[146] Thaddeus Metz, "Toward an African Moral Theory," *Journal of Political Philosophy*, 15, no. 3 (2007), p. 338.

principles should be promoted, and it is inacceptable to undermine such values. The problem of one individual belonging to a community is an issue for all members of that community.[147] To seek redress and rectifying the individual's problems, issues with the community are identified, meaning that problems and redress are part of a collective process. This is part of moral philosophy and is used for practical means, which can create peace and dialogue at the grassroots level.

On the opposite end of the spectrum, the lowest good to friendliness is unfriendliness that abuses communal values of shared identity and goodwill that results in a discordant state of affairs. Individuals may pursue their own objectives but must act with good intentions and still be supportive of others. Unlike Western city-states, individuals are not on their own because they are part of the community.[148] The "awareness" of people's "interdependence" that is "social" rather than focusing on "objects," meaning that the responsibility toward a person's social group, trumps individual rights and privileges to nullify "individual greed" and "self-centeredness."[149] Community living is thus applicable to non-African environments. Afro-communitarianism does, however, deviate from ego-centrism, and it is the African culture that inspires the importance of sharing, caring, objectives, values, and shared interests of the community over the individual. The togetherness, complementarity, and collective responsibility for the community is fundamental. There is a family-like social bond to come together in solidarity to deal with collective problems. This is done, for example, in traditional Igbo culture who come together whenever there is a crisis.[150]

[147] Chimakonam and Ogbonnaya, "Can Afro-Communitarianism Be Useful in Combating the Challenge of Human Interaction Posed by the COVID-19 Pandemic?" p. 3.

[148] In a loose way, individuality and conspicuous consumption have been presented as city-state lifestyles and rural farmstead communities enjoy group-like activities and familiar occupations (Thorstein Veblen, *The Theory of the Leisure Class: An Economic Study of Institutions* (New York, NY: Macmillan, 1899). However, the barbarian treatment of women is not part of Afro-communitarianism or contemporary *ubuntu*. The promotion of cooperation, cultural lifestyles, and togetherness are part of Afro-communitarianism that goes beyond Durkheim's conception of mechanical solidarity or *gemeinschaft* because sharing and caring are also placed as part of communal, and rural, importance without individual motives.

[149] A. Wade Boykin, "The Academic Performance of Afro-American Children." In *Achievement and Achievement Motives*, edited by Janet T. Spence (San Francisco, CA: Freeman, 1983), pp. 321–371.

[150] Innocent I. Asouzu, *The Method and Principles of Complementary Reflection in and beyond African Philosophy* (Calabar: University of Calabar Press, 2004).

A deontological perspective of Afro-communitarian concentrates on preserving positive community relations (for the maintenance of goodwill and shared identity) and avoids acting against such values. From the deontological approach, all forms of violence and hostile actions are impermissible—even if fighting for positive community relations, goodwill, and shared identity—because it would have to breach the backbone of Afro-communitarianism at the initial point of fighting. Actions based on the inclination of logic and reason cannot contrast deontology in any way or else such actions would be deemed unethical. The relational ethics of Afro-communitarianism strive to maintain communal and harmonious relationships and thus consequentialism is repudiated because those in a position to promote communal harmony should provide the first concern to the community where the powerful already held a harmonious connection.[151] Under this deontological perspective, foreign armed intervention is not permissible. Moreover, "an agent may not use any means whatsoever to maximize the net amount of harmony in the world" even if a longer harmony would be the result of violence.[152] This deontological approach is relatively futile for analyzing the role of foreign armed intervention because some form of violence is required, usually to rebut violence for a political settlement, robust multilateral peacekeeping operation or a unilateral or regional humanitarian intervention.

From the consequentialist viewpoint, actions that fail to support positive community relations are only permissible if the outcome sought is to strive toward promoting and/or restoring a more harmonious state of affairs (positive communal relationships). From this approach, if an action fails to promote "shared identity among people grounded on goodwill" that encourages "ill-will," subordination, "division," and a notion of "us versus them," then the action is unjustified (wrong).[153] Under this Metzian reformation of Tutuist *Ubuntu* ethics, violence can be justified to rebut the "wrong" that guides just war theory waging war, conduct in war, and justice after the fighting.[154] Discord can be adopted if it enhances the welfare of communities or helps form a society retain its community to

[151] Metz, "An African Theory of Just Causes for War," p. 136.

[152] Metz, "An African Theory of Just Causes for War," p. 137.

[153] Metz, "Toward an African Moral Theory," p. 338.

[154] Metz, "Toward an African Moral Theory," p. 338. It is important to note that Tutu did not encourage violence with his adoption of *ubuntu* alongside Christianity to promote reconciliation and forgiveness, but did not object to violence in the context of South Africa because friendly alternatives failed to deal with apartness and discrimination. This is why

produce "better individual and collective lives."[155] *Ubuntu* is not distinct to one tribe or location (tribalist) failing to consider the morality and ethics of an extended clan, and *Ubuntu* is not pacifist that fully forbids violence in all situations.[156] Therefore, this interpretation is not based on pacificism to reach a socially harmonious state of affairs. From a consequentialist perspective, discord is morally permissible if the end outcome results in a socially harmonious situation.

Violence can be used in self-defense from Metz's interpretation of *Ubuntu* ethics because violence goes against the greatest good of social harmony and thus it can be rebutted to form a less disharmonious situation. Barriers to communal progress can be rebutted with morally justified violence *jus ad bellum*.[157] Violence can be morally permissible to exercise the right to self-governance, as exemplified by Cabral and Frantz Omar Fanon, to improve the state of affairs and would not be justified if the situation was not progressed.[158] When considering actions in self-defense to discord, violence can be initiated after nonviolent measures to restore social harmony, and violence is stopped if it is ineffective or accomplishing social harmony is no longer required.[159]

Like with international humanitarian law and international human rights, such as war crimes, rape, torture, murder, and apartheid, these acts of severe discord (enmity) are perpetrated against innocents who have not acted in this manner—and thus violates the identity and solidarity-based relationships.[160] This is wrong even if a better state of harmonious affairs

Metz has reformed the interpretations of *ubuntu* to provide more depth on justified violence in Africa (African just war theory).

[155] Colin Tinei Chasi, "*Ubuntu* and Freedom of Expression: Considering Children and Broadcast News Violence in a Violent Society," *Journal of Media Ethics*, Vol. 30, No. 2 (2015), p. 104.

[156] Metz, "A Life of Struggle as Ubuntu," p. 2.

[157] Ronald Olufemi Badru, "An African Philosophical Account of Just War Theory," *Ethical Perspectives*, Vol. 26, No. 2 (2019), p. 171.

[158] Conversely, if there is harmonious state of affairs, then violence cannot be conducted to improve a situation (Luís Cordeiro-Rodrigues, "African Perspectives on Just War," *Philosophy Compass*, Vol. 17, No. 3 (March 2022), pp. 3–4).

[159] Cordeiro-Rodrigues, "Towards a Tutuist Ethics of War," p. 431.

[160] An economic blockade by a naval force, cutting the supply of water or the construction of a dam on a main river threatening one side do not constitute aggression from a Western perspective, but would require a rebuttal because they would qualify as severe discord under Afro-communitarian principles (Metz, "An African Theory of Just Causes for War," pp. 138, 144–146). Therefore, activities that require rebuttal are not always militaristic.

is reached in the aftermath. In this way, the action(s) is only justified if the rightness of actions is defined by identity, solidarity, and/or friendship that form relationships. Parties that fall outside of the community are not to be treated with enmity or discordance though. It is the promotion of positive communal relationships that measures the permissibility of the action (even if it initially conducts violence to try and bring a more harmonious state of affairs by restoring shared identity and goodwill). Therefore, Afro-communitarianism prefers nonviolence, but for the consequentialist version—if affairs are not promoting shared identity and goodwill (negative communal relations)—then violence can be morally permissible.

Taking Afro-communitarian relational ethics into consideration, the justification of violence can be underlined. There are three African responses on deciding to wage violence: (1) consequentialism; (2) analyze peace and war (the situation) and its impact on the people to decide whether entering war is permissible or not; and (3) enter war to rebut wrongs perpetrated.[161] These responses can be linearly clarified. If there is antisocial contradiction of communion, and thus a large extent of a discordant state of affairs, then violence is only justified if it is directed at the initial participants of dissonance with a least amount of discord to rebut it; and "no greater discord" should be adopted or else it is "unjust."[162] In this way, violence is permissible only if it is compulsory to defend a community with discord.[163] An aggressor threatening or attacking an innocent party can be rebutted with comparable violence because it would not degrade the rebutter's capacity for social/communal harmony.[164] Put simply, *Ubuntu* ethics can deal with unfriendly action proportionality.[165] Therefore, *Ubuntu* may permit violence if the outcome results in social harmony.[166]

In other words, military conflict may be morally permissible if a culture or community is under suppression, but Afro-communitarianism is opposed to Western forms of waging war to deter or punish aggressors, or

[161] Cordeiro-Rodrigues, "African Perspectives on Just War," p. 9.

[162] Metz, "An African Theory of Just Causes for War," p. 132.

[163] Ugwuanyi, "Towards an African Theory of Just War," p. 56.

[164] Eventually, severe forms of violence can only be justified when it is fundamental to deter the initiator of discord.

[165] Thaddeus Metz, "Ubuntu as a Moral Theory and Human Rights in South Africa," *African Human Rights Law Journal*, Vol. 11, No. 2 (January 2011), p. 544. https://hdl.handle.net/10520/EJC51951.

[166] Cordeiro-Rodrigues, "Towards a Tutuist Ethics of War," p. 431.

protecting a territory from an invasion.[167] I accept this Afro-communitarian approach because waging war or violence must only be permitted if necessary (heinous crimes, harm, and subordination of a group/community) and as a last resort (not for pure state relative gains but only after communities have engaged in—greatly attempted or would prove fruitless—conflict mediation, negotiation, and potential arbitration). Reconciliation between belligerent parties and the prospects of restored communal relations must be feasible in aftermath of violence being waged. I am more so sympathetic to the *Ubuntu* interpretation for foreign armed invasion. This African moral philosophy tries to do good by rebutting violence, but the comparable forms of violence advocated need to be judged on rebutting violence and reaching a social harmonious state of affairs rather than solely testing the Western principle of proportionality (against military necessity) *jus in bello*.

The concept of the just cause can be explained from *Ubuntu* principles. With *Ubuntu*, an armed struggle of liberation is morally permissible—by any single or group of actors pertaining a just cause—if a disharmonious situation becomes more harmonious or discord eradicates a discordant situation and results in a harmonious state of affairs.[168] It is the efforts to rebut harm and subordination that are of significant importance for Afro-communitarians. Luban has similarly worked on the just cause of force to protect basic human rights beyond the state.[169] This may include the Wall in the Western Bank Barrier of Israel separating Palestine from alleged threats of terrorism, but in reality also heavily denies Palestinians from basic resources that abuses access to water, which distorts the right to life. Here, the concept of "sharing" is central for Luban and Afro-communitarian principles to work on harm and subordination issues.

If discord is directed to a hostile party, it can be aimed to protect or compensate the victims (innocents). Innocents should be protected even if the guilty parties are part of a community and future long-term harmonious relations would be constrained. Substantial discord that justifies the regulation on the use of force includes killing, amputations, or psychological damage at individual and collective extents.[170] The response to discord

[167] Metz, "An African Theory of Just Causes for War," p. 132. This significantly differs to international law and the rule of self-defense legitimizing the use of force against aggression (Article 51 of the Charter of the United Nations, 1945).

[168] Cordeiro-Rodrigues, "African Perspectives on Just War," p. 4.

[169] Luban, "Just War and Human Rights," pp. 160–181.

[170] Metz, "An African Theory of Just Causes for War," p. 139.

against large enmity-violence must be conducted with the minimal necessary and measures of feasibility to rebut comparable violence and/or prevent further harm and subordination from the initiator of violence. Initiators of violence can be rebutted with proportionate forms of armed force, including by justifiable military intervention in the commitment of states and permitting rebels to fight brutal governments.[171] In other words, comparable force is only permissible even if substantial discord is needed to rebut a wrongdoer of violence and/or get them to stop and be fearful of future malevolent acts.

For example, permissible responses to rebut violence rest on a number of armed groups emerging to fight colonialism, genocide, and discrimination, such as the People's Movement for the Liberation of Angola (MPLA) in Angola against French occupation, Tutsi rebels in Rwanda, and the Arakan Liberation Army in the Rakhine State of Myanmar, respectively. However, for the consequentialist approach of Afro-communitarianism, if actions (including violence) result in relationships of enmity, in a state of affairs when individuals do not respect the valued objectives of others and do not support others, then that action is not morally acceptable.

Based on the above criteria and brief examples that will be explored in the subsequent section of this theoretical chapter, the consequentialist perspective of Afro-communitarianism permits violence if unfriendliness is dominating communal relations and thus requires rebuttal.[172] To rebut enemy-like behavior, violence is morally permissible if it results in a harmonious state of affairs and reduces (or removes) the discordant situation. These actions of violence for these justified reasons can only proceed if there are no amicable options. Hence, violence is only morally acceptable if it can weaken the enemy (of Afro-communitarian values) or result in better harmonious communal relations (state of affairs). The action(s) promoting violence must have the objective to promote a better harmonious situation and rebut a disharmonious/discordant state of affairs.

Communal harmony is considered the upmost good so violence may be morally permissible if no friendly alternatives restore this situation. There can be a situation where there is high enmity-like relations and violence, but the violence initiated determines a state of affairs that is less discordant than the prior situation. Violence that is routine merely enhances

[171] Deane-Peter Baker, "Rebellion and African Ethics," *Journal of Military Ethics*, Vol. 15, No. 4 (2016), pp. 288–298.

[172] Metz, "Ubuntu as a Moral Theory and Human Rights in South Africa," pp. 532–559.

vengeance, hate, and anger, so under Afro-communitarianism, violence must be initiated as the final option when friendly alternatives have been exhausted. The outcome is of social harmony with friendly means, so violence is likely to contravene future positive communal relationships.

An example would be of Mandela (ANC) in South Africa that would qualify conforming with consequentialist Afro-communitarian ethics. The 1913 Natives Land Act legally held that most land belonged to white civilians, which was followed by further apartheid legal statutes and the banning of political assembly. In the 1930s, the Dutch Christians prescribed apartheid that was promoted by the Dutch Reformed Church missionaries that then gained broader political values in the 1940s.[173] The National Party government thus willingly harmed and subordinated black people. Throughout the 1960s, Mandela contended that sabotage conducted by the outlawed APC's paramilitary wing, uMkhonto weSizwe [Spear of the Nation] (MK), against enforcers of the apartheid was the best outcome to restore racial relations in the future.[174] This was a justifiable method to rebut white governmental discordance against black people.[175] Mandela and MK refuted to abandon physical violence in the 1970s and 1980s.[176] If the violence from apartheid was nonexistent, then MK would not have responded with discord.[177]

Mandela and the African National Congress initially responded to apartheid with black nonviolent protesting for approximately 15 years, but this resistance was ineffective so the prohibited Congress party deemed violence as morally permissible because it was utilized as a last resort. Tutu understood these ventures of exhausting "nonviolent avenues" related to the armed struggle in South Africa.[178] Mandela used principles of violence, similar to the LOAC principle of military necessity, with sabotage by targeting electricity power stations, transportation links, telephone

[173] Christian beliefs are said to have initially justified apartheid (Saul Dubow, *Apartheid – 1948 – 1994* (Oxford: Oxford University Press, 2014).

[174] Nelson Rolihlahla Mandela, *Long Walk to Freedom* (London: Abacus, 1994).

[175] However, as the Truth and Reconciliation Commission found, violence was not justified when white people who were not part of enforcing apartheid were targeted in mainly black townships.

[176] Metz, "A Life of Struggle as Ubuntu," p. 2.

[177] Nelson Rolihlahla Mandela, *Conversations with Myself* (London: Pan Macmillan, 2010), p.79.

[178] John Allen, *Rabble-Rouser for Peace: The Authorized Biography of Desmond Tutu* (London: Rider, 2007).

communication lines, and other governmental infrastructure that advocated apartheid-based racial discrimination.[179] The violence was thus coordinated as a last resort because unarmed peaceful protests proved fruitless and the political struggle of liberation required coordinated and targeted forms of permissible violence to rebut the initial apartheid discord of harms and subordination of namely black people. Mandela did not accept his release from prison in exchange of the APC – MK withdrawing from hostilities because the apartheid would have remained. Mandela did opt for force, but only after peaceful protests did not work and used the least amount of force, with initially sabotage, required to pursue freedom and the equality of all races in South Africa[180] (followed by the next phase of violence). Mandela waged phases of proportional violence to rebut wrongs once peaceful protests failed with the objective to negotiate peace and called off violence when a settlement had arisen.[181]

If relating to Western interpretations of *jus ad bellum*, Mandela acted in self-defense of the oppressive apartheid regime that abused basic human rights from the apartness of black access to rights and services from white privilege. Although most accounts of Mandela are rightfully praiseworthy, he was heavily criticized for joining the table to talk peace with the white government because he could have postponed the talks to include economic justice to span beyond basic civil and political liberties. The government only provided reparations (with TRC recommendations) to a few thousand civilians that faced serious human rights abuses.[182] To end the violence early, Mandela and his political comrades were happy to accept initially democracy and civil liberty and have economic and property rights restored in the future.

Although these acts of violence managed by Mandela and the APC – MK were justifiable on the whole, the Truth and Reconciliation Commission revealed that ANC enthusiasts did sometimes target civilians in mainly black townships.[183] MK combatant Aboobaker Ismail claimed at an amnesty hearing that MK did not target white civilians as "a racist war,"

[179] Mandela, *Long Walk to Freedom*, p. 338.

[180] Mandela, *Long Walk to Freedom*, pp. 325, 336, 441.

[181] Mandela, *Long Walk of Freedom*.

[182] Metz, "A Life of Struggle as Ubuntu," pp. 16–17.

[183] Padraig O'Malley, "ANC Killed Mostly Civilians," *O'Malley: The Heart of Hope*, March 21, 2003. Due to retribution from blacks against whites, Tutu was criticized alongside the post-apartheid settlement of inadequate economic reparations (Chasi, "Tutuist Ubuntu and Just War," pp. 236–237.

but the Truth and Reconciliation Commission Report found that most casualties from MK fighting were civilians, such as 52 civilians and 19 security forces being killed between 1976 and 1984.[184] MK held noble intentions by engaging with sabotage and targeting governmental security forces, but the killing of civilians undermined Mandela's strategy of targeting governmental facilities and installations. Despite this criticism, overall, the principles of Afro-communitarianism justified violence in South Africa against apartheid.

Although Tutu did not write or say much about just war, he did identify that disharmony, disunity, alienation, and an apartness in the apartheid rule needed fighting—just like Jesus of Nazareth for reconciliation of the world.[185] Tutu claimed that God wanted human interdependence, but when there is contravention to it and violation of the rule of law, then humans must "resort to violence" to fight for justice and restore peace.[186] Tutu did not speak of violence to rebut discord, but he certainly condemned violence if there was a disharmonious state of affairs and nonviolent measures had been exhausted.[187] After a conflict, *Ubuntu* moral philosophy encourages all parties involved to engage in reconciliation.[188] Therefore, *Ubuntu* is able to justify violence if it is conducted with a sincere effort to change a social disharmonious state of affairs to social harmony—that does not contravene post-conflict reconciliation.[189] Alongside truth and reconciliation, ceasefires and peace agreements would be commended by *Ubuntu* ethics because it fortifies the cessation of violence from all parties and negotiate peace—moving to a more harmonious state of affairs. *Ubuntu* would move beyond a ceasefire; however, by encouraging all sides to expose their wrongdoing and stop them—thus leading to reconciliation.

The permissible forms of violence can be hierarchized and initiated from the less severe modes moving to the subsequent if a positive state of

[184] South African Truth and Reconciliation Commission, *Truth and Reconciliation Commission of South Africa Report – Volume Six* (Kenwyn, Cape Town: Juta & Co Ltd, March 2003), p. 277, paras. 52–53.

[185] Tutu, *The Rainbow People of God*, pp. 61–62.

[186] Desmond Mpilo Tutu and Beyers Naudé, "Our Common Humanity," in *50 Years of the Freedom Charter*, edited by Raymond Suttner and Jeremy Cronin (Pretoria: University of South Africa Press, 2006), pp. 232–234.

[187] Cordeiro-Rodrigues, "Towards a Tutuist Ethics of War," p. 430.

[188] Metz, "A Life of Struggle as Ubuntu," p. 15.

[189] Cordeiro-Rodrigues, "Towards a Tutuist Ethics of War," p. 426.

affairs is not reached and the situation remains a disharmonious one. There are four stages, which are sabotage, guerrilla warfare, terrorism, and open revolution. First, sabotage comprises an attempt to obstruct, destabilize, demoralize, or destroy governmental property and national military munitions, which can include arson-attacks and explosions, to weaken the operations of governance.[190] Second, guerrilla warfare involves irregular armed combatants fighting against usually larger sized regular national armed forces and thus the violence conducted entails sabotage, but also targets to kill enemy armed forces with unorthodox methods.[191] Third, terrorism entails (usually from a nonstate actor) engaging with the threat or use of violence against a civilian population to inflict fear and intimidation against its host government for the achievement of a political, social, and/or religious objective(s).[192] Examples of terrorism include assassinations; the hijacking of vehicles, naval ships, and aircraft; kidnappings; bombings; the threat of bombs; computer-based cyber-attacks; and the threat and use of biological, chemical, radiological, and/or nuclear weapons.[193] Guerrillas and insurgents often use the same tactics as terrorists.[194] Therefore, terrorism includes the targeting of civilians that spans beyond attacking governmental property (sabotage) and killing foe combatants (guerrilla warfare). Fourth, open revolution is unrestrained violence that is not limited, and the attacks are open to all persons and property to accomplish an objective(s). It is important to note that every stage of violence is justifiable after the prior phase fails.[195]

If there are friendly methods of resolving disputes (or in Afro-communitarian for this book, disharmonious communal relations), such as diplomacy or legal avenues, then they must be exhausted to accomplish the goal of positive harmonious affairs for the initial stage of violence to be justified. If relating this to the Charter of the United Nations, diplomacy

[190] David Hardiman, *Non Cooperation in India: Nonviolent Strategy and Protest, 1920–22* (Oxford: Oxford University Press, 2021), p. 272.

[191] Mao Tse-tung, *On Guerrilla Warfare*, translated by Samuel B. Griffith (Mineola, New York: Dover Publications, 2017), pp. 41–50.

[192] Bruce Hoffman, *Inside Terrorism: Revised and Expanded Edition* (New York: Columbia University Press, 2006), pp. 31, 34–35.

[193] Abdul Karim Bangura, "Terrorism and Islam in Africa," in *Terrorism in Africa: The Evolving Front in the War on Terror*, edited by Jon Davis, (Lanham, MD: Lexington Books, 2010), pp. 114–115.

[194] Hoffman, *Inside Terrorism*, p. 35.

[195] Gwilym David Blunt, *Global Poverty, Injustice, and Resistance* (Cambridge: Cambridge University Press, 2020), p. 186.

and negotiations must be tried under Chap. 7 of its Charter and then sanctions can be attempted if a threat to peace and security remains.[196] However, in my view, sanctions are a form of violence because targeting a regime impacts on accessing money and movement (travel) with a no-fly zone and can lead to poverty for many ordinary, and innocent, civilians.[197]

The four staged forms of violence proposed by the consequentialist Afro-communitarian approach are not part of vengeance or retributive allegations against a wrongdoer that warrants punishment. Instead, restorative justice can be attempted to adopt forgiveness. An example rests on the Truth and Reconciliation Commission in South Africa that promoted amnesty from jail terms in exchange for nationally documented truth-telling and perpetrators appealing for forgiveness from the victim's families for heinous acts committed during the apartheid era. By applying *Ubuntu*, it was romanticized to show how South Africans were forgiving toward predominantly white perpetrators of crime during the times of apartheid in the Truth and Reconciliation Commission.[198] This was to alleviate the negative impacts of society; create social harmony between races in South Africa rather than have the amnesty serve as a trade-off forcing forgiveness; and promote truth-telling from the perpetrators of human rights violations.[199] Chairman Archbishop Tutu stressed that comparison, openness, and hospitality are needed for everyone—even if they have violated

[196] Chapter 7 of the Charter of the United Nations, Article 41.

[197] The United Nations Security Council authorized sanctions against the Saddam Hussein and Colonel Muammar al-Gaddafi authoritarian regimes in Iraq and Libya that significantly hindered the economy, causing impoverishment and unemployment for many civilians, seizure of oil and foreign financial assets, violation of the airspace of the sovereign territories with no-fly zones and restricted the freedom of movement respectively (UN Security Council Resolution 660, "Alarmed by the Invasion of Kuwait." UN Doc. S/RES/660, August 2, 1990, adopted 2,963rd meeting; UN Security Council Resolution 778, "Iraq to Withdraw from Kuwait," UN Doc. S/RES/778, November 29, 1990, adopted 2,932nd meeting; UN Security Council Resolution 1970, "Situation in the Libyan Arab Jamahiriya and Condemnation of Violence," UN Doc. S/RES/1970, February 26, 2011, adopted 6,491st meeting; UN Security Council Resolution 1973, "On the Establishment of a Ban on Flights in the Libyan Arab Jamahiriya Airspace," UN Doc. S/RES/1973, March 17, 2011, adopted 6,498th meeting).

[198] Kgatla, "Relationships are Building Blocks to Social Justice," p. 2.

[199] For the wrongdoers, Tutuist *ubuntu* ethics encourages the persuasion of aggressors to repent by fully disclosing their evil acts perpetrated to generate sorrow for bad actions to restore humanity and limit negativity (D. Lama and Desmond Mpilo Tutu, *The Book of Joy* (Hutchinson: Avery, 2016).

human rights because people are bound through other people.[200] Friendly-like relations and actions are preferred to accomplish the outcomes of shared identity and goodwill because actions of ill-will would contravene these collective communal obligations. Violence is only permissible, if necessary, as a final resort, and when the enemy surrenders and/or provides a path for viable negotiation or a political settlement, hostilities must be stopped straight away.

Internal Struggle and Anti-colonial Cases in Context

A number of African struggles for liberation against European colonialization used violence against disharmonious occupation that eventually resulted in a less discordant, and more harmonious, state of affairs.[201] Examples of anti-colonial liberation struggles can be presented. The Soviet-supported artido Africano para a Independência de Guiné e Cabo Verde [African Party for the Independence of Guinea and Cape Verde] (PAIGC) in Guinea-Bissau initially protested peacefully against Portuguese colonialism but then turned to more violent means in the 1960s war of independence due to the reaction of Portuguese forces during the Pidjiguiti Massacre on August 3, 1959, killing a minimum of 25 unarmed protestors.[202] Although Amílcar Lopes da Costa Cabral fought for national liberation, he sought the cultural right of the people to reclaim their narrative rather than the rule of self-determination to govern itself.[203] Cabral argued that if violence does not improve conditions of the situation for the people under colonialism, then revolution would not be justified.[204] Also, against Portuguese colonial rule, the Frente de Libertação de Moçambique [Liberation Front of Mozambique] (FRELIMO) in Mozambique started as a nationalist movement in its fight for independence and later became a socialist political party. MPLA fighters waged a war of independence

[200] Tutu, *The Rainbow People of God*, p. 122.

[201] Luís Cordeiro-Rodrigues, "Towards a Tutuist Ethics of War: *Ubuntu*, Forgiveness and Reconciliation," *Politikon: South African Journal of Political Studies*, Vol. 45, No. 3 (June 2018), p. 431.

[202] Femi Akomolafe, *Black Damage: Why Africa and Black Communities across the World are Poor and Dysfunctional and the Ways Forward* (London: PublishNation, 2016), p. 147.

[203] Guy Martin, *African Political Thought* (New York: Palgrave Macmillan, 2012), p. 78.

[204] Cabral, Amílcar Lopes da Costa, "Unity and Struggle," in *Amílcar Cabral Speeches and Writings* (2nd edition), edited by Mark Adams and Chris Cocks (Pretoria: Unisa Press, 2004).

against the Portuguese armed forces and defeated the Frente Nacional de Libertação de Angola [National Liberation Front of Angola] (FNLA) and the União Nacional para a Independência Total de Angola [National Union for the Total Independence of Angola] (UNITA) during the civil war.[205] Armed struggle is thus justified to protect an indigenous culture, so violence is permissible to rebut severe discordance that highly contravened culture in these contexts of Portuguese colonialism. It is debatable whether culture constitutes a Western human right, but culture pertains minority rights and partially the right to self-determination and governance.

Cultural imperialism attempted to destroy the cultural heritage of colonialized states. For example, fascism under the dictatorship of the Estado Novo State claiming that Guinea-Bissau and Angola held culture similar to Portugal as its mainland.[206] For Frantz Omar Fanon, the colonial settlers (with a specific example of the French in Algeria), dehumanized and taught the oppressed that their status was inferior to their colonial masters, but overtime the oppressed could learn of psychological exclusion to fight colonialism.[207] If one uses violence against colonialism, the subjects to colonialism learn to realize they are no longer inferior to become liberated (adopting a Marxian approach of true consciousness replacing class conflict with colonialism) so violence enhances emancipation as a therapeutic form of violence.[208] Fanon argued that "decolonization is always a violent phenomenon," meaning that power struggles in colonized states can only be resolved through violent struggle.[209]

Furthermore, a variety of peaceful and then violent liberation movements fought against British colonial rule in India. The revolutionary resistance commenced with initial nonviolence that was met with the robust use of force from the British Indian Army. This can be exemplified with the Jallianwala Bagh Massacre and Chauri Chaura Incident, respectively. On April 13, 1919, the Jallianwala Bagh Massacre, Amritsar, Punjab, concerned a peaceful protest against indefinite detentions without trial (the Rowlatt Act) that resulted in the British Indian Army firing under the

[205] William Martin James III, *A Political History of the Civil War in Angola 1974–1990* (New Brunswick, NJ: Transaction Publishers, 2011).

[206] Cordeiro-Rodrigues, "African Perspectives on Just War," p. 4.

[207] Frantz Omar Fanon, *The Wretched of the Earth* (London: Penguin, 1961).

[208] Fanon's Marxian perspective of the colonial exploitation of false consciousness (replacing capitalists/bourgeoise with inferiority to colonial settlers) was to undertake the psychoanalysis of the situation forming a true consciousness for revolution to change the status quo.

[209] Fanon, *The Wretched of the Earth.*

instruction and command of General Michael Francis O'Dwyer to kill an estimated 379 unarmed civilians and approximately 1200 wounded.[210] This was followed by the Chauri Chaura Incident on February 4, 1922, comprising infuriated farmers throwing stones at the police in reprisal of the latter firing air bound gunshots at unarmed protesting farmers against the local police and zamindars (feudal landlords collecting taxes) committing atrocities resulting in the sub-inspector being lynched and setting fire to the local police station.[211] Three civilians were killed, and there were 24 British Indian governmental servant casualties that compelled Mahatma Gandhi to withdraw the peaceful Non-Cooperation Movement.[212] After several occasions of the British Indian Army killing unarmed peaceful protestors, the Hindustan Socialist Republican Association (HSRA) extreme left-wing Indian revolutionary council engaged in violence as a liberation struggle against British colonialism. HSRA radicals attempted to rebut British colonial violence and oppression with the resort to violence, which included the Kakori train robbery[213] and terrorism, namely bombings of the Viceroy and the assassination of General O'Dwyer by Udham Singh.[214] India eventually gained independence from British colonial rule on August 15, 1947, which separated India and Pakistan.[215]

Even failed enmity-like violence against colonialism have been studied. This includes the Maji Maji rebellion in July 1905 in Ruanda-Urundi (German East Africa) of armed Islam and animist Africans against Germany's occupation and policies forcing indigenous people to cultivate cotton for exportation that resulted in a German victory and death of up to 300,000 of the population from mainly famine due to German scorched-earth policy.[216] Moreover, the 1950s Mau Mau uprising in Kenya com-

[210] Savita Narain, *Jallianwala Bagh Massacre, 1919* (Atlanta, GA: Lancer, 2013).

[211] Arvind Chauhan, "Chauri Chaura a Subaltern Revolt that Receded into Oblivion," *The Times of India*, August 20, 2022.

[212] Radhey Shyam Chaurasia, *History of Modern India: 1707 A.D. to up to 2000 A.D.* (New Delhi: Atlantic, 2002), p. 355.

[213] Pradnya Bivalkar, *The Becoming of a Hero: Identity Conflicts in Contemporary Hindi Cinema: The Protagonist as a Site for Political, Social and Religious Conflicts* (Tübingen: Tübingen Library Publishing, 2023), p. 187.

[214] Adrija Roychowdhury, "Udham Singh: The Witness to Jallianwala Bagh who Swore to Bring an End to British Rule," *Indian Express*, October 14, 2021.

[215] Barney White-Spunner, *Partition: The Story of Indian Independence and the Creation of Pakistan in 1947* (Manhattan, New York City, NY: Simon & Schuster, 2017).

[216] Klaus Bachmann and Gerhard Kemp, "Was Quashing the Maji-Maji Uprising Genocide? An Evaluation of Germany's Conduct Through the Lens of International Criminal Law." *Holocaust and Genocide Studies*, Vol. 35, No. 2 (July 2021), p. 243.

prised Kikuya, Embu, and Meru combatants against British armed authorities, allied European colonialists, and the Kenyan Regiment with the latter capturing the Mau Mau leader, Field Marshal Dedan Kimathi, to cease the forest-based rebellion.[217]

Therefore, African moral philosophy has provided a newer approach to just war ethics.[218] The morality of armed conflict has been displayed by consequentialist Afro-communitarian ethics. Yet, most of this literature and examples have undertaken a theoretical analysis or how to deal with violence internally against oppression or colonialism.

Counterarguing Afro-communitarian Ethics: From Deontology and Individualism

Ubuntu has received several criticisms that are important to note. The term translated to "humanness" has been received as vague from a definitional aspect insofar that people claim to know *Ubuntu* whenever they see it for undertaking certain decisions.[219] In addition, Metz recognizes that some may contend that *Ubuntu* is grounded on collectivist values to respect the communal and societal interests, responsibilities, and

[217] Elizabeth Isichei, *The Religious Traditions of Africa* (London: Bloomsbury, 2004), pp. 291–293.

[218] Colin Tinei Chasi, "Ubuntu and Freedom of Expression: Considering Children and Broadcast News Violence in a Violent Society," *Journal of Media Ethics*, Vol. 30, No. 2 (2015), pp. 91–108; Deane-Peter Baker, "Rebellion and African Ethics," *Journal of Military Ethics*, Vol. 15, No. 4 (2016), pp. 288–298; Chasi, "Tutuist Ubuntu and Just War," pp. 232–244; Sharon Omotoso, "African Womanist View of Just War Theory in Tunde Kelani's The Narrow Path," *African Notes: Bulletin of the Institute of African Studies, University of Ibadan*, Vol. 42, Nos. 1 & 2, (2018), pp. 56–74; Luís Cordeiro-Rodrigues, "African Views of Just War in Mandela and Cabral," *The Journal of Speculative Philosophy*, Vol. 32, No. 4 (2018), pp. 657–673; Uchena Okeja, "War by Agreement: A Reflection on the Nature of Just War," *Journal of Military Ethics*, Vol. 18, No. 3 (2019), pp. 189–203; Danny Singh and Luís Cordeiro-Rodrigues, "Introduction: International and Comparative Perspectives to Just War Theory," in *Comparative Just War Theory: An Introduction to International Perspectives*, edited by Luís Cordeiro-Rodrigues and Danny Singh (Lanham: Rowman & Littlefield, 2020), pp. 1–11; Thaddeus Metz, "An African Theory of Just Causes for War," in *Comparative Just War Theory: An Introduction to International Perspectives*, edited by Luís Cordeiro-Rodrigues and Danny Singh (Lanham: Rowman & Littlefield, 2020), pp. 131–157.

[219] Yvonne Mokgoro, "Ubuntu and the Law in South Africa," *Buffalo Human Rights Law Review*, Vol. 4, No. 3 (January 1998), pp. 15–23.

compulsions that would run the risk of tainting liberal ideals and rights of "individual freedom."[220] Furthermore, the traditional foundation of *Ubuntu* was based on the ideology of small rural communities during pre-colonial times based on spiritual relationships, including deceased ancestors, which would be hard to apply to modern large industrialized societies that have many secular pluralized cultures.[221] Kgata also argues that *Ubuntu* is a moral philosophy of life based on the tripartite interconnectivity of human beings with God and land to apply all the time and it cannot be conveniently applied to circumvent accountability.[222] Under this premise, *Ubuntu* cannot be related to a foreign context, *e.g.,* with Western law. This depiction of *Ubuntu* would endanger its applicability to foreign armed interventions, which is the scope of this book. My response is that even if taking concepts of religion into consideration, the principles of justice and fairness can be applied all the time. Although I agree that Western secular law and even morality are different to *Ubuntu*, but the values of *Ubuntu* in Afro-communitarianism can be applied that excludes specific reference to God via a partial Metzian reformation of *Ubuntu*.

Another criticism is that if the role of the community and social harmony has so much importance with many African moral philosophies, including *Ubuntu*, *Ibuanyidanda*, Akan, and Igbo, then in terms of peace, Africa as a continent has been ravaged with numerous armed conflicts.[223] Under a "moral" political economy perspective, grand corruption is also plaguing the continent where greedy kleptocrats redistribute state resources, jobs, and services to the "haves" leaving an infuriated "have nots."[224] It seems that many leaders fail to apply these African principles, nor care for the welfare of the entirety of their civilians. Total war has been commonplace in Africa, comprising the destruction of the enemy, all its property and the population are targeted with the unlimited use of force.[225]

[220] Metz, "Ubuntu as a Moral Theory and Human Rights in South Africa," p. 533.

[221] Metz, "Ubuntu as a Moral Theory and Human Rights in South Africa," p. 533.

[222] Kgatla, "Relationships are Building Blocks to Social Justice," p. 2.

[223] One could also make the argument that *ubuntu* should not be the preferred moral philosophy for examining Afro-communitarianism because there are many types of African moral theory. However, what I have tried to convey in this chapter is that for the few I have examined, they share the same traits and principles with *Ubuntu* but I do not intend to downplay the other many African normative dimensions left out of this book.

[224] Danny Singh, "Anticorruption, Cultural Norms, and Implications for the APUNCAC," *Laws*, Vol. 10, No. 2 (April 2021), 23, pp. 4–5.

[225] Ugwuanyi, "Towards an African Theory of Just War," p. 60.

It is fair to argue that many wars within the African context were "unAfrican" because they did not adopt basic African moral theory because many civilians and mass starvation have been deployed as tactics.[226]

Comparison of Western Just War Theory With Afro-communitarianism

Like traditionalists, the African philosophy on the morality of war focuses on collectivism but not in terms of international standards, norms, respect for international law and expected ethics and responses of the international community, e.g., *jus cogens* and *erga omnes*.[227] From an Afro-communitarian perspective, the justification of violence is similar to traditionalists, but the focus on social harmony differs from morally "innocent bystanders (civilians)"[228] to "non-discordant people."[229] Unlike Western approaches to just war theory and contemporary international law (including the Charter of the United Nations), state sovereignty is to be preserved and violation of sovereignty can redress self-defense,[230] but this is difficult to find on rules of statehood alone in African moral philosophy *jus ad bellum*. African ethics would, instead, focus on maintaining community values and propose friendly alternatives (until their exhaustion or futileness) so that shared solidarity, identity, values, and humanness can be achieved. Moreover, African ethics would also support aspects of the

[226] One of many examples would be Nigerian Civil War (1967–1970) when the Nigerian armed, navy and air forces imposed a blockade of telecommunications, foreign currency affairs, mail, airfields, seaports to interdict food, relief supplies and medicines that starved over two million Biafran civilians to death with famine (Emmanuel Neba-Fuh, *Triumph of Racism: The History of White Supremacy in Africa and How Shithole Entered the United States Presidential Lexicon* (Kansas City, MO: Miraclaire Publishing, 2021), p. 412).

[227] *Jus cogens* is the Latin term for peremptory customary non-derogable norms in international law that includes the most heinous crimes ranging from piracy on the high seas, the right to life, torture, slavery, genocide, and acts of aggression. These crimes would warrant a response from the international community because a violation of peremptory norms is an attack against all (*erga omnes*) and thus warrants an international response towards all. For a comprehensive overview on these customary international law concepts, see Alexander Orakhelashvili, *Peremptory Norms in International Law* (Oxford: Oxford University Press, 2006).

[228] Walzer, *Just and Unjust Wars*, 1977, pp. 119, 128, 137.

[229] Thaddeus Metz, "An African Theory of Just Causes for War," in *Comparative Just War Theory: An Introduction to International Perspectives*, edited by Luís Cordeiro-Rodrigues and Danny Singh (Lanham, MD: Roman & Littlefield, 2020), p. 137.

[230] Charter of the United Nations, 1945, Article 51.

revisionist approach to determine wrongdoing and justified combatants. This is for the justified side to engage in permissible violence if friendliness fails to retain relations and required violence to rebut enmity-like violence to bring about an eventual harmonious and less discordant state of affairs. It is important to note that these aims on communal progress are to develop the personhood that is absent in Western interpretations of just war theory. These ethics can resort to violence if alternative means are absent or exhausted.

The outlined forms of *jus ad bellum* will be explained in the deontological and consequentialist approaches to Afro-communitarianism that is followed by the hierarchized stages of violence *jus in bello* while respecting humanity and chivalry and military necessity if endorsing sabotage as a strategy.

However, Afro-communitarianism contains differences with military necessity and proportionality when justifiable violence to rebut violence may also target civilians with higher stages of violence, such as guerrilla warfare, terrorism, and open revolution are in stark contrast with Western just war ethics and LOAC *jus in bello*. It should be noted that the consequentialist approach of Afro-communitarian ethics endorses violence against an initiator of discord if they engage in severe violence, harm, and subordination, but the violence orchestrated must be comparable to justify the rebuttal of violence and cease once a political solution or negotiations materialize. This approach starkly differs to the work of Western just war theorists. For instance, McMahan argues that the use of force can be justifiably used to retaliate against an unjust attack to deter it even if the response uses substantially more violence.[231] Initiating war can be justifiable against an aggressor with the use of force for the purpose of instilling fear to deter other parties from future aggression against the state.[232] This

[231] McMahan, "The Ethics of Killing in War," pp. 712–713. The danger of this rests on a humanitarian intervention of powerful unilateral actors or multilateral organizations that possess superior arsenal, arms and military tactics, including asymmetrical warfare, which can conduct extremely high forms of violence and bombardment against an aggressor of violence. This does protect a community from extinction, but the severity of the foreign military operation is likely to result in a difficult future state of affairs between the endangered community and aggressor once the international forces or mission leaves.

[232] Thomas Hurka, "Proportionality and Necessity," in *War: Essays in Political Philosophy*, edited by Larry May (New York: Cambridge University Press, 2008), pp.131–132; Jeff McMahan, "Aggression and Punishment," in *War: Essays in Political Philosophy*, edited by Larry May (New York: Cambridge University Press, 2008), pp. 78–79.

Western-based approach of just war theory and realist deterrence do not conform to Afro-communitarian principles because of the use of lethal military force to rebut aggression. It may be justifiable as the means, but the ends of excessive (and non-comparable force) are not justifiable. Therefore, the actual or the threat of excessive violence would be unjustly disproportionate that Afro-communitarians would assess with extreme caution and only engage with higher forms of violence if the severe acts of discord, harm, and subordination could not be rebutted with lower forms of violence to reach comparable discord.

In Western interpretations of the just cause, war is justified to punish aggressors, but with normative Afro-communitarian relational theory, war may be justified partially to help the humanness, reconciliation, and love of animal-like behavior of aggressors because they are also dehumanized by undertaking such actions.[233] By undertaking the principle of "charity" even against aggressors (or blatant severe, and unjustified, discordance), Afro-communitarianism offers an approach to *jus in bello* by ensuring that war should be conducted in a way that does not violate the potential of reconciliation in the aftermath. If considering *in bello*, moderate forms of violence that do not hinder future relations and aim to encourage future harmonious communal relations are morally permissible.[234]

Afro-communitarian ethics would also be loosely receptive with state-building ideals *jus post bellum*. However, these African ethics would be reluctant to endorse retributive post-war justice *jus post bellum* because punishing alleged wrongdoers is a form of victor's justice that would not create restorative justice, truth, or reconciliation for a better harmonious state of affairs. If war criminals are relinquished from responsibility or are merely imprisoned from the retributive justice model, nothing is done for the viability of reconciliation in the aftermath. Punishment is not compulsory to justify against wrongdoers per se, but it can be used to rehabilitate perpetrators and compensate victims. Based on these preferences for restorative justice, Tutu focused more on forgiveness and reconciliation via restorative justice *post bellum* that was opposed to retributive criminal tribunals.[235] These similarities and differences cannot be grasped until *Ubuntu* ethics is understood, which is immediately covered in the subsequent part of this chapter.

[233] Kenneth Kaunda, *Kaunda on Violence* (London: Collins, 1980), pp. 88, 117; Desmond Mpilo Tutu, *No Future Without Forgiveness* (New York: Random House, 1999), p. 35.

[234] Cordeiro-Rodrigues, "Towards a Tutuist Ethics of War," pp. 431–432.

[235] Cordeiro-Rodrigues, "Towards a Tutuist Ethics of War," p. 433.

Conclusion

A viable criticism of Western-based just war theory legitimizes different types of war to protect a world order cemented on universal moral norms and justice.[236] In addition, the rules are unclearly applied due to the contention between military necessity and proportionality. Other inaccuracies rest on weak military estimations, which are famously presented by the Prussian military theorists, Carl von Clausewitz. He contended that all causes and activities of war are smeared with "fog" and "uncertainty" that is due to military commanders unaware of the ground of the battlefield, the distinction from foe combatants and civilians, and the actual size of the enemy force and arsenal.[237] These are viable criticisms of *jus ad bellum* and *jus in bello*. *Jus post bellum* has similarly focused on maintaining the liberalist international order to ensure that the alleged horrors of communism and military authoritarianism do not reemerge after the post-Cold War era by prescribing liberal statebuilding and post-war justice.

Based on these criticisms, I argue that the over focus on Western-based contemporary just war theory promote wars and neoliberal reconstruction as the endgame. This downplays the true estimation of civilian casualties and the competence of the oppositional armed forces. War as a last resort as articulated from Christian theological ethics is slowly deteriorating overtime, which is why the decolonialization of war ethics is needed to provide as alternative non-Western approach to mitigate and legitimize violence truly as a final option. Afro-communitarian ethics can circumvent the geopolitics of realist (national security and foreign policy interests) versus liberalist (universal norms, law, and justice) foreign armed intervention, which includes humanitarian intervention for geopolitical reasons. The African ethics of moral philosophy can, instead, focus on retaining and/or repairing friendly communal relations to promote a more harmonious and less discordant state of affairs.

Violence may be needed with its consequentialist approach to achieve these two outputs, but as a last resort, which legitimizes the use of hierarchized stages of violence to rebut a disharmonious state of affairs and then immediately cease violence once violence has been rebutted. This was evident with the decades of peaceful protests in South Africa against

[236] Valerie Morkevičius, "Power and Order: The Shared Logics of Realism and Just War Theory," *International Studies Quarterly*, Vol. 59, No. 1 (March 2015), pp. 19–21.

[237] Carl Philipp von Clausewitz, *On War* (New York: Knopf, 1993), p. 117.

discriminatory apartheid rule that were followed by stages of sabotage, guerrilla warfare, and terrorism that Mandela ordered an end to when viable negotiations were offered by the white government.[238] Reconciliation was promoted with the Truth and Reconciliation Commission to foster restorative justice that achieved a better harmonious and less hostile state of affairs rather than engage with post-war accountability of crimes *just post bellum*. These African ethics have also been applied in a range of anti-colonial struggles, and there is no reason why this morality of war cannot be functional for assessing foreign armed intervention. The remaining chapters will provide an ethical analysis, from an Afro-communitarian consequentialist perspective, of the actual wars presented and reasons explaining why such foreign interventions are justified as right or unjustified as wrong. In doing so, an examination of foreign intervention and African moral philosophy are intertwined.

References

Aihiokhai, Simonmary Asese. "Remembering Bénézet Bujo, who Offered a Vision of African Theological Imagination." *National Catholic Reporter*, November 21, 2023. https://www.ncronline.org/opinion/guest-voices/remembering-b-n-zet-bujo-who-offered-vision-african-theological-imagination.

Akomolafe, Femi. *Black Damage: Why Africa and Black Communities across the World are Poor and Dysfunctional and the Ways Forward*. London: PublishNation, 2016.

Allen, John. *Rabble-Rouser for Peace: The Authorized Biography of Desmond Tutu*. London: Rider, 2007.

Aquinas, Thomas. *Summa Theologiae*, II-II. London: R & T Washbourne, 1911.

Asouzu, Innocent I. *The Method and Principles of Complementary Reflection in and beyond African Philosophy*. Calabar: University of Calabar Press, 2004.

Asouzu, Innocent I. *Ibuanyidanda: New Complementary Ontology: Beyond World-immanentism, Ethnocentric Reduction and Impositions*. Zürich: LIT Verlag, 2007.

Bâ, Sylvia Washington. *The Concept of Négritude in the Poetry of Léopold Sédar Senghor*. Princeton, NJ: Princeton University Press, 1973.

Bachmann, Klaus, and Gerhard Kemp. "Was Quashing the Maji-Maji Uprising Genocide? An Evaluation of Germany's Conduct through the Lens of International Criminal Law." *Holocaust and Genocide Studies*, Vol. 35, No. 2 (July 2021), pp. 235–249. https://doi.org/10.1093/hgs/dcab032.

[238] Guerrilla warfare was justifiably used to rebut the apartheid regime (Metz, "An African Theory of Just Causes for War," p. 133).

Badru, Ronald Olufemi. "An African Philosophical Account of Just War Theory." *Ethical Perspectives*, Vol. 26, No. 2 (2019), pp. 153–181. https://doi.org/10.2143/EP.26.2.3286746.

Baker, Deane-Peter. "Rebellion and African Ethics." *Journal of Military Ethics*, Vol. 15, No. 4 (2016), pp. 288–298. https://doi.org/10.1080/15027570.2017.1284462.

Bangura, Abdul Karim. "Terrorism and Islam in Africa." In *Terrorism in Africa: The Evolving Front in the War on Terror*, edited by Jon Davis, pp. 103–132. Lanham, MD: Lexington Books, 2010.

Beukes, Jacques Walter, and Laurika Elouise Beukes. "Proposing a Social Justice Approach to Diaconia for a South African Context." *Religions*, Vol. 14, No. 668 (May 2023), pp. 1–17. https://doi.org/10.3390/rel14050668.

Bivalkar, Pradnya. *The Becoming of a Hero: Identity Conflicts in Contemporary Hindi Cinema: The Protagonist as a Site for Political, Social and Religious Conflicts*. Tübingen: Tübingen Library Publishing, 2023.

Blunt, Gwilym David. *Global Poverty, Injustice, and Resistance*. Cambridge: Cambridge University Press, 2020.

Boykin, A. Wade. "The Academic Performance of Afro-American Children." In *Achievement and Achievement Motives*, edited by Janet T. Spence, pp. 321–371. San Francisco, CA: Freeman, 1983.

Boyle, Joseph. "Traditional Just War Theory and Humanitarian Intervention." *Nomos – American Society for Political and Legal Philosophy*, Vol. 47 (2006), pp. 31–57. https://www.jstor.org/stable/24220031.

Buber, Martin. *I and Thou*, 2nd ed. New York: Charles Scribner's Sons, 1958.

Bujo, Bénézet. *African Theology in Its Social Context*. Eugene, OR: Wipf & Stock, 1992.

Bujo, Bénézet. *Foundations of an African Ethic: Beyond the Universal Claims of Western Morality*. Spring Valley, NY: Crossroad Publishing, 2001.

Cabral, Amílcar Lopes da Costa. "Unity and Struggle." In *Amílcar Cabral Speeches and Writings*, 2nd ed., edited by Mark Adams and Chris Cocks. Pretoria: Unisa Press, 2004.

Calpin, G. H. *The South African Way of Life: Values and Ideals of a Multi-racial Society*. New York: Columbia University Press, 1953.

Chasi, Colin Tinei. "*Ubuntu* and Freedom of Expression: Considering Children and Broadcast News Violence in a Violent Society." *Journal of Media Ethics*, Vol. 30, No. 2 (2015), pp. 91–108. https://doi.org/10.1080/23736992.2015.1020378.

Chasi, Colin Tinei. "Tutuist Ubuntu and Just War." *Politikon: South African Journal of Political Studies*, Vol. 45, No. 2 (2018), pp. 232–244. https://doi.org/10.1080/02589346.2017.1301022.

Chauhan, Arvind. "Chauri Chaura a Subaltern Revolt that Receded into Oblivion." *The Times of India*, August 20, 2022. https://timesofindia.indiatimes.com/

city/lucknow/chauri-chaura-a-subaltern-revolt-that-receded-into-oblivion/articleshow/93674041.cms.

Chaurasia, Radhey Shyam. *History of Modern India: 1707 A.D. to up to 2000 A.D.* New Delhi: Atlantic, 2002.

Chimakonam, Jonathan O., and Victor C.A. Nweke. "An Examination of Nigerian, Sri Lankan, and Guatemalan Civil Wars in Light of the Law of Armed Conflict." In *Comparative Just War Theory: An Introduction to International Perspectives*, edited by Luís Cordeiro Rodrigues and Danny Singh, pp. 81–94. Lanham, MD: Rowman & Littlefield, 2020.

Chimakonam, Jonathan O., and L. Uchenna Ogbonnaya. "Can Afro-Communitarianism Be Useful in Combating the Challenge of Human Interaction Posed by the COVID-19 Pandemic?" *International Journal of Environmental Research and Public Health*, Vol. 19, Issue 21, 14255 (October 2022), pp. 1–13. https://doi.org/10.3390/ijerph192114255.

Clausewitz, Carl Philipp von. *On War*. New York: Knopf, 1993.

Cordeiro-Rodrigues, Luís. "African Views of Just War in Mandela and Cabral." *The Journal of Speculative Philosophy*, Vol. 32, No. 4 (2018a), pp. 657–673. https://www.muse.jhu.edu/article/713674.

Cordeiro-Rodrigues, Luís. "Towards a Tutuist Ethics of War: *Ubuntu*, Forgiveness and Reconciliation." *Politikon: South African Journal of Political Studies*, Vol. 45, No. 3 (June 2018b), pp. 426–435. https://doi.org/10.1080/02589346.2018.1480148.

Cordeiro-Rodrigues, Luís. "African Perspectives on Just War." *Philosophy Compass*, Vol. 17, No. 3 (March 2022), pp. 1–11. https://doi.org/10.1111/phc3.12808.

Cordeiro-Rodrigues, Luís, and Thaddeus Metz, "Afro-Communitarianism and the Role of Traditional African Healers in the COVID-19 Pandemic," *Public Health Ethics*, Vol. 14, No. 1 (March 2021), pp. 59–71. https://doi.org/10.1093/phe/phab006.

Cordeiro-Rodrigues, Luís, and Danny Singh. *Comparative Just War Theory: An Introduction to International Perspectives.* Lanham, MD: Roman & Littlefield, 2020.

Coupland, Robin M. "The SIrUS Project: Towards a Determination of which Weapons Cause 'Superfluous Injury or Unnecessary Suffering.'" In *The Changing Face of Conflict and the Efficacy of International Humanitarian Law*, edited by Helen Durham and Timothy L.H. McCormack, pp. 99–118. The Hague: Kluwer Law International, 1999.

Djukić, Dražan, and Niccolò Pons. "Entries: Distinction." In *The Companion to International Humanitarian Law*, eds. Dražan Djukić and Niccolò Pons, pp. 307–308. Leiden: Brill Nijhoff, 2018.

Doyle, Michael. "Kant, Liberal Legacies, and Foreign Affairs." *Philosophy and Public Affairs*, Vol. 12, No. 3 (Summer 1983), pp. 205–235. https://www.jstor.org/stable/2265298.

Doyle, Michael. "International Ethics and the Responsibility to Protect." *International Studies Review*, Vol. 13, No. 1 (March 2011), pp. 72–84. https://doi.org/10.1111/j.1468-2486.2010.00999.x.

Drew, Allison. "Visions of Liberation: The Algerian War of Independence and Its South African Reverberations." *Review of African Political Economy*, Vol. 42, No. 143 (February 2015), pp. 22–43. https://doi.org/10.1080/03056244.2014.1000288.

Dubow, Saul. *Apartheid – 1948 – 1994.* Oxford: Oxford University Press, 2014.

Edelstein, David M. "Foreign Militaries, Sustainable Institutions, and Postwar Statebuilding." In *The Dilemmas of Statebuilding: Confronting the Contradictions of Postwar Peace Operations*, edited by Roland Paris and Timothy D. Sisk, pp. 81–103. London: Routledge, 2009.

Etzioni, Amitai. "Communitarianism." In *Encyclopedia of Community: From the Village to the Virtual World*, edited by Karen Christensen and David Levinson, pp. 224–228. Thousand Oaks, CA: Sage, 2003.

Fabre, Cécile. *Cosmopolitan War.* Oxford: Oxford University Press, 2012.

Fagothey, Austin. *Right and Reason: Ethics in Theory and Practice*, 3rd ed. Saint Louis, MO: The C.V. Mosby Company, 1963.

Fanon, Frantz Omar. *The Wretched of the Earth.* London: Penguin, 1961.

Feldman, David. "The Economics of Ideology: Some Problems of Achieving Rural Socialism in Tanzania." In *Politics and Change in Developing Countries: Studies in the Theory and Practice of Development*, edited by Colin Leys, pp. 85–111. Cambridge: Cambridge University Press, 1969.

Fortin, Katharine. "Armed Groups and the DoD Manual: Shining a Light on Overlooked Issues." In *The United States Department of Defense Law of War Manual: Commentary and Critique*, edited by Michael A. Newton, pp. 383–402. Cambridge: Cambridge University Press, 2018.

Fukuyama, Francis. *The End of History and the Last Man.* New York: Free Press, 1992.

Gade, Christian B. N. "The Historical Development of the Written Discourses on *Ubuntu*." *South African Journal of Philosophy*, Vol. 30, No. 3 (2011), pp. 303–329. https://doi.org/10.4314/sajpem.v.30i3.69578.

Gade, Christian B. N. "What is *Ubuntu*? Different Interpretations among South Africans of African Descent." *South African Journal of Philosophy*, Vol. 31, No. 3 (2012), pp. 484–503. https://doi.org/10.1080/02580136.2012.10751789.

Gasser, Hans-Peter. "Geneva Conventions I–IV (1949)." In *The Law of Armed Conflict and the Use of Force: The Max Planck Encyclopedia of Public International Law* – Thematic Series Volume 2, edited by Frauke Lachenmann and Rüdiger Wolfrum, pp. 394–405. Oxford: Oxford University Press, 2017.

Gill, Terry D. "Trapped: Three Dilemmas in the Law of Proportionality and Asymmetric Warfare." In *Yearbook of International Humanitarian Law 2015*, edited by Terry D. Gill, pp. 153–180. The Hague: Asser Press, 2016.

Golash, Deidre. *The Case against Punishment: Retribution, Crime Prevention, and the Law*. New York: New York University Press, 2005.

Gyeke, Kwame. "Traditional Political Ideas: Their Relevance to Development in Contemporary Africa." In *Person and Community: Ghanian Philosophical Studies, I*, pp. 243–255. Washington, DC: Council for Research in Values and Philosophy, 1992.

Gyekye, Kwame. *Tradition and Modernity: Philosophical Reflections on the African Experience*. New York, NY: Oxford University Press, 1997.

Gyekye, Kwame. *Beyond Cultures: Perceiving a Common Humanity*. Washington, DC: The Council for Research in Values and Philosophy, 2004.

Gyeke, Kwame. "African Ethics." In *The Stanford Encyclopedia of Philosophy*, edited by Edward N. Zalta (Fall 2011 Edition), https://plato.stanford.edu/entries/african-ethics/.

Hardiman, David. *Non Cooperation in India: Nonviolent Strategy and Protest, 1920–22*. Oxford: Oxford University Press, 2021.

Hawley, Michael C. "Can Just Wars Be Fought Proportionately? A Critique of *In Bello* Proportionality." *Journal of Military Ethics*, Vol. 22, No. 2 (September 2023), pp. 89–102. https://doi.org/10.1080/15027570.2023.2257916.

Henckaerts, Jean-Marie, and Louise Doswald-Beck. *Customary International Humanitarian Law – Volume II: Practice, Part 1*. Cambridge: Cambridge University Press, 2005.

Hoffman, Bruce. *Inside Terrorism: Revised and Expanded Edition*. New York: Columbia University Press, 2006.

Holzgrefe, J.L. "The Humanitarian Intervention Debate." In *Humanitarian Intervention: Ethics, Legal, and Political Dilemmas*, edited by J.L. Holzgrefe and Robert. O. Keohane, pp. 15–52. Cambridge: Cambridge University Press, 2003.

Hurka, Thomas. "Proportionality in the Morality of War." *Philosophy & Public Affairs*, Vol. 33, No. 1 (January 2005), pp. 34–66. https://doi.org/10.1111/j.1088-4963.2005.00024.x.

Hurka, Thomas. "Proportionality and Necessity." In *War: Essays in Political Philosophy*, edited by Larry May, pp. 127–144. New York: Cambridge University Press, 2008.

International Committee of the Red Cross. *Geneva Convention Relative to the Treatment of Prisoners of War (Third Geneva Convention)*, 12 August 1949, 75 United Nations Treaty Series (UNTS) 135.

International Committee of the Red Cross. *Protocol Additional to the Geneva Conventions of 12 August 1949, and relating to the Protection of Victims of International Armed Conflicts (Protocol I)*, 8 June 1977a, 1125 UNTS 3–4.

International Committee of the Red Cross. Protocol Additional to the Geneva Conventions of 12 August 1949, and relating to the Protection of Victims of Non-International Armed Conflicts (Protocol II), 8 June 1977b, 1125 UNTS 609–610.

Isichei, Elizabeth. *The Religious Traditions of Africa*. London: Bloomsbury, 2004.

Jabavu, Noni. *Drawn in Color: African Contrasts*. London: John Murray, 1961.

James III, William Martin. *A Political History of the Civil War in Angola 1974–1990*. New Brunswick, NJ: Transaction Publishers, 2011.

Janzekovic, John. *The Use of Force in Humanitarian Intervention: Morality and Practicalities*. Aldershot, Hamps: Ashgate, 2006.

Jones, Charles A. *More than Just War: Narratives of the Just War Tradition and Military Life*. London: Routledge, 2013.

Kaunda, Kenneth. *Kaunda on Violence*. London: Collins, 1980.

Kgatla, Selaelo T. "Relationships are Building Blocks to Social Justice: Cases of Biblical Justice and African Ubuntu." *HTS Teologiese Studies/Theological Studies*, Vol. 72, No. 1, a3239 (October 2016), pp. 1–6. https://doi.org/10.4102/hts.v72i1.3239.

Kinsella, Helen M. *The Image before the Weapon: A Critical History of the Distinction between Combatant and Civilian*. Ithaca, NY: Cornell University Press, 2011.

Kleffner, Jann K. "Scope of Application of International Humanitarian Law." In *The Handbook of International Humanitarian Law*, 3rd ed., edited by Dieter Fleck, pp. 201–257. Oxford: Oxford University Press, 2013.

Kolb, Robert, and Richard Hyde. *An Introduction to the International Law of Armed Conflicts*. Oxford: Hart Publishing, 2008.

Lama, D., and Desmond Mpilo Tutu. *The Book of Joy*. Hutchinson: Avery, 2016.

Lanier, David E. "Who is my Neighbor?" *Biblical Illustrator Magazine*, April 9, 2013, pp. 1–10.

Letseka, Moeketsi. "How Would *Ubuntu* Respond to the Crises in the World Today?" *London School of Economics and Political Science*, November 15, 2023. https://blogs.lse.ac.uk/africaatlse/2023/11/15/how-would-Ubuntu-respond-to-the-crises-in-the-world-today/.

Luban, David. "Just War and Human Rights." *Philosophy and Public Affairs*, Vol. 9, No. 2 (Winter 1980), pp. 160–181. http://www.jstor.org/stable/2265110.

Luban, David. "Will Syria Redefine the Just War?" *Just Security*, September 24, 2013. https://www.justsecurity.org/1035/syria-redefine-war/.

Mandela, Nelson Rolihlahla. *Long Walk to Freedom*. London: Abacus, 1994.

Mandela, Nelson Rolihlahla. *Conversations with Myself*. London: Pan Macmillan, 2010.

Maquet, Jacques Jérôme Pierre. *Africanity: The Cultural Unity of Black Africa*, translated by Joan K. Rayfield. New York: Oxford University Press, 1973.

Martin, Guy. *African Political Thought*. New York: Palgrave Macmillan, 2012.

Martin, Francisco Forrest, Stephen J. Schnably, Richard J. Wilson, Jonathan S. Simon, and Mark V. Tushnet. *International Human Rights and Humanitarian Law: Treaties, Cases and Analysis.* Cambridge: Cambridge University Press, 2006.

Matolino, Bernard. *Afro-Communitarian Democracy.* Lanham, MD: Lexington Books, 2019.

McMahan, Jeff. "War as Self-Defense." *Ethics & International Affairs*, Vol. 18, No. 1 (March 2004a), pp. 75–80. https://doi.org/10.1111/j.1747-7093.2004.tb00453.x.

McMahan, Jeff. "The Ethics of Killing in War." *Ethics*, Vol. 114, No. 4 (July 2004b), pp. 693–733. https://doi.org/10.1086/422400.

McMahan, Jeff. "Aggression and Punishment." In *War: Essays in Political Philosophy*, edited by Larry May, pp. 67–84. New York: Cambridge University Press, 2008.

McMahan, Jeff. *Killing in War.* Oxford: Oxford University Press, 2009.

Metz, Thaddeus. "Toward an African Moral Theory." *Journal of Political Philosophy*, Vol. 15, No. 3 (May 2007), pp. 321–341. https://doi.org/10.1111/j.1467-9760.2007.00280.x.

Metz, Thaddeus. "Human Dignity, Capital Punishment, and an African Moral Theory: Toward a New Philosophy of Human Rights." *Journal of Human Rights*, Vol. 9, No. 1 (February 2010), pp. 81–99. https://doi.org/10.1080/14754830903530300.

Metz, Thaddeus. "Ubuntu as a Moral Theory and Human Rights in South Africa." *African Human Rights Law Journal*, Vol. 11, No. 2 (January 2011), pp. 532–559. https://hdl.handle.net/10520/EJC51951.

Metz, Thaddeus. "Developing African Political Philosophy: Moral-Theoretic Strategies." *Philosophia Africana*, Vol. 14, No. 1 (September 2012), pp. 61–83. https://doi.org/10.5840/philafricana20121419.

Metz, Thaddeus. "A Life of Struggle as Ubuntu." In *Nelson Rolihlahla Mandela: Decolonial Ethics of Liberation and Servant Leadership.* Trenton, NJ: Africa World Press, 2015a, pp. 1–20. https://philarchive.org/archive/METMAUv1.

Metz, Thaddeus. "A Theory of National Reconciliation: Some Insights from Africa." In *Theorizing Transitional Justice*, edited by Claudio Corradetti, Nir Eisikovits and Jack Rotondi, pp. 119–135. Surrey: Ashgate, 2015b.

Metz, Thaddeus. "An Overview of African Ethics." In *Themes, Issues and Problems in African Philosophy*, edited by I. Upokolo, pp. 61–76. Cham: Palgrave Macmillan, 2017.

Metz, Thaddeus. "An African Theory of Just Causes for War." In *Comparative Just War Theory: An Introduction to International Perspectives*, edited by Luís Cordeiro-Rodrigues and Danny Singh, pp. 131–155. Lanham, MD: Roman & Littlefield, 2020.

Metz, Thaddeus, and Joseph B. R. Gaie. "The African Ethic of *Ubuntu*/Botho: Implications for Research on Morality." *The Journal of Moral Education*, Vol. 39, No. 3 (August 2010), pp. 273–290. https://doi.org/10.1080/0305724 0.2010.497609.

Metz, Thaddeus, and Sarah Clark Miller. "Relational Ethics." In *The International Encyclopedia of Ethics*, edited by Hugh LaFollette, pp. 1–10. Hoboken, NJ: Wiley-Blackwell, 2016.

Miller, David. *Principles of Social Justice*. Cambridge, MA: Harvard University Press, 1999.

Mnyaka, Mluleki, and Mokgethi Motlhabi. "The African Concept of *Ubuntu/Botho* and its Social-Moral Significance." *Black Theology: An International Journal*, Vol. 3, No. 2 (April 2005), pp. 215–237. https://doi.org/10.1558/blth.3.2.215.65725.

Mofuoa, Khali Victor. "The Exemplary Ethical Leadership of King Moshoeshoe of Basotho of Lesotho in the Nineteenth Century Southern Africa." *Journal of Public Administration and Governance*, Vol. 5, No. 3 (2015), pp. 21–35. https://doi.org/10.5296/jpag.v5i3.8129.

Mokgoro, Yvonne. "Ubuntu and the Law in South Africa," *Buffalo Human Rights Law Review*, Vol. 4, No. 3 (January 1998), pp. 15–23. https://digitalcommons.law.buffalo.edu/bhrlr/vol4/iss1/3.

Morkevičius, Valerie. "Power and Order: The Shared Logics of Realism and Just War Theory." *International Studies Quarterly*, Vol. 59, No. 1 (March 2015), pp. 11–22. https://doi.org/10.1111/isqu.12152.

Narain, Savita. *Jallianwala Bagh Massacre, 1919*. Atlanta, GA: Lancer, 2013.

Neba-Fuh, Emmanuel. *Triumph of Racism: The History of White Supremacy in Africa and How Shithole Entered the United States Presidential Lexicon*. Kansas City, MO: Miraclaire Publishing, 2021.

Nkondo, Gessler Muxe. "Ubuntu as a Public Policy in South Africa." *International Journal of African Renaissance Studies*, Vol. 2, No. 1 (September 2007), pp. 88–100. https://doi.org/10.1080/18186870701384202.

O'Malley, Padraig. "ANC Killed Mostly Civilians." *O'Malley: The Heart of Hope*, March 21, 2003. https://omalley.nelsonmandela.org/index.php/site/q/03lv02424/04lv02730/05lv02918/06lv02938.htm.

Ogbonnaya, A. Okechukwu *On Communitarian Divinity: An African Interpretation of the Trinity*. New York: Paragon House, 1994.

Okeja, Uchenna. "War by Agreement: A Reflection on the Nature of Just War." *Journal of Military Ethics*, Vol. 18, No. 3 (November 2019), pp. 189–203. https://doi.org/10.1080/15027570.2019.1690115.

Okolo, Chukwudum Barnabas. "The African Person: A Cultural Definition." *Indian Philosophical Quarterly*, Vol. 16, No. 1 (January 1989), pp. 67–74. https://www.unipune.ac.in/snc/cssh/ipq/english/IPQ/16-20%20volumes/16%2001/PDF/16-1-5.pdf.

Omotoso, Sharon. "African Womanist View of Just War Theory in Tunde Kelani's The Narrow Path." *African Notes: Bulletin of the Institute of African Studies, University of Ibadan*, Vol. 42, Nos. 1 & 2 (January 2018), pp. 56–74.

Orakhelashvili, Alexander. *Peremptory Norms in International Law*. Oxford: Oxford University Press, 2006.

Ozumba, G.O., and Jonathan O. Chimakonam. *Njikoka Amaka: Further Discussion on the Philosophy of Integrative Humanism*. Calabar: 3rd Logic Option, 2014.

Paris, Roland. *At War's End: Building Peace After Civil Conflict*. Cambridge: Cambridge University Press, 2004.

Pattison, James. "The Case for the Nonideal Morality of War: Beyond Revisionism versus Traditionalism in Just War Theory." *Political Theory*, Vol. 46, No. 2 (2018), pp. 242–268. https://doi.org/10.1177/0090591716669394.

Ramose, Mogobe B. "An African Perspective on Justice and Race." *Polylog: Forum for Intercultural Philosophy*, 2001. https://them.polylog.org/3/frm-en.htm.

Ranganathan, Shyam. "Just War and the Indian Tradition: Arguments from the Battlefield." In *Comparative Just War Theory: An Introduction to International Perspectives*, edited by Luís Cordeiro Rodrigues and Danny Singh, pp. 173–190. Lanham, MD: Rowman & Littlefield, 2020.

Rawls, John Bordley. *A Theory of Justice*. Cambridge, MA: Harvard University Press, 2001.

Reichberg, Gregory M. *Thomas Aquinas on War and Peace*. Cambridge: Cambridge University Press, 2017.

Rodin, David. *War and Self-Defense*. Oxford: Clarendon, 2002.

Roedder, Christopher J., and Darren Moellendorf. *Jurisprudence*. Lansdowne: Juta, 2004.

Römer, Jan. *Killing in a Gray Area between Humanitarian Law and Human Rights: How Can the National Police of Colombia Overcome the Uncertainty of Which Branch of International Law to Apply?* Berlin: Springer, 2010.

Roychowdhury, Adrija. "Udham Singh: The Witness to Jallianwala Bagh who Swore to Bring an End to British Rule." *Indian Express*, October 14, 2021. https://indianexpress.com/article/research/udham-singh-the-witness-to-jallianwala-bagh-who-swore-bring-an-end-to-british-rule-7571522/.

Ruch, E. A., and K. Chukwulozie Anyanwu. *African Philosophy: An Introduction to the Main Philosophical Trends in Contemporary Africa*. Rome: Catholic Book Agency, 1981.

Shue, Henry. "Eroding Sovereignty: The Advance of Principles." In *The Morality of Nationalism*, 3rd ed., edited Robert McKim and Jeff McMahan, pp. 340–359. Oxford: Oxford University Press, 1997.

Shutte, Augustine. *Ubuntu: An Ethic for the New South African*. Cape Town: Cluster Publications, 2001.

Singh, Danny, and Luís Cordeiro-Rodrigues. "Introduction: International and Comparative Perspectives to Just War Theory." In *Comparative Just War Theory: An Introduction to International Perspectives*, edited by Luís Cordeiro-Rodrigues and Danny Singh, pp. 1–11. Lanham: Rowman & Littlefield, 2020.

Singh, Danny. "Anticorruption, Cultural Norms, and Implications for the APUNCAC." *Laws*, Vol. 10, No. 2 (April 2021), 23, pp. 1–17. https://doi.10.3390/laws10020023.

Smith, Edwin William. *The Blessed Missionaries: Being the Phelps-Stokes Lectures Delivered in Cape Town in 1949 (with Foreword by Sir Herbert Stanley)*. Oxford: Oxford University Press, 1950.

South African Truth and Reconciliation Commission. *Truth and Reconciliation Commission of South Africa Report – Volume Six*. Kenwyn, Cape Town: Juta & Co Ltd, March 2003. https://www.gov.za/sites/default/files/gcis_document/201409/trc0.pdf.

Strohmeyer, Hansjörg. "Collapse and Reconstruction of a Judicial System: The United Nations Missions in Kosovo and East Timor." *American Journal of International Law*, Vol. 95, No. 1 (January 2001), pp. 46–63. https://doi.org/10.2307/2642036.

Sullivan, E. Thomas, and Richard S. Frase. *Proportionality Principles in American Law: Controlling Excessive Government Actions*. Oxford: Oxford University Press, 2009.

Táíwò, Olúfẹ́mi. "Against African Communalism." *Journal of French and Francophone Philosophy*, Vol. 24, No. 1 (October 2016), pp. 81–100. https://doi.org/10.5195/jffp.2016.759.

Tse-tung, Mao. *On Guerrilla Warfare*, translated by Samuel B. Griffith. Mineola, New York: Dover Publications, 2017.

Tutu, Desmond Mpilo. *The Rainbow People of God: The Making of a Peaceful Revolution*. New York: Doubleday, 1994.

Tutu, Desmond Mpilo. *No Future Without Forgiveness*. New York: Random House, 1999.

Tutu, Desmond Mpilo, and Beyers Naudé. "Our Common Humanity." In *50 Years of the Freedom Charter*, edited by Raymond Suttner and Jeremy Cronin (Pretoria: University of South Africa Press, 2006), pp. 232–234.

Ugwuanyi, Lawrence Ogbo. "Towards an African Theory of Just War." *Revista de Estudios Africanos* [Journal of African Studies], Vol. 1 (November 2020), pp. 51–65. https://doi.org/10.15366/reauam2020.1.003.

United Nations. *Charter of the United Nations*. 1 United Nations Treaty Series XVI, October 24, 1945.

United Nations Security Council Resolution 660. "Alarmed by the Invasion of Kuwait." UN Doc. S/RES/660, August 2, 1990, adopted 2,963rd meeting.

United Nations Security Council Resolution 778. "Iraq to Withdraw from Kuwait." UN Doc. S/RES/778, November 29, 1990, adopted 2,932nd meeting.

United Nations Security Council Resolution 1970. "Situation in the Libyan Arab Jamahiriya and Condemnation of Violence." UN Doc. S/RES/1970, February 26, 2011, adopted 6,491st meeting.

United Nations Security Council Resolution 1973. "On the Establishment of a Ban on Flights in the Libyan Arab Jamahiriya Airspace." UN Doc. S/RES/1973, March 17, 2011, adopted 6,498th meeting.

United States Army Field Manual. *The Law of Land Warfare*. Department of the Army Field Manual, FM 27–10, July 1956.

Veblen, Thorstein. *The Theory of the Leisure Class: An Economic Study of Institutions*. New York, NY: Macmillan, 1899.

Verhoef, Heidi, and Claudine Michel. "Studying Morality within the African Context." *The Journal of Moral Education*, Vol. 26, No. 4 (1997), pp. 389–407. https://doi.org/10.1080/0305724970260401.

Vitoria, Francisco de. "On the Evangelization of Unbelievers (1534–1535)." In *Colonial Latin America: A Documentary History*, edited by Kenneth Mills, William B. Taylor and Sandra Lauderdale Graham, pp. 65–77. Denver, CO: Rowman & Littlefield, 2002.

Walzer, Michael. *Just and Unjust Wars: A Moral Argument with Historical Illustrations*. New York: Basic Books, 1977.

Walzer, Michael. *Just and Unjust Wars: A Moral Argument with Historical Illustrations*, 4th ed. New York: Basic Books, 2006.

White-Spunner, Barney. *Partition: The Story of Indian Independence and the Creation of Pakistan in 1947*. Manhattan, New York City, NY: Simon & Schuster, 2017.

CHAPTER 3

Rwanda, the United Nations, France, and Weak Intervention

Introduction

This chapter commences with an overview of European colonialism in East Africa, principally Rwanda that was also shared with neighboring Burundi. Within this section, ethnic polarization of Hutu and Tutsi groups from colonial influences, preferences, and divide and rule strategy is brought to attention. This is followed by the Hutu social revolution vying for independence and Hutu rule resulting in their governance, clashes with Tutsis, and an outpour of Tutsi refugees, later establishing the Rwandan Patriotic Front (RPF) in, namely, neighboring Uganda.[1] Subsequently, the October 1990 invasion from the RPF to Rwanda forming the civil war is presented that is followed by international mediation and interventionist efforts to foster a more harmonious state of affairs between both ethnicities. The interventions include a UN observer mission and the deployment of the United Nations Assistance Mission for Rwanda (UNAMIR) in 1993 that attempted to monitor the Arusha Accords negotiating a power-sharing government. This is followed by the shorter-term causes of the genocide in April 1994, principally the assassination of the Rwandan and Burundi Hutu presidents, Juvénal Habyarimana and Cyprien Ntaryamira, with both Hutu and Tutsi sides blaming one

[1] Tom Streissguth, *Rwanda in Pictures* (Minneapolis, MN: Lerner Publishing Group, 2008), p. 28.

D. Singh, *Applied Afro-Communitarian Ethics and Foreign Armed Intervention*, https://doi.org/10.1007/978-3-031-64110-7_3

another, and a weak Chap. 6 mandate of UNAMIR without authorization to protect civilians in danger.[2]

The main part applies the principles of Afro-communitarianism to validate the failed attempts of peaceful negotiations with the Arusha Accord to end the civil war, the abortive call of UNAMIR's Force Commander (Roméo Antonius Dallaire) for additional troops, and the RPF's acceptability of directing violence to rebut enmity-behavior from the Hutu-dominated national armed forces, Presidential Guard and Interahamwe. The presentation of these African consequentialist ethics is directed to the RPF, the United Nations, and the French-led Opération Turquoise. It is contended that the Hutu militia and its media instruments attempted to construct a less discordant state of affairs but a more harmonious state of affairs did not originally embark when Paul Kagame, a Tutsi RPF leader, seized power. This is because victor's justice was dubiously employed to punish Hutu génocidaires over RPF crimes in Rwanda and neighboring Zaire.[3] Furthermore, it is argued that the UN peacekeeping force failed to conduct permissible force due to its weak mandate and the lack of political will from major powers, principally the Permanent Members of the United Nations Security Council (P–5), resulting in the reduction and removal of international troops from the country.[4] Finally, France's UN-authorized Opération Turquoise supported a demilitarized passage for Hutus fleeing the RPF that resulted in many génocidaires, including the Interahamwe, engaging in the First Congo War.

[2] Linda Melvern, "United Nations Observer Mission Uganda – Rwanda (UNOMUR) and United Nations Assistance Mission for Rwanda I (UNAMIR I)," in *The Oxford Handbook of United Nations Peacekeeping Operations*, edited by Joachim Alexander Koops, Norrie MacQueen, Thierry Tardy and Paul D. Williams (Oxford: Oxford University Press, 2015), p. 468.

[3] Victor Peskin, "Beyond Victor's Justice? The Challenge of Prosecuting the Winners at the International Criminal Tribunals for the Former Yugoslavia and Rwanda," *Journal of Human Rights*, Vol. 4, No. 2 (2005), pp. 225–226.

[4] Tamar Gutner, *International Organizations in World Politics* (Thousand Oaks, CA: Sage, 2017), p. 73.

Colonialism of German East Africa and Ruanda-Urundi

In the early 1880s, European explorers entered East Africa. At the end of the nineteenth century, the German and then Belgian colonialists provided favored Tutsis greater access to governmental posts, clergy membership, and education than Hutus. Both the Germans and Belgians supported Tutsi dominance despite their 15 percent minority population over the 84 percent Hutu population and 1 percent Twa.[5]

As part of the Berlin Conference in 1884 permitting Europeans to occupy the entirety of Africa, the German Empire seized possession of the kingdoms of Rwanda and Urundi and absolved them into the Protectorate of German East Africa while renouncing territorial claims over Uganda that Britain assumed. Rwanda had limited resources so colonializers preferred indirect rule through the royal Tutsi monarchy kingdomship. King Rwabugiri created a royal army with arms provided by Germany and banned the majority of foreigners, principally Arabs, from entering Rwanda. In 1899, Germany started colonialism in Rwanda. European colonial policy engaged with "ethnogenesis" that exaggerated ethnic distinctions to create division. The policy adopted preferred the Hamitic thesis stressing that Africa is valued if the people can be traced to the origins of Caucasians. From the nineteenth century, anecdotal evidence suggests that Hamites comprised a Caucasian racial subgroup of white invaders instead of Black sub-Saharan African indigenes. The Tutsis originated from the lost Ham tribe that migrated from Ethiopia. Tutsis were classified as Hamites and thus colonial governors promoted them as the aristocratic superior race.

Due to the defeat of Germany in World War I, in 1919, the League of Nations mandated that the Belgium Trusteeship seize control over Rwanda.[6] Due to Belgium's colonial rule, French became widely spoken in Rwanda. The Belgians created an ethnogenesis policy to distinguish greater differences between Hutus and Tutsis based on ethnicity to establish a monopolized Tutsi rule. This formalized distinction between

[5] Stephen Kinzer, *A Thousand Hills, Rwanda's Rebirth and the Man Who Dreamed It* (Hoboken, NJ: John Wiley & Sons, 2008), p. 24. It must be noted that the Belgians initially supported Tutsi dominance via an indirect colonial rule, but changed allegiance to Hutu after World War II once they started gaining political emancipatory popularity.

[6] Jean-Marie Kagabo, *Democratic Engineering in Rwanda and Burundi* (Kampala: Fountain Publishers, 2018), p. 130.

Hutu, Tutsi, and the minority Twa groups derived from the Belgian policy of ethnic identification cards in 1926.[7] Belgian colonizers officially made the identity cards part of the consensus in 1933 to reveal all Tutsi, Hutu, and Twa identities.[8] It was now harder to change to other group identities. During the 1930s, Hutu peasants suffered from shortages of land and severe poverty that was exacerbated by Belgium's forced taxes and labor.[9] From ethnic polarization, Hutus were liable for forced labor and Tutsis were granted admission to the Arusha administrative school.[10]

From the Hamitic thesis, it was believed that Tutsi were far more intelligent than Hutu and were the only race to enter the administration, agricultural departments, and medical and veterinary services.[11] This ethnicization policy was part of colonial indirect rule to ensure that Hutus engaged in hard forced labor to protect the favored Tutsis who held a monarchy system for centuries. These Socio-Darwinist initiatives provided Tutsis with better access to education, jobs, governmental service, and the church. Unlike the Germans, the Belgians found the feudal patron-client system that allowed Hutu to obtain status complicated and thus abolished the land, cattle, and army tripartite chieftainship with a mono-structure of Tutsi chiefs, resulting in rigid ethnic polarization.[12] Tutsis were thus benefitting from this colonial system and it was a cost-effective and easy way for the Belgians to extract Rwandan coffee.

When the taxation system arose after World War II, Hutus remained in hard agricultural labor and also had to pay tax while Tutsi chiefs collected a section of agricultural goods cultivated on Hutu-owned farmlands.[13] The Catholic Church now started to Hutus with some having the opportunity to enter education and space to voice grievances.

In the 1950s, state-based jobs were blocked for Hutu by Tutsi preferences. The United Nations decolonization movement exerted pressure on

[7] Isaac A. Kamola, "Coffee and Genocide: A Political Economy of Violence in Rwanda," *Transition*, No. 99 (2008), p. 64.

[8] Gregory H. Stanton, "Could the Rwandan Genocide Have Been Prevented?" *Journal of Genocide Research*, Vol. 6, No. 2 (2004), p. 213.

[9] Audrey Richards, *Economic Development and Tribal Change: A Study of Immigrant Labor in Buganda* (Cambridge: East African Institute of Social Research, 1954).

[10] Rachel van der Meeren, "Three Decades in Exile: Rwandan Refugees 1960–1990," *Journal of Refugee Studies*, Vol. 9, No. 3 (September 1996), p. 254.

[11] van der Meeren, "Three Decades in Exile: Rwandan Refugees 1960–1990," pp. 253–254.

[12] van der Meeren, "Three Decades in Exile: Rwandan Refugees 1960–1990," pp. 254–255.

[13] Kamola, "Coffee and Genocide," p. 64.

the Belgian colonialists to assist Rwanda and Burundi toward independent democracies. The Belgians attempted to integrate Hutus into the coffee trade to market coffee without the colonial government restricting them from doing so. In 1956, this strategy was institutionalized with the Travail~Fidélité~Progrès au Rwanda (TRAFIPRO) [Work–Fidelity–Progress in Rwanda] in Gitarama (the central-south of Rwanda). This provided a platform for Hutu politicians and entrepreneurs, but the institution was southern-based to benefit the Hutu elite within that region. It was here that "Hutu Power" would emerge to counter the Hutu elite. When assessing the principles of Afro-communitarian ethics, it can be contended that Tutsi dominance and indirect colonial rule did not result in a less discordant state of affairs, especially for ethnic Hutus.

Hutu Social Revolution, Independence, and the Coffee Economy

As a response to centuries of Tutsi aristocracy and colonialists favoring Tutsi dominance, Hutu Rwandans formed an uprising that grew stronger in the late 1950s through to Rwanda's independence in July 1962 when Grégoire Kayibanda won the election of the newly independent Rwanda. The southern businessman, Kayibanda, led the TRAFIPRO institution in 1957 and went on to organize the Mouvement Social Muhutu political party that was succeeded by the Parti du Mouvement et l'Emancipation Hutu (PARMEHUTU) [Party of the Movement and Hutu Emancipation].[14] Instead of examining the role of the Belgian colonial administration and the promotion of indirect rule favoring Tutsis and the Hutu elite in southern Rwanda, racial discrimination was prioritized. A Hutu Power revolution advocating Hutu supremacy with the November 1959 Hutu Social Revolution resulted in approximately 120,000 Tutsis, and pro-monarchy political supporters, fleeing massacres into neighboring Uganda, Burundi, Zaire, and Tanzania.[15]

[14] Kamola, "Coffee and Genocide," pp. 64–65.

[15] Jonathan R. Beloff and Samantha Larkin, "Peace and Compromise, Idealism and Constraint: The Case of the Arusha Peace Accords in Rwanda and Burundi," *Genocide Studies and Prevention: An International Journal*, Vol. 13, No. 2 (June 2019), p. 131. Many of the refugee's children formed the Rwandan Patriotic Front that fought against Hutu autocracy in the civil war beginning in October 1990.

By retaining Hutu power, Hutus "organized massacres" throughout the 1960s.[16] Kayibanda changed TRAFIPRO into a state-based marketing institution that bought "coffee from local farmers in seventy locations" across Rwanda, but excluded northern businessmen.[17] Moreover, Kayibanda continued to isolate Tutsis as the principal enemy and thus were repudiated of employment and entering the military and education. In 1973, universities purged on Tutsis and Public Safety Committees orchestrated premeditated mass violence against Tutsis. It can be argued that the Hutu Power revolution was exercised as the highest form of violence from the principles of Afro-communitarian ethics to create a more harmonious state of affairs and better communal relations, but greater north and south Hutu division and inequality left the situation in a more discordant state of affairs—especially with violence perpetrated against Tutsis.

In July 1973, Major-General Habyarimana initiated a bloodless coup. The coup was backed by Hutu business elites located in northern Rwanda, and France committed to military support as an agreement.[18] This support permitted Habyarimana to chair his Mouvement Révolutionnaire National pour le Développement (MRND) [National Revolutionary Movement for Development] party. The resentment of the north-south divide intensified that later formed an opportunity for Major-General Habyarimana to transfer authority and the shift of grievance from southern to northern-based Hutu. Once in office, Habyarimana immediately eradicated the state-ran TRAFIPRO institution and, unlike Kayibanda, engaged with international development aid and foreign investment.

While Habyarimana was engaging in economic repair and cementing a patronage-based system, the refugee crisis and oppositional rebellion intensified. The Front originated in Uganda and attained support from, namely, Rwandan refugees.[19] The refugees in Uganda joined rebellion

[16] Emily A. Milnes, "The Rwandan Genocide: A Study for Policymakers Engaged in Foreign Policy, Diplomacy, and International Development," *Pepperdine Policy Review*, Vol. 13, No. 5 (May 2021), pp. 2–3.

[17] Kamola, "Coffee and Genocide," p. 65.

[18] Stefano Recchia, "A Legitimate Sphere of Influence: Understanding France's Turn to Multilateralism in Africa," *Journal of Strategic Studies*, Vol. 43, No. 4 (March 2020), p. 518.

[19] Hannah Spens-Black, "Rwandan Women at War: Fighting for the Rwandan Patriotic Front," in *War and Women Across Continents: Autobiographical and Biographical Experiences*, edited by Shirley Ardener, Fiona Armitage-Woodward and Lidia Dina Sciama (New York: Berghahn Books, 2016), p. 132.

groups in an attempt to topple Apollo Milton Obote and Idi Amin Dada Oumee from power. The Rwandan Patriotic Front supported Yoweri Museveni with General Fred Gisa Rwigyema and Paul Kagame who were part of the initial 26 original fighters. RPF leaders wanted negotiation for power-sharing, the integration of RPF forces into a national army, the repatriation of an estimated 700,000 refugees, including their citizenship granted by Habyarimana, a democracy, and a veto above the main governmental function.[20]

Despite these problems, Habyarimana's main focus was on restoring the Rwandan economy. Economic liberalism attempted to entice investment and tackle rural poverty with privatization policies that increased international aid and foreign capital investment drastically. Despite good trading in coffee amounting to 86 percent of the country's total revenue, including the increase of prices for it, coffee sales collapsed within the 1986–1987 fiscal year from 14 billion Rwandan Franc (RwF) to 5 billion and crashed further in 1989 from the lack of renegotiating the International Coffee Agreement.[21] The incentives of farmers cultivating coffee were undermined and unemployment significantly increased.[22] Habyarimana knew of the weak economy, land shortages, and his inability to satisfy clans in the north and Hutu and Tutsi in southern Rwanda.[23]

In the late 1980s, Rwanda was in $1 billion debt due to buying coffee from rural farmers that were greatly higher than international rates. The international coffee market capitulated. Alongside the refugee problem, high poverty in Rwanda mounted socioeconomic problems that also caused the conflict.[24] The International Monetary Fund (IMF) and the World Bank drafted Structural Adjustment Programs (SAPs). As part of SAPs, the World Bank imposed macroeconomic reforms based on the liberalization of trade, elimination of agricultural subsidies, and engaging in the privatization of state companies. To meet these World Bank

[20] Joel Stettenheim, "The Arusha Accords and the Failure of International Intervention in Rwanda," in *Words Over War: Mediation and Arbitration to Prevent Deadly Conflict*, edited by Melanie Burton, John H. McGuiness and Margaret E. Greenberg (Lanham, MD: Rowman & Littlefield, 2000), p. 225.

[21] Kamola, "Coffee and Genocide," p. 67.

[22] Out of the unemployed, many were armed and trained into Hutu paramilitary groups involved in the 1994 genocide.

[23] van der Meeren, "Three Decades in Exile: Rwandan Refugees 1960–1990," p. 257.

[24] Christina Fisanick, *Rwanda Genocide: At Issue in History* (Chicago, IL: Greenhaven Press, 2004), p. 101.

conditionalities, Rwanda decided to devalue its RwF currency by 40 percent in November 1990 and 15 percent in June 1991, which resulted in considerable inflation.[25] Household income per capita fell from 1989 to 1993 from $330 to $200, respectively, which marked a decrease of 40 percent within these four years.[26] Due to economic turmoil, the Rwandan administration could no longer finance social services, schools started to close, civil servants lost their posts, and malaria and malnutrition spread. The poor economic climate hit Rwandan peasants hard. At the same time with a poor economy, Hutu dominance expanded. With a poor economy, a shortage of land, and politicians deciding to engage in mass killings for their political advantage, ordinary peasants believed that a stark reduction of civilians would have left more resources and land for surviving people.[27] Habyarimana, leading a poor economy, decided to avoid repatriating Tutsi refugees due to land shortage and the mythology of Tutsis reseizing political power and influence.[28]

The Rwandan Civil War

On October 1, 1990, Habyarimana was faced with an invasion of northern Rwanda by General Rwigyema and the Rwandan Patriotic Army (military wing of RPF Tutsi-rebels) (an estimated 7000 total combatants) from Uganda and almost took Kigali.[29]

France, Zaire, and Belgium deployed forces to help Habyarimana. On October 4, 1990, Opération Noroît was deployed without multilateral endorsement,[30] comprising 300 Foreign Legionnaire paratroopers and Marines deployed in Kigali to support the Hutu government against the Tutsi rebels' attempted coup.[31] President François Mitterrand increased the 300 soldiers to 600 troops to strengthen Habyarimana's resistance to

[25] Kamola, "Coffee and Genocide," pp. 67–68.

[26] Stettenheim, "The Arusha Accords and the Failure of International Intervention in Rwanda," p. 217.

[27] Gérard Prunier, *The Rwanda Crisis 1959–1994: History of a Genocide* (London: Charles Hurst, 1995).

[28] van der Meeren, "Three Decades in Exile: Rwandan Refugees 1960–1990," p. 258.

[29] However, on the second day of fighting, Rwigyema was killed.

[30] The Operation did not attain authorization from the United Nations Security Council.

[31] Recchia, "A Legitimate Sphere of Influence," p. 511.

the Tutsi rebels.[32] The French-speaking Zairian President, Mobutu Sese Seko Kuku Ngbendu wa za Banga, deployed several hundred senior Presidential Guard forces to help his long-lasting friend, Habyarimana, and bolster ties with Paris and Brussels. Paris then provided another 600 armed forces and facilitated more than $10 million worth of military supplies.[33] France successively blocked the Rwandan Patriotic Front insurgency in 1990 and Ugandan expansionism which is why both entities blamed France for the civil war and genocide.[34]

Habyarimana's national armed forces were disorganized and France amended the 1975 France-Rwandan Accord to include heavily assisting the FAR.[35] FAR was expanded from 5200 soldiers in 1990 to 35,000 in 1993.[36] France and Zaire supported FAR troops to push RPF rebels back into Uganda.

President Mitterrand persuaded Habyarimana to undertake steps toward democratization for continual military and economic assistance. In July 1991, Habyarimana amended the national constitution to hold multiparty elections that resulted in over 15 parties contesting while the far-right "Hutu Power" Coalition pour la Défense de la République (CDR) [Coalition for the Defense of the Republic] political party criticized any negotiation with the Rwandan Patriotic Front. The National Revolutionary Movement for Development party formed the Interahamwe militia and then the Akazu elite created the Impuzamugambi militia of the Coalition for the Defense of the Republic.[37] The political wings used violent extremism and paramilitary organizations that intimidated oppositional parties and thus Habyarimana faced a dilemma of combating RPF rebels, rescuing the economy, and dealing with political dissidents. The International Monetary Fund and World Bank continued pouring loans of millions of

[32] Daniella Kroslak, *The French Betrayal of Rwanda* (Bloomington, IN: Indiana University Press, 2007), pp. 127–131.

[33] Stettenheim, "The Arusha Accords and the Failure of International Intervention in Rwanda," p. 221.

[34] Mel McNulty, "French Arms, War and Genocide in Rwanda," *Crime, Law & Social Change*, Vol. 33 (March 2000), p. 111.

[35] C. Prabavathi, "External Involvement and the 1994 Genocide in Rwanda," in *Facets of Contemporary History*, edited by M. Thilakavathy and R.K. Maya (Triplicane, Chennai: MJP Publishers, 2015), pp. 65–66.

[36] McNulty, "French Arms, War and Genocide in Rwanda," p. 110.

[37] Both militias received training in secret camps by FAR troops and were armed with machetes, grenades, and Kalashnikovs shipped to the Rwandan government (Stanton, "Could the Rwandan Genocide Have Been Prevented?" p. 215).

dollars into the Rwandan National Bank to pay off its huge debt with valuable currency, but Habyarimana used most of the funds to buy weapons to deal with the immanent Tutsi-rebel problem.[38] Habyarimana attempted to combat rural poverty with economic liberalism but failed to bring about a more harmonious state of affairs and division within extremist far-right Hutu Power groups politically challenged his leadership. The disharmonious state of affairs was also evident with continued violence from RPF forces.

From October 1990 to April 1994, Habyarimana spent an estimated $112 million on arms and ammunition from these states (France, Egypt, and South Africa) potentially from World Bank loans.[39] Melvern has argued that a variety of states sold machetes to the Hutu génocidaires to conduct the mass murder of Tutsis.[40] France also trained and supported the pro-Hutu Interahamwe[41] (the MRND youth wing) and Impuzamugambi militias and armed Hutu civilians and many of the weapons supplied from the aforementioned countries were provided to the Interahamwe and MRND loyalists.[42] Overall development aid continued to support the Hutu supremacist government up until 1994, despite racial discrimination directed toward Tutsis.[43]

The Signing of the Arusha Accords

On July 8, 1993, Radio Télévision Libre des Mille Collines (RTLM) began broadcasting that incited ethnic hatred and concerns over the Arusha Accords. Ethnic hatred and violence had now intensified nationwide. On August 4, 1993, Habyarimana signed the Arusha Accords with the Rwandan Patriotic Front and five oppositional parties to end the

[38] Kamola, "Coffee and Genocide," pp. 68–69.

[39] Isaac A. Kamola, "The Global Coffee Economy and the Production of Genocide in Rwanda," *Third World Quarterly*, Vol. 28, No. 3 (April 2007), p. 586.

[40] Linda Melvern, *A People Betrayed: The Role of the West in the Rwandan Genocide* (London: Zed Books, 2009).

[41] The Interahamwe militia used the phrase "those who work together" to justify the "work" of killing Tutsis.

[42] Alison Des Forges, *Leave None To Tell The Story: Genocide in Rwanda* (New York: International Federation of Human Rights), p. 93.

[43] Peter Uvin, *Aiding Violence: The Development Enterprise in Rwanda* (West Hartford, CT: Kumarian Press, 1998).

three-year-long civil war. The war between the Rwandan government and the Rwandan Patriotic Front was declared to be "brought to an end."[44]

Despite the ceasefire, the genocide was already planned because the Interahamwe targeted peasants and unemployed men to create a hit list of Tutsis and moderate Hutus. The Accords attempted to cease decades of fighting deriving from ethnic tensions and prior Belgian colonial policies to segregate the identity of Hutu, Tutsi, and Twa.

As part of the political criteria, it was formally agreed that the Rwandan government would adopt power-sharing by creating the interim government to be headed by Faustin Twagiramungu within 37 days, including the Rwandan Patriotic Front, and establish an interim parliament.[45] During this initial period awaiting Twagiramungu's inauguration, Madame Agathe Uwilingiyimana would assume caretaker governor responsibility. Uwilingiyimana recommended that Rwanda achieve a democracy within a short timeframe given the dictatorship. In addition, it was agreed to repatriate and reintegrate internally displaced persons (IDPs) and refugees[46] and establish an integrated army by merging the RPF forces with the pre-existing FAR troops.[47] Yet, the Akazu held senior posts in the armed forces, and other CDR and MRND extremists trained and arranged local Interahamwe militia nationwide. Habyarimana would retain presidential authority until the Broad-Based Transitional Government was formally established.[48] The nationalistic "Hutu Power" thought remained strong with the intention to thwart power-sharing and destroy Tutsis and moderate Hutu opposed to the ideology. Based on this rationale, the Hutu Power movement appealed to many who feared Tutsi power and a return to the colonial caste system.[49]

The United States and the United Kingdom claimed that 4500 troops would be too expensive for deployment.[50] These peacekeeping intentions

[44] Arusha Accords, "Peace Agreement between the Government of the Republic of Rwanda and the Rwandese Patriotic Front," Annex I, *United Nations Peacemaker*, August 4, 1993, Article 1. The original text of the Arusha Accords is in French.

[45] Arusha Accords, "Peace Agreement," Articles 6–7.

[46] However, as part of the Arusha Accords, if refugees were absent for over one decade, then they had no right to reclaim their ancestral land (van der Meeren, "Three Decades in Exile: Rwandan Refugees 1960–1990," p. 258).

[47] Arusha Accords, "Peace Agreement," Article 2 (IV–V).

[48] Arusha Accords, "Peace Agreement," Article 8.

[49] Mahmood Mamdani, *When Victims Become Killers: Colonialism, Nativism, and the Genocide in Rwanda* (Princeton, NJ: Princeton University Press, 2001), p. 189.

[50] Melvern, *A People Betrayed*, p. 106.

were different from the broad objectives of the Accords and the United States amended the draft resolution to disregard disarming civilians, which would have included Hutu extremists (the hard-liners), and was against a large peacekeeping operation.[51] Therefore, the United Nations Secretary-General recommended that UNAMIR would comprise 2548 troops rather than deploy a fully armed military intervention for an initial "period of six months" to implement the Arusha Accords.[52]

The objectives of UNAMIR rested on supporting the Rwandan Armed Forces and gendarmerie by securing Kigali with a secure weapon zone. The mandate of UNAMIR was weak, held poor equipment and a lack of ammunition, and had taken six months for the deployment of UNAMIR to replace French forces and did not permit the peacekeeping force to shoot at Hutu militia or FAR forces. Therefore, the narrow mandate that was eventually agreed by the United Nations Security Council mandated the deployment of lightly armed peacekeeping troops that did not have the authorization to use force.[53] UNAMIR was to retrieve weapons and the Canadian General, Roméo Antonius Dallaire, was appointed as its Force Commander.

On October 22, 1993, Dallaire arrived as UNAMIR's Force Commander in Kigali and was joined by 21 military staff five days later and the Special Representative in Rwanda appointed was Jacques-Roger Booh-Booh who arrived on November 23, 1993.[54] UNAMIR's contingents started to arrive from Bangladesh, Belgium, Ghana, and additional states.[55] RTLM called for Rwanda's Prime Minister Uwilingiyimana to be assassinated.

[51] Koenraad van Brabant, "Security and Protection in Peacekeeping: A Critical Reading of the Belgian Inquiry into Events in Rwanda in 1994," *International Peacekeeping*, Vol. 6, No. 1 (1999), p. 144.

[52] UN Security Council Resolution 872, "Establishing the United Nations Assistance Mission for Rwanda (UNAMIR)," UN Doc. S/RES/872, October 5, 1993, adopted 3288th meeting, para. 2.

[53] Brent Beardsley, "UN Peacekeepers in Rwanda were Ill-Equipped," interview by Michael Dobbs, *Genocide Prevention Project* (Washington, DC: National Security Archive, April 30, 2013).

[54] Gösta Ingvar Carlsson, Han Sung-Joo and Rufus M. Kupolati, "Report of the Independent Inquiry into the Actions of the United Nations during the 1994 Genocide in Rwanda," S/1999/1257, December 15, 1999, p. 9.

[55] Emily A. Willard, "New Documents Shed Light: Why Did Peacekeepers Withdraw during Rwanda's 1994 Genocide?" *Genocide Studies and Prevention: An International Journal*, Vol. 12, No. 3 (December 2018), p. 145.

Dallaire's Cable and the United Nations Secretariat

On January 11, 1994, "Dallaire sent a telegram" titled "Request for Protection for Informant" to the Canadian Major-General Maurice Baril, the Secretary-General's Military Adviser in charge of the United Nations Department of Peacekeeping Operations Military Division based in New York on vital information obtained from a top-level Interahamwe militia trainer.[56] The informant was instructed to register all the names of Tutsis in the capital, Kigali. With this command, the informant was suspicious that the government was planning an extermination phase.[57] It was suggested that his Hutu men were able to "kill up to 1,000 Tutsis" within "20 minutes" and the "Interahamwe-armed militia of MRND" trained 1700 combatants in Rwandan Government Forces (RGF) that were dispersed "in groups of 40 throughout Kigali."[58] In addition, the informant claimed that there was a large weapons cache, holding a minimum of 135 weapons (namely AK-47s and G3 automatic rifles) and would show UNAMIR in exchange for his evacuation after potential interim asylum in a foreign embassy.[59] In the cable, Dallaire informed that action could be undertaken within the subsequent 36 hours, but suggested that the informant could be trapping UNAMIR and the reliability of the informant was questionable.

After a few additional telegrams, the United Nations Secretariat decided that it could not agree on the operation of hunting down the alleged large weapons cache, delivered from a debatable French aircraft, because it stretched beyond the mandate of UNAMIR and could result in the use of force and repercussions.[60] Dallaire's initial plea for further equipment and supplies to act against the weapons caches (resulting in the massacre of Tutsis),[61] and an expanded mandate was thus denied. Therefore, the information contained in Dallaire's cable was not presented to the United Nations Security Council members.

[56] Gösta Ingvar Carlsson, "The UN Inadequacies." *Journal of International Criminal Justice*, Vol. 3, No. 4 (September 2005), p. 839.

[57] Willard, "New Documents Shed Light," p. 145.

[58] Roméo Antonius Dallaire, "Outgoing Code Cable," January 11, 1994, paras. 1, 5–6.

[59] In retrospect, the United Nations-based independent inquiry found it unacceptable that nothing was done to follow up on the location of the large weapons cache.

[60] Willard, "New Documents Shed Light," p. 145.

[61] Noam Schimmel, "What Caused the Rwandan Genocide Against the Tutsi?" *Peace Review: A Journal of Social Justice*, Vol. 32, No. 3 (2020), p. 350.

Habyarimana was approached by the United Nations, but denied all instigations and claimed he would investigate the activities of the potential Hutu militia. Yet, there was no pressure placed on Habyarimana to investigate the matter. Given the weakness of UNAMIR's directive to investigate and seize the weapons caches, the United Nations Independent Inquiry on Genocide in Rwanda held that it should have been raised and reconsidered by the United Nations Security Council to revise the weak mandate.[62]

Despite Dallaire's early warning evidence, and, namely, the January 11, 1994, cable, senior UN Secretariat officials placed the Rwandan context as a non-emergency in a black file or black box.[63] Proper consideration of the telegram would have provided a more robust early warning from the Department of Peacekeeping Operations to the Secretariat for presentation to the Security Council members.[64]

Weapons were found and confiscated by peacekeepers, but information on the locations of arms was shared with the Rwandan government. During this period, the Broad-Based Transitional Government power-sharing initiative of the Arusha Accords was seriously marred with violence, political assassinations, and reprisal killings. On February 22, 1994, the Rwandan Minister of Public Works and Secretary-General of the Parti Social Démocrate, Félicien Gatabazi, was shot dead by gunmen in Kigali and as revenge, a group of Gatabazi's supporters in Butare, his hometown, abducted Martin Bucyana of the rival CDR "from his car and chopped him to pieces with machetes."[65]

On February 27, 1994, Dallaire repeated the plea to the Department of Peacekeeping Operations to seize weapons caches, witnessed by a

[62] Carlsson, Sung-Joo and Kupolati, "Report of the Independent Inquiry into the Actions of the United Nations during the 1994 Genocide in Rwanda."

[63] Touko Piiparinen, "Beyond the Mystery of the Rwanda 'Black Box': Political Will and Early Warning," *International Peacekeeping*, Vol. 13, No. 3 (November 2006), pp. 334–335. The January cable might have been taken out at the time and put back in after (as a cover up) to mirror conspiracy theories, but UN officials denied the black file's existence (Piiparinen, "Beyond the Mystery of the Rwanda 'Black Box,'" pp. 335–336).

[64] Perhaps the "black box" was a metaphor for the institutionalized practice of the United Nations Secretariat officials withholding some details when filing cases for the Security Council.

[65] Lindsey Hilsum, "Rwanda Tribal Rampage Feared after Two Politicians are Killed," *The Guardian*, February 23, 1994.

deployed Senegalese UNAMIR soldier, that the Interahamwe were hiding across the country, but Baril refused the request once more.[66]

On March 1, 1994, the United Nations Secretary-General, Boutros Boutros-Ghali, threatened to withdraw UNAMIR due to the lack of progress in implementing the Arusha Accords. In fairness to Boutros-Ghali, he reported to the United Nations Security Council on March 30, 1994, concerning the deteriorating security and humanitarian circumstances due to a political stalemate, but the Council only extended UNAMIR's mandate by up to four months.[67]

April 6, 1994, Assassination and Genocide

Despite the signing of the Arusha Accords, Habyarimana's plane was shot down by surface-to-ground missiles at 8:30 pm on April 6, 1994, when returning from Dar es Salaam, Tanzania, to Kigali Airport with Cyprien Ntaryamira, the President of Burundi. Ingvar Carlsson, Sweden's Former Prime Minister and chief of the United Nations Independent Inquiry on Genocide in Rwanda, reported that within one hour of the assassination, roadblocks were erected by mainly the Interahamwe militias in Kigali who checked the ethnic identity of people with the identity cards and the killing commenced against identified Tutsis.[68]

A day later, both sides blamed each other. RPF leaders blamed Hutu extremists and Hut hard-liners believed that Kagame was behind the assassination. RTLM was privately owned with financial links to the Rwandan president and his extremist family members who started calling for Tutsi extermination.[69] *Kangura* (newspaper), like RTLM, called for the death of anyone who was in opposition to Hutu Power and would be deemed as accomplices of Tutsis and RPF allies. Hutu moderates and the intelligentsia were deemed as Tutsi sympathizers who attempted the negotiation of peace and were thus deemed as traitors and against the true Hutu population. This was to ensure Tutsi massacres as part of the national policy of

[66] Stanton, "Could the Rwandan Genocide Have Been Prevented?" p. 212.

[67] Carlsson, "The UN Inadequacies," p. 839.

[68] Carlsson, "The UN Inadequacies," p. 837; Stanton, "Could the Rwandan Genocide Have Been Prevented?" p. 214.

[69] Fisanick, *Rwanda Genocide*, p. 21.

extremist Hutu politicians, armed forces, and businesspersons who had taken over the Rwandan government.[70]

In relation to anti-Tutsi propaganda, the Hutu skillfully provided the message to kill or else be killed that instilled "fear among Hutu" resulting in distrust over ethnicity and the belief that if RPF forces seized the country, Hutus "would be murdered or again put under colonial-like control."[71] Hutu extremists media exercised the freedom of speech which is why the United States did not shut down RTLM's radio coverage.

Moreover, the morning after the plane shooting, on April 7, 1994, Madame Agathe, the Prime Minister of Rwanda and moderate Hutu, received 10 Belgian peacekeepers prior to 3 am with the duty to escort her to Radio Rwanda to publicly address civilians to stop fighting in a national broadcast. Madame Agathe and the ten peacekeepers were brutally killed.

From this point, the Interahamwe and FAR began mass killings. Moreover, Hutu extremists, FAR, and the Presidential Guard killed other Hutu moderate politicians "in their homes," particularly the Interahamwe and FAR engaged in mass murders, rape, and torture against Tutsis across Rwanda.[72] On April 8–14, 1994, Belgian, French, and American governments helped evacuate their nationals out of Rwanda and closed their embassies.[73] France and Belgium had historical interests in Rwanda but had now deserted the country.

The United States carried the "Somalia Syndrome" and lack of engagement in international peace support operations as per Bill Clinton with American Congress consultations of the issued Presidential Decision Directive (PDD) 25 even prior to the Somalia calamity.[74]

Within the initial week of the genocide, all UN, aid and development missions shut their offices and all embassies closed, excluding China. In the next weeks, the killings spread nationwide that included priests killing

[70] Jennie E. Burnet, "Review – From War to Genocide: Criminal Politics in Rwanda, 1990–1994 by André Guichaoua and Don E. Webster." *African Conflict and Peacebuilding Review*, Vol. 7, No. 2 (Fall 2017), p. 120.

[71] Margo G. Evilsizor and Fletcher D. Cox, "Pathways and Barriers for Women's Mobilization during Civil War: Nepal, Colombia, and Rwanda in Comparative Perspective," *Peace & Change: A Journal of Peace Research*, Vol. 46, No. 1 (January 2021), pp. 85–86.

[72] Willard, "New Documents Shed Light," p. 146.

[73] Milnes, "The Rwandan Genocide," p. 4. L'operation Amaryllis [Operation Amaryllis] was the French military process that evacuated French and foreign nationals out of Rwanda.

[74] United States National Security Council, *Presidential Decision Directive 25* (Washington, DC: The White House, May 3, 1994).

women and children hiding in churches. Priests and ministers in Catholic and Anglican churches engaged and supported in the killing, torture, and rape of Tutsis within these places of worship.[75] There were reportedly more conflict-based rapes than any other previous civil war.[76] During this process of propaganda and the use of women as lookouts, machetes, knives, and axes were used to brutally kill Tutsis and moderate Hutus. In relation to the latter, politicians who wanted democracy were murdered with a speedy hunt for all desiring power-sharing, which also included journalists, lawyers, clerks, teachers, students, and civil society activists who were killed with door-to-door operations.[77]

Moreover, there are other cited occurrences of UNAMIR troops being unable to prevent massacres despite their presence due to being outnumbered by militias and the weakness of the mandate to shoot to protect civilians.[78] Dallaire claimed that he only had food, water, and petrol supplies to last for a couple of days.[79] This meant that civilians going to UNAMIR posts could not be protected. The United Nations Secretariat quickly considered withdrawing all UNAMIR's troops rather than raising the numbers and strengthening its mandate within the United Nations Security Council. To its credit, the Organization of African Unity held strong political will during the Arusha Accords and its troops remained once fighting broke out.

One of the biggest monumental sites for the genocide that stand today is the series of events that unfolded at Nyamata Catholic Church, which hosts a memorial. On April 11, 1994, an estimated 10,000 Tutsis and Hutu moderates entered the Church and barricaded the entrance doors.[80] However, the Interahamwe militia and Rwandan armed forces engraved holes in the church walls to throw grenades inside and then people within the church were shot or butchered to death with machetes.[81] The bones

[75] Chris McGreal, *Chaplains of the Militia: The Tangled Story of the Catholic Church During Rwanda's Genocide* (London: Guardian Shorts Book 12, 2014).

[76] Laura Elizabeth Sjoberg, *Gendering Global Conflict: Toward a Feminist Theory of War* (New York: Columbia University Press, 2013), p. 219.

[77] Linda Melvern, The Security Council: Behind the Scenes." *International Affairs*, Vol. 77, No. 1 (January 2001), p. 107.

[78] Carlsson, "The UN Inadequacies," p. 843.

[79] Dallaire, *Shake Hands with the Devil*, p. 107.

[80] Elisabeth King, *From Classrooms to Conflict in Rwanda* (Cambridge: Cambridge University Press, 2014), p. 70.

[81] Denis Walls, *A Year in Rwanda: An Anecdotal and Informative Account of Life as a Volunteer in this Small African Nation* (Cairns, QLD: Lulu, 2012), p. 147.

and remains of the 10,000 who died and an additional 40,000 are buried at the Nyamata Genocide Memorial. Similarly, the Ntarama Church holds 5000 bodies as a genocidal memorial site.[82] Additional killings included medical staff at hospitals and patients, but 74 nurses and 56 doctors also engaged in the genocide.[83]

Despite evidence of these ongoing atrocities, on April 12, 1994, the United States justified the significant drawdown of UNAMIR rather than deploying reinforcements that the peacekeeping operation requested.[84] Belgium declared its full troop withdrawal from UNAMIR and America and Britain decided that intervention in the chaotic environment of Rwanda was inappropriate.[85]

On April 17, 1994, Dallaire's faxed cable from Kigali to the United Nations Secretariat, namely, Maurice Baril, at New York, described the massacre as disorganized, irrational, independent, and spread attacks by militias questionably beyond governmental control.[86] This statement did not indicate that the militias were acting on orders from the Hutu government, including the transitional government led by senior military officer Colonel Théoneste Bagosora influencing the Crisis Committee and centrally controlling and instigating the genocide.[87] Two days later, on April 19, 1994, the interim President, Théodore Sindikubwabo, addressed Rwandan national radio by insulting people who were not killing Tutsis ("working"), informed them to move "out of the way and let us work," and went to Butare to supervise exterminating Tutsis.[88] While the United Nations was withdrawing battalions from UNAMIR, the security situation was worsening. A Hutu inner circle created a secret power structure around the Akazu, including Colonel Théoneste Bagasora and Tharcisse Renzaho, to control the interim administration to eliminate Tutsis and Hutu moderates to solve the Rwandan Patriotic Front problem.[89]

[82] John Steward, *From Genocide to Generosity: Hatred Heals on Rwanda's Hills* (Carlisle, Cumbria: Langham, 2015), pp. 35–36.

[83] Williams Buningwire, "Kwibuka 28: Ministry of Health Pays Tribute to Patients, Former Staff," *KT Express*, April 13, 2022.

[84] Willard, "New Documents Shed Light," p. 144.

[85] Melvern, "The Security Council," p. 109.

[86] Roméo Antonius Dallaire, "UNAMIR Outgoing Cable: Most Immediate – The Military Assessment of the Situation as of April 1994," April 17, 1994.

[87] Prunier, *The Rwanda Crisis*.

[88] Human Rights Watch, "Let Them Stand Aside for Us and Let Us Work," *Human Rights Watch*, March 1999.

[89] Guichaoua, *From War to Genocide*, pp. 255–256.

On April 21, 1994, the United Nations Security Council unanimously voted in favor of reducing troops from 2548 to 270.[90] The remaining peacekeepers were not resupplied. A UN Secretary-General Special Report reiterated the failures of UNAMIR and efforts to implement the Arusha Accords that was apparent with the Council's vote for the Alternative II option of withdrawing the majority of the remaining 1515 UNAMIR troops (from the initial 2165) to an estimated 270 personnel.[91] To his credit, Boutros-Ghali did propose Alternative I that both the Rwandan Government Forces and RPF would not agree on a ceasefire within a short-term period.[92] Based on this accurate assessment, Boutros-Ghali recommended an "immediate and massive reinforcement of UNAMIR and change in its mandate to that it would be equipped and authorized to coerce the opposing forces into a ceasefire" that "would require several thousand additional troops" with potential "enforcement powers under Chap. 7 of the Charter of the United Nations."[93] The latter mandate proposed would have comprised a peace-enforcing mission by preventing the massacres of civilians with resort to force.

Late April 1994, Boutros-Ghali requested, with a letter, to the United Nations Security Council to overturn its decision for Member States that disregarded the Alternative I option to undertake forceful action to restore peace and security in Rwanda.[94] The letter provided an update from Dallaire and Booh-Booh on the "deterioration of the situation in Kigali and other parts of Rwanda," largely based on firing from both RGF and RPF sides that amounted to 200,000 deaths "during the last three weeks" to question the option preferred by the Security Council regarding Resolution 912.[95] Alongside "uncontrolled military personnel," the rise in radical civilian groups entering the violence could not be rebutted with

[90] UN Security Council Resolution 912, "Condemnation of the Ensuing Large-scale Violence in Rwanda," UN Doc. S/RES/912, April 21, 1994, adopted 3368th meeting.

[91] Boutros Boutros-Ghali, "Special Report of the Secretary-General on the United Nations Assistance Mission for Rwanda," S/1994/470, April 20, 1994, paras. 5, 7, Alternative II: paras. 15–16.

[92] Boutros-Ghali, "Special Report of the Secretary-General on the United Nations Assistance Mission for Rwanda," Alternative I: para. 13.

[93] Boutros-Ghali, "Special Report of the Secretary-General on the United Nations Assistance Mission for Rwanda," Alternative I: para. 13. Alternative III (para. 19) rested on "the complete withdrawal of UNAMIR."

[94] Boutros Boutros-Ghali, "Letter Dated April 29, 1994, From the Secretary-General Addressed to the President of the Security Council," S/1994/518, April 29, 1994.

[95] Boutros-Ghali, "Letter Dated April 29, 1994," paras. 1–5.

"UNAMIR's present capacity."[96] Based on this premise, Boutros-Ghali urged the Council "to re-examine" its decision on the alternative options presented (II being preferred) to recommend Alternative I, requiring "a commitment of human and material resources on a scale which Member States have so far proved reluctant to contemplate."[97] The United Nations Secretary-General also informed that the violence needed deterring to bring about a ceasefire to prevent conflict due to the rise of refugees in Rwanda's neighboring countries.[98]

The Security Council did not rapidly act on the letter but claimed it would do so later. This was fitting, especially given that Rwanda shockingly remained as a non-permanent member of the Council even though it was undergoing civil war and a genocide.[99] It was obvious that the Rwandan interim government, with Sindikubwabo overseeing the genocide, would not support Alternative I and was happy that the UN peacekeepers were drastically downsizing to 270 troops with Alternative II. It is thus ironic that the United Nations insisted on its unilateral role, and control, but it downsized and withdrew its forces. Debatably, the Rwandan representative when deciding on Resolution 912 encouraged some of the other non-permanent members to want the same. Despite the mass killings, the Security Council still avoided the term "genocide." Kofi Annan and Boutros-Ghali argued that the problem with the atrocities committed in Rwanda did not rest on the lack of information, intelligence, or early warning, but on the basis of futile political will of the major states within the United Nations Security Council.[100]

On May 17, 1994, the United Nations Security Council sanctioned a 5500 force but the troops were delayed, and America failed to deploy "50 armored personnel carriers."[101] A five-battalion force was mandated, but only a few African states stressed a meager commitment to contribute, on

[96] Boutros-Ghali, "Letter Dated April 29, 1994," para. 7.

[97] Boutros-Ghali, "Letter Dated April 29, 1994," para. 8.

[98] Boutros-Ghali, "Letter Dated April 29, 1994," para. 8.

[99] Schimmel, "What Caused the Rwandan Genocide Against the Tutsi?" p. 352.

[100] Kofi Atta Annan, *Towards a Culture of Prevention. Statements by the Secretary-General of the United Nations* (New York: Carnegie Commission on Preventing Deadly Conflict, 1999), p. 11; Boutros Boutros-Ghali, "Interview with Touko Piiparinen," Paris, April 15, 2005.

[101] Milnes, "The Rwandan Genocide," p. 4.

the condition of receiving monetary and logistical help.[102] Alongside attempting to increase the force size of UNAMIR, the Resolution also imposed a weapons embargo on Rwanda, but arms still entered the country from France's previous contracts with the interim government.

It was not until June 10, 1994, that America used the term "genocide," but most of the massacres were completed by then.[103] The rapid withdrawal of UNAMIR troops meant that the peacekeeping operation was too weak to act against armed Hutu militia and FAR forces. On July 25, 1994, UNAMIR was left with 550 troops, which was only 10 percent of its mandated size, to protect civilians containing a nationwide population of over 6.7 million people.[104] Therefore, two months after the United Nations Secretary-General Report, the revised mandate authorized by the United Nations Security Council did not spark an acceptable reaction, as a form of foreign armed intervention, thus the United Nations assuming unilateral control and the burden of responsibility had failed. The Report issued by Boutros-Ghali acknowledged the pitfalls of the United Nations system and the paralysis of the international community from the lack of political will. Leading powers chose to do nothing. This can be explained from a realist perspective in international relations because Rwanda lacked natural resources and geographical strategic importance for America and European allies, Russia, and China to act. These powers "did not care about" Rwanda,[105] because there was no relative gain envisioned.

It was the Rwandan Patriotic Front, not the United Nations, that had taken control of Rwanda on July 18, 1994, and established "a multilateral ceasefire" and a day later formed the five-year transitional Government of National Unity.[106] According to UN estimates, a total of 800,000 Tutsi and some Hutu moderates were killed, which is contrasted with Rwandan government figures at one million, over 100 days and the Tutsi deaths constituted 75 percent of the total Rwandan Tutsi population.[107] The genocide resulted in an estimated 1.5–2 million Tutsis, referred to as Banyarwanda, to Uganda, Burundi, Zaire, and Tanzania.[108] The United

[102] UN Security Council Resolution 918, "On the Situation in Rwanda," UN Doc. S/RES/918, May 17, 1994, adopted 3377th meeting.

[103] Stanton, "Could the Rwandan Genocide Have Been Prevented?" p. 220.

[104] Carlsson, "The UN Inadequacies," p. 841.

[105] Schimmel, "What Caused the Rwandan Genocide against the Tutsi?" p. 351.

[106] Carlsson, "The UN Inadequacies," p. 841.

[107] King, *From Classrooms to Conflict in Rwanda*, p. 70.

[108] Milnes, "The Rwandan Genocide," p. 1.

Nations estimated that Rwanda's population reduced from "7.9 million to 5 million" due to the high number of deaths and influx of refugees to neighboring countries.[109]

The speed of the genocide exceeded the Nazis extermination policy of Jews during World War II by five times and thus would not have been feasible to do so without foreign weapons supplies.[110] When assessing Afro-communitarian ethics, the Rwandan interim government failed to resort to a less discordant state of affairs and foster better communal relations because FAR still received several shipments of weapons from principally France despite the United Nations arms embargo. France, as a foreign actor, thus failed to bring a harmonious state of affairs and develop better communal relations between Hutu and Tutsi due to illegally arming pro-Hutu hard-liners plotting and eventually massacring Tutsis.

Opération Turquoise and the Spillover to Eastern Zaire

By July 1994, the Rwandan Patriotic Front had advanced from Kigali and Gitarama to Ruhengeri and Gisenyi in the north-east and Butare in the south of Rwanda. In the final days of the genocide, génocidaires were surrounded by the Rwandan Patriotic Army. As a response to save the fleeing Hutu génocidaires still engaged in the genocide toward eastern Zaire, the French deployed a heavily armed intervention.

Opération Turquoise comprised a Chap. 7 UN-mandated 2468-strong French and 32 Senegalese temporary multilateral force with over 100 armored personnel carriers, 10 helicopters, 12 fighter bombers, and 120 mm battery mortars that provided a humanitarian safe zone in Kibuye, Gikongoro, and Cyangugu (referred to as Zone Turquoise).[111] French armed forces entered from Cyangugu, south-west Rwanda, and north-west, Gisenyi. On July 4, 1994, the Rwandan Patriotic Front took Kigali and ended the genocide by installing a ceasefire on July 18, with the Hutu administration and civilians fleeing the country. Fighting continued for another month. France's humanitarian zone provided support to evacuate

[109] Stettenheim, "The Arusha Accords and the Failure of International Intervention in Rwanda," p. 216.

[110] McNulty, "French Arms, War and Genocide in Rwanda," p. 108.

[111] United Nations Security Council Resolution 929, "French-led Multilateral Operation to Secure Rwanda," UN Doc. S/RES/929, June 22, 1994, adopted 3392nd meeting.

foreigners and "secure retreat" for former FAR forces, Hutu leaders, and the Interahamwe with minimal policing, resulting in their weapons also crossing to Zaire.[112]

In the safe zones, French troops ensured that Hutu governmental armed forces and the Rwandan Patriotic Front would not clash to allow a safe passage for fleeing refugees. The Operation helped save between 10,000 and 15,000 lives in west Rwanda[113] and assisted 1.5–2 million Hutu refugees. This included perpetrators of the genocide such as the Interahamwe militias with food and medicines to flee to the forests in the Kivu provinces of eastern Zaire and kill and raid the local population that was a major cause of the First Congo War.[114] France's Operation was potentially the biggest cluster of "fugitive murderers ever assembled" in history that were protected, sheltered, and fed by international aid agencies.[115] Zairian President Mobutu welcomed Hutu refugees and received Hutu extremists as guests and permitted the Mai Mai militia groups to help create political and military bases in eastern Zairian Hutu refugee camps to kill ethnic Tutsis over the Rwandan border and in Zaire.[116] The local Tutsis, Banyamulenge, population could thus be targeted.

In eastern Zaire, the Tutsis were primarily supported by Uganda's President Yoweri Kaguta Museveni and Rwanda's Defense Minister Paul Kagame and also Burundi, Angola, and Eritrea. The support permitted an attack by the organized Zairian Tutsis and, namely, Rwanda and Uganda in an attempt to oust Mobutu from power by joining with local forces headed by the English-speaking Laurent-Désiré Kabila pitted against the Zairian military dictator. These combined forces named the Alliance of Democratic Forces for the Liberation of Congo (ADFLC) headed west for the capital, Kinshasa, to fight the Zairian armed forces and allied Sudanese, Chadian, ex-FAR, and Interahamwe forces. The rebellion had taken control over most of Zaire within a few months. This invasion attempted to destroy the camps that resulted in the Interahamwe, with new army

[112] Kovras, "The UN's Moral Responsibility in the 'Spill-Over' of Genocide," pp. 151–152.

[113] Recchia, "A Legitimate Sphere of Influence," p. 521.

[114] Simon Denyer, "Hutu Militia Spread Terror in Congo's East," *Reuters*, August 10, 2000. The Kivu provinces are located in eastern Congo, which borders Rwanda, Uganda, and Burundi.

[115] Melvern, *A People Betrayed*, p. 224.

[116] Mobutu's authoritarian rulership utilized Kivu and the eastern provinces to attain patronage circles to control the Congo (William S.K. Reno, *Warlord Politics and African States* (London: Lynne Reiner, 1998)).

uniforms and radios, moving further into the Congolese forests on their killing and stealing spree.[117]

While being treated for prostate cancer in Switzerland, Mobutu could not control the rebellion headed by Kabila Laurent Nkunda, and despite France's aid, Mobutu's government and army fell. Consequently, Kabila took control of Zaire and renamed the state, the Democratic Republic of Congo (DRC). The First Congo War resulted in an estimated 250,000 civilian deaths, 220,000 refugees who went missing, and 20,000 armed combatant fatalities. RPF forces also committed massacres against Hutu refugees in camps in Zaire, but the Tutsi rebels did not attempt to exterminate the entirety of the Hutu population.[118] The spillover to the Second Congolese War has been Africa's deadliest conflict to date. The total deaths, which included the Second Congo War, amounted to over 5.4 million, which is Africa's worst war and is comparable to the destruction of World War II.

Post-war Rwanda: The Politics of Paul Kagame and ICTR

The Rwandan Patriotic Front now retains full political governance and opponents have disappeared, arbitrarily detained, or been killed, which in turn limits freedom of expression.[119] Hutu civil action was met with Tutsi (ruling) suspicion, but it was the colonial preference for Tutsis that formed Hutu emancipatory politics, becoming a country ravaged by ethnic violence. The Rwandan Patriotic Front intended to form a country based on pluralistic values to sway away from ethnic hatred, but the alleged democracy that has been installed by the Government of National Unity restricts major Hutu engagement. The Rwandan Patriotic Front governs, and heads, a one-party *de facto* state led by Kagame. Rwanda is supposedly democratic, and despite Kagame being celebrated as a "warlord democrat," elections are biased, that include prohibiting opposition parties,

[117] Denyer, "Hutu Militia Spread Terror in Congo's East."

[118] Hitchcott, "Visions of Civil War and Genocide in Fiction from Rwanda," p. 155. RPF leaders did not intend on exterminating all Hutus as evident with Bizimungu, a Hutu, serving as President after the genocide for the Rwandan Patriotic Front political party for almost six years.

[119] Milnes, "The Rwandan Genocide," p. 12.

assassinating or detaining critics, and electoral fraud.[120] If a political opponent steps out of line, they are deemed by Kagame as "useless characters" and "whoever betrays the country will pay the price" that was evident with the brutal killing of Patrick Karegeya, the ex-intelligence chief in 2014.[121] This means a less discordant state of affairs has not been fully reached due to the lack of Hutu political participation, which is largely due to re-genocide suspicion.

Despite an illiberal peace held by Kagame and coercion against political opponents, the Rwandan Patriotic Front has instituted a social harmonious state of affairs politically for women. The Front did not include the defeated FAR forces, but the 2003 Constitution did install a Ministry of Gender and the Promotion of Women to enable women's participation with exclusively quota-based female councils. Rwanda's first post-war election in 2003 saw women successively obtain 48 percent of the country's parliamentary seats and, in 2017, women made up 64 percent of the parliament.[122] When analyzing the successful female candidates, it can be argued that Kagame favored Anglophone Tutsis brought up in neighboring Uganda and thus Tutsis and Hutus born in Rwanda still face political barriers.[123] As part of communitarian ethics, African feminism has been instrumental in Stiwanism. Stiwanism attempts to engage in the global social transformation by women that aims for an equal partnership with men without reversing gendered roles, but by both sexes working in both best interests simultaneously to form a more harmonious community.[124] It can, however, cynically be argued that Kagame adopted this approach to demonstrate women's participation in post-war Rwandan politics for good international press and to consolidate power.

By the request of the Rwandan government, the International Criminal Tribunal for Rwanda (ICTR) was established by UN Security Council

[120] Lars Waldorf, "Apotheosis of a Warlord: Paul Kagame," in *Warlord Democrats in Africa: Ex-Military Leaders and Electoral Politics*, edited by Anders Themnér (London: Zed Books, 2017), p. 68.

[121] Waldorf, "Apotheosis of a Warlord: Paul Kagame," p. 68.

[122] Evilsizor and Cox, "Pathways and Barriers for Women's Mobilization During Civil War," p. 86.

[123] Marie Elizabeth Berry, "Barriers to Women's Progress After Atrocity: Evidence from Rwanda and Bosnia-Herzegovina," *Gender & Society*, Vol. 31, No. 6 (December 2017), p. 849.

[124] Muhammad Alkali, Rosli Talif, Wan Roselezam Wan Yahya and Jariah Mohd Jan, "Dwelling or Duelling in Possibilities: How (Ir)relevant are African Feminisms?" *Journal of Language Studies*, Vol. 13, No. 3 (September 2013), p. 242.

Resolution 955 with the mandate to prosecute grave breaches of international humanitarian law taking place in Rwanda between January 1, 1994, and December 31, 1994.[125] A total of 75 cases were heard and 93 people were prosecuted until the Tribunal's formal closing on December 31, 2015.

The initial case at the Tribunal was Jean-Paul Akayesu, a Republican Democratic Movement politician, mayor, and former school teacher based in Taba.[126] As the mayor of the Taba community during the genocide, Akayesu permitted policemen and others under his jurisdiction to engage in raping and torturing Tutsi women who sought Akayesu's protection.[127] Akayesu was found guilty on September 2, 1998, in Trial Chamber I for genocide, inciting genocide, and crimes against humanity for murder, torture, extermination, and rape, but not guilty of complicity in war crimes and genocide. The accused was sentenced to a single term of life imprisonment and is incarcerated in Benin.

A major case was the trial against Jean Kambanda, Rwandan former prime minister, who was the first head of state to claim guilty to the crime of genocide before an international court who was not permitted to enjoy state or diplomatic immunity.[128] On September 4, 1998, ICTR's Trial Chamber I eroded the rule of immunity that considered the element of special intent (*dolus specialis*) that enforced criminal accountability to redress impunity and the severity of genocide as the highest international *atrocity* crime.[129] Kambanda argued duress under his role and blamed the Rwandan military and claimed he was a puppet to them once he was dragged from the bank to take over the assassinated Uwilingiyimana, but this appeal on October 19, 2000, failed to dismiss the sentence of life imprisonment.

The International Criminal Tribunal for Rwanda also hosted a landmark case that put the media officials on trial. Although Ferdinand

[125] UN Security Council Resolution 955, "On Establishment of an International Tribunal for Rwanda and the Adoption of the Statute of the Tribunal," S/RES/955, November 8, 1994, adopted 3453rd meeting, para. 1.

[126] ICTR, *Prosecutor v. Akayesu*, Case No. ICTR 96–4, Judgment (1998).

[127] Julia Volkmann-Benkert, "Protection of Women Against Sexual Violence in Armed Conflict," in *Ethics and Human Rights in a Globalized World*, edited by Klaus Hoffman-Holland (Tübingen: Mohr Siebeck, 2009), p. 162.

[128] ICTR, *Kambanda vs Prosecutor*, Case No. ICTR 97-23-A.

[129] Giuliana Ziccardi Capaldo, *The Global Community: Yearbook of International Law and Jurisprudence 2016* (Oxford: Oxford University Press, 2017), p. 458.

Nahimana, Jean–Bosco Barayagwiza, and Hassan Ngeze were indicted separately, they were jointly tried for crimes that included public and direct incitement to commit genocide, persecution, and extermination qualifying as crimes against humanity and war crimes.[130] Nahimana, an MRND member, established an initiative committee in 1992 that created RTLM to broadcast a year later from July 1993. Barayagwiza, a lawyer and one of the founding members of CDR, was part of the committee and acting Director of Political Affairs that sat in the Ministry of Foreign Affairs. Ngeze was also a founding CDR member and, in 1990, acted as the Editor-in-Chief for the *Kangura* newspaper. After conviction and submitted appeals, on November 28, 2007, Nahimana was sentenced to serve a reduced 30 years in jail, Barayagwiza to be imprisoned for 32 years (but died during jail time), and Ngeze to serve 35 years behind bars.[131]

The main shortcoming of the International Criminal Tribunal for Rwanda rested on victor's justice. Allegations of victor's justice favoring Tutsis over Hutus. The Tribunal was unwilling to prosecute any forces of the Rwandan Patriotic Front for war crimes and/or crimes against humanity perpetrated in 1994 because they killed thousands of mainly Hutu civilians (although incomparable to the genocide itself), but Hutu victims and families also deserved justice.[132] Based on favoring what side to prosecute, ultimately Hutu entering investigation and prosecution processes, it is evident that internationally supported post-war justice failed to reach better communal relations and a more friendly state of affairs between Tutsi and Hutu. As part of *Ubuntu*, punishment in the form of vengeance or victory does not improve the lives of all parties involved, and thus reconciliation is the preferred approach.[133] There is little evidence to suggest that prosecuting Hutus has resulted in reconciliation with Tutsis.

[130] ICTR, *Prosecutor v. Ferdinand Nahimana, Jean–Bosco Barayagwiza and Hassan Ngeze, "The Media Case,"* ICTR-99-52-T, Trial Chamber I Judgment and Sentence, December 3, 2003.

[131] International Crimes Database, "The Prosecutor v. Ferdinand Nahimana, Jean–Bosco Barayagwiza and Hassan Ngeze," 2013.

[132] Human Rights Watch, "Rwanda: International Tribunal Closing Doors: Governments Should Bring Remaining Genocide Suspects to Justice," *Human Rights Watch*, December 23, 2015.

[133] Thaddeus Metz, "Human Dignity, Capital Punishment, and an African Moral Theory: Toward a New Philosophy of Human Rights," *Journal of Human Rights*, Vol. 9, No. 1 (February 2010), p. 86.

Assessing Afro-communitarian Ethics in Rwanda

Hutus identified that the status quo of the Tutsi monarchy system was later left to remain by Germany and then initially Belgium as colonialists. Hutus could not change the status quo, which was a discriminatory and discordant state of affairs for them living under a feudal-style system working with hard farm labor while Tutsis enjoyed elitist and administrative roles. For Hutus that attained status and cows in the north of Rwanda, a route was feasible to rebut a disharmonious state of affairs without resorting to violence, but their status was stripped by the Tutsis. Under Afro-communitarianism (and especially its consequentialist perspective), the next stage permitting violence could be generated.

During the early 1960s, Kayibanda headed a Hutu emancipatory political party to fight for an independent republic—that was publicized in its 1957 PARMEHUTU manifesto, several conflicts broke out during the 1960s that resulted in thousands of Tutsis fleeing the country. However, Hutus targeted Tutsi civilians rather than attacking Tutsi-based governmental infrastructure and thus the stage of sabotage was skipped for immediate forms of warfare and an open revolution. Despite Hutus gaining political power and control over Rwanda as an independent republic in 1962, ethnic conflicts persisted right through the 1960s, resulting in an estimated half a million Tutsis fleeing Rwanda to its neighboring states. Therefore, after the Hutu open revolution ridding of Tutsi aristocracy and Belgian colonialism, the Hutu government had an opportunity to restore a more harmonious and less discordant state of affairs between the Hutus and Tutsis. Yet, the Hutu government failed to do this and thus the communal, and relational, ethics of *Ubuntu* (solidarity, caring, sharing, compassion, identity, and forgiveness) were neglected due to prematurely opting for violence to rebut enmity-like violence from the Tutsi aristocracy (open revolution).

The Tutsi refugees attempted dialogue in a non-violent, and peaceful, manner with Habyarimana, but he denied their return despite the Arusha Accords. Due to the breakdown of friendly alternatives, Tutsi refugees armed and formed the Rwandan Patriotic Front in 1988 to engage in violence to rebut the violence from the oppressive Hutu government. It can be argued that once the Hutu government came into power, the power shift from north to south Hutus was the priority that ignored the reintegration of Tutsis that blatantly failed the ethics of Afro-communitarianism on promoting a more harmonious state of affairs and less discordant situation and bolstering communal relations in a friendly way (and only resorting to violence if peaceful means collapse).

In 1990, RPF rebels entered north-east Rwanda to wage a civil war. The rebels engaged in sabotage (targeting Hutu armed forces), guerilla warfare (of a small RPF force against a national Rwandan army), debatably terrorism (with the assassination of Habyarimana and Ntaryamira), and held a political motive to establish a power-sharing agreement with the Hutu government. These forms of violence were thus partially, at least, justified under Afro-communitarian ethics (namely, its consequentialist version) to bring a more harmonious and less discordant situation after initial non-violent dialogue with Habyarimana proved futile due to his denial of Tutsi refugee's return and his intentions of massacring the Tutsi population.

When analyzing Afro-communitarian ethics in line with the foreign armed intervention, the assessment is interesting and, indeed, critical of external intervener's geopolitical interests.[134]

After the invasion of RPF rebels, France—as a traditional ally of the Hutu government and Habyarimana—immediately responded with Opération Noroît on October 4, 1990, that was deployed to protect French nationals in Rwanda, but French troops, in reality, helped the Rwandan armed forces to defeat RPF rebels by the close of October 1990 and their leader, Rwigyema, was killed on the second day of the civil war. France also provided weapons and permitted the sale of weapons from other countries via credit finance from French banks to profess President Mitterrand and his son's support for Habyarimana to save the French-speaking Hutu government fighting English-speaking RPF rebels. France wanted to retain their Francophone policy in Africa by defeating Anglophonic groups to assert French regional hegemony in Africa. France's foreign armed intervention with Senegalese allies contravened Afro-communitarian ethics. France did not attempt to promote a more harmonious state of affairs and a less discordant situation because it was one-sided in helping the Hutu government with Opération Noroît, its weapons supply, and military support during the genocide and assistance to fleeing Hutu génocidaires with Opération Turquoise to safely enter Zaire (resulting in two civil wars in succeeding Congo). It is clear that France's interventions did not rebut violence but made it more discordant

[134] This is why the African philosophical theory of war needs evaluation from a political science and international relations perspective.

by assisting Hutu forces to engage in warfare (by targeting Tutsi civilians with massacres) with little mediation.

In relation to the United Nations, they initially observed the Arusha Accords in 1993 with the deployment of UNAMIR. The mandate of UNAMIR was weak and the rules of engagement comprised using force in self-defense and did not permit the use of force to defend unarmed civilians. This mandate did little to help the retreating Tutsi civilians being massacred en masse by Hutu armed forces and paramilitary organizations. Dallaire issued a cable to the United Nations Secretariat system concerning suspected weapons caches and Hutu death squads containing lists of Tutsis in Kigali, but the United Nations only informed Dallaire to investigate further. After the outbreak of the genocide, Belgian peacekeepers were killed and Brussels withdrew their contingent from UNAMIR, resulting in other states doing the same. The United States also stressed the importance of complying with its PDD 25 National Security Council policy of avoiding contributing to international peacekeeping missions. These factors significantly reduced the force size in subsequent UN Security Council resolutions with Rwanda still astonishingly voting with its non-permanent seat. Almost one million Tutsis and Hutu moderates were massacred in 1994 and thus the foreign armed intervention from the United Nations was too weak due to its mandate and withdrawal of troops from poor political will of powerful states. There was no means of permissible violence utilized by UNAMIR to protect the Tutsi civilian population and Hutu moderates supporting the Broad-Based Transitional Government initiative of the Arusha Accords. Therefore, the role of the United Nations did not conform with the ethics of Afro-communitarianism because the world organization failed with its foreign armed intervention to bring about a less discordant state of affairs because it was the Rwandan Patriotic Front that brought an end to the genocide to instill victor's justice and the political suppression of Hutu opposition.

Conclusion

The United Nations and UNAMIR peacekeepers did not deter a disharmonious state of affairs. The United Nations did not only fail the principles of Afro-communitarian ethics, but the foreign *lightly* armed intervention did the reverse by making the protection of the Arusha Accords ceasefire, as part of a traditional peacekeeping mandate, and the implementation of the Broad-Based Transitional Government part of its mandate. These objectives of the international community pressured Habyarimana to eventually sign the Arusha Accords (that he regularly detested) due to France wanting democratization and thus Habyarimana played lip service, while the Akazu were plotting the genocide, to continue receiving French and international arms shipments. Therefore, the Arusha Accords exacerbated violence from Hutu hard-liners, including the Interahamwe, the Akazu, the Presidential Guard, extremist FAR troops, and the media (*Kangura* and RTLM) to kill Tutsis and Hutu moderates (wanting power-sharing) to avoid the alleged risk, and fear, of pre-colonial Tutsi rule.

In relation to the failure of the United Nations to bring about a less discordant state of affairs, and in our opinion, increasing hostile communal relations between Hutu and Tutsi (due to supporting the Arusha Accords) did not have proper early detection. Poor uncovering mechanisms were largely due to the belief of internal, and spontaneous, "machete" violence that would rapidly phase out, and it was the Arusha Accords and the lack of will from political parties in Rwanda that were the main causes of violence. With UNAMIR, logistical challenges and correspondence issues between its Force Commander Dallaire (including the January 11, 1994, cable) and the United Nations Headquarters hindered the activities of the peacekeeping operation.

After the Holocaust, the winning Grand Alliance of World War II (United States, Britain, Russia, and also France) covenanted "Never Again" and preserved this pledge in the United Nations Convention on Genocide, 1948, but the United States and its main allies failed these promises in Rwanda.[135] Ironically, the French supported the genocide through arming, training, and saving Hutu armed forces and politically affiliated militias. The United States could have deployed troops for a unilateral mission—as France did in July 1994 with Opération Turquoise—with or without UN consent (e.g., Kosovo in 1999) or join UNAMIR forces to halt the occurring genocide.[136]

Due to pivotal permanent members of the United Nations Security Council over several phases deciding to significantly reduce the force size, the genocide continued. It was the Rwandan Patriotic Front that had to

[135] Kroslak, *The French Betrayal of Rwanda*.

[136] Samantha Power, "Bystanders to Genocide: Why the United States Let the Rwandan Tragedy Happen," *Atlantic Monthly*, Vol. 288, No. 2 (September 2001), pp. 102–103.

bring an end to the atrocities by militarily defeating FAR forces.[137] The United Nations system failed and the continual lack of political will by its Member States, namely, European nations and America, to commit to UNAMIR (even when a later mandate encouraged more troops). Almost the entirety of UNAMIR troops were withdrawn and only Dallaire and a few African battalions remained. The remaining 456 UNAMIR volunteers stayed and saved 25,000 fleeing civilian lives by guarding churches, hotels, and stadiums.[138] Based on this fact, surely a 4500-strong UNAMIR force with a clear and robust Chap. 7 mandate would have saved many more lives than the remaining, and indeed courageous, 456 troops. A better early warning system would have improved the ability of non-permanent UN Security Council members to understand the genocide before the withdrawal of UNAMIR to form an urgency to save lives rather than withdrawing troops.

Rwanda has been selected as a case study to analyze the role of foreign armed intervention because it was the biggest failure in UN history and amounted to a death toll, including its spillover to the Congo, comparable to World War II. Ethnic fragmentation between Tutsi and Hutu groups in Rwanda has expanded to neighboring states and this animosity remains to plague East African social and communal relations. This is evident after the genocide when the International Criminal Tribunal for Rwanda engaged in victor's justice by avoiding prosecuting any RPF member for war crimes committed in 1994 and Kagame cemented power by restricting Hutu political parties and coercively dealing with criticism.

Based on this conclusion, there are some fundamental lessons learned for foreign armed intervention in small ethnically divided countries like Rwanda that are generated from Afro-communitarian ethics. Third parties, notably foreign armed intervention, must preserve their utmost commitment if they accept their involvement and control of authority. The command structure must be efficient and transparent between the administration, politics, and military deployment of third-party international arrangements.

In addition, any power-sharing agreement must examine its spoiler management strategy and envision how total spoiler groups, like the Coalition pour la Défense de la République, will rally militias to engage in

[137] Marie Elizabeth Berry, *War, Women and Power: From Violence to Mobilization in Rwanda and Bosnia-Herzegovina* (Cambridge: Cambridge University Press, 2018), p. 59.

[138] Stanton, "Could the Rwandan Genocide Have Been Prevented?" p. 222.

mass violence. In the case of Rwanda, the burden rested on the United Nations and the world organization must accept its failure of world governance, notably in maintaining international peace and security, and its great powers also share this responsibility and fiasco. In small countries that have ethnically divided societies from traditional and colonial legacies, foreign armed intervention can be a lot stronger to save lives by rebutting violence with more robust enmity-like violence through stronger mandates. However, stronger mandates require greater political will of international actors and the deployment of their soldiers, equipment, and other resources. Weak Chap. 6 UN mandates and a lack of political will ultimately fail to curtail violence and bring about a political and social harmonious state of affairs.

References

Alkali, Muhammad, Rosli Talif, Wan Roselezam Wan Yahya, and Jariah Mohd Jan. "Dwelling or Duelling in Possibilities: How (Ir)relevant are African Feminisms?" *Journal of Language Studies*, Vol. 13, No. 3 (September 2013), pp. 237–253. http://journalarticle.ukm.my/6605/1/4234-9747-1-SM.pdf

Annan, Kofi Atta. *Towards a Culture of Prevention. Statements by the Secretary-General of the United Nations*. New York: Carnegie Commission on Preventing Deadly Conflict, 1999.

Arusha Accords. "Peace Agreement between the Government of the Republic of Rwanda and the Rwandese Patriotic Front." Annex I, *United Nations Peacemaker*, August 4, 1993. https://peacemaker.un.org/sites/peacemaker.un.org/files/RW_930804_PeaceAgreementRwanda-RwandesePatrioticFront.pdf.

Beardsley, Brent. "UN Peacekeepers in Rwanda were Ill-Equipped." Interview by Michael Dobbs, *Genocide Prevention Project*. Washington, DC: National Security Archive, April 30, 2013.

Beloff, Jonathan R., and Samantha Larkin. "Peace and Compromise, Idealism and Constraint: The Case of the Arusha Peace Accords in Rwanda and Burundi." *Genocide Studies and Prevention: An International Journal*, Vol. 13, No. 2 (June 2019), pp. 129–147. https://doi.org/10.5038/1911-9933.13.2.1696.

Berry, Marie Elizabeth. "Barriers to Women's Progress After Atrocity: Evidence from Rwanda and Bosnia-Herzegovina." *Gender & Society*, Vol. 31, No. 6 (December 2017), pp. 830–853. https://doi.org/10.1177/0891243217737060.

Berry, Marie Elizabeth. *War, Women and Power: From Violence to Mobilization in Rwanda and Bosnia-Herzegovina*. Cambridge: Cambridge University Press, 2018.

Boutros-Ghali, Boutros. "Special Report of the Secretary-General on the United Nations Assistance Mission for Rwanda." S/1994/470, April 20, 1994a. https://digitallibrary.un.org/record/197542?ln=en.

Boutros-Ghali, Boutros. "Letter Dated April 29, 1994, From the Secretary-General Addressed to the President of the Security Council." S/1994/518, April 29, 1994b. https://digitallibrary.un.org/record/197576?ln=en.

Boutros-Ghali, Boutros. "Report of the Secretary-General on the Situation in Rwanda." S/1994/640, May 31, 1994c.

Boutros-Ghali, Boutros. "Interview with Touko Piiparinen," Paris, April 15, 2005. Cited in Piiparinen, Touko. "Beyond the Mystery of the Rwanda 'Black Box': Political Will and Early Warning." *International Peacekeeping*, Vol. 13, No. 3 (November 2006), pp. 334–349. https://doi.org/10.1080/13533310600824033.

Buningwire, Williams. "Kwibuka 28: Ministry of Health Pays Tribute to Patients, Former Staff." *KT Express*, April 13, 2022. https://www.ktpress.rw/2022/04/kwibuka-28-ministry-of-health-pays-tribute-to-patients-former-staff/.

Burnet, Jennie E. "Review – From War to Genocide: Criminal Politics in Rwanda, 1990–1994 by André Guichaoua and Don E. Webster." *African Conflict and Peacebuilding Review*, Vol. 7, No. 2 (Fall 2017), pp. 119–121. https://doi.org/10.2979/africonfpeacrevi.7.2.07.

Capaldo, Giuliana Ziccardi. *The Global Community: Yearbook of International Law and Jurisprudence 2016*. Oxford: Oxford University Press, 2017.

Carlsson, Gösta Ingvar, Han Sung-Joo, and Rufus M. Kupolati. "Report of the Independent Inquiry into the Actions of the United Nations during the 1994 Genocide in Rwanda." S/1999/1257, December 15, 1999. https://www.securitycouncilreport.org/atf/cf/%7B65BFCF9B-6D27-4E9C-8CD3-CF6E4FF96FF9%7D/POC%20S19991257.pdf.

Carlsson, Gösta Ingvar. "The UN Inadequacies." *Journal of International Criminal Justice*, Vol. 3, No. 4 (September 2005), pp. 837–846. https://doi.org/10.1093/jicj/mqi057.

Dallaire, Roméo Antonius. "Outgoing Code Cable." January 11, 1994a. https://nsarchive2.gwu.edu/NSAEBB/NSAEBB53/rw011194.pdf.

Dallaire, Roméo Antonius. "UNAMIR Outgoing Cable: Most Immediate – The Military Assessment of the Situation as of April 1994." April 17, 1994b.

Dallaire, Roméo Antonius. *Shake Hands with the Devil: The Failure of Humanity in Rwanda*. London: Arrow Books, 2003.

Des Forges, Alison. *Leave None To Tell The Story: Genocide in Rwanda*. New York: International Federation of Human Rights, 1999.

Denyer, Simon. "Hutu Militia Spread Terror in Congo's East." *Reuters*, August 10, 2000. https://www.iol.co.za/news/africa/hutu-militia-spread-terror-in-congos-east-46778.

Evilsizor, Margo G., and Fletcher D. Cox. "Pathways and Barriers for Women's Mobilization during Civil War: Nepal, Colombia, and Rwanda in Comparative Perspective." *Peace & Change: A Journal of Peace Research*, Vol. 46, No. 1 (January 2021), pp. 71–97. https://doi.org/10.1111/pech.12449.

Fenton, Neil. *Understanding the UN Security Council: Coercion or Consent?* Burlington, NC: Ashgate, 2004.

Guichaoua, André. *From War to Genocide: Criminal Politics in Rwanda, 1990–1994*. Translated by Don E. Webster. Madison, WI: University of Wisconsin Press, 2015.

Gutner, Tamar. *International Organizations in World Politics*. Thousand Oaks, CA: Sage, 2017.

Hitchcott, Nicki. "Visions of Civil War and Genocide in Fiction from Rwanda." *Research in African Literatures*, Vol. 48, No. 2 (Summer 2017), pp. 152–165. https://doi.org/10.2979/reseafrilite.48.2.11.

Human Rights Watch. "Let Them Stand Aside for Us and Let Us Work." *Human Rights Watch*, March 1999. https://www.hrw.org/legacy/reports/1999/rwanda/Geno11-4-02.htm.

Human Rights Watch. "Rwanda: International Tribunal Closing Doors: Governments Should Bring Remaining Genocide Suspects to Justice." *Human Rights Watch*, December 23, 2015. https://www.hrw.org/news/2015/12/23/rwanda-international-tribunal-closing-its-doors/.

International Crimes Database. "The Prosecutor v. Ferdinand Nahimana, Jean–Bosco Barayagwiza and Hassan Ngeze." 2013. https://internationalcrimesdatabase.org/Case/152/Nahimana-et-al/.

International Criminal Tribunal for Rwanda. *Prosecutor v. Akayesu*, Case No. ICTR 96–4, Judgment, 1998.

International Criminal Tribunal for Rwanda. *Kambanda vs Prosecutor*, Case No. ICTR 97-23-A.

International Criminal Tribunal for Rwanda. *Prosecutor v. Ferdinand Nahimana, Jean–Bosco Barayagwiza and Hassan Ngeze, "The Media Case."* ICTR-99-52-T, Trial Chamber I Judgment and Sentence, December 3, 2003.

Kagabo, Jean-Marie. *Democratic Engineering in Rwanda and Burundi*. Kampala: Fountain Publishers, 2018.

Kamola, Isaac A. "The Global Coffee Economy and the Production of Genocide in Rwanda," *Third World Quarterly*, Vol. 28, No. 3 (April 2007), pp. 571–592. https://doi.org/10.1080/01436590701192975.

Kamola, Isaac A. "Coffee and Genocide: A Political Economy of Violence in Rwanda." *Transition*, No. 99 (2008), pp. 54–72. https://www.jstor.org/stable/20204261.

Kinzer, Stephen. *A Thousand Hills, Rwanda's Rebirth and the Man Who Dreamed It*. Hoboken, NJ: John Wiley & Sons, 2008.

Kovras, Iosif. "The UN's Moral Responsibility in the 'Spill-Over' of Genocide from Rwanda to the Democratic Republic of the Congo." *African Journal of International and Comparative Law*, Vol. 19, No. 1 (March 2011), pp. 145–163. https://doi.org/10.3366/ajicl.2011.0007.

Kroslak, Daniella. *The French Betrayal of Rwanda*. Bloomington, IN: Indiana University Press, 2007.

Mamdani, Mahmood. *When Victims Become Killers: Colonialism, Nativism, and the Genocide in Rwanda*. Princeton, NJ: Princeton University Press, 2001.

McGreal, Chris. *Chaplains of the Militia: The Tangled Story of the Catholic Church during Rwanda's Genocide*. London: Guardian Shorts Book 12, 2014.

McNulty, Mel. "French Arms, War and Genocide in Rwanda." *Crime, Law & Social Change*, Vol. 33 (March 2000), pp. 105–129, https://doi.org/10.1023/A:1008394219703.

Melvern, Linda. "The Security Council: Behind the Scenes." *International Affairs*, Vol. 77, No. 1 (January 2001), pp. 101–111. https://doi.org/10.1111/1468-2346.00180.

Melvern, Linda. *A People Betrayed: The Role of the West in the Rwandan Genocide*. London: Zed Books, 2009.

Melvern, Linda. "United Nations Observer Mission Uganda – Rwanda (UNOMUR) and United Nations Assistance Mission for Rwanda I (UNAMIR I)." In *The Oxford Handbook of United Nations Peacekeeping Operations*, edited by Joachim Alexander Koops, Norrie MacQueen, Thierry Tardy and Paul D. Williams, pp. 462–472. Oxford: Oxford University Press, 2015.

Metz, Thaddeus. "Human Dignity, Capital Punishment, and an African Moral Theory: Toward a New Philosophy of Human Rights." *Journal of Human Rights*, Vol. 9, No. 1 (February 2010), pp. 81–99. https://doi.org/10.1080/14754830903530300.

Milnes, Emily A. "The Rwandan Genocide: A Study for Policymakers Engaged in Foreign Policy, Diplomacy, and International Development." *Pepperdine Policy Review*, Vol. 13, No. 5 (May 2021), pp. 1–16. https://digitalcommons.pepperdine.edu/ppr/vol13/iss1/5.

Peskin, Victor. "Beyond Victor's Justice? The Challenge of Prosecuting the Winners at the International Criminal Tribunals for the Former Yugoslavia and Rwanda." *Journal of Human Rights*, Vol. 4, No. 2 (2005), pp. 213–231. https://doi.org/10.1080/14754830590952152.

Piiparinen, Touko. "Beyond the Mystery of the Rwanda 'Black Box': Political Will and Early Warning." *International Peacekeeping*, Vol. 13, No. 3 (November 2006), pp. 334–349. https://doi.org/10.1080/13533310600824033.

Power, Samantha. "Bystanders to Genocide: Why the United States Let the Rwandan Tragedy Happen." *Atlantic Monthly*, Vol. 288, No. 2 (September 2001), pp. 84–108.

Prabavathi, C. "External Involvement and the 1994 Genocide in Rwanda." In *Facets of Contemporary History*, edited by M. Thilakavathy and R.K. Maya, pp. 61–76. Triplicane, Chennai: MJP Publishers, 2015.

Prunier, Gérard. *The Rwanda Crisis 1959–1994: History of a Genocide*. London: Charles Hurst, 1995.

Recchia, Stefano. "A Legitimate Sphere of Influence: Understanding France's Turn to Multilateralism in Africa." *Journal of Strategic Studies*, Vol. 43, No. 4 (March 2020), pp. 508–533. https://doi.org/10.1080/01402390.2020.1733985.

Reno, William S.K. *Warlord Politics and African States*. London: Lynne Reiner, 1998.

Richards, Audrey. *Economic Development and Tribal Change: A Study of Immigrant Labor in Buganda*. Cambridge: East African Institute of Social Research, 1954.

Schimmel, Noam. "What Caused the Rwandan Genocide against the Tutsi?" *Peace Review: A Journal of Social Justice*, Vol. 32, No. 3 (2020), pp. 350–356. https://doi.org/10.1080/10402659.2020.1867352.

Sjoberg, Laura Elizabeth. *Gendering Global Conflict: Toward a Feminist Theory of War*. New York: Columbia University Press, 2013.

Spens-Black, Hannah. "Rwandan Women at War: Fighting for the Rwandan Patriotic Front." In *War and Women Across Continents: Autobiographical and Biographical Experiences*, edited by Shirley Ardener, Fiona Armitage-Woodward and Lidia Dina Sciama, pp. 127–146. New York: Berghahn Books, 2016.

Stanton, Gregory H. "Could the Rwandan Genocide Have Been Prevented?" *Journal of Genocide Research*, Vol. 6, No. 2 (2004), pp. 211–228. https://doi.org/10.1080/1462352042000225958.

Stettenheim, Joel. "The Arusha Accords and the Failure of International Intervention in Rwanda." In *Words Over War: Mediation and Arbitration to Prevent Deadly Conflict*, edited by Melanie Burton, John H. McGuiness and Margaret E. Greenberg, pp. 213–236. Lanham, MD: Rowman & Littlefield, 2000.

Steward, John. *From Genocide to Generosity: Hatred Heals on Rwanda's Hills*. Carlisle, Cumbria: Langham, 2015.

Streissguth, Tom. *Rwanda in Pictures*. Minneapolis, MN: Lerner Publishing Group, 2008.

United Nations. *The Convention on the Prevention and Punishment of the Crime of Genocide*. Paris, United Nations Treaty Series, Vol. 78, December 9, 1948, p. 277.

United Nations Security Council Resolution 872. "Establishing the United Nations Assistance Mission for Rwanda (UNAMIR)." UN Doc. S/RES/872, October 5, 1993, adopted 3,288th meeting.

United Nations Security Council Resolution 912. "Condemnation of the Ensuing Large-scale Violence in Rwanda." UN Doc. S/RES/912, April 21, 1994, adopted 3,368th meeting.

United Nations Security Council Resolution 918. "On the Situation in Rwanda." S/RES/918, May 17, 1994, adopted 3,377th meeting.

United Nations Security Council Resolution 929. "French-led Multilateral Operation to Secure Rwanda." UN Doc. S/RES/929, June 22, 1994, adopted 3,392nd meeting.

United Nations Security Council Resolution 955. "On Establishment of an International Tribunal for Rwanda and the Adoption of the Statute of the Tribunal." UN Doc. S/RES/955, November 8, 1994, adopted 3453rd meeting.

United States National Security Council. *Presidential Decision Directive 25.* Washington, DC: The White House, May 3, 1994. https://irp.fas.org/offdocs/pdd25.htm.

Uvin, Peter. *Aiding Violence: The Development Enterprise in Rwanda.* West Hartford, CT: Kumarian Press, 1998.

van Brabant, Koenraad. "Security and Protection in Peacekeeping: A Critical Reading of the Belgian Inquiry into Events in Rwanda in 1994." *International Peacekeeping*, Vol. 6, No. 1 (1999), pp. 143–153. https://doi.org/10.1080/13533319908413761.

van der Meeren, Rachel. "Three Decades in Exile: Rwandan Refugees 1960–1990." *Journal of Refugee Studies*, Vol. 9, No. 3 (September 1996), pp. 252–267. https://doi.org/10.1093/jrs/9.3.252.

Volkmann-Benkert, Julia. "Protection of Women against Sexual Violence in Armed Conflict." In *Ethics and Human Rights in a Globalized World*, edited by Klaus Hoffman-Holland, pp. 155–178. Tübingen: Mohr Siebeck, 2009.

Waldorf, Lars. "Apotheosis of a Warlord: Paul Kagame." In *Warlord Democrats in Africa: Ex-Military Leaders and Electoral Politics*, edited by Anders Themnér, pp. 68–94. London: Zed Books, 2017.

Walls, Denis. *A Year in Rwanda: An Anecdotal and Informative Account of Life as a Volunteer in this Small African Nation.* Cairns, QLD: Lulu, 2012.

Willard, Emily A. "New Documents Shed Light: Why Did Peacekeepers Withdraw during Rwanda's 1994 Genocide?" *Genocide Studies and Prevention: An International Journal*, Vol. 12, No. 3 (December 2018), pp. 143–162. https://doi.org/10.5038/1911-9933.12.3.1611.

CHAPTER 4

ECOMOG, PMCs, the United Nations, and Britain in Sierra Leone

Introduction

This chapter engages with the short-term build-up of the devastating Sierra Leonean civil war. It will report on the diamond trade in West Africa and the collaboration of Charles Taylor's National Patriotic Front of Liberia (NPFL) that collaborated with the Revolutionary United Front (RUF) to control Sierra Leone's southern diamond mines. Former Sierra Leonean Army Corporal Foday Saybana Sankoh led RUF rebels. The rebels protested against the allegedly corrupt and inept single-party government by commanding the rebels to engage in mass killings, amputation of civilians' hands, fingers, and feet, systematic rapes, forced abduction and labor for additional recruits that included children, and enforced diamond mining (for the exchange of diamonds for weapons with Taylor). During the civil war (1991–2002), approximately 50,000 civilians were killed, children were stopped from attending school, thousands were amputated, assaulted, and raped, and over half of the civilian "population was displaced."[1] Children constituted 700,000 of Sierra Leone's 1.8 million

[1] Maarten Voors, Peter Van Der Windt, Kostadis J. Papiaoannou, and Erwin Bulte, "Resources and Governance in Sierra Leone's Civil War," *The Journal of Development Studies*, Vol. 53, No. 2 (May 2017), p. 281.

D. Singh, *Applied Afro-Communitarian Ethics and Foreign Armed Intervention*, https://doi.org/10.1007/978-3-031-64110-7_4

displaced persons.[2] At this time, unemployment was high, the economy was stagnated, and unemployed youth were victim to corrupt political elites who forced them to work as thugs during political campaigns in exchange for narcotics. This chapter will demonstrate that the forms of violence conducted by the RUF were not tolerable, under Afro-communitarianism, to confront a corrupt and waning government because the attacks primarily harmed civilians, which falls beyond the four permitted forms of violence. Although the RUF began with political messages to guarantee free compulsory education, disperse diamond wealth to the people of Sierra Leone, and challenge the corrupt Freetown elite, most RUF activity was largely for socioeconomic and partially political, rather than ideological, reasons.

Subsequently, the chapter provides coverage of the Nigerian-led intervention of the Economic Community of West African States Monitoring Group (ECOMOG) peacekeepers that intensified fighting with the rebels and soldiers that provided ammunition and support to the rebels ('Sobels'). This is followed by a description of the coup formed by a military junta, the National Provisional Ruling Council, which hired several private military contractors (PMCs), simply known as foreign mercenaries, including the South African Executive Outcomes. The latter regained territory in diamond mining areas and thus the RUF rebels turned toward further violent means to secure negotiations for a political settlement at Abidjan, Côte d'Ivoire. However, violence escalated and the United Nations supported its observer mission with a peacekeeping force that increased in size. The United Nations peacekeeping force and role in the Disarmament, Demobilization and Reintegration (DDR) of ex-combatants alongside amnesty and the renewed political status of the RUF were negotiated. These peacebuilding terms were signed by both Sierra Leonean President Ahmad Tejan Kabbah and Sankoh of the RUF at Lomé, Togo.

Another coup emerged from the Armed Forces Revolutionary Council that demanded Sankoh's release to form a joint military junta running Sierra Leone. ECOMOG did force the united military junta out of office that reformed a civilian government. During this time, a splinter of the Armed Forces Revolutionary Council called the West Side Boys engaged in looting and control over the Occra Hills area and later in

[2] United Nations Security Council, "Security Council Extends Sierra Leone Mission Until 13 June, Commends West African Peacekeeping Force," *UN Security Council Press Release SC/6653*, March 11, 1999.

hostage-taking of foreign personnel. This included British armed forces, and thus Britain (a former colony) with Operations Palliser and Barras ended the civil war. It will be argued that the attempts from the United Nations were predominantly peaceful and warranted a more harmonious state of affairs, but were thwarted with the departure of Executive Outcomes and India and Jordan and accusations that Nigerian forces were engaged in profiting from illegal diamond mining. Britain's involvement was more forceful with permissible violence that countered UN approaches to oppose RUF enmity-behavior and bring about a less harmonious state of affairs. Once the fighting ceased, the UN and foreign forces remained to see out DDR that was marred with a lack of services for many youth wanting to disband and disarm in exchange for petty cash and a vocational training program.

Political Economy and Demographics of Sierra Leone

Young people were suppressed and marginalized in Sierra Leonean communities, while an economy based on patronage impacted on aid during and post-civil war period.[3] Even though the mining industry brought some wealth in mainly the east, it was unevenly distributed, catering for politicians, chiefs in diamond-rich areas, and traders from Lebanon. Common Sierra Leoneans held a low standard of living and high levels of impoverishment and economic decline in the 1980s. The local chiefdom system formed patron–client relations for rural civilians to access property or attain political rights, and excluded young men felt marginalized with little hope of entering the economy.[4] Sierra Leone was thus an "oppressive state apparatus" based on "client-patron relationships" or a "shadow state."[5]

[3] Richard Fanthorpe and Roy Maconachie, "Beyond the 'Crisis of Youth'? Mining, Farming, and Civil Society in Post-War Sierra Leone," *African Affairs*, Vol. 109, No. 435 (April 2010), p. 251.

[4] Edward Sawyer, "Remove or Reform? A Case for (Restructuring) Chiefdom Governance in Post-conflict Sierra Leone," *African Affairs*, Vol. 107, No. 428 (July 2008), pp. 387–403.

[5] Alfred B. Zack-Williams, "Sierra Leone: The Political Economy of Civil War, 1991–98," *Third World Quarterly*, Vol. 20, No. 1 (February 1999), p. 144.

All People's Congress Rulership Under Siaka Stevens

A one-party rulership was retained by Siaka Probyn Stevens from 1968 to 1985 with the All People's Congress (APC) that deterred competition from its rival political party, the Sierra Leone People's Party (SLPP). Stevens' APC administration was publicly perceived as corrupt, inefficient, and nepotistic.[6] In 1971, Stevens transformed politics into a one-party de facto government that instilled violence in southern and eastern Sierra Leone.

During 14 years of Stevens's leadership, he plundered the majority of state resources, attributing this to the breakdown of state institutions. Stevens tried to intercept the complexity of politics of diamond areas for his own advantage, by ensuring that loyal chiefs retained power in chieftain elections to access mining licenses in principal diamond plots. Stevens established an entirely informal networked market to control the Kono District, which was "diamond rich."[7] In 1980, Stevens emptied the state treasury to develop a huge hotel to host an Organization of African Unity (OAU) Summit.

Stevens turned to the International Monetary Fund (IMF) for support and negotiated a Structural Adjustment Policy (SAP) with the condition of disbanding an estimated 16,000 civil servants, constituting over 40 percent of the state's entire work force, as austerity measures to manage the debt.[8] This borrowing policy devalued the Sierra Leonean leone and state deregulation, as a condition for receiving aid, and intensified prevalent inflation, high unemployment rates and widespread poverty.[9] Consequently, the state further weakened and his Congress relied on a patronage system of loyal supporters. Economic decline was severe in 1985 so Stevens handed over power to the handpicked Major General Joseph Saidu

[6] Christopher W. Mullins, "Variations in War Crimes During the Sierra Leone Civil War," *International Criminal Justice Review*, Vol. 33, No. 2 (2020), p. 3.

[7] Zack-Williams, "Sierra Leone: The Political Economy of Civil War," p. 145.

[8] William S.K. Reno, "African Weak States and Commercial Alliances," *African Affairs*, Vol. 96, No. 383 (April 1997), p. 170; William S.K. Reno, "War, Markets, and the Reconfiguration of West Africa's Weak States," *Comparative Politics*, Vol. 29, No. 4 (July 1997), p. 502.

[9] Alfred B. Zack-Williams, "Sierra Leone: The Deepening Crisis and Survival Strategies," in *Beyond Structural Adjustment in Africa: The Political Economy of Sustainable and Democratic Development*, edited by Julius E. Nyang'oro and Timothy M. Shaw (New York: Praeger, 1992), pp. 149–168.

Momoh as a measure to prevent his long-serving lieutenant, Sorie Ibrahim Koroma, from shifting policies.

The Legacy of Bad Governance from Stevens to Momoh

After Stevens plummeted the economy and placed the state in debt, the system of looting state resources was inherited by Momoh. When Momoh succeeded Stevens, the former appointed foreign companies to destroy local monopolies and exploited diamonds while promising mineral wealth across the mining sector for the country but failed to break away from the predatory system. The officers' corps of the Republic of Sierra Leone Military Forces (RSLMF) were all virtually northerners. Corruption continued to mar the national armed forces with policies on ethnicizing soldiers and austerity that resulted in competing PMCs entering Sierra Leone to fill the security vacuum.[10]

In November 1986, Momoh penned a 40.53 million IMF Special Drawing Rights (SDR)[11] SAP with the International Monetary Fund in exchange for conditions.[12] In 1987, a state of economic emergency was declared by Momoh and thus he clamped down on corruption and the smuggling of diamonds and gold. In the late 1980s, Libyan President Colonel Muammar al-Muhammad Abu Minyar Gaddafi hosted, trained, and armed Charles McArthur Ghankay Taylor and Foday Sankoh in Libya. Gaddafi held anti-West foreign policy against Western dominance in West Africa. RUF rebels grew out of a student protest that coercively emerged with military organization, financing, and arms from NPFL units in Liberia and were trained and heavily assisted by Libya.[13] Momoh continued with Stevens's inherited corrupt practices that also deliberately weakened the

[10] Herbert M. Howe, "Private Security Forces and African Stability," *The Journal of Modern African Studies*, Vol. 36, No. 2 (June 1998), p. 314.

[11] IMF SDR is not a separate currency and thus its value rests on five currencies, including the United States dollar, the euro, British pound sterling, Japanese yen, and Chinese renminbi.

[12] Alfred B. Zack-Williams, "Sierra Leone: Crisis and Despair," *Review of African Political Economy*, Vol. 49 (Winter 1990), p. 29.

[13] Kieran Mitton, "Irrational Actors and the Process of Brutalization: Understanding Atrocity in the Sierra Leonean Conflict (1991–2002)," *Civil Wars*, Vol. 14, No. 1 (March 2012), pp. 104–122.

armed forces, which resulted in the appeal of the Revolutionary United Front to marginalized civilians.[14]

Charles Taylor and the Revolutionary United Front Invasion of Sierra Leone

In late 1989, Charles Taylor led his 50-man National Patriotic Front of Liberia (NPFL) army that invaded Liberia and had taken most of the state, parts of Sierra Leone and regions in Guinea and Côte d'Ivoire.[15] Taylor's aim was for his NPFL forces to fight the Liberian Samuel Doe government, but the newly established ECOMOG fought the movement that was later deployed over the border to Sierra Leone.[16] The Revolutionary United Front also fought the Liberian-based Doe government by supporting the Patriotic Front with combat operations. Sierra Leonean President Joseph Momoh hosted Nigerian combat planes, through ECOMOG at Lungi International Airport, and deployed the Sierra Leonean military to assist ECOMOG.[17] Taylor was resentful of Sierra Leone acting as a "peacemaker" and permitting ECOMOG "to use its airport to bomb territories controlled by his NPFL faction."[18] Taylor wanted revenge against Sierra Leone. The emergent RUF were inspired by Gaddafi's Third Way advocated in his Green Book and training in Benghazi comprising guerilla warfare.[19] Momoh was also losing his patron–client based system, which included soldiers and political associates, leaving an opportunity for RUF rebels to loot diamond mines.[20]

The ideology of the Revolutionary United Front comprised the desire to reclaim minerals and resources for the public, thus growing civic support. RUF rebels formed loyalty to fight for free education, enhanced healthcare, and state protectionist policy from international capitalists,

[14] Once Momoh was ousted from power in 1992, challenges intensified for the Republic of Sierra Leone Military Forces and the successive governments until 2002.

[15] Reno, "War, Markets, and the Reconfiguration of West Africa's Weak States," p. 498.

[16] James Okolie-Osemene, "Sierra Leone: Mapping the Disarmament, Demobilization – Remobilization and Reintegration of Ex-Combatants. Prospects for Sustainable Peace," *Conflict Studies Quarterly*, 34 (January 2021), p. 28.

[17] John Lewis Hirsch, "War in Sierra Leone," *Survival*, Vol. 43, No. 3 (2001), p. 147.

[18] Zack-Williams, "Sierra Leone: The Political Economy of Civil War," p. 147.

[19] Paul Richards, *Fighting for the Rainforest: War, Youth and Resources in Sierra Leone* (Oxford: International African Institute/James Currey, 1996).

[20] Reno, "War, Markets, and the Reconfiguration of West Africa's Weak States," p. 502.

which would, at face value, qualify as motivations for violence to bring about better communal relations and a less discordant state of affairs. The RUF manifesto appealed to the rural populace lacking education and a government that exploited the countryside for the benefit of the Freetown elite. Therefore, the lead-up to the civil war constituted decades of grievances against rural civilians, a corrupt Freetown elite, lack of development in the countryside and huge diamond deposits located in agrarian land that mobilized the backing of the Revolutionary United Front.[21]

The civil war in Sierra Leone commenced on March 23, 1991, when an estimated 100–250 lightly armed RUF combatants led by Sankoh, which included Sierra Leonean disputants, Liberian fighters backing Charles Taylor and some Burkina Faso-based mercenaries, invaded Bomaru, Kailahun District, eastern Sierra Leone, from Liberia against 3000 Sierra Leonean soldiers.[22] This district was a command center where the Revolutionary United Front held their operations to challenge the governance of the All People's Congress chaired by Major-General Joseph Saidu Momoh.[23] RUF combatants tapped the state's diamond mining regions in the eastern part.[24] Many rebel veterans of Sierra Leonean descent involved in the invasion were intellectuals trained in Libya. In April 1991, it was discovered that the rebellion had been initiated by the Revolutionary United Front, under the directorship of Foday Sankoh, a former Sierra Leonean Army Corporal. The Revolutionary Front claimed to fight the Freetown political and business elite that looted all state resources.

Infiltration of the alluvial diamond fields merely protracted the civil war and Taylor needed a close relationship with the Revolutionary United Front to militarily and financially fight the Liberian government to take control. Although Sankoh operated centralized control regarding diamond deals, he relied on a border relationship with Taylor to sell and trade

[21] Kendra Dupuy and Helga Malmin Binningsbø, *Buying Peace with Diamonds? Power-sharing Agreements in Sierra Leone*, PRIC Policy Brief 7 (Oslo: International Peace Research Institute, 2008), p. 1.

[22] William S.K. Reno, "The Failure of Peacekeeping in Sierra Leone," *Current History*, Vol. 100, Vol. 646 (May 2001), p. 219; Christopher W. Mullins and Nishanth Visagaratnam, "Sexual and Sexualized Violence in Armed Conflicts," in *Criminology and War: Transgressing the Borders*, edited by Sandra Walklate and Ross McGarry (London: Routledge, 2015), pp. 139–157; Cornelia Nuxoll, "We Listened to it Because of the Message: Juvenile RUF Combatants and the Role of Music in the Sierra Leone Civil War," *Music & Politics*, Vol. 9, No. 1 (Winter 2015), p. 2.

[23] Zack-Williams, "Sierra Leone: The Political Economy of Civil War," p. 143.

[24] Reno, "War, Markets, and the Reconfiguration of West Africa's Weak States," p. 501.

in exchange for weapons, medicine, food, "petrol and diesel."[25] Therefore, Taylor provided weapons in exchange for diamonds. Diamonds from Sierra Leone entered Liberia and Côte d'Ivoire. Many private foreign weapons and diamonds dealers profited handsomely from the civil war.

Revolutionary United Front

Alongside support from a disgruntled youth, in terms of bolstering robust support, RUF rebels appealed to the Sierra Leonean soldiers. The armed forces were poorly equipped and poorly paid salaried, often not paid for months, and thus the Revolutionary United Front appealed to the military to loot state resources and engage in tyrannous atrocities against unarmed civilians.[26] Moreover, the Revolutionary United Front coercively recruited young people to avoid being killed. RUF recruits were frequently given drugs and forced to harm or kill their own relatives, making it difficult for them to be repatriated home from RUF bush camps. The Revolutionary United Front was an insurgency produced as a "sectarian intellectual response to the perceived corruption of a metropolitan patrimonial elite.[27] The Revolutionary United Front liked to listen to roots reggae music as marginalized youth and students because it held Marxist and liberal meaning as a form of protest against social injustice, poverty, and corruption.[28] Emerging from reggae music, Rastafarian dialogue and salutes were utilized by RUF rebels.[29] The RUF rebels' anthem titled "Footpaths to Democracy" was intended to display the grievances of impoverished and hungry people; underline that minerals were being looted by foreign lands; and describe how the APC were failing the country with the president stealing diamonds and gold, while the Revolutionary United Front was fighting to save it.[30]

[25] Zoe Marks, "Rebel Resource Strategies in Civil War: Revisiting Diamonds in Sierra Leone," *Political Geography*, Vol. 75 (November 2019), p. 5.

[26] Hirsch, "War in Sierra Leone," p. 146.

[27] Richards, *Fighting for the Rainforest*, p. XXV.

[28] Nuxoll, "We Listened to it Because of the Message," pp. 6–7.

[29] Paul Richards, *No Peace, No War: An Anthropology of Contemporary Armed Conflicts* (Oxford: James Currey, 2005), p. 3.

[30] Dena Montague, "The Business of War and the Prospects for Peace in Sierra Leone." *The Brown Journal of World Affairs*, Vol. 9, No. 1 (Spring 2002), pp. 229–237; Lansana Gberie, *A Dirty War in West Africa: The Revolutionary United Front and the Destruction of Sierra Leone* (London: Hurst, 2005).

RUF rebels captured state weapons caches and targeted "commercial mining sites" to devastate access for the national foreign exchange.[31] RUF rebels created forest bases to hit principal state economic regions. During the mid-1990s, US $300–400 million worth of diamonds per annum was produced by Sierra Leone that enticed several players due to the lucrative business.[32] However, the mining infrastructure was destroyed as a form of sabotage for military and political advantage.

Coup d'État: National Provisional Ruling Council and Rise of Foreign Mercenaries

The strategy in Sierra Leone varied. International engagement, namely foreign armed intervention, initially attempted to fight and conquer the Revolutionary United Front. ECOMOG forces were struggling against the increasing numbers of the Revolutionary United Front and thus expensive Private Military Contractors (PMCs) were hired by the Sierra Leonean government from the early 1990s. The Sierra Leonean government contracted 12 PMCs between 1991 and 1999 to deal with the increased violence of non-state actors.[33] At the outset of 1992, over 10,000 civilians were killed, 300,000 people were displaced, 400,000 were trapped, and 200,000 fled to Guinean refugee camps.[34]

The weak Momoh APC government was overthrown in April 1992 by the National Provisional Ruling Council headed by Captain Valentine Esegrabo Melvin Strasser. NPRC soldiers were unpaid and frustrated junior officers that marched toward Freetown to oust Momoh.[35] Strasser received loans from the International Monetary Fund, the European Union the International Labor Organization, and the African Development Bank to spread funds among a rapidly increased army, which like RUF

[31] Marks, "Rebel Resource Strategies in Civil War," p. 6.

[32] Montague, "The Business of War and the Prospects for Peace in Sierra Leone."

[33] Christopher M. Faulkner, Joshua E. Lambert, and Jonathan M. Powell, "Reassessing Private Military and Security Company (PMSC) 'Competition' in Civil War: Lessons from Sierra Leone," *Small Wars & Insurgencies*, Vol. 30, No. 3 (June 2019), p. 644.

[34] Zack-Williams, "Sierra Leone: The Political Economy of Civil War," p. 149.

[35] The majority of NPRC troops were under 30 years old and listened to revolutionary "reggae and rap music" (Nuxoll, "We Listened to it Because of the Message," p. 7). Street art emerged in Freetown, with Bob Marley and Peter Tosh and their revolutionary lyrics written on walls.

rebels, conscripted children.[36] The soldiers needed immediate training. Consequently, the National Provisional Ruling Council had to appoint Frontline Security Service, British Gurkha Security Guards, and Executive Outcomes as private mercenaries for army training and countering RUF rebels.[37]

South African mercenaries, ex-South African Defense Force members based in Pretoria that forcefully influenced the National Union for the Total Independence of Angola (UNITA) to accept the 1994 Lusaka Protocol, also trained Sierra Leonean soldiers.[38] Executive Outcomes cost US $1.7 million per month. In 1994, the National Provisional Ruling Council attempted to defeat RUF rebels by increasing the army's force size to 14,000 that targeted unemployed youth and armed gangs affiliated with politicians.[39]

However, RUF rebels continued to control the diamond fields in the Kono District and conducted attacks in January 1995. Moreover, the Revolutionary United Front attacked mining centers, namely on the southeast coastline, which included Koidu and Sierra Rutile Limited, to disrupt approximately 40 percent of Sierra Leone's national foreign income per annum.[40] The attack on Sierra Rutile, in January 1995, engaged in the taking of hostages, including the chief of a PMC, G4S, Peter White, managing "an open cast titanium dioxide mine"[41] to drive ECOMOG out of the country.

In July 1995, Executive Outcomes utilized Russian helicopters to secure control over diamond areas for Strasser after multiple battles with the Revolutionary United Front.[42] While the Executive Outcomes secured the majority of towns and diamond areas,[43] the Revolutionary United Front progressed to within 45 kilometers of Freetown, the capital. Young

[36] Zack-Williams, "Sierra Leone: The Political Economy of Civil War," p. 149.

[37] This PMC bloc also trained the Kamajor militia.

[38] In 1989, Executive Outcomes was established by a South African ex-Lieutenant Colonel, Luther Eeben Barlow, of the South African Defense Force with experience countering anti-apartheid attempts, including training the South African army (Reno, "African Weak States and Commercial Alliances," pp. 176–179). After the apartheid era came to a close, Executive Outcomes looked to profit in other protracting African wars, such as Angola and Sierra Leone.

[39] Reno, "The Failure of Peacekeeping in Sierra Leone," p. 220.

[40] Marks, "Rebel Resource Strategies in Civil War," p. 6.

[41] Michael Sheridan, "Sierra Leone Kidnappers Threaten to Kill Britons," *The Independent*, January 21, 1995.

[42] Reno, "War, Markets, and the Reconfiguration of West Africa's Weak States," p. 504.

[43] Reno, "The Failure of Peacekeeping in Sierra Leone," p. 220.

NPRC soldiers were suspected of diamond smuggling and there were debates as to whether a civilian government would be better than military rule.

On January 16, 1996, a dispute between the governance of the Supreme Council of State and RUF leaders commenced. The disagreement had taken place prior to multiparty elections. It was contested whether the elections should proceed with or without junta forces. Consequently, Strasser was forcibly replaced in a bloodless coup by the Chief of the Defense Staff, Brigadier Julius Maada Wonie Bio. At this time, the Revolutionary United Front engaged in their initial amputation regime to prevent civilians from voting for Kabbah once more by chopping off their hands, fingers, feet, and arms, making them legally incompetent to vote.[44]

Ahmad Kabbah and the Abidjan Peace Accord

In February 1996, Sierra Leone held its first multiparty democratic elections. In March 1996, the National Provisional Ruling Council "reluctantly" surrendered power to Kabbah's civilian SLPP government.[45] The national army remained tainted by NPRC loyalism, recruitment was based on political and ethnic patronage, and the army traditionally secured APC rule. From May to October 1996, Executive Outcome's continued onslaught against the Revolutionary United Front, including the destruction of their headquarters, pressed the rebels back and persuaded Sankoh to engage with an eventual peace agreement.

As part of negative peace, in late November 1996, Kabbah and the Revolutionary United Front signed the Abidjan Accord, which was OAU headed, as a trade-off to disarm RUF rebels in exchange for the removal of Executive Outcomes. To comply with the Abidjan Peace Accord, in January 1997, Kabbah banished Executive Outcomes from Sierra Leone to comply with the five-week withdrawal clause.[46] Although the Revolutionary United Front influenced the withdrawal of Executive Outcomes, the desire for withdrawing regional forces, and the transformation of the RUF to a political party in exchange for amnesty, police, judicial, and electoral reforms, Sankoh refused the permission of UN

[44] Sierra Leone Truth and Reconciliation Commission, *Witness to the Truth: Report of the Sierra Leone Truth and Reconciliation Commission*, 2004, p. 591.

[45] Zack-Williams, "Sierra Leone: The Political Economy of Civil War," p. 143.

[46] Abidjan Peace Accord, "Peace Agreement," Article 12.

peacekeepers to monitor the ceasefire.[47] Consequently, the war continued less than two months after the Abidjan Accord.[48]

After rice subsidies were largely cut from Sierra Leone's security forces, army indiscipline increased. Consequently, Kabbah relied on a civil fighting force comprising local hunters and volunteers called the Kamajors that emerged after 1993, and this quasi-domestic armed force clashed with the national armed forces. The Kamajors comprised Mende hunters of southeast Sierra Leone and the allied Civil Defense Forces supported the fight against RUF rebels.[49] The Mendes included an estimated 30 percent of Sierra Leone's population that supported the Sierra Leone People's Party. The Kamajors accused the Sierra Leonean army of being Sobels, which refers to undisciplined soldier rebels that looted property and worked in the diamond fields for moonlighting opportunities. Sobels were thus state soldiers by day, but rebels at night. Based on the Sobels analogy, the Sierra Leonean army were largely rebels that stole civilian livestock for food, looted homes, and killed bodyguards.[50]

The lack of political will of international powers and regional actors' full engagement hindered foreign armed intervention to thwart a disharmonious state of affairs. This hostility was largely intensified by RUF rebels fighting ECOMOG forces, a withdrawn Executive Outcomes, and subsequent battles with UN peacekeepers and governmental forces.

The Military Coup of the Armed Forces Revolutionary Council and RUF Alliance

On May 25, 1997, resentful junior military officers called the Armed Forces Revolutionary Council (AFRC), headed by Johnny Paul Koroma, that allied with RUF forces took office by ousting the Sierra Leone People's Party from power that deposed Kabbah from office.[51] This opportunity had arisen from the Economic Community of West African States (ECOWAS) becoming more engaged in Liberia, from mid-1997, which provided space for the junta. Once established, the coalition

[47] Okolie-Osemene, "Sierra Leone," pp. 31–32.

[48] Gberie, *A Dirty War in West Africa*.

[49] The Kamajors emerged in 1993 fighting around Sierra Leone's second largest town, Bo, to defeat RUF rebels in battles because the Sierra Leonean army was incapable of doing so.

[50] Sierra Leone Truth and Reconciliation Commission, *Witness to the Truth*, p. 312.

[51] Zack-Williams, "Sierra Leone: The Political Economy of Civil War," p. 143; Okolie-Osemene, "Sierra Leone," p. 28.

appended the Constitution of Sierra Leone, including the progression for an independent judiciary, and almost all magistrates were exiled. The People's Army established its civilian-led courts called the People's Revolutionary Courts and military courts. AFRC disbanded all political parties and implemented a ruling council of military officers.

When the People's Army were prevented from entering Freetown by ECOMOG forces, they engaged in mass looting, shooting, bombing, mining, and burning that killed many civilians and destroyed private properties. This nine-month fight involved the Civil Defense Forces chaired by the Kamajors confronting the coalition forces with violence.[52] This conflict resulted in prevalent human rights violations, which included summary executions when both parties attempted to control the Kono and Kenema diamond fields and Dara and Zimmi garrison towns.[53] It was later reported by the Sierra Leone Truth and Reconciliation Commission that the Kamajors beheaded people and killed girls if they were smartly dressed due to allegations of having relationships with soldiers.[54]

As a response to the coup, Kabbah fled to neighboring Guinea in exile. A restoration of the Kabbah government rested on Nigerian-led ECOWAS, comprising a strategy on dialogue, the implementation of sanctions, and the robust use of force. ECOWAS had undertaken leadership in an attempt to restore the return of Kabbah to power. In February 1998, an intense battle commenced in Freetown to oust the united junta from power, but the Revolutionary United Front remained in Sierra Leone. It was the pro-SLPP Kamajor specialized hunters of the Civil Defense Forces that helped to defeat the allied AFRC–RUF coalition to try to reinstate Kabbah's presidency.[55]

[52] Mende-language songs were released for the local market. The content covered atrocities of the civil war, looting, displacement, property damage, and civilian suffering (Nuxoll, "We Listened to it Because of the Message," p. 13).

[53] Zack-Williams, "Sierra Leone: The Political Economy of Civil War," p. 158.

[54] Sierra Leone Truth and Reconciliation Commission, *Witness to the Truth*, pp. 7–8, 367–368.

[55] Danny Hoffman, "West-African Warscapes – Violent Events as Narrative Blocs: The Disarmament at Bo, Sierra Leone," *Anthropological Quarterly*, Vol. 78, No. 2 (Spring 2005), p. 335.

The West Side Boys and Hostage-Taking

To add to the problem of the united military junta, another armed youth group emerged. In early 1998, AFRC loyalists in Tumbodu, north of Koidu, spread the initial name the "West Side Ni**az" and the leaders respected the music of American rap-star Tupac Amaru Shakur (2Pac), as evidenced with Tupac's pictures in downtown Freetown.[56] Tupac's songs and album *Me Against the World* were popular for the youth to illustrate social marginalization. The role of Bai Bureh courageously fighting British colonial rule, and its forces, in northern Sierra Leone was also covered by the young rebellion. The West Side Boys (WSB) splintered as a faction from the Armed Forces Revolutionary Council and became a group of 400–600 rebels in 1999–2000. The ideology of music to fight corruption, poverty, and political oppression was instrumental for rebels—initially NPRC then RUF and WSB forces—that formed social cohesion, togetherness, and revolution, thus intending to create a more harmonious state of affairs. Yet, the ideology was different from the coercive reality.

Heavy drug use within the young WSB group was widely reported. This included marijuana, crack cocaine, smoke-heroin, diazepam, and ephedrine. Marijuana was locally grown and extremely popular, and drugs were used solely for recreational purposes, not militarily.[57] Rather than being depicted as renegades with no real long-term agenda, the West Side Boys used well-framed military techniques. They had previous experience of training with the Sierra Leonean army to shape their objectives, while politicians and military commanders used the group as part of political and military strategies.[58]

The Sierra Leonean army formed a military government with the Armed Forces Revolutionary Council. Yet, the West Side Boys was a guerrilla movement that transformed "into a government militia," which eventually reintegrated into the armed forces or disappeared.[59] Sierra Leonean

[56] Mats Utas and Magnus Jörgel, "The West Side Boys: Military Navigation in the Sierra Leone Civil War," *The Journal of Modern African Studies*, Vol. 46, No. 3 (September 2008), p. 493.

[57] However, drugs may have been used to enhance courage when fighting, and to relax when faced with death and the leaders wanted to enhance the image of WSB as ferocious rebel soldiers (David Keen, *Conflict and Collusion in Sierra Leone* (London: Palgrave Macmillan, 2005), p. 231).

[58] Utas and Jörgel, "The West Side Boys," pp. 487–488.

[59] Utas and Jörgel, "The West Side Boys," p. 489.

armed forces also later reintegrated into the West Side Boys and CDF. The West Side Boys comprised the youth who wanted status with an opportunity to be reintegrated within the national armed forces. WSB leaders came from the Wilberforce village in Freetown. The West Side Boys were raised by fathers who were soldiers at the Wilberforce Barracks. Freetown is based in western Sierra Leone and the barracks were also stationed in the western part of Freetown in mainly Wilberforce. The location was one of the main reasons for the 'West Side' given in the name. Johnny Paul Koroma was highly respected and commanded the West Side Boys.

Revolutionary United Front and ECOMOG Clashes

Alongside the rise of WSB and its loyalty to former AFRC commanders, the Revolutionary United Front engaged with its brutal operations. In February 1998, the Revolutionary United Front promoted a campaign on Operation Pay Yourself that originated from the Koidu area.[60] The Revolutionary United Front cadres retained loyalty to Sankoh. Sankoh ordered the Revolutionary United Front to loot everything with Operation Pay Yourself, leading to theft, mass rape, and the burning and looting of villages on the march to Freetown.[61] AFRC's Chairman, Koroma, also instructed the alliance to loot whatever AFRC–RUF forces wanted to pay themselves.[62]

In March–April 1998, Nigerian peacekeepers of ECOMOG intervened to press RUF rebels and AFRC combatants out from the capital and then seized control over the diamond-rich Kono District, which permitted the reinstallation of the Kabbah administration. In response, AFRC forces began targeting civilians and private property. These soldiers ousted from Kono started rebel attacks within villages and closed in on Freetown.

Despite the retaliatory violence from the revolutionary coalition, the Nigerian-led foreign armed intervention paved the way for Kabbah's return from exile to Freetown in the hope of confront a discordant state of affairs. Therefore, the AFRC–RUF coalition ruled for a year and a half

[60] Human Rights Watch, "Human Rights Abuses Committed by Members of the AFRC/RUF," *Human Rights Watch* (August 1998).

[61] Paul Collier and Marguerite Duponchel, "The Economic Legacy of Civil War: Firm-Level Evidence from Sierra Leone," *Journal of Conflict Resolution*, Vol. 57, No. 1 (February 2013), p. 73.

[62] Sierra Leone Truth and Reconciliation Commission, *Witness to the Truth: Report of the Sierra Leone Truth and Reconciliation Commission*, 2004.

until they were driven out of Freetown. The Revolutionary United Front retreated to their Kono, Koinadugu, and Kailahun districts. The deposed AFRC units fled to Kono, eastern Sierra Leone.[63]

When Kabbah was restored to office, he contracted several PMCs, including the preexisting Sandline International and Cape International Corporation. The latter trained and supported anti-RUF militias, namely the Civil Defense Forces coordinated by Chief Samuel Hinga Norton and Kamajors militia in local communities to push RUF rebels back from key areas.[64] This prevented the Revolutionary United Front from seizing Freetown. The South African mercenaries and the Kamajors had retaken aluminum and rutile mines located in south-east Sierra Leone.[65] Moreover, Pacific Architects & Engineers provided logistical assistance for ECOMOG peacekeepers. In response to the attacks conducted by ECOMOG forces, the Sierra Leonean military, and CDF militias on AFRC forces, the revolutionary coalition (both AFRC and RUF) rapidly killed civilians and burned buildings in eastern Freetown.[66] In mid-1998, the exiled Kabbah managed to retake Freetown. Therefore, the intentions of ECOMOG were positive, but the outcome of their foreign armed intervention resulted in further hostility, thus failing the principles of Afro-Communitarian ethics.

The policy of ECOWAS altered when ECOMOG's leader, the Nigerian General Sani Abacha, died in June 1998. Abacha's successor, General Abubakr, informed Kabbah that ECOMOG would remain with high Nigerian commitment to conquer the Revolutionary United Front. However, Nigerian forces were increasingly killed and ECOMOG personnel were undermined from a lack of logistics. Sankoh thus gained leverage and he was supported from both "Liberia" and "Burkina Faso."[67]

[63] Utas and Jörgel, "The West Side Boys," p. 492.

[64] Faulkner, Lambert, and Powell, "Reassessing Private Military and Security Company (PMSC) 'Competition' in Civil War," p. 651.

[65] Hirsch, "War in Sierra Leone," p. 156.

[66] Utas and Jörgel, "The West Side Boys," pp. 487–488.

[67] Hirsch, "War in Sierra Leone," p. 152.

The Arrival of the United Nations and Continued Rebel Activity

In July 1998, the United Nations Observer Mission in Sierra Leone (UNOMSIL) was established. UNOMSIL held 70 unarmed observer forces, under the security of ECOMOG, with a mandate to disarm fighters and engage in restructuring domestic security forces.[68] Despite these efforts, however, RUF rebels had taken over half of Sierra Leone and attempted to reseize Freetown in December 1998, which included driving ECOMOG forces out of the diamond fields in the Kono District.[69]

In late December 1998, the rebels (with help from coalition forces) captured strategic areas. The rebels' alliance with the Armed Forces Revolutionary Council granted further offensive attacks, and ammunition to take control of some territories, but lacked the economic funds to engage in the corporate side of mining. The Revolutionary United Front's transitional leader, Samuel Bockarie (Mosquito), tried to outsource mining and security overseas to broker deals, including with France, to finance the war. This strategic initiative intensified fighting over the Kono District. During his arrest, Sankoh was willing to negotiate mining deals with foreign companies, thus replicating Kabbah's civilian approach. RUF commanders continued to police the theft of "government diamonds" with its police and security units, but many RUF combatants were cashing out with the disarmament process.[70]

In January 1999, the Revolutionary United Front raided Freetown and almost defeated the majority Nigerian contingent of ECOMOG. Consequently, UNOMSIL staff evacuated to Conakry and suddenly downsized its personnel until ECOMOG regained Freetown to begin the process of installing a civilian government later that month.[71] However, a three-week campaign called "Operation No Living Thing" was conducted by AFRC–RUF forces to capture Freetown with mass looting and assault. The most heinous war crimes perpetrated by the Revolutionary United Front and AFRC also included murder, abducting

[68] United Nations Security Council Resolution 1181, "Establishing the United Nations Observer Mission in Sierra Leone (UNOMSIL): The Situation in Sierra Leone," UN Doc. S/RES/1181, July 13, 1998, adopted 3902nd meeting, para. 6.

[69] Reno, "The Failure of Peacekeeping in Sierra Leone," p. 221.

[70] Marks, "Rebel Resource Strategies in Civil War," p. 8.

[71] United Nations Peacekeeping, "Sierra Leone – UNOMSIL Background," *United Nations*, 2000.

children as militants or sexual slaves, and forced displacement by burning villages down.[72] The Revolutionary United Front engaged in its amputation regime by chopping arms, hands, and legs off women and children to campaign for "no living thing," preventing anyone from supporting the United Nations Mission in Sierra Leone (UNAMSIL) or ECOWAS.[73] AFRC forces were initially ill equipped, but by targeting the armed forces, they obtained weaponry to take Freetown in January 1999. During these events, the West Side Boys who splintered from AFRC forces and allegiance to its commanders were highly active. The Armed Forces Revolutionary Council retained a large following of youth who "were socially marginalized" who transformed to soldiers, including "ex-convicts" freed by the May 1997 coup and January 1999 fighting from "Padema Road jail."[74]

After the Lomé Agreement, UNAMSIL was initially mandated to implement the Accords, disarm all warring belligerents, and assist with the RUF militia-to-party process with an estimated 6000 peacekeeping troops and "260 military observers," with the United Nations Secretariat holding a budget of more than $600 million per year.[75] Nigeria, India, and Jordan provided most of UNAMSIL's troops. The purpose of UNAMSIL's deployment was to assist the Sierra Leonean government, the Revolutionary United Front, ECOMOG, ECOWAS, and UNOMSIL in implementing the Lomé Peace Agreement of July 7, 1999.[76]

The Lomé Peace Agreement

The Lomé Accord included DDR of former combatants, which included child soldiers, by the Sierra Leonean government through the rapid establishment of the National Committee for Disarmament, Demobilization and Reintegration (NCDDR).[77] This Committee recommended that the ex-fighters of AFRC, RUF, and Kamajor pro-government combatants and

[72] Mullins, "Variations in War Crimes During the Sierra Leone Civil War," p. 7.

[73] Hirsch, "War in Sierra Leone," p. 150.

[74] Utas and Jörgel, "The West Side Boys," p. 497.

[75] United Nations Security Council Resolution 1270, "Establishing the United Nations Mission in Sierra Leone (UNAMSIL)," UN Doc. S/RES/1270, October 22, 1999, adopted 4054th meeting, para. 9.

[76] United Nations Security Council Resolution 1270, "Establishing UNAMSIL," para. 1.

[77] United Nations Security Council Resolution 1270, "Establishing UNAMSIL," paras. 3, 8b.

loyal Sierra Leonean armed forces qualified as recognized belligerent forces surrender their weapons and ammunition.[78]

Alongside the role of the National Committee, ECOMOG troops, UNOMSIL, and community stakeholders contributed to statebuilding.[79] As part of the DDR program, United Nations Security Council Resolution 1270, authorized in late October 1999, also called for the immediate disbandment of and surrender of weapons from RUF rebels, ex-Sierra Leonean military forces, former AFRC troops, the Civil Defense Forces, and all other irregular militias.[80] RUF and CDF combatants and the Sierra Leonean army would be able to integrate into a new armed force.[81] The Resolution encouraged the repatriation of the Revolutionary United Front and AFRC leaders to Freetown with active roles, ensuring that their combatants engaged in the immediate DDR process.[82] As part of disarming, RUF rebels would be offered positions in the government and be granted the legitimacy to establish their own political party. Furthermore, the Lomé Peace Accord included DDR and UNOMSIL staff holding protection, UNAMSIL chairing the Ceasefire Monitoring Committee, the arrangement of a special fund as reparations for victims, and the release of all prisoners of war and "abductees."[83] However, despite the Lomé Accord and mandated UN peacekeepers, violence was not reduced among AFRC–RUF forces.[84]

As part of the Lomé peace process and negotiations with Sankoh during his house arrest, the RUF leader negotiated a power-sharing agreement that would grant him the role of Vice President of Sierra Leone until

[78] Okolie-Osemene, "Sierra Leone," p. 34.

[79] Okolie-Osemene, "Sierra Leone," p. 20.

[80] United Nations Security Council Resolution 1270, "Establishing UNAMSIL," para. 4. Moreover, United Nations Security Council Resolution 1260 also encouraged RUF rebels to "immediately" disband and "participate fully" in the DDR program to correspond with the Lomé Peace Accord (United Nations Security Council Resolution 1260, "On the Provisional Expansion and Strengthening of the Political, Civil Affairs, Information, Human Rights and Child Protection Elements of the UN Observer Mission in Sierra Leone (UNOMSIL)," UN Doc. S/RES/1260, August 20, 1999, adopted 4035th meeting, para. 8).

[81] The Lomé Agreement, "Peace Agreement between the Government of Sierra Leone and the Revolutionary United Front of Sierra Leone," July 7, 1999, Article XVII, 2.

[82] United Nations Security Council Resolution 1270, "Establishing UNAMSIL," para. 5.

[83] The Lomé Agreement, Articles II, 1., XIII, 1 (i-ii), XXI, XXIX.

[84] Caitriona Dowd and Clionadh Raleigh, "Mapping Conflict across Liberia and Sierra Leone," *Accord: An International Review of Peace Initiatives*, Issue 23 (March 2012), p. 14.

his later arrest in May 2000.[85] UNAMSIL was mandated to help with elections to support the Lomé Peace Accord and had the backing of a Chap. 7 mandate for its peacekeepers to move freely to protect endangered civilians.[86] Furthermore, the United Nations Security Council provided scope for ECOMOG to continue securing its operational areas, namely around Freetown and Lungi to protect the Sierra Leonean government, implement the Lomé Peace Agreement, and engage in UNAMSIL's coordinated disbarment and demobilization process.[87] The Lomé Accord did not include the West Side Boys/AFRC in the text (and only included the Revolutionary United Front as the rebels) and thus the Occra Hills soldiers started taking hostages in retaliation for exclusion from the Accord.[88] RUF rebels abused the Lomé Accord several times, which included attacking UN peacekeepers with British soldiers deployed in the capital to evacuate UK nationals and secure the airport for more UN personnel.

As part of the Lomé Accord, in November 1999, ECOMOG received assistance by UNAMSIL that slowed down the influence of the West Side Boys within the Occra Hills area. The DDR process engulfed the West Side Boys, with many surrendering as part of demobilization. It appeared that the key ex-army leaders did not want to side with the Revolutionary United Front. This resulted in other socially marginalized youth to derail the government. Subsequently, during the peace process, the former army leaders were reintegrated into senior government, military, or political positions. Koroma was deemed a criminal and thus could not return to Freetown for a government post, but he held leverage to do so by supporting the West Side Boys.

[85] Corrina Schuler, "Sierra Leone: A Rebel Leader of Rag-Tag Terrorists," *Christian Science Monitor*, September 17, 1999; Tony Karon, "Sankoh a Hot Potato in Government Hands," *CNN*, May 17, 2000.

[86] United Nations Security Council Resolution 1270, "Establishing UNAMSIL," paras. 8i, 14.

[87] United Nations Security Council Resolution 1270, "Establishing UNAMSIL," para. 11.

[88] BBC News, "World: Africa: Sierra Leone Who are the Kidnappers?" BBC News, August 6, 1999.

The Use of Militias to Fight the Revolutionary United Front

The United Nations peacekeepers were also weakened and fragmented at this time. The Kenyan contingent of UNAMSIL failed to enforce the Lomé Agreement terms because they handed over their weapons to RUF rebels in November 1999 and the UN's Guinea unit forcefully surrendered "several tons of ammunition," around 50 AK-47 assault rifles and other guns in January 2000.[89] India played a major role that initially led UNAMSIL from December 1999 with an assertive Force Commander, Major-General Vijay Kumar Jetley, who was criticized for his treatment of soldiers from other nations, particularly the Nigerian contingent.

In January 2000, an estimated 1000 WSB soldiers cooperated with the DDR process and child soldiers were released in February 2000. Despite progress, however, the Revolutionary United Front remained a threat to the government in Freetown and Koroma sided with the Freetown administration to impose the role of the West Side Boys as a strategic player in the Occra Hills region to protect the capital from ongoing RUF rebels. The West Side Boys, allied with the Sierra Leonean armed forces and CDF (mainly Kamajors), played a significant role in May 2000 in stalling an advancing RUF from Occra Hills to Waterloo.[90] WSB combatants were growing stronger at this point. Kabbah was afraid of another coup and thus formed an amnesty for the West Side Boys and their leader, Koroma, for the young militia to contribute as a security force. The security initiative moved swiftly to parts of Freetown to thwart Sankoh and RUF rebels.

On May 6, 2000, the West Side Boys arrested RUF rebels in Freetown, and a day later, Koroma announced a state of emergency calling for a peace rally, located at the National Stadium, for the entire Sierra Leonean armed forces (former soldiers and Kamajors) to find the Revolutionary United Front. Five Five commanded WSB Units to target the RUF rebels and imprisoned several of its main commanders. As part of the peace task force, the West Side Boys had access to weapons from Sierra Leonean army stores and the alleged peace demonstration, and thus many civilians allied with a large group of WSB soldiers. On May 8, 2000, the soldiers and civilians marched to Spur Road at Sankoh's residence where many RUF leaders had taken refuge, and RUF rebels fired back. The fight from

[89] Reno, "The Failure of Peacekeeping in Sierra Leone," p. 222.

[90] Keen, *Conflict and Collusion in Sierra Leone*, p. 264.

the allied WSB, Sierra Leonean armed forces, and Kamajors outgunned the Revolutionary United Front, but Sankoh and his seniors fled and were captured a few days later.[91] The West Side Boys got what they wanted: to avert social marginalization by returning to Freetown and being reintegrated within the Sierra Leonean armed forces. Yet, the West Side Boys began looting the city.

There was a conspiracy that Kabbah had used Koroma to control the West Side Boys to protect strategic areas close to Freetown to defeat the Revolutionary United Front. However, it may be argued the other way round. There is anecdotal evidence that Five Five, Gullit, and Bazzy were approached by senior RUF commanders a few weeks earlier to request Koroma to ally with Sankoh in a united coup. Even though Koroma did not mind being rid of Kabbah again, Koroma certainly did not want Sankoh to be Sierra Leone's president.

The Hostage Crisis and Role of the British

During this time, Koroma had recognized that UNAMSIL were also difficult to defeat. In May 2000, the final Nigerian-led ECOMOG forces left the country and thus the Revolutionary United Front retained control of diamond fields located in the east of Sierra Leone by kidnapping and disarming over "500 Kenyan and Zambian" UN "peacekeepers" in Makeni town.[92] In addition, 23 Indian troops were taken as hostages by the rebels.[93] The United Nations had to negotiate with Charles Taylor for their release. During the hostage crisis, the contingents within UNAMSIL and its leadership became disjointed, but were swayed to act more coercively. However, the interests of foreign armed intervening states conflicted between the United Nations, United Kingdom, America, and France. The United States was largely involved in Liberia to provide secure conditions for an election in 1997. US investment in Liberia was unprecedented aside from during the Cold War when Washington supported Sergeant Samuel Doe to rival the Soviet Union as a means of accessing the Roberts International Airfield and a large "electronic communications facility"

[91] Utas and Jörgel, "The West Side Boys," p. 503.

[92] Hirsch, "War in Sierra Leone," p. 158; Reno, "The Failure of Peacekeeping in Sierra Leone," pp. 219, 222–223.

[93] Alan Bullion, "India in Sierra Leone: A Case of Muscular Peacekeeping?" *International Peacekeeping*, Vol. 8, No. 4 (2001), pp. 81–82.

located near Monrovia.[94] The United States also supported ECOMOG in Liberia, and America perceived Sierra Leone as Britain's obligation. Although France distanced itself from Sierra Leone, Paris was largely involved in Liberia. France engaged with its economic interests of timber and pursued them by vetoing UN Security Council-drafted sanctions against Liberia rebel factions. Timber exports were then excluded from UN-based sanctions on Liberia.

Kofi Atta Annan, the UN Secretary-General at the time, pleaded with the British, as an ex-colonial power, to thwart RUF rebels from taking Freetown. Tony Blair, Britain's Prime Minister at the time, decided that British nationals residing in Sierra Leone were seriously endangered and required assistance. Britain held strong political will to support the democracy of Sierra Leone, including paying for the majority of the costs of the 1996 election, which was marred by widespread RUF atrocities. As part of Operation Palliser, the United Kingdom dispatched 700 military "forces in Freetown" in response to the Revolutionary United Front kidnapping of more than 350 UNAMSIL peacekeepers, including one British army officer.[95] At this point in time, the Revolutionary United Front held an estimated 4000 well-armed combatants against 2000–3000 "poorly trained" Sierra Leonean soldiers, had taken control of over 40 percent of Sierra Leone, and was taking parts of the capital.[96] On May 7, 2000, the United Kingdom Ministry of Defense deployed under 1000 forces of the Parachute Regiment of the 1st Battalion (1 PARA) via three aircraft from Brize Norton, Oxfordshire, to Senegal, and a day later took control of Lungi (Freetown) International Airport to help evacuate British, European Union, and Commonwealth citizens.[97] The British Commander, Brigadier-General David Julian Richards, adopted the strategy of encouraging Koroma's now pro-government WSB forces to drive RUF rebels out of Freetown.[98]

[94] Hirsch, "War in Sierra Leone," p. 154.

[95] Karon, "Sankoh a Hot Potato in Government Hands"; Hirsch, "War in Sierra Leone," p. 153.

[96] Peter Alexander Albrecht, "Foundational Hybridity and Its Reproduction: Security Sector Reform in Sierra Leone," PhD thesis (Copenhagen: Copenhagen Business School, Department of Business and Politics, 2012), p. 133.

[97] David Carter, "Sierra Leone 2000 – Death and Diamonds: Operation Palliser," *Britain's Small Wars*, 2000.

[98] David H. Ucko, "Can Limited Intervention Work? Lessons from Britain's Success Story in Sierra Leone," *Journal of Strategic Studies*, Vol. 39, Nos. 5–6 (2016), p. 854.

Now that the Revolutionary United Front was virtually defeated, in late May 2000, the West Side Boys had lost its political use. Consequently, Koroma did not want to deal with WSB soldiers as his burden because he had changed his alliance in an attempt to join the Sierra Leonean government. More WSB joined the government's call to be vetted for a new national armed force. However, some WSB still remained in the Occra Hills region.

Several further instances of hostage-taking occurred. In July 2000, Operation Kukhri, consisting of Indian, British, Ghanaian, and Nigerian soldiers, deployed over 2000 troops to free 222 Indian peacekeepers and 11 military observers" that were being held by RUF rebels in the Kailahun District, eastern Sierra Leone.[99]

UNAMSIL believed that WSB would align with the Revolutionary United Front to combat the United Nations peacekeepers. On July 22, 2000, UNAMSIL cracked down on illicit Occra Hills checkpoints. This weakened the West Side Boys. This was evident on August 3, 2000, when Colonel Rambo and his 88 militiamen demobilized at the center in Lungi.[100] More WSB soldiers followed, but leader Foday Kallay executed members that wanted to disarm. On August 25, 2000, 11 troops of the "British Short-Term Training Team were taken hostage" by the West Side Boys at Mageni base and five were rescued on August 30, 2000.[101] However, Kallay held no political or military strategy, so negotiations fell through. On September 10, 2000, the United Kingdom, as the ex-colonial ruler and a permanent member of the United Nations Security Council, stepped in with Operation Barras and raided the West Side Boys' camp to save the remaining six British soldiers (five Royal Irish Regiment troops and one Sierra Leonean Army Liaison Officer) and 20 civilian prisoners held hostage by the West Side Boys.[102] The British killed an estimated 25 members of the militia and one British soldier was killed in the process. Over the next few days, a CDF called the Gbethis defeated the remaining WSB members.

In late October 2000, the United Kingdom decided to extensively increase its military presence, including British headquarters located in

[99] Douglas Farah, "UN Rescues Hostages in Sierra Leone," *The Guardian*, July 20, 2000.

[100] Utas and Jörgel, "The West Side Boys," p. 505.

[101] Bullion, "India in Sierra Leone," p. 79.

[102] Reno, "The Failure of Peacekeeping in Sierra Leone," p. 224; William Fowler, *Operation Barras* (London: Orion Publishing Group, 2022).

Freetown. Britain redeployed 500 Royal Marine Commanders via the Mediterranean, but this was not part of UNAMSIL. To comply with Security Sector Reform (SSR), British soldiers increased to 400 troops and trained 3000 Sierra Leonean armed forces and intended to train another 3000.[103] At this time, Annan wanted to enforce peace with robust measures in the spirit of the Brahimi Report by enacting robust Chap. 7 mandates that would put the failed UN peacekeeping operations in Somalia and Rwanda in the past.[104] In doing so, Annan wanted to stretch the rules of engagement for peacekeepers to fire in self-defense to "counter force with force," meaning that sovereignty could no longer defend the clause of non-intervention.[105]

On March 30, 2001, the United Nations Security Council decided to expand the peacekeeping troop size to 17,500.[106] Yet, the United Nations and Sierra Leonean government lacked a long-term strategy to put an end to the conflict. Apposite security and humanitarian assistance arrived after the coup headed by Johnny Paul Koroma in May 1997, and prior to this, attention was paid to the Liberian civil war. The Sierra Leonean armed forces reported low resources and the conditions facing UNAMSIL relied on poor logistical support against the well-armed RUF rebels.[107] Annan similarly claimed that UNAMSIL was poorly trained and equipped.[108]

Despite the Abidjan and Lomé Peace Agreements, and multiple ceasefires between the Revolutionary United Front and Ahmad Tejan Kabbah, Sierra Leone remained in economic despair alongside a displaced population.[109] The United Nations and ECOWAS attempted to enforce the Lomé Agreement, but these efforts were undermined.[110] At this time, Sankoh was arrested and jailed once more so a new leader was sought.

[103] Bullion, "India in Sierra Leone," pp. 79, 89.

[104] Lakhdar Brahimi, "Report of the Panel on United Nations Peace Operations," *United Nations General Assembly – Security*, A/55/305 – S/2000/809, August 21, 2000, para. 53 (p. 10).

[105] Kofi Atta Annan, "UN's Millennium Summit About Action – Annan," *Reuters*, September 4, 2000.

[106] United Nations Security Council Resolution 1346, "Concerning the Situation in Sierra Leone," S/RES/1346, March 30, 2001, adopted 4306th meeting, para. 2.

[107] Gberie, *A Dirty War in West Africa*.

[108] Michael Ellison and Ewan MacAskill, "Annan Disparages UN Efforts in Sierra Leone," *The Guardian*, May 13, 2000.

[109] Hirsch, "War in Sierra Leone," p. 145.

[110] For a comprehensive overview on these problems, which includes RUF rebels and the West Side Boys detaining and disarming UNAMSIL contingents and conflict of commands

Disarmament, Demobilization, and Reintegration

DDR in Sierra Leone commenced in May 2001 and was installed by the government and aided primarily by the World Bank. The disarmament stage commenced by collecting, registering, disabling, and destroying all arms and ammunition.[111] The DDR initiative was principally funded by the United Nations and the World Bank and reached 45 reception centers to disarm 72,490 combatants and collect more than 30,000 weapons.[112] When disarmament finished in early 2002, it had collected "42,330 weapons and 1.2 million pieces of ammunition."[113] Out of the 72,490 combatants disarmed, an estimated 29,000 were beneficiaries of vocational training, 12,000 received help with formal education, and the total cost amounted to US $36.5 million.[114] The highest number of fighters disarmed and demobilized was 28,051 CDF followed by 19,267 RUF rebels in districts including Bo, Bombali, Western Area, Kailahun, Kenema, Kolnadugu, Kono, Moyamba, Port Loko/Kambia, and Tonkoli.[115] Pools of ex-fighters were mapped by the village or town chief, youth coordinator, or NCDDR or DDR skills training centers with these teams randomly selecting candidates. The DDR program appealed to young fighters by offering a petty cash sum of 300,000 Sierra Leonean leone (an estimated US $130 at the time), a sleeping mat, bucket and soap, and potentially skills-based training to emancipate them from hard farming labor, being a mercenary, or "diamond digging."[116]

Moreover, international donors encouraged the participation of militia leaders and commanders in post-war reconstruction and development in

and suspicion within the United Nations contingent troops, consult Reno, "The Failure of Peacekeeping in Sierra Leone," pp. 219, 223–224.

[111] Victor Odame Asiedu and Maria Berghs, "Limitations of Individualistic Peacebuilding in Postwar Sierra Leone," *African Conflict & Peacebuilding Review*, Vol. 2, No. 1 (Spring 2012), pp. 136–151.

[112] Okolie-Osemene, "Sierra Leone," pp. 35–36.

[113] Hoffman, "West-African Warscrapes," p. 335.

[114] Hoffman, "West-African Warscapes," p. 335.

[115] Thokozani Thusi and Sarah Meek, "Disarmament and Demobilization in Sierra Leone," in *Sierra Leone, Building the Road to Recovery*, edited by Mark Malan, Sarah Meek, Thokozani Thusi, Jeremy Ginifer, and Patrick Coker (Pretoria: Institute for Security Studies, 2003), pp. 23–38.

[116] Hoffman, "West-African Warscapes," p. 332.

exchange for them disarming.[117] This provided former RUF combatants, especially commanders, an incentive to continue preaching their collective agrarian ideology to better manage internationally funded projects than the public. The public claimed that the Revolutionary United Front militias provided them with protection and the forced labor imposed by the rebels was misunderstood.[118] It was the remobilization of former fighters that protracted the civil war. This, in turn, required further foreign armed intervention to establish a secure environment for SSR and statebuilding initiatives and thus work toward a more harmonious state of affairs. These programs needed the involvement of the rural youth, and continually still require this to avoid a resurgence of civil war. Although the DDR process was spotty, it did help to eventually disband the majority of rebel forces, the military junta, WSB, Sobels, and RUF rebels to bring the civil war to an end.

UNAMSIL and other state parties worked to bring the Revolutionary United Front to negotiate with Kabbah and end the civil war on January 18, 2002. In May 2002, the Revolutionary United Front officially disbanded and became a political party.[119] The peace agreements worked for short periods and collaboration from PMCs was active throughout the conflict.

Post-Conflict Sierra Leone

From an Afro-Communitarian perspective, it can be contended that although Sierra Leone is no longer in conflict, the country has not reached an adequate state of affairs or better communal relations because some groups remain alienated from the patrimonial system, which was a main grievance that radicalized the youth population during the civil war. The economy remains tarnished. At the close of the civil war, Sierra Leone plummeted to the last place on the United Nations Development Programme's Human Development Index (HDI) and remained there in 2008.[120]

[117] Krijin Peters, *Footpaths to Reintegration: Armed Conflict, Youth and the Rural Crisis in Sierra Leone*. PhD Thesis (Wageningen: University of Wageningen, 2006), p. 89.

[118] Peters, *Footpaths to Reintegration*, pp. 84–97.

[119] Megan H. MacKenzie, *Female Soldiers in Sierra Leone: Sex, Security, and Post-Conflict Development* (New York: New York University Press, 2012).

[120] United Nations Development Programme, *Human Development Indicators* (New York: United Nations Development Programme, 2009).

The Special Court for Sierra Leone was created to host courts in Freetown, The Hague, and New York on January 16, 2002, to try individuals responsible for serious breaches of international humanitarian law (IHL) perpetrated in the country after November 30, 1996, and throughout the civil war. The leaders of the West Side Boys were indicted by the Special Court for Sierra Leone. Koroma, as the leader the AFRC military junta, was on the initial list of indictments for commanding attacks on civilians, UN peacekeepers, and humanitarian aid staff. The specific attacks listed included looting, sexual violence and slavery, rape, and murder as punishment against people refusing to support AFRC–RUF combatants and forcibly conscripting children as soldiers.[121] The Sierra Leonean government accused Koroma of attempting a coup in early 2003 and, later being detained in police custody, he escaped.[122] Koroma reportedly left Freetown for Liberia. Charles Taylor anecdotally executed Koroma in Lofa, but Koroma's deoxyribonucleic acid did not match the remains. Koroma later died in his village, Binkolo, northern Sierra Leone, in August 2017.[123] Subsequently, the commanders of the West Side Boys were indicted for war crimes. This included Bazzy, Gullit, and Five Five, who were sentenced in July 2007 by the Special Court to serve between 45 and 50 years imprisonment.[124] Bomblast remained at the Pademba Road Prison but was later released in 2005.[125]

The Special Court made its final decision on September 26, 2013, at The Hague for the Appeals Chamber that moved to uphold ex-Liberian President, Charles Taylor, with a sentence of 50 years imprisonment. In April 2012, Taylor was found guilty of five counts each for crimes against humanity and war crimes and an additional count of contravening IHL by supporting RUF rebels.[126]

The civil war in Sierra Leone devastated the economy and impacted firms. War slowed down the recovery of the economy and thus the

[121] Special Court for Sierra Leone, "Memorandum for: Confirming Judge, Special Court for Sierra Leone," *Special Court for Sierra Leone: Office of the Prosecutor*, March 6, 2003.

[122] Keen, *Conflict and Collusion in Sierra Leone*, p. 287.

[123] Sierra Express Media, "Johnny Paul Dead and Laid to Rest," *Sierra Express Media*, August 20, 2017.

[124] Utas and Jörgel, "The West Side Boys," p. 509.

[125] Utas and Jörgel, "The West Side Boys," p. 509.

[126] Lansana Gberie, "The Special Court for Sierra Leone Rests – For Good," *Africa Renewal*, April 2014.

intensity of the civil war negatively impacted the size of operational firms.[127] After the civil war, another diamond rush entered the Kono District with the migration of many former combatants, with the hope of fleeing "agrarian poverty," who failed to join the DDR program.[128] Mining advocacy groups have increased with the Movement of Concerned Kono Youth who were weary of DDR failing to reach the Kono District. The District was enraged by the civil war.

Despite more integration of youth, post-war life still remains extremely impoverished because the increase in donor aid merely satisfies the reciprocal expectations of patron–client relations.[129] From 1980 to 2000, Gross Domestic Product (GDP) per capita decreased by 50 percent from "US $300 to $150" and by 2006, 70 percent of the population still "lived under the national poverty line."[130] Skilled workers remain unavailable, which is a major constraint on business infrastructure.[131] A World Bank Business Report found that employers in Sierra Leone find it extremely difficult to attain construction permits, appoint and fire workers, obtain credit and contracts, and engage in cross-border trading, registering property, and closing a business. Post-war reforms and the inclusion of the youth within civil society have not entirely resulted in better communal relations and a more harmonious state of affairs. Disharmonious traits of the civil war persist, with bad governance, judicial corruption, and land and extractive industries (namely bauxite and iron ore) causing inequality, social exclusion, and conflict.[132]

[127] Collier and Duponchel, "The Economic Legacy of Civil War: Firm-Level Evidence from Sierra Leone," *Journal of Conflict Resolution*, Vol. 57, No. 1 (February 2013), p 65.

[128] Fanthorpe and Maconachie, "Beyond the 'Crisis of Youth'?" p. 264.

[129] Fanthorpe and Maconachie, "Beyond the 'Crisis of Youth'?" p. 262.

[130] Collier and Duponchel, "The Economic Legacy of Civil War," pp. 71–72.

[131] World Bank, "Improving the Opportunities for Sustainable Youth Employment in Sierra Leone," *World Bank Technical Report* (Washington, DC: World Bank, 2007).

[132] Joan Baxter and Elke Schäfter, *Who is Benefitting? The Social and Economic Impacts of Three Large Scale Land Investments in Sierra Leone: A Cost Benefit Analysis* (Freetown: Action for Large-scale Land Acquisition Transparency, 2013); Pauline E. Peters, "Conflicts over Land and the Threats to Customary Tenure in Africa," *African Affairs*, Vol. 112, No. 449 (October 2013), pp. 543–562.

Assessing Afro-communitarian Ethics in Sierra Leone

There have been several phases of interventions in Sierra Leone and two main ceasefires that attempted to support the crumbling Sierra Leonean government and find a political solution to the civil war by engaging with the Revolutionary United Front during negotiations. These efforts were made in good faith to counter violence, but the bolstered security support from PMCs and local tribes intensified violence to result in a more disharmonious state of affairs. This, in turn, protracted the armed conflict.

The rulerships of Stevens and Momoh were based on single-party politics. While both APC leaders cemented patron–client relationships that empowered chieftains in rural areas within diamond areas, grand corruption of embezzling the state treasury and patronage politics stagnated the crippling national economy. The political and economic situation left many Sierra Leoneans out of education, unemployed, and frustrated with diamond wealth being exploited by greedy officials and foreign companies. To confront these forms of structural violence, the Revolutionary United Front emerged with a clear and appealing manifesto and anthems to disburse equitable diamond profits and promote free education. Many young Sierra Leoneans joined the Front because they sympathized with the grievances displayed. To counter the growth of the Revolutionary United Front, APC governance increased the number of Sierra Leonean armed forces.

However, a civil war was in the making because Charles Taylor held resentment for the Freetown government that cooperated with ECOMOC planes at Lungi International Airport to attack his NPFL forces and prevent him from seizing Monrovia. Taylor wanted revenge on Sierra Leone and knew of the economic potential he could accomplish to sustain the Liberian civil war and succeed the Doe administration, and thus needed an insurgency that was willing to attempt an overthrow of the Sierra Leonean government. Taylor developed a patron–client relationship with Sankoh and his RUF forces with the exchange of diamonds from the rebel leaders in exchange for weapons and NPFL support to sustain the Sierra Leonean civil war.

With heavy support from Taylor, the Revolutionary United Front conquered diamond-rich areas in Sierra Leone and traded them with Taylor for arms and support. This placed the RUF rebels in an advantageous position to engage in guerrilla warfare against Sierra Leonean armed forces, and then as the civil war intensified, to engage in terrorism by targeting civilians with murder, arson, an amputation regime to prevent civilians from voting, and the forced conscription of children as RUF soldiers. From *Ubuntu* principles, the Revolutionary United Front started with a young movement that held valid grievances against the Sierra Leonean state, but as they were increasingly armed from Taylor the forms of violence were not permissible because they were initially appealing for the welfare of civilians, but then ruthlessly attacked them with operations Pay Yourself and No Living Thing. Therefore, from an Afro-communitarianism perspective, the forms of violence initiated from the Revolutionary United Front were not justified.

The Sierra Leonean government weakened with the devastation of the civil war. To oppose the threat of the RUF rebels controlling diamond-rich areas, the Sierra Leonean armed forces (that were already frustrated with not being paid for months) split into a junta to overthrow the weak and corrupt government. The military coup orchestrated by NPRC forces constituted an open revolution that was justified because it could attempt to revive the Sierra Leonean economy and better fight the Revolutionary United Front. Strasser did obtain some loans and the economy improved and thus he engaged with the paid services of PMCs, which notably included the expensive Executive Outcomes. The South African mercenaries did manage to press RUF rebels away from Freetown and reclaimed some diamond-rich areas, but Captain Strasser was overthrown by his general, Bio, who then relinquished governance to a civilian government headed by SLPP leader Kabbah.

Kabbah wanted to bring about a peaceful solution to the civil war. Under Afro-communitarianism, a diplomatic political solution was sought by Kabbah engaging in dialogue with Sankoh to seek a ceasefire with the Abidjan Accord. The Accord comprised a trade-off of the Revolutionary United Front engaging with disarmament in exchange for the Executive Outcomes leaving Sierra Leone, but Sankoh refused UN peacekeepers' request to observe the ceasefire. Due to the final term being denied, a harmonious state of affairs could not be reached because fighting resumed two months later so Kabbah turned to Kamajor local Mende hunters and CDF forces to fight advancing RUF rebels. The local hunters were also pitted against alleged Sobels and the hunters engaged in heinous human rights abuses, including beheading civilians and killing girls accused of having relations with soldiers. These local hunters should have been vetted because the atrocities committed did not work toward a more harmonious state of affairs, but rather by attempting to counter violence from RUF rebels by supporting Kabbah, the situation was more discordant.

The protracted violence resulted in another coup with Koroma leading AFRC forces allied as a coalition with the Revolutionary United Front, so Kabbah fled to Guinea. The Kamajors still engaged in fighting for Kabbah and relied on ECOWAS to defeat the coalition. The forms of violence from local forces and also the foreign armed intervention from ECOWAS were now effective to oppose AFRC-RUF forces remaining in Freetown and controlling the majority of alluvial diamond-rich areas. To retain this positive position and end the civil war, efforts were made once Kabbah was restored to power. Kabbah welcomed the prospect of UN peacekeepers. The Lomé Agreement provided a ceasefire that included a more exclusive DDR process for RUF, AFRC, Kamajors, local armed forces, and later the West Side Boys. UNAMSIL, which still worked with ECOMOG, was deployed that. The latter continued to secure Freetown and Lungi, but the United Nations had now taken a lead role. However, UN peacekeepers and ECOMOG forces were increasingly attacked by RUF and AFRC forces and UNAMSIL became disjointed with a variety of its contrasting contingents. The civil war did not thus come to a close through the role of the United Nations and Lomé Agreement. Therefore, the United Nations did not provide foreign armed intervention that countered violence to result in a less discordant, and more harmonious, state of affairs.

It was the British forces that responded with Operations Pallister and Barras that raided WSB compounds to deal with a hostage crisis and engaged in the civil war to prevent UNAMSIL from collapsing with its fight against RUF forces. This helped to end the civil war. The British forces thus intervened robustly to oppose violence and bring about a harmonious state of affairs. In the aftermath of the civil war, post-war justice was implemented with the Special Court for Sierra Leone that tried Sierra Leonean and Liberian leaders, including Charles Taylor, for war crimes. However, retributive justice is at odds with *Ubuntu* because forgiveness is largely promoted with truth-telling and reconciliation so community relations can be restored.

Conclusion

Due to Stevens mismanaging state funds, the rural movement of the Revolutionary United Front and urbanized military governments from the National Provisional Ruling Council (1992–1996) and the Armed

Forces Revolutionary Council (1997–1998) had arisen. As a weak state, Sierra Leone was captive to the good credit ratings of the World Bank and the African Development Bank for the attainment of loans (even when the conditions were bad).[133] However, bad governance and resource-related greed do not explain the origin or protracted violence of the Sierra Leonean civil war.[134] Alongside greed, grievance and injustice that resulted in marginalization and social and racial exclusion are other factors that led to the civil war.[135] It has been argued by Paul Collier and his colleagues that diamonds financed the rebellion in Sierra Leone.[136] In contrast, Richards contends that Sierra Leone's failure of state institutions, and not greed, principally initiated and fueled the conflict.[137] However, grievances with the state and greed for alluvial diamonds are simplistic explanations of the civil war. Despite this contestation regarding the main drivers of the conflict, Sierra Leone has a historical legacy of corruption, bad leadership, and poor accountability. It was the Revolutionary United Front that initially formed a manifesto to disperse mineral wealth, promote free education, and eradicate political corruption, thus intending to promote better communal relations with violence.

Conversely, the motives of RUF rebels, under the leadership of Sankoh followed by Sam Bockarie during Sankoh's house arrest and imprisonment (1997–1999), altered to forcibly seize ammunition, appoint child soldiers and civilians, engage in mass rapes, genital mutilation, and the taking of peacekeepers as hostages, loot villages, and amputate many civilians. RUF rebels had seized diamond areas, which protracted the civil war against the Sierra Leonean armed forces and allied ECOMOG and UN peacekeepers to form a more discordant state of affairs.

Subsequently, the strategy shifted in an attempt to induce the insurgency into an expanded power-sharing government. Despite elections in February 1999 for Sierra Leone in Nigeria, the Revolutionary United Front continued to fight ECOMOG peacekeepers. This was why Nigeria, the United States, and the United Kingdom called for updated negotiations with the Revolutionary United Front, resulting in the Accords at

[133] Reno, "African Weak States and Commercial Alliances," p. 171.

[134] Voors et al., "Resources and Governance in Sierra Leone's Civil War," pp. 278–294.

[135] Voors et al., "Resources and Governance in Sierra Leone's Civil War," p. 278.

[136] Paul Collier, Anke Hoeffler, and Dominic Rohner, "Beyond Greed and Grievance: Feasibility and Civil War," *Oxford Economic Papers*, Vol. 61, No. 1 (January 2009), p. 13.

[137] Paul Richards, "To Fight or to Farm? Agrarian Dimensions of the Mano River Conflicts (Liberia and Sierra Leone)," *African Affairs*, Vol. 104, No. 417 (October 2005), p. 588.

Lomé in July 1997, as part of the liberal peace model focusing on political liberalization at this point.[138] The Lomé Peace Agreement was signed to pacify and be sympathetic toward the Revolutionary United Front. Finally, the international approach placed RUF militants before the Special Court for Sierra Leone for war crimes trials. It can be argued that the altering international strategies to combat the Revolutionary United Front that was forming a discordant state of affairs were challenging and uncertain.

The West Side Boys splintered from AFRC forces and exerted extreme forms of violence as a military weapon with its feared menacing group to scare, and deter, the enemy from fighting. The West Side Boys desired social roles to survive within a field of war to kill and protect. They perceived themselves as a revolution for the youth to challenge the patronage elite and escape inequality, and often traded goods looted in the Occra Hills for diamonds. Ironically the West Side Boys fought the Sierra Leonean government for three years, but were rearmed by the government to prevent the Revolutionary United Front from taking Freetown. NPRC, RUF, WSB, and Mende- and Temne-speaking combatants were inspired by reggae, rap, and Bubu music to expose political and social grievances relevant to their condition and discovered methods "to justify their conduct in war."[139] However, the rebels did not distinguish between the ideology of reggae songs and the practice of the violent civil war.

Due to a poor grassroots following, RUF rebels did not really mobilize a civilian following to support a coup of a corrupt government, but engaged with violence through guns purchased with diamonds regularly traded with Taylor to neighboring Liberia to fund his NPFL and cement power.[140] In May 2001, the Sierra Leonean civil war broadened to spill over to bordering Liberia and Guinea.[141] The interests of these bordering states to war were based on competition for resources and posts, which included leaders Taylor in Liberia and Lansana Conte in Guinea. The Revolutionary United Front did the same as the previous Sierra Leonean

[138] For any foreign armed intervention which involves the use of external force, international actors "influence" political guarantees to both politically and practically support a government, so the state complies and agrees with the terms of "external parties" (Aaron Griffiths and Catherine Barnes, "Incentives and Sanctions in Peace Processes," *Accord: An International Review of Peace Initiatives*, Issue 19 (February 2008), p. 12).

[139] Nuxoll, "We Listened to it Because of the Message," p. 13.

[140] Reno, "The Failure of Peacekeeping in Sierra Leone," p. 222.

[141] Comfort Ero, "The Mano River Conflict and the World," *West Africa* (April 30–May 6, 2001).

governments by controlling diamond-mining areas for their own gain rather than dispersing the wealth among poor rural civilians as initially envisioned in their anthem.[142]

ECOMOG was initially deployed to deal with the civil war in Liberia but later helped the Sierra Leonean army repress the Revolutionary United Front and the Kamajor traditional Mende hunters, Executive Outcomes, and UN peacekeepers all engaged as principally foreign actors in the armed intervention.[143] Sierra Leone relied on warlord-based political units in the city of Freetown and hired foreign PMCs and firms rather than rely on state apparatuses.[144] Although foreign armed intervention from ECOMOG, Executive Outcomes (in the earlier phase), UNAMSIL, and British soldiers demonstrated adequate political will to fight the Revolutionary United Front and attempt to uphold the conditions of the Abidjan and Lomé Peace Accords, the civil war was not immediately brought to an end. This was due to the underestimation of the Revolutionary United Front as a rag-tag rebel group that could be curtailed with some foreign armed intervention. As part of foreign armed intervention and the liberal peace model, there were three negotiated peace accords that proposed power-sharing, amnesty, and DDR in Abidjan (November 30, 1996), Conakry (October 23, 1997), and Lomé (July 7, 1999).

The conditions of the Lomé Peace Accord were well negotiated by Sankoh to expel Executive Outcomes and ultimately weakened the press against RUF rebels and placed Sankoh as Vice President. The Indian and Nigerian peacekeeping forces held a disjointed relationship that was met with the withdrawal of Indian and Jordanian peacekeepers. Hence, the foreign armed intervention met the Revolutionary United Front and West Side Boys with enmity and violence, but the gains made were stalled by removing key PMCs from Sierra Leone and a poor command structure within UNAMSIL. It was the British responding to the hostage crisis that ended the rebellion and both SSR and an electoral process have been undertaken to restore communal relations in post-conflict Sierra Leone. The violence in Sierra Leone was highly intense and included foreign armed intervention, namely ECOWAS and UN troops as multilateral

[142] Reno, "The Failure of Peacekeeping in Sierra Leone," p. 222; Montague, "The Business of War and the Prospects for Peace in Sierra Leone."

[143] Mullins, "Variations in War Crimes During the Sierra Leone Civil War," p. 4.

[144] Reno, "War, Markets, and the Reconfiguration of West Africa's Weak States," p. 493.

forces with the use of peace agreements and DDR.[145] Therefore, foreign armed intervention attempted to bring about a more harmonious state of affairs in Sierra Leone. The aftermath of the civil war was supported by the United Nations with the Special Court for Sierra Leone that tried WSB commanders and ex-Liberian President Charles Taylor. However, a growing youth population continues, patron–client relations remain, and poverty looms that is traceable to the conditions of Sierra Leone from the earlier rulership of the All People's Congress with Stevens and Momoh in power.

References

Abidjan Peace Accord. "Peace Agreement between the Government of the Republic of Sierra Leone and the Revolutionary United Front of Sierra Leone." Abidjan, November 30, 1996. https://peacemaker.un.org/sites/peacemaker.un.org/files/SL_961130_PeaceAgreementSierraLeone-RUFSL.pdf.

Albrecht, Peter Alexander. "Foundational Hybridity and Its Reproduction: Security Sector Reform in Sierra Leone." PhD thesis. Copenhagen: Copenhagen Business School, Department of Business and Politics, 2012.

Annan, Kofi Atta. "UN's Millennium Summit About Action – Annan." *Reuters*, September 4, 2000.

Asiedu, Victor Odame, and Maria Berghs. "Limitations of Individualistic Peacebuilding in Postwar Sierra Leone." *African Conflict & Peacebuilding Review*, Vol. 2, No. 1 (Spring 2012), pp. 136–151. https://doi.org/10.2979/africonfpeacrevi.2.1.136.

Baxter, Joan, and Elke Schäfter. *Who is Benefitting? The Social and Economic Impacts of Three Large Scale Land Investments in Sierra Leone: A Cost Benefit Analysis.* Freetown: Action for Large-scale Land Acquisition Transparency, 2013.

BBC News. "World: Africa: Sierra Leone Who are the Kidnappers?" BBC News, August 6, 1999. http://news.bbc.co.uk/1/hi/world/africa/413521.stm.

Brahimi, Lakhdar. "Report of the Panel on United Nations Peace Operations." *United Nations General Assembly – Security*, A/55/305 – S/2000/809, August 21, 2000. https://peacekeeping.un.org/sites/default/files/a_55_305_e_brahimi_report.pdf.

Bullion, Alan. "India in Sierra Leone: A Case of Muscular Peacekeeping?" *International Peacekeeping*, Vol. 8, No. 4 (2001), pp. 77–91. https://doi.org/10.1080/13533310108413921.

[145] Okolie-Osemene, "Sierra Leone," pp. 25–26.

Carter, David. "Sierra Leone 2000 – Death and Diamonds: Operation Palliser." *Britain's Small Wars*, 2000. https://britains-smallwars.com/campaigns/sierra-leone/page.php?art_url=operation-palliser.

Collier, Paul, and Marguerite Duponchel. "The Economic Legacy of Civil War: Firm-Level Evidence from Sierra Leone." *Journal of Conflict Resolution*, Vol. 57, No. 1 (February 2013), pp. 65–88. https://doi.org/10.1177/0022002712464847.

Collier, Paul, Anke Hoeffler, and Dominic Rohner. "Beyond Greed and Grievance: Feasibility and Civil War." *Oxford Economic Papers*, Vol. 61, No. 1 (January 2009), pp. 1–27. https://doi.org/10.1093/oep/gpn029.

Dowd, Caitriona, and Clionadh Raleigh. "Mapping Conflict across Liberia and Sierra Leone." *Accord: An International Review of Peace Initiatives*, Issue 23 (March 2012), pp. 13–18. https://rc-services-assets.s3.eu-west-1.amazonaws.com/s3fs-public/Consolidating_peace_Liberia_and_Sierra_Leone_Accord_Issue_23.pdf.

Dupuy, Kendra, and Helga Malmin Binningsbø. *Buying Peace with Diamonds? Power-sharing Agreements in Sierra Leone.* PRIC Policy Brief 7. Oslo: International Peace Research Institute, 2008.

Ellison, Michael, and Ewan MacAskill. "Annan Disparages UN Efforts in Sierra Leone." *The Guardian*, May 13, 2000. https://www.theguardian.com/world/2000/may/13/sierraleone.unitednations1.

Ero, Comfort. "The Mano River Conflict and the World." *West Africa* (April 30–May 6, 2001).

Fanthorpe, Richard, and Roy Maconachie. "Beyond the 'Crisis of Youth'? Mining, Farming, and Civil Society in Post-War Sierra Leone." *African Affairs*, Vol. 109, No. 435 (April 2010), pp. 251–272. https://doi.org/10.1093/afraf/adq004.

Farah, Douglas. "UN Rescues Hostages in Sierra Leone." *The Guardian*, July 20, 2000. https://www.theguardian.com/world/2000/jul/20/sierraleone.unitednations#:~:text=Backed%20by%20helicopter%20gunships%2C%20hundreds,UN%20officials%20and%20diplomats%20said.

Faulkner, Christopher M., Joshua E. Lambert, and Jonathan M. Powell. "Reassessing Private Military and Security Company (PMSC) 'Competition' in Civil War: Lessons from Sierra Leone." *Small Wars & Insurgencies*, Vol. 30, No. 3 (June 2019), pp. 641–659. https://doi.org/10.1080/09592318.2019.1601869.

Fowler, William. *Operation Barras.* London: Orion Publishing Group, 2022.

Gberie, Lansana. *A Dirty War in West Africa: The Revolutionary United Front and the Destruction of Sierra Leone.* London: Hurst, 2005.

Gberie, Lansana. "The Special Court for Sierra Leone Rests – For Good." *Africa Renewal*, April 2014. https://www.un.org/africarenewal/magazine/april-2014/special-court-sierra-leone-rests-%E2%80%93-good.

Griffiths, Aaron, and Catherine Barnes. "Incentives and Sanctions in Peace Processes." *Accord: An International Review of Peace Initiatives*, Issue 19 (February 2008), pp. 9–13. https://rc-services-assets.s3.eu-west-1.amazonaws.com/s3fs-public/Accord%2019_2Incentives%20and%20sanctions%20in%20peace%20processes_2008_ENG.pdf.

Hirsch, John Lewis. "War in Sierra Leone." *Survival*, Vol. 43, No. 3 (2001), pp. 145–162. https://doi.org/10.1080/00396330412375169943.

Hoffman, Danny. "West-African Warscapes – Violent Events as Narrative Blocs: The Disarmament at Bo, Sierra Leone," *Anthropological Quarterly*, Vol. 78, No. 2 (Spring 2005), pp. 329–353. https://doi.org/10.1353/anq.2005.0025.

Howe, Herbert M. "Private Security Forces and African Stability." *The Journal of Modern African Studies*, Vol. 36, No. 2 (June 1998), pp. 307–331. https://doi.org/10.1017/S0022278X98002778.

Human Rights Watch. "Human Rights Abuses Committed by Members of the AFRC/RUF." *Human Rights Watch*, August 1998. https://www.hrw.org/legacy/reports98/sierra/Sier988-03.htm.

Karon, Tony. "Sankoh a Hot Potato in Government Hands." *CNN*, May 17, 2000. http://edition.cnn.com/2000/WORLD/africa/05/17/leone5_17.a.tm/index.html.

Keen, David. *Conflict and Collusion in Sierra Leone*. London: Palgrave Macmillan, 2005.

MacKenzie, Megan H. *Female Soldiers in Sierra Leone: Sex, Security, and Post-Conflict Development*. New York: New York University Press, 2012.

Marks, Zoe. "Rebel Resource Strategies in Civil War: Revisiting Diamonds in Sierra Leone." *Political Geography*, Vol. 75 (November 2019), pp. 1–11. https://doi.org/10.1016/j-polgeo.2019.102059.

Mitton, Kieran. "Irrational Actors and the Process of Brutalization: Understanding Atrocity in the Sierra Leonean Conflict (1991–2002)." *Civil Wars*, Vol. 14, No. 1 (March 2012), pp. 104–122. https://doi.org/10.1080/13698249.2012.654691.

Montague, Dena. "The Business of War and the Prospects for Peace in Sierra Leone." *The Brown Journal of World Affairs*, Vol. 9, No. 1 (Spring 2002), pp. 229–237. https://www.jstor.org/stable/24590287.

Mullins, Christopher W. "Variations in War Crimes During the Sierra Leone Civil War." *International Criminal Justice Review*, Vol. 33, No. 2 (2020), pp. 1–21. https://doi.org/10.1177/1057567720981621.

Mullins Christopher, W., and Nishanth Visagaratnam. "Sexual and Sexualized Violence in Armed Conflicts." In *Criminology and War: Transgressing the Borders*, edited by Sandra Walklate and Ross McGarry, pp. 139–157. London: Routledge, 2015.

Nuxoll, Cornelia. "We Listened to it Because of the Message: Juvenile RUF Combatants and the Role of Music in the Sierra Leone Civil War." *Music &*

Politics, Vol. 9, No. 1 (Winter 2015), pp. 1–25. https://doi.org/10.3998/mp.9460447.0009.104.

Okolie-Osemene, James. "Sierra Leone: Mapping the Disarmament, Demobilization – Remobilization and Reintegration of Ex-Combatants. Prospects for Sustainable Peace." *Conflict Studies Quarterly*, 34 (January 2021), pp. 20–44. https://doi.org/10.24193/csq.34.2.

Peters, Krijin. *Footpaths to Reintegration: Armed Conflict, Youth and the Rural Crisis in Sierra Leone*. PhD Thesis. Wageningen: University of Wageningen, 2006.

Peters, Pauline E. "Conflicts over Land and the Threats to Customary Tenure in Africa." *African Affairs*, Vol. 112, No. 449 (October 2013), pp. 543–562. https://doi.org/10.1093/afraf/adt047.

Reno, William, S.K. "African Weak States and Commercial Alliances." *African Affairs*, Vol. 96, No. 383 (April 1997a), pp. 165–186. https://doi.org/10.1093/oxfordjournals.afraf.a007824.

Reno, William, S.K. "War, Markets, and the Reconfiguration of West Africa's Weak States." *Comparative Politics*, Vol. 29, No. 4 (July 1997b), pp. 493–510. https://doi.org/10.2307/422016.

Reno, William S.K. "The Failure of Peacekeeping in Sierra Leone." *Current History*, Vol. 100, Vol. 646 (May 2001), pp. 219–225. https://doi.org/10.1525/curh.2001.100.646.219.

Richards, Paul. *Fighting for the Rainforest: War, Youth and Resources in Sierra Leone*. Oxford: International African Institute/James Currey, 1996.

Richards, Paul. *No Peace, No War: An Anthropology of Contemporary Armed Conflicts*. Oxford: James Currey, 2005a.

Richards, Paul. "To Fight or to Farm? Agrarian Dimensions of the Mano River Conflicts (Liberia and Sierra Leone)." *African Affairs*, Vol. 104, No. 417 (October 2005b), pp. 571–590. https://doi.org/10.1093/afraf/adi068.

Sawyer, Edward. "Remove or Reform? A Case for (Restructuring) Chiefdom Governance in Post-conflict Sierra Leone." *African Affairs*, Vol. 107, No. 428 (July 2008), pp. 387–403. https://doi.org/10.1093/afraf/adn039.

Schuler, Corrina. "Sierra Leone: A Rebel Leader of Rag-Tag Terrorists." *Christian Science Monitor*, September 17, 1999. https://reliefweb.int/report/sierra-leone/sierra-leone-rebel-leader-rag-tag-terrorists.

Sheridan, Michael. "Sierra Leone Kidnappers Threaten to Kill Britons." *The Independent*, January 21, 1995. https://www.independent.co.uk/news/sierra-leone-kidnappers-threaten-to-kill-britons-1568935.html.

Sierra Express Media. "Johnny Paul Dead and Laid to Rest." *Sierra Express Media*, August 20, 2017. https://sierraexpressmedia.com/?p=82074.

Sierra Leone Truth and Reconciliation Commission. *Witness to the Truth: Report of the Sierra Leone Truth and Reconciliation Commission*. 2004. http://www.sierraleonetrc.org/.

Special Court for Sierra Leone. "Memorandum for: Confirming Judge, Special Court for Sierra Leone." *Special Court for Sierra Leone: Office of the Prosecutor*, March 6, 2003. https://www.rscsl.org/Documents/Decisions/Other/Koroma/SCSL-03-03-I-001.pdf.

The Lomé Agreement. "Peace Agreement between the Government of Sierra Leone and the Revolutionary United Front of Sierra Leone." July 7, 1999. https://peaceaccords.nd.edu/wp-content/accords/The_Lome_Peace_Agreement-_1999_0.pdf.

Thusi, Thokozani, and Sarah Meek. "Disarmament and Demobilization in Sierra Leone." In *Sierra Leone, Building the Road to Recovery*, edited by Mark Malan, Sarah Meek, Thokozani Thusi, Jeremy Ginifer and Patrick Coker, pp. 23–38. Pretoria: Institute for Security Studies, 2003.

Ucko, David H. "Can Limited Intervention Work? Lessons from Britain's Success Story in Sierra Leone." *Journal of Strategic Studies*, Vol. 39, Nos. 5–6 (2016), pp. 847–855. https://doi.org/10.1080/01402390.2015.1110695.

United Nations Development Programme. *Human Development Indicators*. New York: United Nations Development Programme, 2009.

United Nations Peacekeeping. "Sierra Leone – UNOMSIL Background." *United Nations*, 2000. https://peacekeeping.un.org/sites/default/files/past/unomsil/UnomsilB.htm.

United Nations Security Council. "Security Council Extends Sierra Leone Mission Until 13 June, Commends West African Peacekeeping Force." *UN Security Council Press Release SC/6653*, March 11, 1999. https://press.un.org/en/1999/19990311.sc6653.html.

United Nations Security Council Resolution 1181. "Establishing the United Nations Observer Mission in Sierra Leone (UNOMSIL): The Situation in Sierra Leone." UN Doc. S/RES/1181, July 13, 1998, adopted 3,902nd meeting.

United Nations Security Council Resolution 1260. "On the Provisional Expansion and Strengthening of the Political, Civil Affairs, Information, Human Rights and Child Protection Elements of the UN Observer Mission in Sierra Leone (UNOMSIL)." UN Doc. S/RES/1260, August 20, 1999, adopted 4,035th meeting.

United Nations Security Council Resolution 1270. "Establishing the United Nations Mission in Sierra Leone (UNAMSIL)." UN Doc. S/RES/1270, October 22, 1999, adopted 4,054th meeting.

United Nations Security Council Resolution 1346. "Concerning the Situation in Sierra Leone." UN Doc. S/RES/1346, March 30, 2001, adopted 4,306th meeting.

Utas, Mats, and Magnus Jörgel. "The West Side Boys: Military Navigation in the Sierra Leone Civil War." *The Journal of Modern African Studies*, Vol. 46, No. 3 (September 2008), pp. 487–511. https://doi.org/10.1017/S0022278X08003388.

Voors, Maarten, Peter Van Der Windt, Kostadis J. Papiaoannou and Erwin Bulte. "Resources and Governance in Sierra Leone's Civil War." *The Journal of Development Studies*, Vol. 53, No. 2 (May 2017), pp. 278–294. https://doi.org/10.1080/00220388.2016.1160068.

World Bank. "Improving the Opportunities for Sustainable Youth Employment in Sierra Leone." *World Bank Technical Report*. Washington, DC: World Bank, 2007.

Zack-Williams, Alfred B. "Sierra Leone: Crisis and Despair." *Review of African Political Economy*, Vol. 49 (Winter 1990), pp. 22–33. https://www.jstor.org/stable/4005975.

Zack-Williams, Alfred B. "Sierra Leone: The Deepening Crisis and Survival Strategies." In *Beyond Structural Adjustment in Africa: The Political Economy of Sustainable and Democratic Development*, edited by Julius E. Nyang'oro and Timothy M. Shaw, pp. 149–168. New York: Praeger, 1992.

Zack-Williams, Alfred B. "Sierra Leone: The Political Economy of Civil War, 1991–98." *Third World Quarterly*, Vol. 20, No. 1 (February 1999), pp. 143–162. https://doi.org/10.1080/01436599913965.

CHAPTER 5

NATO's Intervention in Kosovo

Introduction

This chapter begins with a brief context to the dissolution of the Socialist Federal Republic of Yugoslavia (SFRY) in the early 1990s that was followed by secessionist nationalist politics. The main focus engages with the context of Kosovo, which was an autonomous province yet rested under the state sovereignty of Serbia. Once Slobodan Milošević entered office, he wanted to retain his weakening position by appealing to the older loyal nationalists and thus to the significance of Kosovo belonging to the Serbian mainland. This in turn tainted diplomatic and observer efforts of the Organization for Security and Co-operation in Europe (OSCE) and subsequent Rambouillet negotiations. Serbian police continued to enter the province of Kosovo and a well-structured Kosovo League and Liberation Army fought for their sovereign independence and thus engaged in force against Serbian forces. The North Atlantic Treaty Organization (NATO) became weary of the situation and decided to engage in a short bombing campaign to get Milošević to sign the Rambouillet Accord so that Kosovo could determine its own sovereignty in the future, but NATO also swiftly argued that the Serbian regime was engaged in ethnic cleansing of Kosovar Albanian people. However, NATO did not expect Milošević to see out the bombing and therefore the Alliance

D. Singh, *Applied Afro-Communitarian Ethics and Foreign Armed Intervention*, https://doi.org/10.1007/978-3-031-64110-7_5

continued the aerial bombardment over mostly Belgrade for a total of 78 days until Milošević surrendered.

The chapter will demonstrate that the initial non-violence of Kosovar Albanian parallel systems was put in place due to discrimination from Serbia, but this effort turned to violence once weapons were accessible from Albanian state collapse. The subsequent violence of the Kosovo Liberation Army (KLA) did not entirely engage in sabotage regarding targeting governmental constellations because Serbian security forces and civilians were targeted and killed. The former would qualify as military necessity, but the latter undermines the rule of proportionality *jus in bello*. From an *Ubuntu* perspective, it could loosely be contended that the stages of violence after peaceful efforts failed were somewhat followed. However, the intervention of NATO—foreign armed intervention—did engage with sabotage to weaken the military and communications of the Serbian forces, but there were times when civilian workers were also killed. The protracted bombing over Serbia did result in the cessation of large-scale violence between Serbs and Kosovar Albanians, but Serbs residing in the newly independent Kosovo face discrimination, and skirmishes between both police forces remain. On the whole, it will be argued that the intervention of NATO did conform to Afro-communitarian ethics and partially followed the stages of permitted violence. The legality of the bombing campaign that did not seek consultation from the United Nations Security Council was illegal under international law, which may alarm a just war traditionalist theorist, but that is not the burden of Afro-communitarian ethics because positive social relations have somewhat been achieved.

Background to Yugoslav Wars

In Bosnia, after its referendum of independence that was supported by Bosnia and Croatia, civil war emerged between three ethnicities: Bosnian Muslims (Bosniaks) and Bosnian Croats who would form a Federation, and the Bosnian Serbs who boycotted proceedings.[1] To deal with political violence and civil war, the United Nations deployed a protection force called the United Nations Protection Force (UNPROFOR) to provide access for humanitarian convoys and safeguard UN protection/safe areas

[1] Edgar O'Ballance, *Civil War in Bosnia, 1992–94* (Basingstoke, Hampshire: Macmillan Press, 1995).

(safe havens).[2] Bosniaks were besieged by Bosnian Serb (Republika Sprska) armed forces led by General Ratko Mladić and radicalized by Bosnian Serb leader Radovan Karadžić to engage in the ethnic cleansing of Bosniaks seeking refuge and protection in UN safe havens for Muslim refugees, including eastern mountainous towns such as Srebrenica.[3] However, the Dutch battalion of UNPROFOR allegedly assisted people to buses while Serb troops led by Mladić separated the Bosniak men and boys from their female familial counterparts in July 1995.[4] In the Srebrenica massacre, over 8000 Bosniak men and boys were killed by the Bosnian Serb armed forces, which seriously tainted the reputation of the international community's ability to save lives with UN Security Council authorized military intervention.[5] The Dayton Agreement eventually brought an end to the civil war in Bosnia-Herzegovina and negotiated the areas of land and a tripartite consociational political agreement between the Bosniaks, Bosnian Croats, and Bosnian Serbs.[6] However, Kosovo was not invited to participate in the Agreement. The international community was keen to avoid another genocide in the Balkans under the notion 'Never Again.'

A similar scenario, however, emerged in the Kosovo province of Serbia. After Serbian policies of the education curriculum being taught exclusively in the Serbian language and excluding Albanian and the lack of access to health care for the Kosovar Albanian population in Kosovo, a shadow-based political approach for the Kosovar Albanian population was established. The Democratic League of Kosovo was set up to focus on the establishment of health care, education, and basic parallel governmental and social services. Elections were secretly held. However, the Kosovo Liberation Army armed and killed some leaders of the Democratic League of Kosovo and militarily fought with extreme violence against the Serbian

[2] Christopher Mitchell, "Comparing Sanctuary in the Former Yugoslavia and the Philippines," in *Zones of Peace*, edited by Landon E. Hancock and Christopher R. Mitchell (Bloomfield, CT: Kumarian Press, 2007), pp. 125–126, pp. 137–166.

[3] York W. Bradshaw, Joseph F. Healey, and Rebecca Smith, *Sociology for a New Century* (Thousand Oaks, CA: Pine Forge Press, 2001) p. 408.

[4] Paul R. Bartrop, *Genocide: The Basics* (London: Routledge, 2015, pp. 86–87.

[5] Amnesty International, "Bosnia and Herzegovina: 25th Anniversary of Srebrenica Massacre is a Sombre Warning from History," *Amnesty International*, July 9, 2020.

[6] Marc Weller and Stefan Wolff, "Bosnia and Herzegovina Ten Years after Dayton: Lessons for Internationalized State Building," in *International State-Building after Violent Conflict: Bosnia Ten Years after Dayton*, edited by Marc Weller and Stefan Wolff (London: Routledge, 2008), p. 4, pp. 1–13.

armed forces.[7] KLA belligerents also engaged in terrorism and violence against the Yugoslav forces and ethnically Serb civilians.[8] Diplomacy was attempted by the international community, principally the United States and their democratic allies.

Kosovo Terrorism to Counter Violence?

During the 1990s, the Kosovo Liberation Army was deemed a terrorist group, but it was later transformed into a uniformed civilian force.[9] In 1993, the Kosovo Liberation Army was created and fought for the independence of Kosovo by force.[10] Initially, Ibrahim Rugova wanted Kosovar Albanians to form a shadow region and deny Serbian rule and legitimacy via boycotting elections. In May 1992, Rugova won a secret referendum representing the Democratic League of Kosovo. This was needed due to Milošević's policy in 1989 dissolving Kosovo's provincial assembly. The 'Program of Measures' led to discrimination against work or teaching in Albanian so Kosovar Albanians created a parallel education and civil society system.[11] The non-violent way of dealing with Serbian discrimination changed to violence due to the sudden availability of weapons when Albania's economy and control over its government and military collapsed in the early 1990s.

KLA belligerents found it hard to attain Albanian civic support due to their communist background and were perceived by the international community as terrorists. The Kosovo Liberation Army was principally funded by the Albanian diaspora communities located in America and Europe. Alongside this aid, the Liberation Army engaged in illicit narcotics, extortion, and prostitution in European networks for further funds. With such international and illegal financial backing, the Kosovo Liberation Army initially perpetrated violence against lead Albanian figures, including Rugova. Albania formed a resistance to the Kosovo Liberation Army in

[7] Alpaslan Özerdem, "From a 'Terrorist' Group to a 'Civil Defense' Corps: The 'Transformation' of the Kosovo Liberation Army," *International Peacekeeping*, Vol. 10, No. 3 (2003), p. 80.

[8] Jonathan I. Charney, "Anticipatory Humanitarian Intervention in Kosovo," *American Journal of International Law*, Vol. 93, No. 4 (October 1999), p. 834.

[9] The Kosovo Protection Corps (KPC) was mandated by the United Nations Mission in Kosovo (UNMIK) within the sovereign territory of Serbia.

[10] Özerdem, "From a 'Terrorist' Group to a 'Civil Defense' Corps," p. 79.

[11] Özerdem, "From a 'Terrorist' Group to a 'Civil Defense' Corps," p. 98.

late 1997 with guerilla warfare. In early 1998, Adem Jashari, KLA's leader, was killed alongside 58 civilians by Albanian resistance.[12] The Kosovar Albanians, however, accepted the Kosovo Liberation Army. KLA combatants continued with its Kosovo independence quest by conducting military attacks and seized an estimated 40 percent of rural-based Kosovo. In retaliation, from February 1998 to March 1999, the Yugoslav military and police forces responded to KLA forces and the fighting killed an estimated 2000 people, over 400,000 Kosovar Albanians civilians were forcibly displaced, and mass arrests and arbitrary detentions were high.[13] Therefore, Serbian counterterrorism strategy against KLA belligerents pushed thousands of Kosovar "Albanians into the hills" to the dismay of NATO and the international community to restore "peace in the province."[14]

Diplomatic Efforts for the Kosovo Dilemma

If a state commits atrocities against its own citizens, then the international community can act *erga omnes* encouraging all states to respond to the abuses of human rights and international humanitarian law, by individual or collective means, with the non-use of force.[15] For instance, the United Nations Security Council engaged with Kosovo prior to NATO's bombing. Three resolutions of Chap. 7 of the Charter of the United Nations were adopted to permit OSCE for observation purposes.[16] Us envoy Richard Holbrooke reached this agreement with Yugoslav President Milošević (Holbrooke–Milošević Agreement). In October 1998, the Organization for Security and Co-operation in Europe deployed a Verification Mission, with UN Security Council consent, comprising unarmed foreign observers to monitor the conflict between Serbian forces and Kosovar belligerents, and to monitor the agreement of deserting

[12] Özerdem, "From a 'Terrorist' Group to a 'Civil Defense' Corps," p. 80.

[13] Özerdem, "From a 'Terrorist' Group to a 'Civil Defense' Corps," p. 80. This is one reason why NATO stepped in with its robust intervention.

[14] Stephen T. Hosmer, *The Conflict Over Kosovo: Why Milošević Decided to Settle When He Did* (Santa Monica, CA: RAND Corporation, 2001), p. 7.

[15] Charney, "Anticipatory Humanitarian Intervention in Kosovo," p. 835.

[16] United Nations, *Charter of the United Nations*, October 24, 1945, 1 United Nations Treaty Series XVI. The United Nations Security Council resolutions called for mainly the former Yugoslavia and KLA to cease fighting to prevent further human rights abuses—without the use of force from another external organization.

Yugoslav forces and supervise elections in Kosovo.[17] The deal was accepted by Milošević because NATO threatened to bomb Serbia so the Yugoslav President hesitantly reduced and redeployed the Serb security forces present in Kosovo and permitted 2000 OSCE to monitor whether hostilities had ceased.[18]

KLA belligerents reasserted their control of the vacated and redeployed Yugoslav armed forces.[19] At this time, most of the internally displaced persons (IDPs) were repatriated from the Holbrooke–Milošević Agreement.[20] Although the verification mission averted prevalent atrocities, NATO forced OSCE observers to withdraw, which encouraged the offensive of the Serbian security forces. On January 15, 1999, in Racak, the offense of the Yugoslav forces resulted in the deaths of 45 Kosovar Albanians, two months prior to NATO's bombing campaign.[21] This attack countered the role of OSCE's verification mission to keep the peace and ensure Serb troop withdrawal in the province. As a result, the Contact Group (comprising representatives from America, Britain, Russia, France, Germany, Italy, "the European Union Presidency, and the European Commission") wanted to seek peace and order in the region.[22] The Contact Group presented a summons for the representatives of both warring parties to negotiate at Rambouillet, located on the outskirts of Paris, chaired by British and French politicians.

In February 1999, the United States and the international community attempted a peace settlement at Rambouillet. The Rambouillet peace arrangements were installed to provide a transitional peace settlement calling for "substantial self-government for Kosovo" while respecting the sovereign territorial integrity of the former Yugoslavia and considering the presence of an international force for the implementation of the Agreement.[23] Hashim Thaçi was one of KLA's founding members and

[17] Organization for Security and Co-operation in Europe, "OSCE Verification Mission/ OSCE Task Force for Kosovo," *OSCE*, 1999.

[18] Hosmer, *The Conflict Over Kosovo*, p. 7.

[19] Independent International Commission on Kosovo. *Kosovo Report: Conflict – International Response – Lessons Learned*. Oxford: Oxford University Press, 2000, p. 2.

[20] Independent International Commission on Kosovo. *Kosovo Report*, p. 26.

[21] Charney, "Anticipatory Humanitarian Intervention in Kosovo," p. 840. Kosovo-Albanians were also reportedly displaced, but all other atrocities were committed during NATO's initiation of bombing and did not include a mass of people.

[22] Hosmer, *The Conflict Over Kosovo*, p. 7.

[23] Marc Weller, "The Rambouillet Conference on Kosovo," *International Affairs*, Vol. 75, No. 2 (April 1999), p. 233.

later became President of Kosovo. Thaçi accomplished the legitimacy for KLA representation to permit a discussion of its potential transformation to a civil force.[24] NATO threatened that if the Agreement was not met, they would use all means necessary to deter a humanitarian disaster. However, President Slobodan Milošević refused to sign the Agreement.[25] Moreover, the Dayton Agreement did not engage with the Kosovo dilemma in a non-violent and diplomatic manner, which is why Kosovar Albanians sought arms and violence as the only means to appeal for global attention.[26]

Milošević believed that if he had accepted the terms of the Rambouillet Agreement, it would have endangered his leadership (that would have provided self-government for Kosovo).[27] Milošević still wanted to preserve Serbian domination and authority in the Kosovo province (as the heart of the former Yugoslavia) due to it representing Serbian identity and its historic culture, which included Serbian Church Orthodox shrines.[28] Serbs wanted to retain control of this historic province by defeating KLA *alleged* terrorists that threatened to take over the province. When Milošević came to power, he made it clear that Kosovar Serbs would be protected from Kosovar Albanian police officers. Based on this pledge, in 1989, Milošević eradicated Kosovar Albanian autonomy in Kosovo under the previous 1974 Constitution.[29]

Moreover, Milošević engaged in fraud by filling ballot boxes in the 1997 parliamentary elections and wanted to dwell on the Kosovo situation to increase Serbs' nationalist sentiments as a distraction from other issues.[30] Using this political strategy, Milošević campaigned on the Kosovo problem to "play the nationalist card" throughout 1998.[31] Serbs either loved

[24] Neil Cooper, "Security Sector (Lack of) Transformation in Kosovo," in *Arms Control and Contemporary Conflicts: Challenges and Responses*, PSIS Special Studies No. 5 (Geneva: Geneva Center for Security Policy and Program for Strategic and International Security Studies, 2001), pp. 65–127.

[25] Hosmer, *The Conflict Over Kosovo*, p. 1.

[26] Richard Caplan, "International Diplomacy and the Crisis in Kosovo," *International Affairs*, Vol. 74, No. 4 (October 1998), p. 752. Eventually, these June 3, 1999, Kosovo Peace Accords were abandoned by NATO's 78-day bombing campaign.

[27] Hosmer, *The Conflict Over Kosovo*, p. 7.

[28] Dusko Doder and Louise Branson, *Milošević, Portrait of a Tyrant* (New York: The Free Press, 1999), pp. 8, 56.

[29] Hosmer, *The Conflict Over Kosovo*, p. 9.

[30] Obrad Kesic, "Serbian Roulette," *Current History*, Vol. 97, No. 617 (March 1998), pp. 98–101.

[31] Hosmer, *The Conflict Over Kosovo*, p. 11.

or hated Milošević so he attempted to appeal to the admiration from elder and less educated rural-based dwellers that held strong notions of nationalist pride.[32]

Yugoslav armed forces were engaging in ethnic cleansing of Kosovar Albanians in the province. The elite manipulation from Milošević was strong and he used the media to justify attacks against the Kosovar Albanian population to shape a "Greater Serbia."[33] Milošević cunningly promoted war in the Balkans, including Bosnia, Croatia, Slovenia, and Serbia, to keep the populace distracted to increase his power. The North Atlantic Treaty Organization (NATO) allies were wary of another massacre, as in Bosnia, but did not opt for authorization from the United Nations Security Council. This was due to the fear of Moscow and Beijing vetoes that supported the state sovereignty of Serbia and perceived a humanitarian intervention as an encroachment of traditional international law.[34] NATO was faced with either respecting international law or using force to avert prevalent human rights abuses perpetrated by the Yugoslav Army and direction of Milošević against Albanian ethnicity in Kosovo.[35]

Yet, both sides committed atrocities against each other. For instance, the Kosovo Liberation Army (KLA) also engaged in terrorism and hostility directed against the former Yugoslav armed forces and Yugoslav Serbs. The United Nations did not deem or display the Kosovo conflict as a major threat to international peace and security for the United Nations Security Council to consider. Milošević was aware of potential NATO intervention due to their threat to do so after his diplomatic refusal. In retaliation, Milošević created a referendum on whether there should be international action regarding the Kosovo conflict, and with the help of governmental media, 95 percent (out of 75 percent voting) voted against foreign intrusion.[36] Milošević's hegemony and focus on the Kosovo issue expanded his electoral and power bases that did not want international

[32] Robert Thomas, *The Politics of Serbia in the 1990s* (New York: Columbia University Press, 1999), pp. 69–79.

[33] Ian Black, "Milošević Tried to Build Greater Serbia, Trial Told," *The Guardian*, October 2, 2002, https://www.theguardian.com/world/2002/oct/02/warcrimes.milosevictrial.

[34] David M. Malone and Karin Wermester, "Boom and Bust? The Changing Nature of UN Peacekeeping," *International Peacekeeping*, Vol. 7, No. 4 (2000), p. 48.

[35] Charney, "Anticipatory Humanitarian Intervention in Kosovo," p. 834.

[36] Memorandum by the Foreign and Commonwealth Office, "Kosovo: History of the Crisis," *House of Commons*, Select Committee on Foreign Affairs, Fourth Report, May 23, 2000.

intervention so he felt no need to cave to the conditions of the Rambouillet Agreement. Conceding Kosovo as a self-governing province for the Kosovar Albanian community and the deployment of a NATO-led international force would have served against Milošević's grasp on his presidency.

The Kosovar Albanian delegation accepted and signed the Rambouillet Agreement, but the former Yugoslavia wanted to alter nearly all the terms during further negotiations at Paris. The former Yugoslavia eventually refused to sign the text, which was largely based on the political settlement regarding Kosovo and the presence of a NATO-based ground military force.[37] Kosovar Albanians wanted the NATO ground force (of an estimated 38,000 troops), to which the negotiators agreed. Alongside large NATO ground presence, the Yugoslav armed forces and police in the Kosovo province were to be downsized to a maximum of 2500 Yugoslav military forces and 75 border police personnel to function within a meagre 5-kilometer radius within the borders of Kosovo.[38] The Rambouillet Agreement proposed that NATO have full "unrestricted passage" of their aircraft, vehicles, equipment, and vessels on the ground, air, and sea of the former Yugoslavia.[39] NATO would also have been authorized to modify the former Yugoslavia infrastructure, such as buildings, roads, tunnels, bridges, and utility structures.[40] These clauses clearly violated the sovereign territory of the former Yugoslavia. None of these provisions were accepted by Belgrade.

The Kosovar Albanian delegation also proposed that Kosovo would reach a final status (including the Helsinki Final Act) after three years of signing the Rambouillet Agreement, which Belgrade could not accept.[41] The Kosovar Albanian delegation proposed that Kosovo would host a referendum on its independence after three years to the United States Secretary of State, Madeleine Albright, in exchange for signing the Rambouillet Agreement by an agreed deadline. Milošević knew that a referendum would result in the majority in Kosovo wanting independence from the former Yugoslavia.[42] Milošević had cemented his power on the promise that Kosovo would always share a special relationship under the

[37] Hosmer, *The Conflict Over Kosovo*, pp. 12–13.

[38] Rambouillet Agreement, Chapter 2, Article VI (2, a); Chapter 7, Article IV: VJ.

[39] Chapter 7, Appendix B, 8.

[40] Chapter 7, B, 22.

[41] Rambouillet Agreement, Chapter 8, Amendment, Article I (3).

[42] Hosmer, *The Conflict Over Kosovo*, pp. 14–15.

sovereignty of Serbia so he could not sign or withdraw Yugoslav security forces and permit the deployment of NATO forces to undermine the initiation of Milošević's political foundations. NATO's arrival would constitute aggression and Kosovo and Serbian nationalist voters would be lost for Milošević. If Milošević caved to the Rambouillet Agreement, the "ultranationalist Serbian Radical Party" could have defeated him at the next elections.[43] Milošević did not want to be removed from power, which is why he rejected the Agreement because the presence of NATO ground troops would have done that.

Due to Milošević failing to sign the Rambouillet Agreement, the NATO-led Operation Allied Force entailed a 78-day aerial bombing campaign (March 24–June 10, 1999) over Serbia and Kosovo to oppose their crimes of aggression against the Kosovar Albanian population in the Kosovo province. FRY forces engaged with a prevalent ethnic cleansing campaign that continued even when NATO started its bombing intervention. Negotiation with the former Yugoslavia only commenced after the bombing started, which merely entailed the consideration of an oil embargo. It could be argued that a non-forcible remedy was not exhausted, and NATO believed that a short bombing campaign over a few days would force Milošević to sign the Rambouillet Agreement.[44] Perhaps NATO's hegemonic state's realist objective of partitioning Serbia was to weaken it and work toward new post-socialist states and protect the Kosovar Albanian population. The United Nations did not condemn or thoroughly criticize NATO's bombing. Furthermore, Milošević did not falter from the initial rounds of NATO's bombing and the Alliance killed an estimated 500 civilians despite its care with targeted military and dual-use facilities.[45]

During the bombing campaign, cluster bombs and uranium depleted missiles and shells caused environmental damage.[46] In addition, there were notable civilian casualties and property damage reported. NATO's bombs killed fleeing refugees, service workers, journalists, make-up artists, hospital patients, and Chinese Embassy personnel in Belgrade.[47] For example, on April 23, 1999, a NATO missile struck Radio Television Serbia (RTS) in central Belgrade that held 120 civilians at the time of the airstrike. The

[43] Hosmer, *The Conflict Over Kosovo*, p. 17.

[44] Independent International Commission on Kosovo. *Kosovo Report*, p. 2.

[45] Independent International Commission on Kosovo. *Kosovo Report*, p. 65.

[46] Independent International Commission on Kosovo. *Kosovo Report*, pp. 2, 65.

[47] Christine M. Chinkin, "Kosovo: A 'Good' or 'Bad' War?" *American Journal of International Law*, Vol. 93, No. 4 (1999), p. 841.

bombing killed 16 civilians and wounded a minimum of an additional 16 workers, namely, service workers and make-up artists, and also left some non-combatants trapped under rubble prior to their deaths.[48] In relation to just war ethics, this questioned the principle of military necessity by targeting RTS because it held a "Serbian military command and control system" and thus the destruction of the apparatus that retained Milošević's power against the minor objectives of targeting propaganda to support a war without evidence of inciting crimes.[49] A month later, in May 1999, NATO targeted military barracks but inadvertently struck the Chinese Embassy. This was followed by an attack on a hospital in Belgrade that killed three patients, injured a woman giving birth via a cesarean operation, and damaged the neurology department's intensive care ward.[50] Cluster bombs were used and NATO also targeted the New Belgrade heating plant and seven bridges, including Novi Sad Bridge, killing civilians. This attack did not target any military functions or major transportation routes.[51] The intensity of destructive force can stretch beyond the just point of targeting an enemy (or weakening their compound, weapons, or communication structure) to outweigh the harms, most notably collateral damage.[52] NATO was constantly apologetic, but pursued its five-fold objectives. The goals entailed the cessation of atrocities committed by the Yugoslav armed forces and police force in Kosovo; withdrawal of these security forces; deployment of an international-led Kosovo Force (KFOR); repatriation of all refugees; and a Kosovo political settlement agreed by the Serbian parliament.[53]

NATO's bombing campaign was deemed illegal by many powerful states, including Russia, China, and India, due to contravention of Article

[48] Danny Singh, "Undertaking Critical Legal Theory to Examine Just War Intervention: A Smokescreen for Political Ambitions," in *Comparative Just War Theory: An Introduction to International Perspectives*, edited by Luís Cordeiro-Rodrigues and Danny Singh (Lanham, MD: Rowman & Littlefield, 2000), p. 70.

[49] Claudio Cordone and Avner Gidron, "Was the Serbian TV Station Really a Legitimate Target?" *Le Monde Diplomatique*, July 2000.

[50] Owen Bowcott, Martin Walker, and Richard Norton-Taylor, "Belgrade Bitter at Hospital Bombing," *The Guardian*, May 21, 1999.

[51] Human Rights Watch, *Civilian Deaths in the NATO Air Campaign – The Crisis in Kosovo* (New York, Human Rights Watch, 2016), pp. 5, 7, 15, 24.

[52] Michael C. Hawley, "Can Just Wars Be Fought Proportionately? A Critique of *In Bello* Proportionality," *Journal of Military Ethics*, Vol. 22, No. 2 (September 2023), p. 93.

[53] North Atlantic Treaty Organization, "NATO's Role in Kosovo," *NATO*, November 20, 2023.

2 (4) of the Charter of the United Nations against the sovereignty of the former Yugoslavia. NATO circumvented the United Nations Security Council that contravened Article 53 (1) of the Charter of the United Nations for rules of regional arrangements and Article 51 was undermined because a NATO member had not been attacked by the former Yugoslavia.[54] The only exception to the rule of sovereignty within Article 2 (4) of the Charter of the United Nations rests on forcible measures seeking permission from the United Nations Security Council under Chap. 7 or if a state exercises their inherent right to individual or collective self-defense against an attack from another state.[55] NATO's Operation Allied Force clearly abused international law and, namely, the Charter of the United Nations.[56] International law prohibits the use of force from a state or collection of states in conducting an intervention in another state, and in the Kosovo context, there was no UN Security Council permission or self-defense. The Security Council respected the sovereign territory of the former Yugoslavia, and the Council did not praise NATO's bombing afterwards in a resolution that permitted the intervention of foreign states to preserve the peace.[57]

Due to the protracted intensity of the bombing, Milošević withdrew Yugoslav troops from Kosovo on June 11, 1999. At the end of NATO's intervention bombing, an estimated 90 separate bombing incidents killed between 488 and 527 of the Yugoslav civilian population.[58] During the Kosovo War (February 28, 1998–June 11, 1999), more than 13,517 people died or went missing[59] and the Yugoslav and Serb military and police forces forced an estimated 1.45 million Kosovar Albanians into

[54] Carl Ceulemans, "The NATO Intervention in the Kosovo Crisis: March–June 1999," in *Moral Constraints on War: Principles and Cases*, 2nd ed., edited by Brian Coppieters and Nick Fotion (Lanham, MD: Lexington Books, 2008), p. 202, pp. 195–228.

[55] Article 51 of the Charter of the United Nations.

[56] Charney, "Anticipatory Humanitarian Intervention in Kosovo," p. 834.

[57] Charney, "Anticipatory Humanitarian Intervention in Kosovo," p. 835.

[58] International Criminal Tribunal for the former Yugoslavia (ICTY), "Final Report to the Prosecutor by the Committee Established to Review the NATO Bombing Campaign Against the Federal Republic of Yugoslavia," *ICTY*, 2000, p. 20 / para. 53 (Section V: Casualty Figures).

[59] Milka Domanović, "List of Kosovo War Victims Published," *Balkan Transitional Justice*, December 10, 2014.

displacement.[60] There were 863,000 refugees outside of Kosovo.[61] The ethnic cleansing strategy by the Serbs also comprised mass torture, rape, pillaging, and looting that resulted in high displacement rates. There were large numbers of refugees from Kosovo. Civilians were killed and their private property also destroyed, as part of ethnic cleansing, and reprisals from returnees followed during NATO's bombing.[62] Although there were civilian casualties and damage to Serbia amounting to an estimated US $100 billion, Milošević eventually surrendered, and a genocide was averted. The Kosovo Commission held that "the NATO campaign was illegal, yet legitimate" because it bypassed permission from the United Nations Security Council, but allegedly exhausted diplomatic routes and there was no alternative to prevent the atrocities committed by the Yugoslav armed forces.[63] The intervention protected an emerging global moral consensus to save human lives from mass atrocities.[64] Nicholas J. Wheeler stated that NATO was right to save lives with a humanitarian intervention against Serbia rather than wait out international legal approval.[65] Although Milošević withdrew Yugoslav forces from Kosovo and signed the Agreement based on the aborted Rambouillet Agreement, Milošević remained in power to continue violence toward Kosovo, and Serbia suffered with equivalent damage to its economy and infrastructure.[66]

With NATO's breach of international law, humanitarian intervention can intensify violence, create a discordant state of affairs, and contravene human rights. Although the Charter of the United Nations does not legally authorize humanitarian intervention due to its non-consent with another state of incursion, it can be morally permissible, as with NATO. For instance, in 1971, India protected Bengalis from the atrocities committed by the West Pakistani military junta by intervening in East Pakistan to weaken their enemy and help Bangladesh strive for independence, which

[60] Organization for Security and Co-operation in Europe, *Human Rights in Kosovo: As Seen, As Told – An Analysis of the Human Rights Findings of the OSCE Kosovo Verification Mission, October 1998 to June 1999* (Vienna: OSCE, November 5, 1999), p. 13.

[61] Independent International Commission on Kosovo, *Kosovo Report*, p. 32.

[62] Chinkin, "Kosovo: A 'Good' or 'Bad' War?" p. 841.

[63] Independent International Commission on Kosovo, *The Kosovo Report*, p. 186.

[64] Independent International Commission on Kosovo, *The Kosovo Report*, p. 186.

[65] Nicholas J. Wheeler, *Saving Strangers* (Oxford: Oxford University Press, 2000), p. 41.

[66] Independent International Commission on Kosovo, *The Kosovo Report*, p. 103.

thus included reasons beyond humanitarian motives.[67] Most of the United Nations General Assembly condemned India's intervention but Prime Minister Indira Gandhi stressed the desire for the early repatriation of refugees.[68] Even when a state invites external support or is collapsed, external parties have political rather than solely humanitarian interests.

International Favoring of Kosovo in the Aftermath

After NATO completed Operation Allied Force, on June 10, 1999, UN Security Council Resolution 1244 authorized the United Nations Mission in Kosovo (UNMIK) that was headed by Dr Bernard Kouchner, as the Special Representative of the Secretary-General, and supported by KFOR as an international armed force.[69] At this point, crime was very high in Kosovo, mostly perpetrated against minority Serbs, and over half of the Serbs left Kosovo with Serbian forces.[70] The Serbs who remained in Kosovo had to reside in divided cities or enclaves where renewed conflicts were common, especially in the partitioned northern Mitrovic/Kosovska province.[71] The United Nations mandate did not authorize NATO's prior bombing. The Kosovo Liberation Army and other armed resistance groups were to undergo immediate demilitarization from conflict zones to reintegration.[72] KLA belligerents were provided access to the new Kosovo security forces: the Kosovo Protection Corps (KPC) as a professionalized multi-ethnic civilian defense force and the Kosovo Police Service. Demilitarized KLA fighters received a reintegration fund. A UN-based transitional administration planned a new civil defense force without any input from Serbia, which undermined, and threatened, their state sovereignty.[73] The United Nations provided the support so Kosovo could attain its self-governance while *somehow* respecting the sovereign territory of the

[67] Michael Walzer, *Just and Unjust Wars: A Moral Argument with Historical Illustrations* (New York: Basic Books, 1977), pp. 105–106.

[68] Kapil Kak, "Revisiting the 1971 War and the Indian Air Force's Role: India's Interests and Compulsions," in *Role of Indian Air Force in 1971 War*, edited by Jasjit Singh (New Delhi: Center for Air Power Studies, 2013), Chapter 4.

[69] United Nations Security Council Resolution 1244, "On the Situation Relating to Kosovo," UN Doc. S/RES/1244, June 10, 1999, adopted 4011th meeting.

[70] Independent International Commission on Kosovo, *The Kosovo Report*, pp. 94–95.

[71] Independent International Commission on Kosovo, *The Kosovo Report*, pp. 39, 41–42.

[72] UN Security Council Resolution 1244, "On the Situation Relating to Kosovo," para. 15.

[73] Özerdem, "From a 'Terrorist' Group to a 'Civil Defense' Corps," pp. 81–82.

former Yugoslavia, but the latter was impossible due to the atrocities already committed.[74] UNMIK did not contain judicial or police processes. It was only civilian tasks undertaken by some contingents of KFOR international troops that engaged with police work. UNMIK held unlimited authority in Kosovo for its self-government.

The Security Sector Reform (SSR) process[75] had to cater for an estimated 8000–10,000 KLA combatants, but in November 1999, there were over 25,000 registered fighters.[76] After the initial screening process, 16,229 ex-combatants required reintegration and the Reintegration Fund amounted to more than US $14 million.[77] The international political and security support for the civilian administration and training of its security forces helped Kosovo work toward independence. Milošević was now out of favor and lost the September 2000 election, and he forcibly resigned as president a month later.[78] The November 2002 general elections placed Kosovo on track as an independent state. Even though Serbian parliamentarians annulled Kosovo's claim for independence, it was still attained on February 17, 2008, as declared by the Kosovo Assembly and support by the United States and other democratic allies.[79]

Assessing Afro-communitarian Ethics of NATO's Intervention in the Former Yugoslavia

Under Afro-communitarian consequentialist ethics, the stages of violence were followed, and it is not concerned with the legality (legitimate authority) of *jus ad bellum* like traditionalists are. Instead, the burden for Afro-communitarians rests on the stages of violence after diplomacy was

[74] Independent Commission on Kosovo. *Kosovo Report*, pp. 93, 259.

[75] SSR aims to establish functional and professionalized security forces (principally a national armed force and state police) to provide security for an entire population that are subject to civilian control, while utilizing the lowest possible amount of resources (Michael Brzoska, "Security Sector Reform: The Concept," in *Disarmament and Conflict Prevention in Development Cooperation*, edited by Bonn International Center for Conversion (BICC), Report 14 (Bonn: BICC, 2000), p. 39).

[76] Özerdem, "From a 'Terrorist' Group to a 'Civil Defense' Corps," p. 85.

[77] Özerdem, "From a 'Terrorist' Group to a 'Civil Defense' Corps," p. 85.

[78] R. Jeffrey Smith and Peter Finn, "How Milošević Lost His Grip: Leader was Isolated in Final Days," *The Washington Post*, October 14, 2000.

[79] James Ker-Lindsay, *The Foreign Policy of Counter Succession: Preventing the Recognition of Contested States* (Oxford: Oxford University Press, 2012), p. 78.

exhausted.[80] Therefore, the stages of violence from NATO acted rapidly and decisively to counter the ethnic cleansing policy of Serbian political leadership and its armed forces against Kosovar Albanians. Despite the Alliance intensifying the conflict between Serbian security forces and the region of Kosovo, NATO had allegedly complied with the law or armed conflict principle of military necessity to target Serbian military personnel, infrastructure, and communications. Sabotage could conform to the *Ubuntu* stages of violence with the Afro-communitarian consequentialist approach, to oppose Serbian violence against Kosovar Albanians with the aim to create a less discordant situation and more positive and harmonious state of affairs.

If assessed with Afro-communitarian consequentialist ethics, sabotage is permissible to weaken governmental and military infrastructure, including the machinery of the maintenance of power, but RTS should have been targeted in the evening hours and with a warning given to the civilian workers to evacuate prior to NATO's aerial bombardment. This could have better engaged with the permissible violence of sabotage and spared the lives of non-combatants. NATO then engaged in warfare to target Serbian civilians, which may have been unintentional, but at least would qualify as negligence. This would also fail Afro-communitarian principles. Similar to traditional just war theory and under the rule of proportionality, targeting innocent civilians is not permissible. Attacking civilians would exacerbate a discordant state of affairs, which can only be justified if there are few casualties with a warranted open revolution.

NATO did believe, however, that Milošević would have surrendered several days after NATO's operation commenced in late March 1999, and did not expect the airstrikes to drag out over three months.[81] McCarthy has controversially argued that NATO commanders were too tentative to strike military targets for fear of exceeding collateral damage and killing innocent civilians, which dragged the war out due to the restraint that was met with a longer period of ethnic cleansing and further destruction.[82] If

[80] From a political science perspective, criticism can be addressed in this regard insofar as Kosovo, as an autonomous province of Serbia, should have been part of earlier diplomatic negotiations prior to the planning of the Dayton Agreement.

[81] Independent International Commission on Kosovo, *The Kosovo Report*, p. 92.

[82] James P. McCarthy, "Ethical Implications of Kosovo Operations," in *The Sacred and the Sovereign: Religion and International Politics*, edited by John D. Carlson and Erik C. Owens (Georgetown, Washington, DC: Georgetown University Press, 2003), p. 71. McCarthy contends that Milošević was clever to acknowledge NATO's rules of engagement on self-

considering Metz's interpretation of *Ubuntu* ethics, ill will undermines mutual solidarity between a community and groups and thus dishonors relationships.[83] Therefore, the Serbian-led ethnic cleansing policy against Kosovar Albanians required opposition due to the antagonistic relations and ongoing violence between KLA belligerents and Serbian forces.

However, the test of attributing a less discordant state of affairs and a more harmonious situation is less clear because it has been argued that NATO's intervention intensified the atrocities committed by the Yugoslav forces during the bombing campaign after the Alliance made the relatively successful OSCE monitoring forces leave.[84] Under OSCE monitoring in Kosovo, human rights abuses were not prevalent or serious.[85] Furthermore, the contemporary relations between Serbia and Kosovo remain fragmented because the former does not recognize the sovereign independence of the latter and thus civilian and police ethnic clashes remain. It could be argued that a disharmonious state of affairs between both sides still exists, but the separation of the two has reduced violent conflict and notably ethnic cleansing.

Conclusion

The conflict in Kosovo emerged with Albanian influence striving for the right to self-determination, which is why a political league and KLA militants fought for the eventual independence of the Kosovo province. At the same time, Milošević wanted to retain power and thus focused attention on Balkan conflicts, including strife over Kosovo and the protection of Kosovar Serbs, and appealed to nationalists by proposing to retain Yugoslav sovereignty over the province. NATO, and especially the United States, observed the situation, and as part of foreign armed intervention had tolerated initial diplomatic solutions. The Holbrooke–Milošević Agreement permitted unarmed OSCE foreign observers, which did reduce skirmishes between Yugoslav forces and KLA belligerents. However, NATO wanted

restraint, to adhere with *in bello* proportionality, so he stationed military targets in civilian territories. Based on this premise, tentative or weak use of force can be worse in war due to the length of destruction.

[83] Thaddeus Metz, "Human Dignity, Capital Punishment, and an African Moral Theory: Toward a New Philosophy of Human Rights," *Journal of Human Rights*, Vol. 9, No. 1 (February 2010), p. 84.

[84] Charney, "Anticipatory Humanitarian Intervention in Kosovo," p. 840.

[85] Charney, "Anticipatory Humanitarian Intervention in Kosovo," p. 839.

the unarmed monitors to leave and focus on a political solution for the Kosovo problem. The conditions of the subsequent Rambouillet Agreement were hard for Milošević because they provided no consolidation prize if conceding to the presence of foreign ground intervention, the removal of Yugoslav forces from the Kosovo territory, and a political framework for an independent Kosovo. The Agreement would have immediately finished Milošević's political career. Consequently, NATO engaged with what they believed would have been a very short bombing campaign to get Milošević to sign the Agreement. Milošević did not, and the bombing continued for 78 days until his final surrender and withdrawal of Serbian security forces from the Kosovo province.

In terms of Afro-communitarian ethics, diplomacy was not exhausted and other avenues than the one-sided Rambouillet Agreement could have been attempted because the prior OSCE unarmed foreign observers reduced violence. Although NATO's bombing that involved 90 incidents resulted in Milošević's surrender to safeguard the Kosovar-Albanian community, the duration of the bombing intensified violence between the Yugoslav forces and KLA belligerents. The eventual state of affairs was harmonious, but the ethnic hatred between Kosovar Serbs and Kosovar Albanians remains, with the former being discriminately targeted after Kosovo's independence. Better communal relations between two belligerent parties can be accomplished from foreign armed intervention, but asymmetrical warfare, especially in the form of aerial bombing, for a long period creates a lot of damage that leaves behind animosity, especially from the losing or surrendered side.

References

Amnesty International. "Bosnia and Herzegovina: 25th Anniversary of Srebrenica Massacre is a Sombre Warning from History." *Amnesty International*, July 9, 2020. https://www.amnesty.org/en/latest/news/2020/07/bosnia-and-herzegovina-25th-anniversary-of-srebrenica-massacre-is-a-sombre-warning-from-history/.

Bartrop, Paul R. *Genocide: The Basics*. London: Routledge, 2015.

Black, Ian. "Milošević Tried to Build Greater Serbia, Trial Told." *The Guardian*, October 2, 2002. https://www.theguardian.com/world/2002/oct/02/warcrimes.milosevictrial.

Bowcott, Owen, Martin Walker, and Richard Norton-Taylor. "Belgrade Bitter at Hospital Bombing." *The Guardian*, May 21, 1999. https://www.theguardian.com/world/1999/may/21/richardnortontaylor.martinwalker.

Bradshaw, York W., Joseph F. Healey, and Rebecca Smith. *Sociology for a New Century*. Thousand Oaks, CA: Pine Forge Press, 2001.

Brzoska, Michael. "Security Sector Reform: The Concept." In *Disarmament and Conflict Prevention in Development Cooperation*, edited by Bonn International Center for Conversion (BICC), Report 14. Bonn: BICC, 2000.

Caplan, Richard. "International Diplomacy and the Crisis in Kosovo." *International Affairs*, Vol. 74, No. 4 (October 1998), pp. 745–761. https://doi.org/10.1111/1468-2346.00043.

Ceulemans, Carl. "The NATO Intervention in the Kosovo Crisis: March–June 1999." In *Moral Constraints on War: Principles and Cases*, 2nd ed., edited by Brian Coppieters and Nick Fotion, pp. 195–228. Lanham, MD: Lexington Books, 2008.

Charney, Jonathan I. "Anticipatory Humanitarian Intervention in Kosovo." *American Journal of International Law*, Vol. 93, No. 4 (October 1999), pp. 834–841. https://doi.org/10.2307/2555348.

Chinkin, Christine M. "Kosovo: A 'Good' or 'Bad' War?" *American Journal of International Law*, Vol. 93, No. 4 (1999), pp. 841–847. https://doi.org/10.2307/2555349.

Cooper, Neil. "Security Sector (Lack of) Transformation in Kosovo." In *Arms Control and Contemporary Conflicts: Challenges and Responses*, PSIS Special Studies No. 5, pp. 65–127. Geneva: Geneva Center for Security Policy and Program for Strategic and International Security Studies, 2001.

Cordone, Claudio, and Avner Gidron. "Was the Serbian TV Station Really a Legitimate Target?" *Le Monde Diplomatique*, July 2000, https://mondediplo.com/2000/07/03kosovo.

Doder, Dusko, and Louise Branson. *Milošević, Portrait of a Tyrant*. New York: The Free Press, 1999.

Domanović, Milka. "List of Kosovo War Victims Published." *Balkan Transitional Justice*, December 10, 2014. https://balkaninsight.com/2014/12/10/kosovo-war-victims-list-published/.

Hawley, Michael C. "Can Just Wars Be Fought Proportionately? A Critique of *In Bello* Proportionality." *Journal of Military Ethics*, Vol. 22, No. 2 (September 2023), pp. 89–102. https://doi.org/10.1080/15027570.2023.2257916.

Hosmer, Stephen T. *The Conflict Over Kosovo: Why Milošević Decided to Settle When He Did*. Santa Monica, CA: RAND Corporation, 2001.

Human Rights Watch. *Civilian Deaths in the NATO Air Campaign – The Crisis in Kosovo*. New York, Human Rights Watch, 2016. https://www.hrw.org/reports/pdfs/g/general/natbm002.pdf.

Independent International Commission on Kosovo. *Kosovo Report: Conflict – International Response – Lessons Learned.* Oxford: Oxford University Press, 2000.

International Criminal Tribunal for the former Yugoslavia (ICTY). "Final Report to the Prosecutor by the Committee Established to Review the NATO Bombing Campaign Against the Federal Republic of Yugoslavia." *ICTY*, 2000.

Kak, Kapil. "Revisiting the 1971 War and the Indian Air Force's Role: India's Interests and Compulsions." In *Role of Indian Air Force in 1971 War*, edited by Jasjit Singh. New Delhi: Center for Air Power Studies, 2013, Chapter 4.

Ker-Lindsay, James. *The Foreign Policy of Counter Succession: Preventing the Recognition of Contested States.* Oxford: Oxford University Press, 2012.

Kesic, Obrad. "Serbian Roulette." *Current History*, Vol. 97, No. 617 (March 1998), pp. 97–102. https://doi.org/10.1525/curh.1998.97.617.97.

Malone, David M., and Karin Wermester. "Boom and Bust? The Changing Nature of UN Peacekeeping." *International Peacekeeping*, Vol. 7, No. 4 (2000), pp. 37–54. https://doi.org/10.1080/13533310008413862.

McCarthy, James P. "Ethical Implications of Kosovo Operations." In *The Sacred and the Sovereign: Religion and International Politics*, edited by John D. Carlson and Erik C. Owens, pp. 66–76. Georgetown, Washington, DC: Georgetown University Press, 2003.

Memorandum by the Foreign and Commonwealth Office. "Kosovo: History of the Crisis." *House of Commons*, Select Committee on Foreign Affairs, Fourth Report, May 23, 2000. http://www.parliament.the-stationary-off.../pa/cm199900/cmselect/cmfaff/28/9111803.html.

Metz, Thaddeus. "Human Dignity, Capital Punishment, and an African Moral Theory: Toward a New Philosophy of Human Rights." *Journal of Human Rights*, Vol. 9, No. 1 (February 2010), pp. 81–99. https://doi.org/10.1080/14754830903530300.

Mitchell, Christopher. "Comparing Sanctuary in the Former Yugoslavia and the Philippines." In *Zones of Peace*, edited by Landon E. Hancock and Christopher R. Mitchell, pp. 137–166. Bloomfield, CT: Kumarian Press, 2007.

North Atlantic Treaty Organization. "NATO's Role in Kosovo." *NATO*, November 20, 2023. https://www.nato.int/cps/en/natohq/topics_48818.htm.

O'Ballance, Edgar. *Civil War in Bosnia, 1992–94.* Basingstoke, Hampshire: Macmillan Press, 1995.

Organization for Security and Co-operation in Europe. "OSCE Verification Mission / OSCE Task Force for Kosovo." *OSCE*, 1999a. https://www.osce.org/kvm-closed.

Organization for Security and Co-operation in Europe. *Human Rights in Kosovo: As Seen, As Told – An Analysis of the Human Rights Findings of the OSCE Kosovo*

Verification Mission, October 1998 to June 1999. Vienna: OSCE, November 5, 1999b.

Özerdem, Alpaslan. "From a 'Terrorist' Group to a 'Civil Defense' Corps: The 'Transformation' of the Kosovo Liberation Army." *International Peacekeeping*, Vol. 10, No. 3 (2003), pp. 79–101. https://doi.org/10.1080/13533310308559337.

Rambouillet Accords. "Interim Agreement for Peace and Self-Government in Kosovo." S/1999/648, June 7, 1999. https://peacemaker.un.org/sites/peacemaker.un.org/files/990123_RambouilletAccord.pdf.

Singh, Danny. "Undertaking Critical Legal Theory to Examine Just War Intervention: A Smokescreen for Political Ambitions." In *Comparative Just War Theory: An Introduction to International Perspectives*, edited by Luís Cordeiro-Rodrigues and Danny Singh, pp. 61–79. Lanham, MD: Rowman & Littlefield, 2000.

Smith, R. Jeffrey, and Peter Finn. "How Milošević Lost His Grip: Leader was Isolated in Final Days." *The Washington Post*, October 14, 2000. https://www.washingtonpost.com/archive/politics/2000/10/15/how-milosevic-lost-his-grip/298ab05b-ba78-46f5-b6d7-dbf6348b7c5c/.

Thomas, Robert. *The Politics of Serbia in the 1990s.* New York: Columbia University Press, 1999.

United Nations. *Charter of the United Nations.* 1 United Nations Treaty Series XVI, October 24, 1945.

United Nations Security Council Resolution 1244. "On the Situation Relating to Kosovo." UN Doc. S/RES/1244, June 10, 1999, adopted 4,011th meeting.

Walzer, Michael. *Just and Unjust Wars: A Moral Argument with Historical Illustrations.* New York: Basic Books, 1977.

Weller, Marc. "The Rambouillet Conference on Kosovo." *International Affairs*, Vol. 75, No. 2 (April 1999), pp. 211–251. https://doi.org/10.1111/1468-2346.00069.

Weller, Marc, and Stefan Wolff. "Bosnia and Herzegovina Ten Years after Dayton: Lessons for Internationalized State Building." In *International State-Building after Violent Conflict: Bosnia Ten Years after Dayton*, edited by Marc Weller and Stefan Wolff, pp. 1–13. London: Routledge, 2008.

Wheeler, Nicholas J. *Saving Strangers.* Oxford: Oxford University Press, 2000.

CHAPTER 6

United States and Allied Unilateral Intervention in Iraq

Introduction

As in the intervention of Afghanistan, this chapter covers a foreign armed intervention that was part of American foreign policy aligned to the war against terror. However, unlike the context of Afghanistan, the March 2003 Iraq invasion differed because the United States failed to attain direct authorization from the United Nations Security Council, which is a fundamental prerequisite for the narrow exception of initiating war for self-defense or a preventive humanitarian intervention in contemporary international law. The United States opted to deploy UN weapons inspectors. The United Nations is a main legitimate authority and thus permission was obtained for the inspection. However, the inspectors found that there was no concrete evidence of the Saddam regime holding weapons of mass destruction (WMD). Subsequently, the United States molded a coalition of willing states to support the global war on terror. At this point in time, Saddam did not fully declare that Iraq would pursue a WMD program or use chemical weapons once more as a deterrent against its main rival, Iran, and internal opponents (i.e., Shiite minorities and Kurdish communities).[1]

[1] David A. Lake, "Two Cheers for Bargaining Theory: Assessing Rationalist Explanations of the Iraq War," *International Security*, Vol. 35, No. 3 (Winter 2010/11), p. 9; Michael Isikoff and David Corn, *Hubris: The Inside Story of Spin, Scandal, and the Selling of the Iraq War* (New York: Free Rivers Press (Crown Publishers), 2006), p. 375.

D. Singh, *Applied Afro-Communitarian Ethics and Foreign Armed Intervention*, https://doi.org/10.1007/978-3-031-64110-7_6

Despite "joint Coalition and Iraqi military operations," the outcome of the intervention and efforts of advancing de-Ba'athification into a new Iraq political system failed to avoid expanding sectarian violence, crime, killings, and kidnappings.[2] When the intervention commenced, the United States deployed its own team to inspect weapons stockpiles and a potential WMD program to re-justify the invasion but nothing significant was found. However, the Bush administration still ascertained that the invasion was the right decision because Saddam was supporting al-Qaeda and aiming to escape sanctions so he could later pursue a WMD program that could enter the hands of international terrorists.

Military victory was estimated as certain so Washington sought the destruction of Iraq and a new handpicked regime from the Bush administration to replace Saddam and his family.[3] It was estimated by the United States government that the cost of the war would be minimal and the overall intervention and statebuilding mission would be swift.[4] The Pentagon claimed that the war would cost $2 billion monthly to a total of an estimated $50 billion,[5] but the cost was almost $1.8 trillion with over 550,000 deaths that included 4600 US forces, 15 Department of Defense civilians, 3,650 contractors, 282 media staff, and 64 humanitarian workers.[6] Other accounts suggest that the war in Iraq was predicted to cost the Americans over US $3 trillion.[7]

When making an assessment on Afro-communitarian consequentialist ethics, the intervention from the United States and coalition forces did not try to foster better friendship relations with the Saddam Hussein regime and it resulted in a less harmonious state of affairs. UN weapons inspectors did not find any functional WMD in Iraq and thus sour relations and violence intensified. For the Bush administration, even if there was no WMD program and stockpiles had been destroyed in Iraq, Saddam

[2] Anthony H. Cordesman with Emma R. Davies, *Iraq's Insurgency and the Road to Civil Conflict – Volume I* (Westport, CT: Praeger Security International, 2008), p. 355.

[3] Saddam might have believed that Bush was not as coercive as stated due to America's early withdrawals from Lebanon in 1984, the Persian Gulf War in 1991, and Somalia in 1993.

[4] Nick Ritchie and Paul Rodgers, *The Political Road to War with Iraq: Bush, 9/11 and the Drive to Overthrow Saddam* (London: Routledge, 2007).

[5] Mark Thompson, "Adding Up the Cost of Our Never-Ending Wars," *Project on Government Oversight*, December 17, 2019.

[6] Meghann Myers, "Wars in Iraq and Syria Cost Half a Million Lives, Nearly $3T: Report," *Military Times*, March 17, 2023.

[7] Joseph Eugene Stiglitz and Linda J. Barnes, *The Three Trillion Dollar War: The True Cost of the Iraq Conflict* (New York: W.W. Norton, 2008).

could have changed his perspective, so regime change was arguably sought.[8] Peaceful relations and diplomacy did not comply because geopolitical interests prompted the robust intervention as part of Bush's Republican hawks advocating their obscured version of neoconservatism to contain terrorism by spreading democratization in the Middle East region. This strategy is non-compliant with Afro-communitarian ethics. Moreover, the social identity of America's intervention and means of violence dented Afro-communitarianism. This was because the geopolitical interests of deposing an autocrat and creating a rapid democracy with liberal marketization for better oil relations within the Middle East were questionably the main objectives of major Western powers,[9] especially leading private oil companies, rather than bringing a less discordant state of affairs.

This chapter is divided into several parts. The opening section covers the initial Gulf War and the sanctions for disarmament against the Saddam Hussein regime. This is followed by the Clinton administration's policies of containing Iraq and encouraging regime change that were contrasted with the Bush government intending to invade Iraq since early 2001. The neconservative influence within the Bush administration are then examined to enhance an understanding of America's war against terror and the strategic liberal discourse of a slight WMD threat and Saddam's alleged harboring of al-Qaeda. The 2003 invasion of Iraq and findings of the Iraq Survey Group are discussed, followed by an assessment of the occupying powers, forming of the Coalition Provisional Authority (CPA), and response of the Surge and increase of private military contractors to defeat the emergence of terrorist groups. The international strategy and pitfalls of post-conflict reconstruction, Security Sector Reform (SSR), statebuilding, and stabilization are examined. This is needed to develop the argument that the foreign armed intervention resulted in further ethno-sectarian violence and strengthening of the Islamic State (Islamic State of Iraq and the Levant/Syria, ISIS/Da'esh), resulting in the reliance of the Iraqi federal government on Iranian-aligned militias to reclaim lost territories.

[8] This uncertainty and fear are based on the security dilemma thesis.

[9] Danny Singh, "Undertaking Critical Legal Theory to Examine Just War Intervention: A Smokescreen for Political Ambitions," in *Comparative Just War Theory: An Introduction to International Perspectives*, ed. Luís Cordeiro Rodrigues and Danny Singh (Lanham, MD: Rowman and Littlefield, 2020), p. 74.

THE 1990–1991 GULF WAR

Saddam Hussein orchestrated a military coup in the late 1960s with the Ba'ath regime and cemented power by heavily investing in the loyal Republican Guard to protect Iraq from the army and people, which prevented an internal Shi'a coup in March 1991.[10] Throughout the 1980s, America and Iraq held amicable relations and the United States helped Iraq against Iran's revolutionary regime. America did not place sanctions on Saddam when his regime applied poisonous gas against Iran's armed forces between 1984 and 1987 and the Kurdish community in Iraq in the March 1988 Halabja massacre.[11] In the latter event, Saddam gassed Kurdish rebels and used sarin nerve gas in Karbala against Shiite rebels.[12] Yet, at the close of the Cold War period, Saddam headed an anti-American movement developing in the Middle East. At this point in time, Iraq boasted one of the most progressive, prosperous, and educated states in the Gulf region.[13] Saddam heavily invested in state infrastructure and developed a welfare system to try to buy loyalty.[14] The police force, under Saddam, was highly trained and motivated to protect order.[15] Iraq invaded Kuwait in early August 1990, which presented a major threat to America's client states within the Middle East region.

On September 11, 1990, Richard (Dick) Bruce Cheney, the then Secretary of Defense for George Herbert Walker Bush, claimed that America justified intervention in the initial Gulf War due to Iraq controlling 20 percent of global oil reserves after the invasion of Kuwait and bordering Saudi Arabia contained 25 percent of world reserves.[16] Therefore, Saddam's control of key oil reserves in the Persian Gulf had placed Iraq in a position to command global energy policy that had to be

[10] Woods et al., *Iraqi Perspectives Project*, pp. vii–viii.

[11] Bruce W. Jentleson, *With Friends Like These: Reagan, Bush, and Saddam, 1982–1990* (New York: W.W. Norton, 1994), pp. 68–93.

[12] Lake, "Two Cheers for Bargaining Theory," p. 30.

[13] Byman, Daniel. "Constructing a Democratic Iraq: Challenges and Opportunities." *International Security*, Vol. 28, No. 1 (July 2003), pp. 47–48.

[14] Greg Muttit, *Fuel on the Fire: Oil and Politics in Occupied Iraq* (New York: New Press, 2012).

[15] Jesse S.G. Wozniak, "Iraq's Neoliberal Reconstruction and the Continued Relevance of the State," *Sociological Focus*, Vol. 52, No. 4 (October 2019), p. 368.

[16] Michael T. Klare, "Blood for Oil, in Iraq and Elsewhere," in *Why Did the United States Invade Iraq?* edited by Jane K. Cramer and A. Trevor Thrall (London: Routledge, 2012), pp. 129–130.

put to a halt. At this point in time, the main problem between America and Iraq lay in its competition to dominate and influence the Persian Gulf.[17] The United States and its allies responded to Iraq's invasion of Kuwait on August 2, 1990, with the aerial bombardment of Iraq with Operation Desert Storm on January 17, 1991, until Kuwait was liberated on February 28, 1991.[18] During this Operation, a large number of Iraqi Armed Forces deserted their posts and the Central Intelligence Agency (CIA) believed that they would merely swap alliance to the United States due to better equipment.[19] In reality, the Iraqi Armed Forces merely disintegrated. After the First Gulf War, America sparked regime change with the United States encouraging the Shiite minorities in south Iraq to fight the Ba'athist administration; but without external aid, they were crushed by Saddam's armed forces.

Sanctions and Disarmament Against the Saddam Hussein Regime

There was further skepticism about Iraq complying with international standards and rules. In August and November 1990, the United States legitimized sanctions and disarmament against the Saddam Hussein regime with UN Security Resolutions 660 and 678 to condemn the invasion of Iraq and provide states with "all necessary means" to put a halt to the incursion.[20] Since the early 1990s, America had wanted to contain Iraq with multiple protracted sanctions for Baghdad to comply, thus deterring their potential WMD program.[21] Due to these international sanctions, most of Iraq lived in poor conditions after 1991 and oil pipelines deteriorated, resulting in Baghdad failing to cater for its own

[17] Peter Woodard Galbraith, *The End of Iraq: How American Incompetence Created a War without End* (New York: Simon and Schuster, 2006), pp. 9–10).

[18] Richard Winship Stewart, *War in the Persian Gulf: Operations Desert Shield and Desert Storm, August 1990–March 1991* (Washington, DC: Center of Military History, United States Army, 2010), pp. 29–58.

[19] Ali Abdul-Amir Allawi, *The Occupation of Iraq: Winning the War, Losing the Peace* (New Haven, CT: Yale University Press, 2007), pp. 88–90.

[20] United Nations Security Council Resolution 660, "Condemnation of Iraq's Invasion of Kuwait," UN Doc. S/RES/660, August 2, 1990c, adopted 2963rd meeting; United Nations Security Council Resolution 778, "Iraq to Withdraw from Kuwait," UN Doc. S/RES/778, November 29, 1990, adopted 2932nd meeting.

[21] John Joseph Mearsheimer and Stephen Martin Walt, "An Unnecessary War," *Foreign Policy*, Vol. 134 (January–February 2003), pp. 50–59.

reconstruction.[22] As a measure to curtail civilian poverty from strict UN-imposed sanctions after the Gulf War, in December 1996, the United Nations Security Council started the Oil-for-Food program by uplifting some sanctions on oil exporting to permit Iraq to sell oil to pay for food and medicines for civilians.[23]

However, the head of the UN program, Benon Sevan, and beneficiaries in Russia, France, China, and Switzerland were among many individuals accepting bribes in the form of vouchers by Saddam Hussein to earn over $1.7 billion via kickbacks and over $10 billion through illicit oil smuggling.[24] It has widely been contended that the chance of Saddam Hussein holding WMD was the main premise of the United States and its coalition allies to invade Iraq for oil. However, the geopolitical tussle between America and Iraq over the Persian Gulf region might best explain why the war occurred.

The multiple sanctions harmed mainly Iraqi citizens rather than the intended political elite, with many civilians going hungry. As Naomi Klein critically notes, US-led sanctions placed restrictions on Iraq's economy that resulted in a loss for its society.[25] The highly unregulated neoliberal invasion and statebuilding venture starved the Iraqi state, with 30–40 percent remaining unemployed and reconstruction mostly entering the hands of contracted multinational firms rather than Iraq's firms or the public.[26] Therefore, it can be argued that the foreign armed intervention in the form of sanctions was still very punitive and a form of violence due to its severe impact on human security. Neoliberal reconstruction failed to curtail widespread poverty and unemployment due to endemic corruption. From an Afro-communitarian perspective, Western-led sanctions on Iraq were not modes of permissible violence to counter enmity-like violence because the Saddam Hussein regime was not imposing sanctions on the entire West.

[22] Allawi, *The Occupation of Iraq*, p. 114.

[23] United Nations Security Council Resolution 986, "Serious Nutritional and Health Situation of the Iraqi Population," UN Doc. S/RES/986, April 14, 1995, adopted 3519th meeting, para. 10.

[24] Sharon Otterman, "Iraq: Oil for Food Scandal," *Council on Foreign Relations*, October 28, 2005.

[25] Naomi Klein, *The Shock Doctrine: The Rise of Disaster Capitalism* (New York: Picador, 2007).

[26] Patrick Cockburn, *The Jihadis Return: ISIS and the New Sunni Uprising* (New York: OR Books, 2014).

US Foreign Policy: From Clinton's Containment to Bush's Neoconservatism

Now that an examination of the initial Gulf War and sanctions has been carried out, this section focuses on American foreign policy from the Clinton and Bush administrations. The former was based on containing Saddam and the latter on justifying a chosen war with the threat of WMD and Baghdad's allegiance with al-Qaeda.

The Remaining International Threat: The Clinton Years

In the late 1990s, many international observers advised to lift the sanctions despite Saddam failing to fully meet the multiple UN Security Council Resolutions on disarmament.[27] In December 1998, America conducted Operation Desert Fox, comprising four-day strikes on WMD sites, which resulted in the departure of UN weapons inspectors.[28] Clinton wanted regime change in Iraq with the 1998 Iraq Liberation Act, namely, sanctions, but it became more aggressive with the succeeding Bush administration.[29] Clinton merely aimed to destabilize Saddam with determent, containment, and international pressure via multilateral cooperation and role of international institutions, but did not believe that Iraq should be invaded.[30] The Operation also aimed to encourage internal change to overthrow Saddam;[31] but internal opponents were defeated by Saddam's forces.

The Neoconservative Republican Bush Administration: Inspecting the WMD Program

When Bush ran for his initial term in January 2001, which was eight months prior to 9/11, the Bush administration in the National Security Council swore to remove Saddam from power.[32] Clinton was criticized for

[27] Nancy Soderberg, *The Superpower Myth: The Use and Misuse of American Might* (Hoboken, NJ: John Wiley and Sons, 2005), pp. 205–206.

[28] The UN weapons inspectors returned in 2002 when war was likely.

[29] The Bush administration wanted an invasion as a response to 9/11 and the American-led war against terror that advocated regime change of rogue states in the Middle East.

[30] William Jefferson Clinton, *My Life* (New York: Vintage, 2005), p. 778.

[31] Allawi, *The Occupation of Iraq*, p. 71.

[32] Julian Borger, "Bush Decided to Remove Saddam 'On Day One,'" *The Guardian*, January 12, 2004; Ron Suskind, *The One Percent Doctrine: Deep inside America's Pursuit of Its Enemies since 9/11* (New York: Simon and Schuster, 2007), p. 26.

multilateralism and the successive government was pressurized to adopt unilateralism as part of its foreign policy because America was in a position to do so after the Cold War. It has thus cynically been argued that the invasion of Iraq marked US hegemonic power as part of "military interventions by liberal states," forcing foreign-based "democracy promotion…at gunpoint."[33] In other words, liberal ideals were being pressed with violent and punitive measures. The United States National Security Strategy identified that failing fragile states impose a high threat to American national security.[34] It was advocated that economic globalization and democratization could bring stability and international peace to overcome the instability of weak and failed states, thus protecting the United States from external threats.[35] Although Bush and his administration mostly denied forcing democracy in Iraq, the National Security Strategy fully planned the intervention on the liberal peace (rapid democratization and marketization) in which the American government attempted to blend militarization with statebuilding.[36]

Even though the United States and Iraq exercised rationality in going to war, there were "cognitive biases" and "self-delusions" that informed decision-making.[37] This was largely based on miscalculations of costs from the Bush administration and the move away from Clinton's containment policy. Solely relying on containment did not continue because Paul Dundes Wolfowitz, the then US Deputy Defense Secretary, believed it was costly and the Bush administration claimed that sanctions were futile.[38] Wolfowitz claimed that it was "9/11" that framed American foreign policy for "a second war…in the context of dealing with terrorism."[39] It was also

[33] Jeffrey Pickering and Mark Peceny, "Forging Democracy at Gunpoint," *International Studies Quarterly*, Vol. 50, No. 3 (September 2006), p. 556.

[34] United States National Security Council, *The National Security Strategy*, September 2002.

[35] Jeremy M. Weinstein, John Edward Porter, and Stuart E. Eizenstat, *On the Brink: Weak States and US National Security*, Commission for Weak States and US National Security, *Center for Global Development*, July 19, 2005, pp. 6–7.

[36] Federation of American Scientists—Intelligence Resource Program, *National Security Presidential Directive 24* (Washington, DC: The White House, January 20, 2003), pp. 1–2.

[37] Lake, "Two Cheers for Bargaining Theory," p. 9.

[38] Thomas Edwin Ricks, *Fiasco: The American Military Adventure in Iraq* (New York: The Penguin Press, 2006), pp. 17–18.

[39] Shamiran Mako and Alistair D. Edgar, "Evaluating the Pitfalls of External Statebuilding in Post-2003 Iraq (2003–2021)," *Journal of Intervention and Statebuilding*, Vol. 15, No. 4 (August 2021), p. 427.

wrongly estimated that the United States would manage the costs of the intervention in Iraq. Naively, Wolfowitz believed that the increase of Iraqi oil revenues projected to earn US $50–100 billion over the initial few years would "finance its own reconstruction."[40] Richard Norman Perle, the then Chair of the United States Defense Advisory Board, and Cheney, Vice President at the time, believed that the United States would be heralded as liberators by the Iraqis and fighting would cease once Saddam was deposed.[41] Therefore, the United States Defense Department included neoconservatives, such as Paul Wolfowitz and Richard Perle (Donald Rumsfeld's Secretary of Defense key advisor), motivating the rapid democratization of Iraq and regime change.[42]

Consequently, Bush and his Republican hawks prescribed neoconservatism to create a stable democracy in Iraq to contain terrorism, undermine Islamic fundamentalism, and avoid another rogue regime.[43] Neoconservatives believed that terrorism could be contained and authoritarianism transferred to liberal democracies.[44] According to Francis Fukuyama, long-term stability in the Middle East was required by promoting democracy to deter terrorism, instability, and failed states.[45] David Kay, the initial chair of the Iraq Survey Group, had sparked the fear of Saddam possibly selling WMD to a "more dangerous" state and stated that the world would be "far safer with the … removal of Saddam Hussein."[46] Even though Kay did not postulate a clear connection between WMD and terrorism, he suggested that many terrorist organizations and individuals had traveled through Iraq.[47] The neoconservative ideology construed that Saddam would destabilize the Middle East and North Africa region with

[40] Paul Dundes Wolfowitz, "Questions for Paul Wolfowitz," *Center for American Progress*, April 20, 2004.

[41] Lake, "Two Cheers for Bargaining Theory," p. 36.

[42] Ivo H. Daalder and James M. Lindsay, *America Unbound: The Bush Revolution in Foreign Policy* (Washington, DC: Brookings Institution Press, 2003), pp. 46–47.

[43] Lake, "Two Cheers for Bargaining Theory," p. 18. Even though some Iraqis supported the removal of Saddam for Ahmed Abdel Hadi Chalabi of the Iraqi National Congress and Prime Minister Nouri al-Maliki, the support later deteriorated (Toby Dodge, "State and Society in Iraq Ten Years after Regime Change: The Rise of a New Authoritarianism," *International Affairs*, Vol. 89, No.2 (March 2013), pp. 241–257).

[44] Francis Fukuyama, *State Building: Governance and World Order in the Twenty-First Century* (London: Profile Book, 2004).

[45] Fukuyama, *State Building*.

[46] David Kay, "David Kay Testifies Before Senate Committee," *CNN*, January 28, 2004.

[47] Kay, "David Kay Testifies Before Senate Committee."

WMD and his support for international terrorists.[48] Based on this premise, Iraq was an allegedly corrupt and chaotic government that was conducive toward terrorists accessing WMD via trading, so the United States pitched that it had no alternative option than war.[49]

Despite the presentation of intelligence regarding a non-operational or severely inhibited WMD program in Iraq throughout the 1990s, the July 7, 2005, London public transport bombings and rise of al-Qaeda in Iraq (re)marketed a liberal strategic discourse for war to challenge heightened terrorism.[50] The Bush administration referred to the wars sought by Saddam against Iran in the 1980s and Kuwait in the early 1990s that killed many Iraqi citizens.[51] It was also argued that Saddam had initially sponsored Middle East state terrorism since 1979, abused the Biological and Toxin Weapons Convention and Nuclear Nonproliferation Treaty by pursuing and using WMD on regional foes and own civilians, and violated no-fly zones.[52] Therefore, the liberal narrative emphasized that Saddam held a tyrannous regime and even when he was deposed, the increased threats of terrorism justified America's-led foreign armed intervention. Instead of a direct war to change Saddam's regime and create a democracy, the United States could have supported a minority group such as the Kurds, Shiites, or another anti-Ba'ath faction to overthrow Saddam Hussein with fewer financial, military, legal, and internal costs.

However, Bush and his bullish Republican hawks desired a war to show that America would use robust military force to obtain its geopolitical interests—as part of an inevitable conquering of Iraq due to no alternative bargain. The Bush administration would gain political glory for a military win over Iraq, but it was the US public that paid higher costs with military lives lost and the increase of taxes paid to fund the war.[53] Bush had already shown the United States military might when quickly deposing the Taliban in late 2001 in Afghanistan.

[48] Ahsan I. Butt, "Why Did the United States Invade Iraq in 2003?" *Security Studies*, Vol. 28, No. 2 (January 2019), pp. 250–285.

[49] Gordon Guthrie Chang, Kerstin Lueck, and Hugh Bud Mehan, "Evidencing International Threat: Examining Iraq Survey Group's Post-Invasion Verification of Iraq's WMD Threat," Vol. 12, No. 1 (January 2013), pp. 35–37.

[50] C. William Walldorf Jr., "Narratives and War: Explaining the Length and End of US Military Operations in Afghanistan," *International Security*, Vol. 47, No. 1 (July 2022), p. 110.

[51] Feith, *War and Decision*, p. 181.

[52] Feith, *War and Decision*, pp. 14, 52.

[53] Lake, "Two Cheers for Bargaining Theory," p. 17.

After 9/11, the Republican hawks of the Bush administration believed Iraq had some involvement in the terrorist attacks, including ties with al-Qaeda, and called for Baghdad's regime change once more. The terrorist attacks were met with anger and a premise that the United States could not politically encounter another attack of that magnitude. The Bush administration contended that the Iraq invasion was justified due to their potential threat by leading the American public to believe Saddam was creating WMD and was largely supporting al-Qaeda.[54] Dick Cheney claimed that it would be foolish for the United States to wait a few years to invade Iraq because Saddam could develop more sophisticated, and potentially nuclear, weapons by then.[55] At this point, Cheney initiated the 1 percent doctrine that a WMD or its proliferation would be catastrophic for America.[56] Similarly, the United States ex-Under-Secretary for Defense, Douglas Fein, argued that Saddam could have grown stronger and more assertive within the Persian Gulf region with better capability of WMD to attack Kuwait so postponement of war was not possible.[57] Therefore, the United States opted for enmity-like violence via foreign armed intervention to counter a small chance of further terrorist attacks against them.

Although the United States claimed that it held no oil interests in Iraq prior to its invasion and that it aimed to foster peace and stability in the Persian Gulf by eliminating the possibility of WMD, many international observers have argued that the United States intended to reassert control by increasing Iraq's production of oil to lower prices.[58] America declared its fight against international terrorism and it was contested whether the United States later intended to establish a democratic regime in Iraq. The United States allegedly held interests in Iraq for its rich oil reserves. America deployed 100,000 forces near Iraq and called for 75,000 troops to enter the country. Therefore, the reasons for the invasion were to promote the liberalization of Iraq's oil reserves and maintenance of America's world powerhouse status.[59]

[54] Steven Kull, Clay Ramsay and Evan Lewis, "Misperceptions, the Media, and the Iraq War," *Political Science Quarterly*, Vol. 118, No. 4 (2003–04), p. 569.

[55] Richard Bruce Cheney, "Meet the Press: Interview with Vice-President Dick Cheney," *NBC*, March 16, 2003.

[56] Suskind, *The One Percent Doctrine*, p. 62.

[57] Douglas Jay Feith, *War and Decision: Inside the Pentagon at the Dawn of the War on Terrorism* (New York: HarperCollins, 2008), p. 355.

[58] Anas F. Alhajji, "US Energy Policy and the Invasion of Iraq: Does Oil Matter?" *The Journal of Energy and Development*, Vol. 29, No. 2 (Spring 2004), p. 209.

[59] Michael T. Klare, "For Oil and Empire? Rethinking War with Iraq," *Current History*, Vol. 102, No. 662 (March 2003), pp. 129–132.

In May 2002, the United States government wanted war with Iraq to oust Saddam from power. Bush labeled Saddam evil and untrustworthy. As part of the discourse on the war against terror, 'evil' actors such as Afghanistan and Iraq threatened good democratic states, which made the invasions of Afghanistan and Iraq politically viable.[60] In late 2002, the US Department of State and Working Group on Oil and Energy created provisions to privatize Iraqi oil once Saddam was replaced with a new cooperative regime.[61] The Navy Seals captured two oil terminals in Iraq against lightly armed Iraqi Republican Guards. It could be argued that the Bush administration wanted control over Iraq's oil industry for the offering of US energy firms. Iraqi boasted the second highest reserves of orthodox petroleum with "reserves of 112 billion of crude oil" and there were still many unexplored oil reservoirs.[62] The former Minister for Oil in Iraq, Ahmad Abdel Hadi Chalabi, met with senior officials of leading American oil companies and additional American-supported Iraqi expatriates a few months prior to the invasion to privatize the oil sector once Saddam was ousted.[63] Bordering oil-rich countries in the Persian Gulf would provide the United States with most of the global oil supply.[64] It was clear that the US-led foreign armed intervention preserved the discourse of democratizing and liberating Iraq, while downplaying oil motives. As argued by Singh, the objectives of liberating and democratizing Iraq were for the ulterior motive of liberalizing and privatizing oil for the benefit of Western countries, which was largely proven by the lack of evidence for the pursuit of a robust WMD program.[65]

Prior to the invasion, Saddam Hussein was unclear about demolishing "WMD programs," which resulted in a "high risk of" war with America to deter opposition from Kurdish and Shiite minorities and regional rival states, particularly Iran, and potentially Israel.[66] If Saddam had conceded

[60] Adam Hodges, *The "War on Terror" Narrative: Discourse and Intertextuality in the Construction and Contestation of Sociopolitical Reality* (New York: Oxford University Press, 2011), pp. 23–40.

[61] Klare, "Blood for Oil, in Iraq and Elsewhere," pp. 129–130.

[62] Dan Morgan and David B. Ottaway, "In Iraq War Scenario, Oil Is Key Issue," *The Washington Post*, September 15, 2002.

[63] Michael T. Klare, "It's the Oil, Stupid," *The Nation*, April 24, 2003.

[64] Nayna J. Jhaveri, "Pretoimperialism: US Oil Interests and the Iraq War," *Antipode*, Vol. 36, No. 1 (January 2004), pp. 2–11.

[65] Singh, "Undertaking Critical Legal Theory," pp. 73–74.

[66] Lake, "Two Cheers for Bargaining Theory," pp. 9, 29.

to the Americans, then Washington would have had little ground to continue with its war; moreover, America's invasion would have been constituted as clear aggression. When the United States wanted to enforce a settlement in Iraq by declaring victory, the costs were not fully considered that might have resulted in the Bush government avoiding its preventive war with Iraq. If Iraq did not have a WMD, the United States would have easily won the war and would have still probably won if it had, but there would have been higher costs and less certainty of military victory. The United States engaged with the preventive war that did not attain the legitimacy of the United Nations or support from the international community and failed to prove the existence of active WMD in Iraq.[67] The preventive war in Iraq could have been avoided because the costs were high for both sides. The settlement, post-war reconstruction, and governance need to be considered. The Bush administration made errors with the threat of WMD and Saddam did not want to fully declare that Baghdad did not have aspirations for a WMD program, and thus these factors increased the likelihood of war.

The alleged WMD programs promoted by Iraq provoked and justified a response from the United States, but this failed bargaining theory because it did not constitute the main motives of war.[68] However, President Bush stated that America would invade Iraq to take "necessary actions international terrorists and terrorist organizations, including those nations, organizations, or persons who planned, authorized, committed, or aided the terrorist attacks that occurred on September 11, 2001."[69] Therefore, America was planning to wage war on Iraq.

The number of US troops estimated for the Iraq war was very low and was accepted by the public, the media, and political elites.[70] The United States did not obtain permission from the United Nations Security Council to wage war on Iraq. In a study conducted with 3262 Chicago residents via phone and interviews from June 1 to June 30, 2002, 65 percent of the sample stated that an invasion would be viable if supported by the United Nations and American allies.[71] The American public were initially behind the invasion, and the full destruction, of Iraq.

[67] Lake, "Two Cheers for Bargaining Theory," p. 16.

[68] Lake, "Two Cheers for Bargaining Theory," p. 14.

[69] George Walker Bush, "Presidential Letter to Congress," March 18, 2003.

[70] Stiglitz and Barnes, *The Three Trillion Dollar War*, p. 124.

[71] Chicago Council on Foreign Relations, *Worldviews 2002: American Public Opinion & Foreign Policy* (Chicago, IL: Chicago Council on Foreign Relations, June 2002), p. 27.

2003 Invasion of Iraq, the Duelfer Report, and Remaining Terrorist Threat

On March 19, 2003, the United States aerially bombed Iraq and invaded on the ground a day later with a combination of US, UK, Polish, and Australian forces. On April 9, 2003, the coalition forces, under Operation Iraqi Freedom (OIF), seized Baghdad (after a six-day fight). During this battle, more than 2000 Iraqi armed forces and 34 coalition forces were killed. The coalition ousted the Saddam Hussein administration from power in under three weeks, with only a few US military casualties, and the British forces captured Basra with few killed and wounded.[72] President Bush declared victory on May 1, 2003, to signal the triumph of the United States-led coalition of the over 170,000 deployed forces (comprising 130,000 American, 45,000 British, 2000 Australian, and 194 Polish troops).

After major combat operations ceased on May 1, 2003, Iraq became a hub for international statebuilding interventionism, without United Nations Security Council authorization under Chapter VII of the Charter of the United Nations.[73] The reasons why the resistance from Iraq was so weak rests on several main factors. This fragility included Saddam miscalculating international threats due to the fixation on internal threats; inferior equipment and a weak military strategy (including the lack of erected barricades in major cities); poor motivation and desertion within the Republican Guard, Special Republican Guard, and Iraqi Regular Army units; and greater US military capability.[74] Saddam prioritized his focus on a potential internal coup from a Shiite revolt, other domestic security problems, and the eight-year fight with Iran.[75] Moreover, once the US

[72] Jerry M. Sollinger, Laurinda L. Rohn, Richard E. Darilek and Walt L. Perry, *Operation Iraqi Freedom: Decisive War, Elusive Peace* (Santa Monica, CA: RAND Corporation, 2015), pp. 1–5.

[73] Roberto Belloni and Irene Costantini, "From Liberal Statebuilding to Counterinsurgency and Stabilization: The International Intervention in Iraq," *Ethnopolitics*, Vol. 18, No. 5 (July 2019), p. 509.

[74] Stephen T. Hosner, *Why the Iraqi Resistance to the Coalition Invasion was so Weak* (Santa Monica, CA: RAND Corporation, 2007), pp. ix–xiv.

[75] Michael R. Gordon and Bernard E. Trainor, *Cobra II: The Inside Story of the Invasion and Occupation of Iraq* (New York: Pantheon, 2006), p. 55.

forces arrived in Baghdad, the majority of Iraq's armed forces had deserted their barracks and fled to their homes.[76]

Saddam convened senior officials to cooperate and permit UN weapons inspectors access in December 2002,[77] but US suspicion was already too high due to Saddam previously failing to let Washington know that Iraq had no intention of WMD development. The United Nations inspection team chaired by Hans Martin Blix, a Swedish diplomat, stated that it had not discovered WMD.[78] To rectify these efforts of UN Security Council Resolution 1441 that deployed UN weapons inspectors that did not find any concrete WMD or weapons stockpiles,[79] the Duelfer Report issued the findings of an American-led WMD fact-finding mission, called the Iraq Survey Group. The Group was established by the United States Department of Defense and CIA. The Iraq Survey Group was initially headed by the late David Kay and began its search in May 2003. While the Oil-for-Food Program had been terminated and arms embargoes were uplifted, the United States, the United Kingdom, and Northern Ireland had been recognized with international legitimacy as "occupying powers under unified command (the 'Authority')" to create stability, security and an effective administration."[80] The Iraq Survey Group issued its first report in October 2003. Kay claimed that the Iraq Survey Group did not discover "stocks of weapons," but found "dozens of WMD-related program activities." Moreover, concealement from the Saddam regime was found. This included the destruction of hard drives and documents. It was speculated that Iraq may have been planning biological wartime practices.[81]

However, no weapons stockpiles were mentioned in later reports and Kay stated that WMD stockpiles would never be discovered.[82] There was only a program for a long-range missile but there was no clear evidence of

[76] Alpaslan Özerdem, "Insurgency, Militias, and DDR as Part of Security Sector Reconstruction in Iraq: How Not to Do It," *Disasters*, Vol. 43, S1 (January 2010), p. S46.

[77] Lake, "Two Cheers for Bargaining Theory," p. 29.

[78] Hans Martin Blix, "UN Inspectors Found no Evidence of Prohibited Weapons Programs as of March 18 Withdrawal, Hans Blix tells Security Council," *United Nations Security Council Press Release*, SC/7777, June 5, 2003.

[79] UN Security Council Resolution 1441, "The Situation between Iraq and Kuwait," UN Doc. S/RES/1441, November 8, 2002, adopted 4644th meeting.

[80] UN Security Council Resolution 1483, "The Situation between Iraq and Kuwait," UN Doc. S/RES/1483, May 22, 2003, adopted 4761st meeting, paras. 4, 10, 16.

UN Security Council Resolution 1441, "The Situation between Iraq and Kuwait," UN Doc. S/RES/1441, November 8, 2002, adopted 4644th meeting.

[81] David Kay, "Text of David Kay's Unclassified Statement," *CNN*, October 2, 2003.

[82] Chang, Lueck and Mehan, "Evidencing International Threat," p. 32.

a WMD or scientists and plants producing biological, chemical, or nuclear weapons.[83] Kay then resigned for unclear reasons and was replaced by Charles A. Duelfer, but Donald Henry Rumsfeld, the Secretary of Defense, claimed that WMD stockpiles might still be discovered.[84]

Several months later, the Iraq Survey Group closed investigations when all sites were searched and found nothing under the leadership of Duelfer and delivered the findings in late September 2004. The Report was formally released a month later, one month prior to the Presidential Election, and it dismissed all preceding suspicions.

Therefore, like the UN, the Iraq Survey Group did not find physical WMD, but US politicians, including President Bush and Secretary of State Colin Luther Powell, claimed there was an international threat.[85] The efforts of Saddam's cooperation "was too little, too late," with Powell claiming that Iraq was transporting missiles and chemical weapons around Iraq to evade inspectors and held 8500 liters of anthrax.[86] Although Powell claimed that the United States administration had got the accusations of Iraq possessing WMD stockpiles and weapons wrong, he stressed that the "intention" and "the capability" were "retained" while Saddam was cheating to relinquish sanctions.[87]

Similarly, after the reported findings of the Iraq Survey Group, President Bush stressed that America did not find WMD, but Saddam reserved "the capability of making WMD…and "could have passed that capability onto an enemy," which "is a risk" not worth taking "after September the 11th."[88] Bush further elucidated that "Saddam" was "trying to" eradicate "sanctions so he could reconstitute a weapons program" with "the biggest threat facing America" being "terrorists with weapons of mass

[83] David Kay, "David Kay: Exclusive Interview by Tom Brokaw," *Nightly News with Brian Williams*, *NBC*, January 26, 2004.

[84] Chang, Lueck and Mehan, "Evidencing International Threat," p. 32.

[85] Chang, Lueck and Mehan, "Evidencing International Threat," p. 30.

[86] Adrian R. Lewis, *The American Culture of War: The History of United States Military Force from World War II to Operation Enduring Freedom* (New York: Routledge, 2012), p. 430.

[87] Colin Luther Powell, "Although No WMD Found, Saddam Had Intent, Capability, Powell Says," Interview of Secretary of State Colin L. Powell by Warren Strobel of Knight-Ridder, *Global Security*, October 8, 2004.

[88] George Walker Bush, "Remarks by the President at Victory 2004 Rally," *Weekly Compilations of Presidential Documents*, Vol. 40, No. 41 (October 1, 2004), pp. 2209–2216.

destruction."[89] It can be argued that the existential threat of a WMD or functional weapons stockpiles was not discovered in Iraq in material terms, but the international threat was constructed by discourse.[90] At this point in time, Saddam believed that international law—the legality of the war—would prevail because the United States had not attained multilateral backing at the United Nations Security Council and relied on France and Russia to veto America.[91]

Although the inspectors deployed by the United States could not find any evidence to infer a robust WMD program, the 900-page Duelfer Report was issued. The Report supplemented the Republican discourse prior to the 2004 US Presidential Election in which Bush sought a second term in office. The Report thus remained sympathetic to the Bush administration insofar as its conclusion of Saddam Hussein controlling all the strategic decisions for the regime with a main objective from 1991 to 2003 to uplift UN sanctions, while preserving the regime.[92] Despite a lack of evidence, the fear remained of Iraq developing a WMD or sharing technologies with transnational terrorists.[93] A regression analysis study found that Bush lost almost 2 percent of the domestic popular vote in the 2004 election due to the estimated 10,000 US military deaths and injuries.[94] It was the future WMD and both military and technological capabilities of Iraq rather than the suspicion of a preexisting WMD program that committed the Bush administration to war with Iraq,[95] which still held sufficient public support. The WMD allows bargaining from US coercion, which is why Iran has advanced its nuclear programs.

The United States may have reduced likely threats in the Middle East for America and its allies, but the Iraq War has had catastrophic results. The casualties reached an estimated 100,000 fatalities with thousands

[89] George Walker Bush, "The Second Bush-Kerry Presidential Debate," *Commission on Presidential Debates*, October 8, 2004.

[90] Chang, Lueck and Mehan, "Evidencing International Threat," p. 29.

[91] Kevin M. Woods with Michael R. Pease, Mark E. Stout, Williamson Murray, and James G. Lacey, *Iraqi Perspectives Project: A View of Operation Iraqi Freedom from Saddam's Senior Leadership* (Norfolk: VI: The Joint Center for Operational Analysis, 2006), p. 28.

[92] Charles A. Duelfer, *Comprehensive Report of the Special Advisor to the DCI on Iraq's WMD, with Addendums (Duelfer Report)* (Langley, VA: Executive Agency Publications), April 25, 2005.

[93] Lake, "Two Cheers for Bargaining Theory," p. 23.

[94] David Karol and Edward Miguel, "The Electoral Cost of War: Iraq Casualties and the 2004 US Presidential Election," *The Journal of Politics*, Vol. 69, No. 3 (August 2007), p. 633.

[95] Lake, "Two Cheers for Bargaining Theory," p. 24.

displaced from March 2003 to September 2004.[96] It was deemed a preventive war that cost millions of US dollars, led to over 4500 American and coalition casualties, and formed further "anti-Americanism."[97] The US foreign armed intervention failed to establish an effective democratic governance, and also exacerbated hostility toward the West in Iraq and shortcomings in the Middle East.[98] Once the Sunni-dominated Ba'ath party was ousted from power, it was wrongly predicted by US and British politicians that religious or ethnic conflict would be an issue in Iraq. Dan Reiter has tested the rationalist doctrine on war, or what can be referred to as 'bargaining theory' to explain the war.[99] It covers the strategic aspects of war to consider the unavoidable costs of conflict and explain why countries still engage in war when tasked with settling "disagreements."[100] Quite similar to Afro-communitarian ethics, bargaining theory seeks alternatives to war due to its costs. The "strategic interactions" of bargaining theory resulted in America's incursion of Iraq in March 2003. However, the war comprising the United States (and its coalition forces) against Iraq cannot be explained by bargaining theory. The United States did not solely invade Iraq to tap the oil industry and businesses like Exxon Mobil and Halliburton.

The Coalition Provisional Authority, the 'Surge,' and Private Military Contractors

As part of post-war governance in Iraq, the United States headed an understaffed Office for Reconstruction and Humanitarian Affairs (ORHA). Jay Montgomery Garner was in charge and only $25,000 was provided to rebuild Iraqi ministries.[101] The ORHA was replaced by the Coalition Provisional Authority chaired by Ambassador Lewis Paul

[96] Gilbert Burnham, Riyadh Lafta, Shannon Doocy, and Les Roberts, "Mortality after the 2003 Invasion of Iraq: A Cross-section Cluster Sample Survey," *The Lancet*, October 12, 2006, p. 1421.

[97] Lake, "Two Cheers for Bargaining Theory," p. 7.

[98] Belloni and Costantini, "From Liberal Statebuilding to Counterinsurgency and Stabilization," p. 511.

[99] Dan Reiter, "Exploring the Bargaining Model of War," *Perspectives on Politics*, Vol. 1, No. 1 (March 2003), pp. 27–43.

[100] Lake, "Two Cheers for Bargaining Theory," p. 8.

[101] George Packer, *The Assassin's Gate: America in Iraq* (Waterville, ME: Thorndike Press, 2006), p. 143.

Bremer III. The United States handpicked Iraqi leaders who had no backing or public support.[102] These exiled Iraqi elites who led the Authority resulted in the creation of fragile and weak political institutions, ethnic and sectarian fractionalization, and reemerging authoritarianism.[103] This resulted in the ethnic preferences of elites wanting to retain their power after Saddam was deposed.[104] From the outset of the war, rapid liberalization of capital markets left an unregulated economy, and a destructive state.[105] Oil and foreign companies were involved, and with a puppet government, the Iraqi people distrusted the Americans.[106]

Alongside security issues, the political system was in turmoil. Since 2003, Sunni Arabs had been politically excluded due to the legacy of de-Ba'athification and exclusive ethnic consociational power-sharing agreements.[107] The political sectarianized consociational power-sharing system sparked Iraqi public protests from October 2019.[108] In 2019, only 13 percent of Iraqi civilians displayed trust in the parliament and 52 percent claimed that democratic regimes have failed to preserve stability and order.[109]

The Surge and Rise of Private Military Contractors

The hunt for Saddam Hussein continued and efforts to curtail terrorism signaled US foreign policy and its national security interests. On December 30, 2006, under Operation Red Dawn, Saddam Hussein was captured, tried, and hanged for crimes against humanity at the Iraqi Special Tribunal.[110] From January 10, 2007 to July 2008, the United States implemented the New Way Forward (known as the Surge). This strategy headed by General David Petraeus comprised a more robust and coherent

[102] Klein, *The Shock Doctrine.*

[103] Mako and Edgar, "Evaluating the Pitfalls of External Statebuilding in Post-2003," p. 426.

[104] Allawi, *The Occupation of Iraq*, p. 8.

[105] Wozniak, "Iraq's Neoliberal Reconstruction," p. 368.

[106] Wozniak, "Iraq's Neoliberal Reconstruction," p. 366.

[107] Toby Dodge, "The Failure of Peacebuilding in Iraq: The Role of Consociationalism and Political Settlements," *Journal of Intervention and Statebuilding*, Vol. 15, No. 3 (August 2021), pp. 459–475.

[108] Mako and Edgar, "Evaluating the Pitfalls of External Statebuilding in Post-2003 Iraq," p. 425.

[109] Arab Barometer Index V, *Iraq Country Report*, 2019, p. 9.

[110] Simon Cottle, *Global Crisis Reporting: Journalism in the Global Age* (Maidenhead, Berkshire: Open University Press, 2009), p. 5.

plan with over 20,000 additional soldiers, including five brigades, to deal with the increase of insurgencies.[111] The 'Surge' endeavored to curtail the activity of terrorist groups, which resulted in an instant 43 percent increase in violence.[112] The total number of US troops during the Surge amounted to 168,000 at its peak until November 2007 when a troop withdrawal commenced once violence had decreased. The insurgencies included Shia insurgents—the Mahdi Army, Special Groups, and Asa'ib Ahl al-Haq—and Sunni insurgents—Islamic State of Iraq, Ansaru al-Sunnah, and the Islamic Army in Iraq. The purpose was for Iraq to defend itself and retain its alliance in the war against terror by securing neighborhoods and ensuring that Iraq's armed forces would secure the state once the United States left. The Surge was a renewed military victory and thus US disengagement could be planned with the cessation of Operation Iraqi Freedom, resulting in the withdrawal of US troops to leave Iraq in charge of its own security.[113]

Despite the belated efforts of the Surge, it can be contended that post-war peace in Iraq was costly and the situation in Iraq post-2003 was in a less harmonious state of affairs due to the sharp rise in militias and insurgencies. The public eventually turned sour on the war with "No blood for oil!" chants and there were allegations of the Halliburton oil firm truly profiting from the war.[114]

After the alleged success of the Surge in decreasing violence in Iraq, foreign armed intervention remained. Many oil companies and military contractors profited from the Iraq war, but the United States did not gain as much. Approximately 180,000 private military contractors (PMCs) were operational in Iraq, with 355 US PMC deaths, 58 British, and 130 Turkish. Blackwater Worldwide attained a lucrative $21 million contract in 2003 for protecting Ambassador Bremer, the leader of the CPA. In 2007, four Blackwater Worldwide contractors were found guilty of killing 14 unarmed and injuring 17 Iraqi civilians at Nisour Square, Baghdad, but were pardoned of multiple war crimes on December 22, 2020, by the then

[111] Danny Singh, *Investigating Corruption in the Afghan Police Force: Instability and Insecurity in Post-conflict Societies* (Bristol: Policy Press, 2020), p. 61.

[112] Hall Gardner, *Averting Global War: Regional Challenges, Overextension, and Options for American Strategy* (New York: Palgrave Macmillan, 2007), p. 73.

[113] Helene Cooper and Sheryl Gay Stolberg, "Obama Declares and End to Combat Mission in Iraq," *New York Times*, August 31, 2010.

[114] Von Cordula Meyer, "A Lot of Blood for Little Oil," *Spiegel International*, December 6, 2010.

US President, Donald John Trump.[115] Since the weakening of the Islamic State from the Surge, several splinter groups have emerged that function in the Middle East and Asia. These include the Khorasan Chapter that has been active since 2015 in Afghanistan, Iran, Pakistan, and India.[116] From an Afro-communitarian perspective, hostilities escalated and the foreign armed intervention, with the addition of PMCs, failed to counter enmity-like violence from growing regional insurgencies with arms because innocent civilians were also targeted.

Sectarian Violence, the Growth of the Islamic State, and Iraq's Regional Weakness

After the war, Iraq remained plagued by prevalent corruption, sectarian violence, and a deeply opposed Iraqi administration.[117] Similar to the Taliban in Afghanistan, the Islamic State have exploited an absent government, inadequate and corrupt policing (partially due to underpaid police officers, ghost police officers, inadequate training, patronage, and nepotism), dubious PMCs, and weak resources to develop bases in Iraq.[118] Due to weak resourcing, the Americans decided to disband the Iraqi Armed Forces, via Bremer's Order Number 2, which made 400,000 ex-Iraqi soldiers unemployed.[119] Moreover, the then Prime Minister, Nouri Kamil Muhammad-Hasan al-Maliki, considered the demobilization of the Arab Sunni tribal fighters who fought al-Qaeda, thwarting the disarmament and reintegration process.[120] The legality of the sudden disbandment to pave the way for newly trained Iraqi security forces created a movement of dissatisfied and armed youth for militias that retained public legitimacy.[121]

[115] United Nations Human Rights Office of the High Commissioner, "US Pardons for Blackwater Guards an 'Affront to Justice' – UN Experts," December 30, 2020.

[116] Center for Strategic and International Studies, "Islamic State Khorasan (IS-K)," 2018.

[117] Lake, "Two Cheers for Bargaining Theory," p. 19.

[118] Braithwaite, John and Ali Wardak. "Crime and War in Afghanistan: Part I: The Hobbesian Solution." *British Journal of Criminology*, Vol. 53, No. 2 (March 2013), pp. 181, 187–188; Singh, *Investigating Corruption in the Afghan Police Force*, pp. 62, 65, 131, 161, 171, 182.

[119] Lewis Paul Bremer III, "Coalition Provisional Authority Order Number 2: Dissolution of Entities," May 23, 2003.

[120] Al-Marashi, "Demobilization Minus Disarmament and Reintegration."

[121] James Jimmy Smith, "Reconsidering the Role of Militias in Iraq," *Combatting Terrorism Center Sentinel*, Vol. 2, No. 1 (January 2009), pp. 1–3.

This exclusion undermined SSR, leaving a security vacuum for the Islamic State to control large parts of Iraq.

The United States-led coalition anticipated futile resistance, but after years of war, it failed to establish law, order, and authority across Iraq.[122] The underestimation of liberating Iraqis with little effort and cost from the American political elite to the US armed forces transformed crime, looting, and violence into a politically and organized "motivated insurgency."[123] To provide another example, the initially trained Iraqi Security Forces and the Peshmerga clashed, which was evident in the Kurds' referendum for independence on September 25, 2017. The Global Coalition adopted counterterrorism but still failed at effective governance, which is why the Islamic State appeared to fill the security and service void that the CPA and state could not. Hence, the 2003 invasion permitted the rise of militias, and the state security forces did little due to externally driven SSR,[124] and the adoption of a mistrusted political system preferring a group of American-selected Iraqi exiles.

The United States then distanced itself from nation-building and left a quasi-state that resulted in problems such as appointing local Iraqis to the new police force due to a lack of trust and legitimacy of the Iraqi government.[125] High turnover rates were a consequence of distrust and high security risks that left a weak security sector and a power vacuum.[126] The power vacuum and lack of investment for Iraqi people left a state of crime, one the highest in the world, kidnappings, high unemployment of an estimated 75,000 (from the de-Ba'athification process), and weak basic social and health provision.[127] Due to a new weak police force in Iraq, violent non-state actors filled this security and state vacuum.[128]

[122] Adeed Dawisha, *Iraq: A Political History from Independence to Occupation* (Princeton, NJ: Princeton University Press, 2009).

[123] Toby Dodge, "Iraq's Future: The Aftermath of Regime Change," *Adelphi Paper*, 372 (London: Routledge, January 2005), p. 9.

[124] Ibrahim Al-Marashi, "Demobilization Minus Disarmament and Reintegration: Iraq's Security Sector from the United States Occupation to the Covid-19 Pandemic," *Journal of Intervention and Statebuilding*, Vol. 15, No. 4 (2021), pp. 441–458.

[125] Jesse S.G. Wozniak, "We are Going to Prove that We are a Civil and Developed Country: The Cultural Performance of Police Legitimacy and Empire in the Iraqi State," *The British Journal of Criminology*, Vol. 57, No. 4 (July 2017), pp. 906–923.

[126] Wozniak, "Iraq's Neoliberal Reconstruction," p. 366.

[127] Özerdem, "Insurgency, Militias, and DDR," p. S45.

[128] Jesse S.G. Wozniak, "Iraq and the Material Basis of Post-Conflict Police Reconstruction," *The Journal of Peace Research*, Vol. 54, No. 6 (September 2017), pp. 806–818. This also occurred in Sierra Leone.

The Islamic State appealed to disenfranchised communities by providing state-like security and welfare functions.[129] Partly due to the security vacuum and weak political reforms, the Islamic State developed from a segment of al-Qaeda that controlled large parts of Iraq and remains operational in rural Iraq. The Islamic State gained loyalty from followers and promoted resentment over the Shia-driven government and cooperation with America.[130] It developed state-like provision and services to develop its own state and consolidate power, thus reproducing power relations that neoliberal governance failed to create.[131] The Islamic State filled the power and state vacuum by providing resources and stipends for living costs in its controlled territories, and engaged in crime control due to poor state policing and the lack of public support for the political system.

In June 2014, Iraq's army collapsed and its second largest city, Mosul, was conquered by the Islamic State.[132] Consequently, the Iraqi state had to rely on militias to provide security.[133] This response to the Islamic State included the Iraqi state attempting to retake territories. Iraq supported Shia pro-Iranian factions, namely, the Popular Mobilization Forces (PMF), which included the Badr and Hezbollah Brigades, Asaib Ahl al-Haq, and Kata'ib Sayyid al-Shuhada, comprising an estimated 67 armed factions of 204,000 fighters to report to the federal government, but they remained aligned to Iran.[134] These militia groups have been accused of perpetrating human rights violations and sectarian violence, and the Kurds have clashed with these groups over territories.[135]

Moreover, Iran grew stronger and began to influence Iraq with the governance of al-Maliki (2006–2014) and encourage trading in the

[129] Achim Wennmann, "Getting Armed Groups to the Table: Peace Processes, the Political Economy of Conflict and the Mediated State," *Third World Quarterly*, Vol. 30, No.6 (July 2009), p. 1133.

[130] Mona Mahmood, "Life in Mosul One Year On: ISIS with All Its Brutality is More Honest than the Shia Government," *The Guardian*, June 10, 2015.

[131] Wozniak, "Iraq's Neoliberal Reconstruction."

[132] Ranj Alaaldin, *Containing Shiite Militias: The Battle for Stability in Iraq* (Washington, DC: Brookings Institution, 2017), p. 1.

[133] Mako and Edgar, "Evaluating the Pitfalls of External Statebuilding in Post-2003 Iraq," p. 434.

[134] Dilshad Hussein, "The Increase in the Number of Popular Mobilization Forces Members in Iraq 'Worries' Some People…Why?" *Irfaa Sawtak*, May 3, 2023.

[135] Human Rights Watch, "Iraq: Ban Abusive Militias from Mosul Operation," *Human Rights Watch*, July 31, 2016.

economy.[136] Hashd al-Shaabi remained loyal to Iran and responded to the Islamic State. To provide one example, Iran used Iraq's airspace in September 2012 to assist President Bashar Hafez al-Assad's regime in Syria even though the Secretary of State, John Kerry, opposed Iran's foothold in Iraq.[137]

Due to the weakness of Iraq, Iran and Saudi Arabia have competed in a new Arab Cold War and Iran and Russia have retained power in the Middle East and are resentful of US unilateralism and regime change. Russia and Iran are the major players that are supporting al-Assad and were against the foreign armed airstrikes in Libya in 2011, and the eventual toppling of Muammar Muhammad Abu Minyar al-Gaddafi. Russia and sometimes China veto interventions against the Syrian regime.

The United States imposed neoliberalist ideology in Iraq with the use of protracted force to create an "obedient client state."[138] This was not compliant with US national interests because America derailed the United Nations process, with Russia, France, and Germany opposing the incursion. Neoliberal markets were only accessible for firms with robust relationships with the newly devised coalition members.[139] Iran expanded its influence over the weakening Iraq that was captive to economic liberalization, resulting in eventual fragile public support and increasing oppositional Sunni-dominated insurgencies. Iraq has lost its previous status as a major power in the Middle East region.

Assessing Afro-communitarian Ethics in Iraq

The United States identified an enemy, Saddam Hussein and the Ba'ath party, and thus conducted violence to end that regime. Under Afro-communitarianism, the United States believed that it had exhausted sanctions on and disarmament of the totalitarian regime since the 1990s. Sanctions on Iraq in both Gulf wars resulted in an economic crisis and hunger and thus would constitute the initial stage of violence conducted by the United States.

[136] Belloni and Costantini, "From Liberal Statebuilding to Counterinsurgency and Stabilization," p. 511.

[137] John Forbes Kerry, "Speech at US Ambassador to Iraq Confirmation," *C-Span*, September 19, 2012.

[138] Wozniak, "Iraq's Neoliberal Reconstruction," p. 371.

[139] Julian Go, *The Patterns of Empire: The British and American Empires, 1688 to Present* (New York: Cambridge University Press, 2011).

Due to the ineffectiveness of sanctions to cripple the Saddam regime, Washington opted for violence in the form of sabotage (targeting the regime and its military infrastructure with aerial bombing to destroy Baghdad) and open revolution (to change the governance and head an interim government to democratize Iraq). Step-by-step violence was undertaken from the United States and its coalition forces—as the foreign armed intervention—in Iraq. Yet, the initiation of violence under Afro-communitarianism was not to oppose enmity-like violence because Saddam Hussein was not attacking America or engaging in a discordant state of affairs. The only premise to wage violence was based on loose and anecdotal information of Saddam having links with al-Qaeda that would have made the 1 percent risk doctrine of Iraq possessing a WMD—that could reach transnational terrorists to attack America and their democratic allies—feasible.

Although the foreign armed intervention in Iraq engaged with gradual increases of violence, which consequentialist Afro-communitarianism permits if its rules are met, the intervention did not counter violence. Instead, the incursion comprising the overthrow of Saddam Hussein, the de-Ba'athification process, interim government, and democratization intensified sectarian violence and gave rise to transnational terrorism (i.e., the Islamic State). Once Saddam Hussein was deposed from power and the de-Ba'athification process was implemented with an interim administration and election of a new political party, an exit strategy was not viable due to the spread of violence in Iraq. The eventual exit strategy resulted in a less harmonious state of affairs due to the emergence of the Islamic State to fill the political vacuum of weak governance. Hence, the foreign armed intervention conducted by the United States and its coalition forces did not create a more harmonious state of affairs.

It is clear that the extended intervention in Iraq was part of America's realist strategy to contain Iran (with its later international war against terrorism anecdotally accusing Saddam Hussein of supporting al-Qaeda) and prevent the small chance of Baghdad developing WMD and weapons stockpiles that could be intercepted by a transitional terrorist organization. The war on terror pretense was later attached to America's Iraq problem because in early 2001, Republican hawks wanted an intervention in Iraq. The intervention, and foreign armed intervention, did not have the objective of voluntarily making Iraq an amiable ally of America, but instead forced, and coerced, a new cooperative relationship for US security (and debatably economic) benefit. America wanted to contain Iraq and deter future authoritarianism to guarantee that Baghdad would never support terrorists. The outcome of US and coalition forces intervention in Iraq led to a more discordant state of affairs, although Baghdad's relationship with Washington has improved from relations under the authoritarian Ba'ath party. Democratic statebuilding was attempted by America to impart their version of social justice in Iraq that was part of neocolonialism and neoliberalist interests.

Afro-communitarians would be cynical of statebuilding projects because they represent the fabric of Western norms and undermine non-violent dialogue and merely facilitate a less harmonious state of affairs. When considering this Afro-communitarian perspective, it can be exhibited that US and coalition intervention was part of geopolitical interests and foreign policy rather than eradicating the unfriendly acts of Saddam Hussein (e.g., against the Kurdish community) as part of humanitarian intervention to bring a more harmonious state of affairs within the Gulf region. The United States wanted to challenge international terrorism, which Saddam had no real relationship with despite the allegations of him supporting al-Qaeda.

Legally, the March 2003 intervention did not consult the United Nations Security Council and thus was illegal under international law. Active WMD and the creation of new weapons stockpiles were not discovered in the United Nations and Duelfer reports. Saddam Hussein could not convey that he did not hold any powerful WMD to Washington because Iraq was frequently at war with neighboring Iran and internal political opponents posed a threat to the Ba'ath party. Like the legal and political outcomes, from an Afro-communitarian perspective, the foreign armed intervention in Iraq was morally impermissible because the intentions and outcomes were not to reach a more harmonious state of affairs with Iraq and the Gulf region. Rather, the incursion was heavily influenced from neoconservative misinterpretations of the United States Defense Department and advisors that wanted to rid the world system of another despot due to the alleged existential threat of international terrorism. However, even though President Bush and Republican hawks within the American administration did not desire nation-building in Iraq, democratic statebuilding was subsequently promoted.

As part of the statebuilding strategy, neoliberal police reconstruction militarized the Iraqi Police to fight against growing oppositional groups and engage with the Surge. However, the interim government headed by Bremer and SSR failed to provide basic security in Iraq. The United States spent $330 million in Iraq every day and a maximum of $757.8 billion (excluding the interest of borrowed funding) in total.[140] This political and military strategy resulted in a more discordant state of affairs with violence that was no longer fighting a clear enemy. Like in Afghanistan, the United States and its Western allies saw an opportunity to engage in statebuilding by Western actors to democratize Iraq, and to apply international human rights, the rule of law, and economic liberalization.[141] The Bush administration pressed for the democratization of the Middle East to defeat "tyrants" to create freedom and "democratic peace" with the assistance of American "allies."[142] The intention was, in rhetoric, to accomplish social harmony in the Middle East, including Iraq, with the installation of freedom and rights under democracies, but these goals were Western perspectives of social justice and are not representative of Afro-communitarian collective and relativist objectives. Hence, liberalist discourse was used by Bush and his Republican hawks with the 'Freedom Agenda' to oust despots for alleged better peace, free markets and freedom in the Middle East and to counter terrorism. However, the foreign armed intervention held ulterior motives in Iraq's incursion, principally rapid democratization and the promotion of Western viewpoints on social justice.

When terrorism peaked in Iraq from 2004 to 2006, the United States intended to oppose violence with enmity-like violence with the Surge in 2007 that can be justified under Afro-communitarianism because terrorism was a threat for the United States and Western allies, but was resulting in a discordant state of affairs in Iraq. The Surge as foreign armed intervention was thus debatably permissible. This view can even be countered with the premise that once America withdrew forces in December 2011, the Islamic State reemerged in Iraq and spread its bases elsewhere. Ironically, the United States false pretense of terrorism in Iraq and WMD under Saddam Hussein was proven incorrect and the foreign armed intervention on this basis removed Saddam to create more crime and sectarian violence. The removal also later encouraged a vacuum in which the Islamic

[140] Linda J. Bilmes, "Prepared Statement of Prof. Linda J. Bilmes, Kennedy School of Government, Harvard University," in *The Growing Budgetary Costs of the Iraq War: Hearing Before the Committee on the Budget House of Representatives 110th Congress First Session – Serial No. 110–22*, edited by John M. Spratt, Jr. (Washington, DC: United States Government Printing Office, October 24, 2007), p. 34.

[141] The only difference is that the US-led foreign armed intervention in Afghanistan was legitimate with UN Security Council authorization.

[142] White House Press Releases, "Text of President Bush's 2004 State of the Union Address," *The Washington Post*, January 20, 2004.

State could develop. Even the aims of the United States did not thus comply with Afro-communitarianism in this context. However, the initial intervention in the second invasion (March 2003) was not morally permissible because US geopolitical motives—with unclear and later disproved intelligence of Saddam Hussein possessing blueprints of WMD stockpiles and support for al-Qaeda—were largely focused on democratizing the Middle East in an effort to contain terrorism. This did not consider improving the state of affairs in Iraq but rather this neoconservatism intended to forcibly remove Saddam Hussein from power and engage with neoliberal statebuilding and rapid democratization.

America could have contended that they attempted other measures than violence in the early 1990s with sanctions preventing all imports and exports (except for medicines) to weaken Saddam Hussein's Ba'ath party and condemn Iraq's invasion of Kuwait.[143] However, the sanctions persisted until America's second intervention that devastated the Iraqi economy, leaving many parts with poor food security, health care, electricity, and transportation. Many innocent civilians were impoverished, which included hunger, and thus sanctions are a form of enmity-like violence that are targeted against a discordant government, but they also punish civilians. Hence, sanctions do not qualify as friendly alternatives to restore harmonious relations.

Moreover, under traditionalist just war theory, the United States did not act in self-defense and did not have permission from the highest legitimate authority, the United Nations (and principally the Security Council), failing *jus ad bellum*. The foreign armed intervention could have only partially complied with consequentialist Afro-communitarian ethics. The exit strategy in Iraq might have failed even if it was earlier or later, but many have argued, including offensive realists—Mearsheimer and Walt—that the intervention was not required because it was not in American interests to engage with a leading foreign armed intervention.[144] This countered US interests on countering terrorism, ridding the world of despots, and democratizing the Middle East with coercion. These mixed ideals of liberal statebuilding, democratization, and reconstruction were merged with alleged realist interests due to the misinterpretation of neoconservatism

[143] United Nations Security Council Resolution 660, "Condemnation of Iraq's Invasion of Kuwait"; United Nations Security Council Resolution 661, "The Situation between Iraq and Kuwait," UN Doc. S/RES/661, August 6, 1990, adopted 2933rd meeting.

[144] Mearsheimer and Walt, "An Unnecessary War."

(that was actually against social engineering) and getting rid of rogue regimes.[145]

When analyzing the United States-led intervention in Iraq from March 2003, alternative means to violence were attempted and continued after brief airstrikes after 1990 (but these were far from friendly). The United States and allies did, however, engage with gradual increments in violence during the war (*in bello*). America did not act in self-defense or engage in a humanitarian intervention that traditionalist just war theorists would have supported *ad bellum*, and for Afro-communitarians, the initiation of war was not to promote a more harmonious state of affairs, but was for US and Western interests to overthrow Saddam Hussein, contain terrorism and liberalize oil, democratize the Middle East, and contain Iran as part of post-9/11 foreign policy. A more discordant state of affairs and growth of terrorism was the outcome, creating a worse state of affairs in Iraq than before the intervention. US and Iraq military casualties and civilian deaths were also the outcome and the foreign armed intervention did not counter enemy violence, which is still ongoing after the US departure in late 2011. Hence, Afro-communitarian moral philosophy provides more insight to traditionalists on waging war *ad bellum* and the examination of conduct during hostilities *in bello* by assessing the harmonious or disharmonious state of affairs and levels of violence at the outset and close of intervention.

Conclusion

During the 1990s, Iraq destroyed its WMD programs. Yet, it did not effectively communicate that it lacked the capacity or that it not intend to pursue a WMD program.[146] WMD were not found, and previously, after the initial Gulf War, the Iraq Survey Group assessed WMD capabilities, located stockpiles, and destroyed them. However, after the Gulf War, UN weapons inspectors found that Baghdad was proceeding with a nuclear program.[147] Saddam was not in a position to clearly specify that Iraq was not engaging with a WMD program for fear of appearing weak to its rival

[145] Francis Fukuyama, "The Neoconservatism of Francis Fukuyama," *The National Interest*, August 3, 2004; Francis Fukuyama, *After the Neocons: America at the Crossroads* (London: Profile, 2006), p. 63.

[146] Isikoff and Corn, *Hubris*, p. 305.

[147] Etel Solingen, *Nuclear Logics: Contrasting Paths in East Asia and the Middle East* (Princeton, NJ: Princeton University Press, 2007).

Iran and its internal Shiite opposition. It was mostly suspicion of a 1 percent doctrine rather than a reality of destroying WMD and potentially the opportunity to privatize the oil industry that motivated the invasion of Iraq in March 2003. Irrespective of America remaining uncertain of Iraq's capability of producing WMD, the United States planned military intervention well in advance with forces deployed in the Gulf and thus would not retreat. The Republican hawks greatly desired wanted a war with Iraq and an easy military victory with few costs.

In relation to the Western-based principles of just war theory, namely, Aquinas's principles of *jus ad bellum*, the initiation of invasion from the United States and its coalition forces did not function as the legitimate authority and was not waged as a last resort. Nor did Iraq impose a real evident threat to the United States. The self-defense principle was flawed because there was no clear evidence that Saddam held links with or was harboring al-Qaeda to plot another terrorist attack against the United States.[148] Unlike the justification of the invasion in Afghanistan comprising Article 51 of the Charter of the United Nations to defend against further acts of terrorism in immediate response to 9/11, there was no clear self-defense argument regarding the foreign armed intervention in Iraq. Prior to the invasion, Saddam continued to believe that the United States would not invade and thus did not settle for a bargain with the Bush administration.

Taking a Clausewitz view on war into consideration, war is waged to conquer a foe rather than impose values on the enemy.[149] When a foe has been defeated, this does not mean that the losing population will abide by the victorious side's ideals. These costs of the idealistic versions of American-sponsored democratization and Western framework of social justice influenced the post-war situation. This point is relevant to Afro-Communitarian ethics because they strive for a more harmonious state of affairs, but the Iraq post-war governance and reconstruction program tainted communal relations and the trust of international statebuilders. The post-war costs were significant in Iraq, and were heavily underestimated

[148] Karol and Miguel similarly argue that there was no linkage between Saddam's Ba'athist regime and al-Qaeda because WMD stockpiles were not found (Karol and Miguel, "The Electoral Cost of War," p. 646). Despite this evidence, the US public still believed that the invasion was the right decision (from 68 percent prior to the incursion and 57 percent when invaded) (Kull, Ramsay, and Lewis, "Misperceptions, the Media, and the Iraq War," p. 570).

[149] Carl von Clausewitz, *On War*. Translated by Michael Howard and Peter Paret (Princeton, NJ: Princeton University Press, 1976), pp. 74–76.

by Washington, and Bush was initially against occupation and nation-building, which ultimately failed. It can be argued that the 2003 invasion of Iraq marked "foreign-imposed regime change," a "failure of securitized statebuilding," and a lack "of legitimacy in externally-imposed democratization" that undermined local efforts at preserving peace.[150] Washington liberating Iraq to form their own state is a form of ideological colonialism due to the promoted—and debatably forced—democratic standards, rule of law, and international human rights package.

From an Afro-communitarian perspective, the foreign armed intervention of the United States and its coalition forces resulted in a less harmonious state of affairs due to the additional anti-Americanism and overextension of US policy as a Western crusade in the Persian Gulf region. These costs should have been considered prior to waging the avoidable preventive war. Iraq became part of Bush's war against terror, but the same threats were faced by the previous Clinton administration that opted to avoid invading Iraq and focused on containing Saddam. Politically, the US-supported CPA and governance did not obtain public support due to mistrust of American handpicked officials. The occupying Authority was provided with the legitimacy and responsibility to rebuild Iraq's security sector,[151] but Bremer's directive abolished the Iraqi army,[152] and the new security forces were unable to fill the security vacuum that was filled by the Islamic State in June 2014. Consequently, a plethora of Iranian-aligned militias attempted to reclaim territories for the Iraqi federal government, but this has been marred by widespread human rights abuses and sectarian violence, and Iran has further cemented its geopolitical power within Iraq, the latter being controlled by Saddam Hussein. The longer-term economic repercussions of the protracted sanctions since the 1990s did not solely target Saddam and his political and oil elite, but they escalated poverty and the UN-led Oil-for-Food Program was plagued with corruption, thus doing little to combat poverty. Therefore, the multiple sanctions enforced by the West functioned as a form of systemic violence and human insecurity that resulted in a less harmonious state of affairs. Iraq is hindered by sectarian violence and even if its relations with the United States will likely improve in the future, a discordant state of affairs—in terms of poor internal security—will remain in the near future.

[150] Mako and Edgar, "Evaluating the Pitfalls of External Statebuilding in Post-2003 Iraq," pp. 425–426.

[151] UN Security Council Resolution 1483, "The Situation between Iraq and Kuwait."

[152] Bremer, "Coalition Provisional Authority Order Number 2: Dissolution of Entities."

References

Al-Marashi, Ibrahim. "Demobilization Minus Disarmament and Reintegration: Iraq's Security Sector from the United States Occupation to the Covid-19 Pandemic." *Journal of Intervention and Statebuilding*, Vol. 15, No. 4 (2021), pp. 441–458. https://doi.org/10.1080/17502977.2021.1934284.

Alaaldin, Ranj. *Containing Shiite Militias: The Battle for Stability in Iraq*. Washington, DC: Brookings Institution, 2017. https://www.brookings.edu/wp-content/uploads/2017/12/shiite_militias_iraq_english.pdf.

Allawi, Ali Abdul-Amir. *The Occupation of Iraq: Winning the War, Losing the Peace*. New Haven, CT: Yale University Press, 2007.

Anas F. Alhajji, "US Energy Policy and the Invasion of Iraq: Does Oil Matter?" *The Journal of Energy and Development*, Vol. 29, No. 2 (Spring 2004), pp. 209–232. https://www.jstor.org/stable/24808881.

Arab Barometer Index V. *Iraq Country Report*. 2019. https://www.arabbarometer.org/wp-content/uploads/ABV_Iraq_Report_Public-Opinion_2019.pdf.

Belloni, Roberto, and Irene Costantini. "From Liberal Statebuilding to Counterinsurgency and Stabilization: The International Intervention in Iraq." *Ethnopolitics*, Vol. 18, No. 5 (July 2019), pp. 509–525. https://doi.org/10.1080/17449057.2019.1640964.

Bilmes, Linda J. "Prepared Statement of Prof. Linda J. Bilmes, Kennedy School of Government, Harvard University." In *The Growing Budgetary Costs of the Iraq War: Hearing Before the Committee on the Budget House of Representatives 110th Congress First Session – Serial No. 110–22*, edited by John M. Spratt, Jr., pp. 9–50. Washington, DC: United States Government Printing Office, October 24, 2007.

Blix, Hans Martin. "UN Inspectors Found no Evidence of Prohibited Weapons Programs as of March 18 Withdrawal, Hans Blix tells Security Council." *United Nations Security Council Press Release*, SC/7777, June 5, 2003. https://press.un.org/en/2003/sc7777.doc.htm.

Borger, Julian. "Bush Decided to Remove Saddam 'On Day One'." *The Guardian*, January 12, 2004. https://www.theguardian.com/world/2004/jan/12/usa.books.

Braithwaite, John, and Ali Wardak. "Crime and War in Afghanistan: Part I: The Hobbesian Solution." *British Journal of Criminology*, Vol. 53, No. 2 (March 2013), pp. 179–196. https://doi.org/10.1093/bjc/azs065.

Bremer III, Lewis Paul. "Coalition Provisional Authority Order Number 2: Dissolution of Entities." May 23, 2003. https://web.archive.org/web/20040701202042/; http://iraqcoalition.org/regulations/20030823_CPAORD_2_Dissolution_of_Entities_with_Annex_A.pdf.

Burnham, Gilbert, Riyadh Lafta, Shannon Doocy, and Les Roberts. "Mortality after the 2003 Invasion of Iraq: A Cross-section Cluster Sample Survey." *The*

Lancet, October 12, 2006, pp. 1421–1428. https://doi.org/10.1016/S0140-6736(06)69491-9.

Bush, George Walker. "Presidential Letter to Congress." March 18, 2003a. http://www.whitehouse.gov/news/releases/2003/03/20030319-1.html.

Bush, George Walker. "Remarks by President George W. Bush at the 20th Anniversary of the National Endowment for Democracy." *United States Commission on International Religious Freedom*, November 6, 2003b. https://www.uscirf.gov/topics/anti-semitism/president-bush-discusses-freedom-iraq-and-middle-east.

Bush, George Walker. "Remarks by the President at Victory 2004 Rally." *Weekly Compilations of Presidential Documents*, Vol. 40, No. 41 (October 1, 2004a), pp. 2209–2216.

Bush, George Walker. "The Second Bush-Kerry Presidential Debate." *Commission on Presidential Debates*, October 8, 2004b. http://www.debates.org/pages/trans2004c.html.

Butt, Ahsan I. "Why Did the United States Invade Iraq in 2003?" *Security Studies*, Vol. 28, No. 2 (January 2019), pp. 250–285. https://doi.org/10.1080/09636412.2019.1551567.

Byman, Daniel. "Constructing a Democratic Iraq: Challenges and Opportunities." *International Security*, Vol. 28, No. 1 (July 2003), pp. 47–78. https://doi.org/10.1162/016228803322427974.

Center for Strategic and International Studies. "Islamic State Khorasan (IS-K)." 2018. https://www.csis.org/programs/transnational-threats-project/terrorism-backgrounders/islamic-state-khorasan-k.

Chang, Gordon Guthrie, Kerstin Lueck, and Hugh Bud Mehan. "Evidencing International Threat: Examining Iraq Survey Group's Post-Invasion Verification of Iraq's WMD Threat." Vol. 12, No. 1 (January 2013), pp. 29–58. https://doi.org/10.1075/jlp.12.1.02cha.

Cheney, Richard Bruce. "Meet the Press: Interview with Vice-President Dick Cheney." *NBC*, March 16, 2003. https://www.leadingtowar.com/PDFsources_claims_noweapons2/2003_03_16_NBCmtp.pdf.

Chicago Council on Foreign Relations. *Worldviews 2002: American Public Opinion & Foreign Policy*. Chicago, IL: Chicago Council on Foreign Relations, June 2002. https://globalaffairs.org/sites/default/files/2020-11/2002-Chicago-Council-Survey-PDF-Report.pdf

Clinton, William Jefferson. *My Life*. New York: Vintage, 2005.

Clausewitz, Carl von. *On War*. Translated by Michael Howard and Peter Paret. Princeton, NJ: Princeton University Press, 1976.

Cockburn, Patrick. *The Jihadis Return: ISIS and the New Sunni Uprising*. New York: OR Books, 2014.

Cooper, Helene, and Sheryl Gay Stolberg. "Obama Declares and End to Combat Mission in Iraq." *New York Times*, August 31, 2010. https://www.nytimes.com/2010/09/01/world/01military.html.

Cordesman, Anthony H., with Emma R. Davies. *Iraq's Insurgency and the Road to Civil Conflict – Volume I.* Westport, CT: Praeger Security International, 2008.

Cottle, Simon. *Global Crisis Reporting: Journalism in the Global Age.* Maidenhead, Berkshire: Open University Press, 2009.

Daalder, Ivo H., and James M. Lindsay. *America Unbound: The Bush Revolution in Foreign Policy.* Washington, DC: Brookings Institution Press, 2003.

Dawisha, Adeed. *Iraq: A Political History from Independence to Occupation.* Princeton, NJ: Princeton University Press, 2009.

Dodge, Toby. "Iraq's Future: The Aftermath of Regime Change." *Adelphi Paper*, 372. London: Routledge, January 2005.

Dodge, Toby. "State and Society in Iraq Ten Years after Regime Change: The Rise of a New Authoritarianism." *International Affairs*, Vol. 89, No.2 (March 2013), pp. 241–257. https://doi.org/10.1111/inta.2013.89.issue-2.

Dodge, Toby. "The Failure of Peacebuilding in Iraq: The Role of Consociationalism and Political Settlements." *Journal of Intervention and Statebuilding*, Vol. 15, No. 3 (August 2021), pp. 459–475. https://doi.org/10.1080/17502977.2020.1850036.

Duelfer, Charles A. *Comprehensive Report of the Special Advisor to the DCI on Iraq's WMD, with Addendums (Duelfer Report).* Langley, VA: Executive Agency Publications, April 25, 2005.

Federation of American Scientists – Intelligence Resource Program. *National Security Presidential Directive 24.* Washington, DC: The White House, January 20, 2003. https://irp.fas.org/offdocs/nspd/nspd-24.pdf.

Feith, Douglas Jay. *War and Decision: Inside the Pentagon at the Dawn of the War on Terrorism.* New York: HarperCollins, 2008.

Fukuyama, Francis. *State Building: Governance and World Order in the Twenty-First Century.* London: Profile Book, 2004a.

Fukuyama, Francis. "The Neoconservatism of Francis Fukuyama." *The National Interest*, August 3, 2004b. https://nationalinterest.org/article/the-neoconservatism-of-francis-fukuyama-2725.

Fukuyama, Francis. *After the Neocons: America at the Crossroads.* London: Profile, 2006.

Galbraith, Peter Woodard. *The End of Iraq: How American Incompetence Created a War without End.* New York: Simon and Schuster, 2006.

Gardner, Hall. *Averting Global War: Regional Challenges, Overextension, and Options for American Strategy.* New York: Palgrave Macmillan, 2007.

Go, Julian. *The Patterns of Empire: The British and American Empires, 1688 to Present.* New York: Cambridge University Press, 2011.

Gordon, Michael R., and Bernard E. Trainor, *Cobra II: The Inside Story of the Invasion and Occupation of Iraq*. New York: Pantheon, 2006.

Hodges, Adam. *The "War on Terror" Narrative: Discourse and Intertextuality in the Construction and Contestation of Sociopolitical Reality*. New York: Oxford University Press, 2011.

Hosner, Stephen T. *Why the Iraqi Resistance to the Coalition Invasion was so Weak*. Santa Monica, CA: RAND Corporation, 2007.

Human Rights Watch. "Iraq: Ban Abusive Militias from Mosul Operation." *Human Rights Watch*, July 31, 2016. https://www.hrw.org/news/2016/07/31/iraq-ban-abusive-militias-mosul-operation.

Hussein, Dilshad. "The Increase in the Number of Popular Mobilization Forces Members in Iraq 'Worries' Some People…Why?" *Irfaa Sawtak*, May 3, 2023. https://www.irfaasawtak.com/iraq/2023/05/03/.

International Center for Transitional Justice. "Iraqi Voices: Attitudes Toward Transitional Justice and Social Reconstruction." 2004. https://www.ictj.org/sites/default/files/ICTJ-Iraq-Voices-Reconstruction-2004-English.pdf.

Isikoff, Michael, and David Corn, *Hubris: The Inside Story of Spin, Scandal, and the Selling of the Iraq War*. New York: Free Rivers Press (Crown Publishers), 2006.

Jentleson, Bruce W. *With Friends Like These: Reagan, Bush, and Saddam, 1982–1990*. New York: W.W. Norton, 1994.

Jhaveri, Nayna J. "Pretoimperialism: US Oil Interests and the Iraq War." *Antipode*, Vol. 36, No. 1 (January 2004), pp. 2–11. https://doi.org/10.1111/j.1467-8330.2004.00378.x.

Karol, David, and Miguel, Edward. "The Electoral Cost of War: Iraq Casualties and the 2004 US Presidential Election." *The Journal of Politics*, Vol. 69, No. 3 (August 2007), pp. 633–648. https://doi.org/10.1111/j.1468-2508.2007.00564.x.

Kay, David. "Text of David Kay's Unclassified Statement." *CNN*, October 2, 2003. https://edition.cnn.com/2003/ALLPOLITICS/10/02/kay.report/.

Kay, David. "David Kay: Exclusive Interview by Tom Brokaw." *Nightly News with Brian Williams, NBC*, January 26, 2004a. http://www.msnbc.msn.com/id/4066462/.

Kay, David. "David Kay Testifies Before Senate Committee." *CNN*, January 28, 2004b. https://transcripts.cnn.com/show/se/date/2004-01-28/segment/02.

Kerry, John Forbes. "Speech at US Ambassador to Iraq Confirmation." *C-Span*, September 19, 2012. https://www.c-span.org/video/?308270-us-ambassador-iraq-confirmation.

Klare, Michael T. "For Oil and Empire? Rethinking War with Iraq." *Current History*, Vol. 102, No. 662 (March 2003a), pp. 129–135. https://doi.org/10.1525/curh.2003.102.662.129.

Klare, Michael T. "It's the Oil, Stupid." *The Nation*, April 24, 2003b. https://www.thenation.com/article/politics/its-oil-stupid/.

Klare, Michael T. "Blood for Oil, in Iraq and Elsewhere." In *Why Did the United States Invade Iraq?* edited by Jane K. Cramer and A. Trevor Thrall, pp. 129–144. London: Routledge, 2012.

Klein, Naomi. 2007. *The Shock Doctrine: The Rise of Disaster Capitalism*. New York: Picador.

Kull, Steven, Clay Ramsay, and Evan Lewis. "Misperceptions, the Media, and the Iraq War." *Political Science Quarterly*, Vol. 118, No. 4 (2003–04), pp. 569–598. https://doi.org/10.1002/j.1538-165X.2003.tb00406.x.

Lake, David A. "Two Cheers for Bargaining Theory: Assessing Rationalist Explanations of the Iraq War." *International Security*, Vol. 35, No. 3 (Winter 2010/11), pp. 7–52. https://doi.org/10.1162/ISEC_a_00029.

Lewis, Adrian R. *The American Culture of War: The History of United States Military Force from World War II to Operation Enduring Freedom*. New York: Routledge, 2012.

Mahmood, Mona. "Life in Mosul One Year On: ISIS with All Its Brutality is More Honest than the Shia Government." *The Guardian*, June 10, 2015. https://www.theguardian.com/world/2015/jun/10/mosul-residents-one-year-on-isis-brutality.

Mako, Shamiran. "Subverting Peace: The Origins and Legacies of de-Ba'athification in Iraq." *Journal of Intervention and Statebuilding*, Vol. 15, No. 4 (August 2021), pp. 476–493. https://doi.org/10.1080/17502977.2020.1850036.

Mako, Shamiran, and Alistair D. Edgar. "Evaluating the Pitfalls of External Statebuilding in Post-2003 Iraq (2003–2021)." *Journal of Intervention and Statebuilding*, Vol. 15, No. 4 (August 2021), pp. 425–440. https://doi.org/10.1080/17502977.2021.1958292.

Mearsheimer, John Joseph, and Stephen Martin Walt. "An Unnecessary War." *Foreign Policy*, Vol. 134 (January–February 2003), pp. 50–59. https://www.mearsheimer.com/wp-content/uploads/2019/07/A0032.pdf.

Morgan, Dan and, David B. Ottaway. "In Iraq War Scenario, Oil Is Key Issue." *The Washington Post*, September 15, 2002. https://www.washingtonpost.com/archive/politics/2002/09/15/in-iraqi-war-scenario-oil-is-key-issue/ba43d2a9-abe5-4371-8f2c-445e262778a1/.

Meyer, Von Cordula. "A Lot of Blood for Little Oil." *Spiegel International*, December 6, 2010. https://www.spiegel.de/international/world/us-involvement-in-iraq-a-lot-of-blood-for-little-oil-a-732984.html.

Muttit, Greg. *Fuel on the Fire: Oil and Politics in Occupied Iraq*. New York: New Press, 2012.

Myers, Meghann. "Wars in Iraq and Syria Cost Half a Million Lives, Nearly $3T: Report." *Military Times*, March 17, 2023. https://www.militarytimes.com/news/your-military/2023/03/17/wars-in-iraq-and-syria-cost-half-a-million-lives-nearly-3t-report/.

Otterman, Sharon. "Iraq: Oil for Food Scandal." *Council on Foreign Relations*, October 28, 2005. https://www.cfr.org/backgrounder/iraq-oil-food-scandal.

Özerdem, Alpaslan. "Insurgency, Militias, and DDR as Part of Security Sector Reconstruction in Iraq: How Not to Do It." *Disasters*, Vol. 43, S1 (January 2010), pp. 40–59. https://doi.org/10.1111/j.1467-7717.2009.01098.x.

Packer, George. *The Assassin's Gate: America in Iraq*. Waterville, ME: Thorndike Press, 2006.

Papagianni, Katia. "Participation and State Legitimacy." In *Building States to Build Peace*, edited by Charles T. Cal, and Vanessa Wyeth, pp. 49–71. Boulder, CO: Lynne Reiner, 2008.

Pickering, Jeffrey, and Mark Peceny. "Forging Democracy at Gunpoint." *International Studies Quarterly*, Vol. 50, No. 3 (September 2006), pp. 539–560. https://doi.org/10.1111/j.1468-2478.2006.00413.x.

Powell, Colin Luther. "Although No WMD Found, Saddam Had Intent, Capability, Powell Says." Interview of Secretary of State Colin L. Powell by Warren Strobel of Knight-Ridder. *Global Security*, October 8, 2004.

Reiter, Dan. "Exploring the Bargaining Model of War," *Perspectives on Politics*, Vol. 1, No. 1 (March 2003), pp. 27–43. https://doi.org/10.1017/S1537592703000033.

Ricks, Thomas Edwin. *Fiasco: The American Military Adventure in Iraq*. New York: The Penguin Press, 2006.

Ritchie, Nick, and Paul Rodgers. *The Political Road to War with Iraq: Bush, 9/11 and the Drive to Overthrow Saddam*. London: Routledge, 2007.

Singh, Danny. *Investigating Corruption in the Afghan Police Force: Instability and Insecurity in Post-conflict Societies*. Bristol: Policy Press, 2020a.

Singh, Danny. "Undertaking Critical Legal Theory to Examine Just War Intervention: A Smokescreen for Political Ambitions." In *Comparative Just War Theory: An Introduction to International Perspectives*, edited by Luís Cordeiro Rodrigues and Danny Singh, pp. 61–79. Lanham, MD: Rowman and Littlefield, 2020b.

Smith, James Jimmy. "Reconsidering the Role of Militias in Iraq." *Combatting Terrorism Center Sentinel*, Vol. 2, No. 1 (January 2009), pp. 1–3. https://ctc.westpoint.edu/wp-content/uploads/2010/06/Vol2Iss1-Art6.pdf.

Soderberg, Nancy. *The Superpower Myth: The Use and Misuse of American Might*. Hoboken, NJ: John Wiley and Sons, 2005.

Solingen, Etel. *Nuclear Logics: Contrasting Paths in East Asia and the Middle East*. Princeton, NJ: Princeton University Press, 2007.

Sollinger, Jerry M., Laurinda L. Rohn, Richard E. Darilek, and Walt L. Perry. *Operation Iraqi Freedom: Decisive War, Elusive Peace*. Santa Monica, CA: RAND Corporation, 2015.

Stewart, Richard Winship. *War in the Persian Gulf: Operations Desert Shield and Desert Storm, August 1990–March 1991*. Washington, DC: Center of Military History, United States Army, 2010.

Stiglitz, Joseph Eugene, and Linda J. Barnes. *The Three Trillion Dollar War: The True Cost of the Iraq Conflict.* New York: W.W. Norton, 2008.

Suskind, Ron. *The One Percent Doctrine: Deep inside America's Pursuit of Its Enemies since 9/11.* New York: Simon and Schuster, 2007.

Thompson, Mark. "Adding Up the Cost of Our Never-Ending Wars." *Project on Government Oversight*, December 17, 2019. https://www.pogo.org/analysis/2019/12/adding-up-the-cost-of-our-never-ending-wars.

United Nations Human Rights Office of the High Commissioner. "US Pardons for Blackwater Guards an 'Affront to Justice' – UN Experts." *United Nations Human Rights Office of the High Commissioner*, December 30, 2020. https://www.ohchr.org/en/press-releases/2020/12/us-pardons-blackwater-guards-affront-justice-un-experts.

United Nations Security Council Resolution 660. "Condemnation of Iraq's Invasion of Kuwait." UN Doc. S/RES/660, August 2, 1990, adopted 2,963rd meeting.

United Nations Security Council Resolution 661. "The Situation between Iraq and Kuwait." UN Doc. S/RES/661, August 6, 1990, adopted 2,933rd meeting.

United Nations Security Council Resolution 778. "Iraq to Withdraw from Kuwait." UN Doc. S/RES/778, November 29, 1990, adopted 2,932nd meeting.

United Nations Security Council Resolution 986. "Serious Nutritional and Health Situation of the Iraqi Population." UN Doc. S/RES/986, April 14, 1995, adopted 3,519th meeting.

United Nations Security Council Resolution 1441. "The Situation between Iraq and Kuwait." UN Doc. S/RES/1441, November 8, 2002, adopted 4,644th meeting.

United Nations Security Council Resolution 1483. "The Situation between Iraq and Kuwait." UN Doc. S/RES/1483, May 22, 2003, adopted 4761st meeting.

United States National Security Council. *The National Security Strategy.* September 2002. https://georgewbush-whitehouse.archives.gov/nsc/nss/2002/text/index.html.

Walldorf Jr., C. William. "Narratives and War: Explaining the Length and End of US Military Operations in Afghanistan." *International Security*, Vol. 47, No. 1 (July 2022), pp. 93–138. https://doi.org/10.1162/isec_a_00439.

Weinstein, Jeremy M., John Edward Porter, and Stuart E. Eizenstat. *On the Brink: Weak States and US National Security.* Commission for Weak States and US National Security. *Center for Global Development*, July 19, 2005. https://www.cgdev.org/publication/brink-weak-states-and-us-national-security.

Wennmann, Achim. "Getting Armed Groups to the Table: Peace Processes, the Political Economy of Conflict and the Mediated State." *Third World Quarterly*, Vol. 30, No.6 (July 2009), pp. 1123–1138. https://doi.org/10.1080/01436590903037416.

White House Press Releases. "Text of President Bush's 2004 State of the Union Address," *The Washington Post*, January 20, 2004. https://www.washingtonpost.com/wp-srv/politics/transcripts/bushtext_012004.html.

Wolfowitz, Paul Dundes. "Questions for Paul Wolfowitz." *Center for American Progress*, April 20, 2004. https://www.americanprogress.org/article/questions-for-paul-wolfowitz/.

Woods, Kevin M., with Michael R. Pease, Mark E. Stout, Williamson Murray, and James G. Lacey. *Iraqi Perspectives Project: A View of Operation Iraqi Freedom from Saddam's Senior Leadership*. Norfolk: VI: The Joint Center for Operational Analysis, 2006.

Wozniak, Jesse S.G. "We are Going to Prove that We are a Civil and Developed Country: The Cultural Performance of Police Legitimacy and Empire in the Iraqi State." *The British Journal of Criminology*, Vol. 57, No. 4 (July 2017a), pp. 906–923. https://doi.org/10.1093/bjc/azw046.

Wozniak, Jesse S.G. "Iraq and the Material Basis of Post-Conflict Police Reconstruction." *The Journal of Peace Research*, Vol. 54, No. 6 (September 2017b), pp. 806–818. https://doi.org/10.1177/0022343317704502.

Wozniak, Jesse S.G. "Iraq's Neoliberal Reconstruction and the Continued Relevance of the State." *Sociological Focus*, Vol. 52, No. 4 (October 2019), pp. 359–376. https://doi.org/10.1080/00380237.2019.1668322.

CHAPTER 7

African-Led Military Interventions

Introduction

The conflicts and foreign armed intervention in Rwanda and Sierra Leone have been applied to Afro-communitarian ethics. This chapter thematically examines a range of African states that did not contain strong Western-based intervention, for example, from the United Nations (UN), United States (US), or the North Atlantic Treaty Organization (NATO). The chapter will engage with the roles held by the African Union (AU) and the Economic Community of West African States (ECOWAS). The African Union can legitimately authorize, endorse, and engage in military intervention on behalf of its African member states,[1] and ECOWAS operates as a regional security organization that can obtain permission from the United Nations Security Council to adopt enforcement action.[2] Several AU military interventions within the African continent will be examined to consider the suggestions of whether Afro-communitarian ethics or Western legal and political theories determine such interventions. The contexts that are analyzed comprise the role of the African Union in Burundi, Darfur, and Somalia and ECOWAS in Mali and Liberia.

[1] Article 4 (h) of its Constitutive Act of the African Union.
[2] Article 53 (1) of the Charter of the United Nations.

D. Singh, *Applied Afro-Communitarian Ethics and Foreign Armed Intervention*, https://doi.org/10.1007/978-3-031-64110-7_7

The African Union as a Regional Peacekeeping Organization

The African Union succeeded the Organization of African Unity in July 2002 to conduct regional African armed peace interventions. This model was tested in Burundi and Darfur, western Sudan. It is debated whether the African Union should resort to military force to deal with political crises within the African continent. In May 2003, the African Standby Force (ASF) was created with a Military Staff Committee to have the authority of managing regional peacekeeping operations.[3] To deal with crises, ASF brigades would manage political crises within the African Union and regional military guidance. The African Union can then mandate a resolution that can deploy a force within 30 days of that resolution.[4] Moreover, a regional observer mission can be deployed, but with a UN Mission, or a standalone observer group. Furthermore, a regional peacekeeping operation can be mandated for complex missions under Chapter VI of the Charter of the United Nations for preventive deployment and peacebuilding. This structure is to tackle low-level spoilers or a robust AU military intervention in the event of genocide if the international community fails to act promptly. The latter can be deployed within 14 rather than 30 days. Article 4 (h) of the Charter of the African Union can resort the Union in an intervention within a Member State if the Assembly decides that war crimes, crimes against humanity, and/or genocide have been committed.

The African Union's Peace and Security Council operates with collective security. This Council provides an early warning system for rapid responses to African conflicts that is usually within 30–90 days dependent on the operation.[5] The Peace and Security Council has 15 members, and 5 of these have one state per region (Central, North, South, East, and West Africa) to hold three-year elected terms, while the 10 other states serve two-year terms. The Council or a member of the Union can recommend extensions.[6] However, under international law, the African Union

[3] Paul D. Williams, "The African Union: Prospects for Regional Peacekeeping after Burundi and Sudan," *Review of African Political Economy*, Vol. 33, No. 108 (June 2006), p. 352.

[4] Williams, "The African Union," p. 352.

[5] African Charter on Human and Peoples' Rights (Banjul Charter), "Charter of the African Union," adopted June 27, 1981, OAU Doc. CAB/LEG/67/3 rev. 5, 21 I.L.M. 58 (1982), 2 (1).

[6] Charter of the African Union, 4 (h), 4 (j).

requires permission from the United Nations Security Council.[7] A Standby High Readiness Brigade (SHIRBRIG) was to comprise 2,200 armed forces, contain a headquarters, and have four lightly armed infantry battalions, engineers, military police, helicopters, medial units, and civilian logistical and administrative support.[8]

The African Union in Burundi

Burundi hosts a population of an estimated eight million people. Its ethnic representation comprises "85 per cent Hutu, 14 per cent Tutsi and 1 per cent Twa."[9] The civil war commenced in 1993 and ended in 2005. It involved elongated ethnic hostility between Hutus and Tutsis, resulting in approximately 300,000 deaths and the forcible displacement of 1.2 million people.[10] The civil war was caused by long ethnic tensions between Hutu and Tutsi ethnic groups, and throughout the conflict, both groups recruited children as soldiers. Burundi attained independence from Belgium in 1962 (as with Rwanda), which welcomed multiparty elections. Burundi began its independence with a series of military dictatorships. During the 1960s through to the 1980s, thousands of Tutsi refugees in Rwanda fled Hutu emancipation political activism and violence to neighboring Burundi and Uganda.

State power and socioeconomic privilege were unequally distributed on ethnic lines. The state judiciary and armed forces have been privatized and controlled by a small number of people. From a political economy perspective, the "have nots" that did not gain from the unfair distribution of resources, jobs, and services were frustrated and aggrieved with marginalization. The minority Tutsi group held most influence in the Burundi armed forces prior and post-independence.[11] Like in Rwanda, Tutsi power ignited several Hutu uprisings. For instance, in 1972, Hutu rebels located in Tanzania entered south Burundi and systematically killed 2,000–3,000

[7] Charter of the United Nations, 1945, Chapter VIII, Article 53 (1).

[8] Williams, "The African Union," pp. 352–353.

[9] Isiaka Alani Badmus, "The African Mission in Burundi (AMIB)," *India Quarterly*, Vol. 73, No. 1 (March 2017), p. 5.

[10] Eric Demers, "The Burundian Civil War – 10 Years On," *Norwegian Refugee Council*, May 2, 2003.

[11] Rene Lemarchand, *Burundi: Ethnic Conflict and Genocide* (Cambridge: Cambridge University Press, 1995).

Tutsis that was met with retaliation from the armed forces killing 100,000–200,000 Hutu civilians.[12] A decade later in September 1987, a violent coup placed the Tutsi Major Pierre Buyoya in power.[13]

In Burundi, the political system reached democratization with the initial transparent, free, and fair democratic elections in June 1993. The Hutu-led Front pour la Démocratie au Burundi [Front for Democracy in Burundi] (FRODEBU) party headed by Melchior Ndadaye defeated the Tutsi-based Union pour le progress national [Union for National Progress] (UPRONA) party. The PALIPEHUTU insurgency continued under Kabora Kossan and split into the National Forces of Liberation (FNL). FNL did not want to join the Hutu government because they wanted all Burundian Tutsis exterminated or totally disempowered. However, Tutsis still dominated the Burundian armed forces, and the extremists imposed more of a threat for Ndadaye. On October 21, 1993, Tutsi military officers orchestrated a coup d'état that was backed by half of the army to kill Ndadaye and his party members. Reprisals occurred with Hutus killing Tutsi. To fight back, the armed forces, gendarmerie, and militia groups massacred Hutu officials and peasants, which resulted in 300,000 deaths, namely, civilians.[14] Consequently, Hutu and Tutsi started killing each other across Burundi.

To succeed Ndadaye, Cyprien Ntaryamira, another Hutu politician, served as the head of state. Yet, on April 6, 1994, Ntaryamira was killed, alongside Rwandan President, Juvénal Habyarimana, when their airplane traveling from Tanzania to broker peace was fired at with surface-to-air missiles over Kigali.[15] Both Hutu extremists and Tutsis blamed each other for the assassination of both Hutu presidents.[16]

At this point and after the Rwandan genocide in the summer of 1994, the refugee crisis impacted on neighboring Zaire and Burundi. The Rwandan government changed to a Tutsi-based one, headed by Paul Kagame, and Hutu génocidaires fled to eastern Zaire (now the Democratic Republic of Congo) with the help of the French military-based Opération

[12] Marc Manirakiza, "Nation-building in Burundi: A History and its Impacts on the Future," *Conflict Trends*, 2 (January 2005), pp. 45–46.

[13] Badmus, "The African Mission in Burundi (AMIB)," p. 5.

[14] Alex J. Bellamy and Paul D. Williams, "Who's Keeping the Peace? Regionalization and Contemporary Peace Operations," *International Security*, Vol. 29, No. 4 (April 2005), p. 189.

[15] Victor O. Okocha, *Leadership and Development Crises in Africa: A New Approach to an Old Challenge* (Pittsburgh, PA: Dorrance Publishing, 2018), p. 168.

[16] Okocha, *Leadership and Development Crises in Africa*, p. 169.

Turquoise providing safe zones. The Burundian Civil War thus spilled over from the Rwandan Civil War, later genocide and the Second Congolese War from the refugee crises of both Tutsis and Hutus to ignite further fighting after the assassination of Ndadaye.

To deal with the growing violence in Burundi, the United Nations attempted to broker a political solution in September 1994 that created a coalition administration with FRODEBU having a president and UPRONA a prime minister. In October 1994, a Hutu political leader, Sylvestre Ntibantunganya was installed as president, but radicals in his party feared a coup and UPRONA withdrew from the coalition. Violence continued. In November 1995, regional talks commenced, but the idea of the deployment of peacekeeping forces was rejected by the armed forces of Burundi.[17] Ntibantunganya was overthrown by the military on July 25, 1996, resulting in Buyoya assuming presidency.[18] Economic sanctions were endorsed by regional leaders, so Buyoya withdrew from the Arusha peace process, but later revived it after permitting FRODEBU to rejoin the government by May 1998.

Nelson Rolihlahla Mandela succeeded former Tanzanian President Julius Kambarage Nyerere after his demise to renegotiate the Arusha Agreement, which attained all 19 delegations (including 6 initial Tutsi reluctant parties) to sign by September 2000. Yet, no ceasefire was implemented, and thus African states were reluctant to contribute forces. In August 2000, the Arusha Agreement was signed, and the contested armed groups signed several regionally based ceasefires in late 2000, which provided the mandate for the deployment of the African Mission in Burundi (AMIB).[19] Mandela negotiated with South Africa to deploy the South African Protection Support Detachment (SAPSD) in late October 2001, reaching approximately 700 personnel.[20] The Burundian armed forces opposed the South African forces, but the South African troops stabilized the capital, Bujumbura, protected Hutu politicians, and supported the

[17] Henri Boshoff, "Historical Overview," in *The Burundi Peace Process: From Civil War to Conditional Peace*, edited by Henri Boshoff, Very Waldemar and George Rautenbach (Pretoria: Institute for Security Studies, 2010), pp. 3–9.

[18] Adekeye Adebajo, *UN Peacekeeping in Africa: From the Suez Crisis to the Sudan Conflicts* (Boulder, CO: Lynne Rienner, 2011).

[19] Arusha Peace and Reconciliation Agreements for Burundi, "Arusha Agreement," August 28, 2000.

[20] Badmus, "The African Mission in Burundi (AMIB)," p. 7.

peace negotiations, but could not protect civilians. South Africa had undertaken leadership and planning of the mission.

An international peacekeeping operation was eventually agreed with the United Nations loose ceasefires in late 2002 signed by the Burundian government, Conseil National pour la Défense de la Démocratie—Forces pour la Défense de la Démocratie [National Council for the Defense of Democracy—Forces for the Defense of Democracy] (CNDD–FDD) rebellion group, and NFL to be conducted by the United Nations or AU. The United Nations remained reluctant to deploy a mission due to the non-existence of an agreed peace agreement, and thus the African Union deployed AMIB on April 2, 1993, which was near the end of the civil war, and it lasted until June 2004. The African Union realized that insecurity in Burundi would mark instability in the Great Lakes area.

The amounted troops of the African Mission in Burundi that replaced the South African mission stood at 2,870 and peaked at 3,128 armed forces, and they were arranged from South Africa, Ethiopia, and Mozambique to enter Burundi for one year, with South Africa staying in Burundi once a UN-sanctioned operation succeeded the AU mission.[21] After one year of operation, the mandate and potential six-month renewal instructed to facilitate a ceasefire agreement and create new military and police structures.[22] The Arusha Agreement called for AMIB to arrive in December 2002, but ultimately poor funding from African states and reliance on the deployment of South African troops resulted in the AU Mission being transferred over to a UN peacekeeping operation.[23] AMIB was centered within the United Nations Operation in Burundi (ONUB) from June 1, 2004.

In 2004, the African Union budget was an estimated US$32 million, but at the close of AMIB's operation, it cost $134 million and thus had to rely heavily on external donor funding.[24] Burundi was deemed stable from AMIB so that ONUB was implemented that held US$333.2 million

[21] Williams, "The African Union," p. 353. Mozambique and Ethiopia only deployed troops due to British and American financial support. The military observers were deployed from Burkina Faso, Mali, Gabon, Togo, and Tunisia.

[22] AMIB also monitored DDR to stabilize the country to allow a UN peacekeeping operation.

[23] The lack of capacity and weak political will of the African Union's Members States hindered AMIB.

[24] Badmus, "African Mission in Burundi (AMIB)," p. 13.

as annual budgets as a multidimensional peacekeeping operation in Burundi.[25] South Africa remained in Burundi until September 2004. The reason was to await the arrival of AMIB's Ethiopian battalion.[26] AMIB troops were rebadged, and Pakistan, Nepal, and Kenya deployed their contingents.[27]AMIB did well, given its reinforcements and strong political will from the African Union to deploy resources, but the Disarmament, Demobilization and Reintegration of former combatants (DDR) process failed.[28] This security initiative envisioned that AMIB would demobilize and disarm an estimated 20,000 ex-fighters, secure humanitarian convoys, and protect repatriating politicians. The rules of engagement for AMIB troops rested on only using force in self-defense. AMIB secured almost 95 percent of Burundi by the end of its operation.[29] Political violence diminished, but general crime increased in late 2003 despite AMIB ensuring the ceasefire was implemented. The armed leaders were protected by AMIB to return to Burundi to engage in the peace process.

DDR was not truly implemented via World Bank–funded support until December 2004, which was six months after the termination of AMIB's mandate. In Dar es Salaam, on September 7, 2006, a peace agreement was signed between Pierre Nkurunziza of the new CNDD–FDD government and FNL to finalize the cessation of fighting, FNL combatants to obtain temporary immunity and demobilized and reintegrated into the new Burundian army. ONUB ceased in December 2006 and was replaced with the United Nations Integrated Office in Burundi to support its government.[30]

Multilateral Peacekeeping in Sudan

In Darfur, land disputes over free cultivation emerged in the 1980s and, in 2003, a rebellion with the secularist Sudan Liberation Movement/Army (SLM/A) launching their grievances against ruling Islamic elites of the

[25] United Nations Security Council Resolution 1545, "On the Situation in Burundi," UN Doc. S/RES/1545, May 21, 2004, adopted 4,975th meeting.

[26] Williams, "The African Union," p. 354.

[27] Badmus, "The African Mission in Burundi (AMIB)," p. 12.

[28] Badmus, "The African Mission in Burundi (AMIB)," p. 1.

[29] Festus Aboagye, "The African Mission in Burundi: Lessons Learned from the First African Union Peacekeeping Operation," *Conflict Trends*, No. 2 (January 2004), pp. 9–15.

[30] United Nations Security Council Resolution 1719, "The Situation in Burundi," UN Doc. S/RES/1719, October 25, 2006, adopted 5,554th meeting.

Khartoum government. The Naivasha peace process (Comprehensive Peace Agreement) from January 2004 concerned the north and south Sudan grievances against exclusion of non-Arab civilians, and young aggrieved men gathered arms in the western region, notably Darfur, to be included in the process. Khartoum decided to eliminate the rebels instead of including them.

Similar to the succession by a UN peacekeeping operation, in 2004, the African Union installed a regional peacekeeping force in Darfur due to funding from NATO, the European Union, and the Group of Eight (G8). When AMIB in Burundi was slowly withdrawing, the African Mission in Sudan (AMIS) began operations in Sudan that included a protection force, military observers, police forces, and humanitarian and civilian entities.[31] The United Nations Security Council refused a military force to protect civilians from mass killings so opted for sanctions, a weapons embargo, a no-fly zone and transferred the case to the International Criminal Court (ICC) to inspect allegations of war crimes, crimes against humanity and genocide perpetrated in Darfur since July 1, 2002, which is when the Rome Statute arrived into force.[32] A Commission of Inquiry into atrocity crimes found that there were 1.65 million internally displaced persons (IDPs) in Darfur, over 200,000 refugees in neighboring Chad, and many villages were destroyed in Darfur.[33] However, in mid-2005, the sanctions did not work that revived Kofi Annan's ethical question on genocide in Rwanda amounting the mass deaths of Tutsis without rapid UN Security Council action, but if the prompt action was present, should a coalition have stood idle.[34]

Single powerful states that hinted at R2P were the United States (US), United Kingdom (UK), and France, but Egypt (with an army nearby) did not indicate any intentions to prevent the mass killings. France had 1,000 forces in neighboring Chad and 200 at the border with Sudan, but made it clear Paris was more concerned about supporting the Marshal Idriss

[31] Paul D. Williams, "Military Responses to Mass Killing: The African Union Mission in Sudan," *International Peacekeeping*, Vol. 13, No. 2 (2006), pp. 168–183.

[32] International Criminal Court, "Situation in Darfur, Sudan," *International Criminal Court*, ICC-02/05 Investigation, March 2005.

[33] Report of the Independent Commission of Inquiry on Darfur to the Secretary-General, "Pursuant to Security Council Resolution 1564 (2004) of September 18, 2004," February 1, 2005, S/2005/60, E. 226.

[34] Nicholas J. Wheeler, *Saving Strangers: Humanitarian Intervention in International Society* (Oxford: Oxford University Press, 2000), p. 294.

Déby Itno regime rather than averting the mass killings in Darfur.[35] Tony Blair did not deploy UK standby troops.

On September 9, 2004, US Secretary of State, Colin Luther Powell, from findings of the State Department's Atrocities Documentation Team (ADT) accused the Sudanese government led by Omar Hassan Ahmad al-Bashir and Janjaweed Sudanese Arab militia group pressing the rebellion back in Darfur of perpetrating genocide, but genocide is "not there yet."[36] The United States was more concerned about its war on terror, was under scrutiny over bogus humanitarian debates regarding the invasion of Iraq in March 2003, and thus did not want to, as a state or with the United Nations Security Council, engage in Sudan to deal with the atrocities committed within the Darfur region. George Walker Bush was voted a second term as president in November 2004, and Sudan was pushed down the pecking order.[37] Despite these notable variables warranting a robust foreign armed intervention in Darfur, the political will of great powers were lacking and thus it was AU troops that entered.

After the rebuttal of a UN multidimensional peacekeeping operation, the African Union deployed a weak AMIS force to Darfur to respond against the mass killing of civilians. NATO was consulted by AMIS for logistical support, but the Alliance did not deploy its own forces for the purpose of a humanitarian intervention (even though NATO can respond to ethnic cleansing as in Kosovo). The International Crisis Group (ICG) recommended NATO to deploy a 12,000–15,000 force within two months, and if not consented to do so by the Sudanese government, then 40,000 troops should be deployed.[38]

AMIS worked with UNMIS and humanitarian non-governmental organizations (NGOs). The initial troop size of the Sudan Mission started with 150 troops, but later mandates increased the size to approximately 7,000 personnel, comprising Nigerian, Rwandan, and Senegalese troops.[39] During this period, AMIS I held approximately 60–80 military observers

[35] Williams, "Military Responses to Mass Killing," p. 173.

[36] Samuel Totten and Erik Markusen, "Research Note: The US Government Darfur Genocide Investigation," *Journal of Genocide Research*, Vol. 7, No. 2 (June 2005), pp. 279–290. https://doi.org/10.1080/14623520500127571.

[37] Williams, "Military Responses to Mass Killing," p. 173.

[38] International Crisis Group, *The AU's Mission in Darfur: Bridging the Gaps*, Africa Briefing No. 6 (Nairobi: ICG, July 6, 2005), pp. 12–13.

[39] United Nations Security Council Resolution 1564, "Report of the Secretary-General on the Sudan," UN Doc. S/RES/1564, September 18, 2004, adopted 5,040th meeting.

with protection provided by the 300 forces of a Protection Force to secure the observer personnel and civilians.[40] This mandate and deployed force size was, however, too ambitious due to the might of the estimated 20,000-strong Janjaweed militia functioning in Darfur against a small deployed AMIS. In an attempt to protect civilians and humanitarian observers from the mismatch, AMIS was increased to 3,320 troops, which included 2,341 armed forces.[41] Yet, the renewed force could only protect select areas in Darfur.

In February 2005, the Intergovernmental Authority on Development (IGAD) was committed to deploy 10,500 peacekeepers in Sudan, which was permitted by the African Union. The mandate of IGAD to use force beyond self-defense and engage in an operation without the consent of a host government was unclear. However, many African states conformed to non-intervention and the norm of respecting state sovereignty by avoiding an incursion that did not have consent of a host government.[42] The African Union adopted this culture of avoiding specific intervention in Darfur. In March 2005, the United Nations Mission in South Sudan (UNMIS) was deployed to monitor and implement the January 9, 2005, Comprehensive Peace Agreement between the Sudanese government and Sudan People's Liberation Army, share oil revenues, and produce a timetable for south Sudan's referendum for independence.[43] As of July 2005, an estimated 300,000 were killed and almost 3 million were impacted from displacement, sickness, and malnourishment due to attacks committed by the Janjaweed militia and Sudanese armed forces.[44]

AMIS II further expressed its intentions to deploy 7,000 forces by late September 2005 and AMIS III with 12,000 personnel by spring 2006.[45] Yet, on February 1, 2006, AMIS only had 4,185 forces alongside 1,390 civilian police.[46] The United Nations was then discussed to undertake full

[40] African Union, "Communiqué," Communication XIII, July 27, 2004, para. 8.

[41] Williams, "Military Responses to Mass Killing," p. 176.

[42] A humanitarian intervention would be an example of undermining the respect for state sovereignty.

[43] United Nations Security Council Resolution 1590, "Establishment of UMMIS," UN Doc. S/RES/1590, March 24, 2005, adopted 5,151st meeting.

[44] United Nations, "Explainer: How Darfur Became a 'Humanitarian Calamity and Catastrophic Human Rights Crisis'," *United Nations*, December 14, 2023.

[45] Williams, "The African Union," p. 354.

[46] African Union, *Current Status of the AU Military Deployment in Darfur* (Darfur Integrated Task Force), Information Update No. 02/06, February 1, 2006.

operations in Sudan—but the United Nations Department of Peacekeeping Operations (DPKO) of the United Nations Secretariat claimed that it could assume this responsibility in January 2007. It was, however, estimated by the United Nations that AMIS funds would cease by late March 2006. AMIS was militarily deployed from Nigeria, Rwanda, and Senegal, but held low funds to cater for US $465 million per year in operational costs.[47]

Sudan was against a UN force, and the African Union could not sustain funding due to unexpected longer commitments.[48] Therefore, the Peace and Security Council of the African Union extended the mandate of AMIS until September 30, 2006. It would partner a UN operation if the Sudanese government did not object to it and held its traditional DPKO tenets: consent, impartiality, and self-defense. It was clear that civilians in Darfur were victim to mass scale war crimes and crimes against humanity, but genocide was disputed by the United Nations Secretary-General, Kofi Atta Annan, as crimes against humanity to avoid bringing the situation to the immediate attention of the United Nations Security Council. At the close of December 2007, the African Union mission was replaced by the United Nations.

The African Union in Somalia

Somalia was a failed and fragile state for a few decades. The civil war in Somalia intensified in 1988 with opposition to Major-General Mohamed Siad Barre's governance that existed since the 1977 Ogaden War with Ethiopia to regain the Ogaden region in Ethiopia.[49] In March 1978, Somalia's armed forces lost the war, and on April 9, 1978, defense leaders launched a coup d'état. The attempted coup did not seize power, but oppositional resentment of Barre increased. Antigovernmental groups emerged with the Somali National Movement (SNM). Guerilla warfare was frequent, and in 1988, SNM fighters attacked Somali armed forces. The national army retaliated by aerially bombing Burau and Hargeisa in northern Somalia.

[47] Williams, "The African Union," p. 355.

[48] Bereng Mtimkulu, "The African Union and Peace Support Operations," *Conflict Trends: Focus on Peacekeeping*, No. 4 (January 2005), p. 36.

[49] Debora Valentina Malito, "Neutral in Favor of Whom? The UN Intervention in Somali and the Somaliland Peace Process," *International Peacekeeping*, Vol. 24, No. 2 (2017), p. 287.

In December 1990, a coalition pressed back Somali armed forces from the capital, Mogadishu. Barre fled and the United Somali Congress (USC) (from central and southern areas) gained the capital. The United Somali Congress failed to fully control central Somalia, and its wings split in late January 1991. Ali Mahdi Muhammad controlled the state as transitional president. The split USC wings comprised USC/Somali Salvation Alliance (SSA) headed by Ali Mahdi and USC/Somali National Alliance (SNA) chaired by General Mohammed Farah Hassan Aidid. Clans continued fighting, and the United Nations acted on Ali Mahdi's letter to deploy a foreign armed intervention. Both USC wings were in a full-scale armed conflict. At this time (1991–1992), famine and other diseases resulted in over 300,000 deaths in south Somalia.[50]

Mogadishu had no functional government in the 1990s, and thus basic judicial, security, and political infrastructure was very weak, and human security, education, and food were also scarce. This is why terrorism groups emerged to provide security by filling the void.

The United Nations and the United States preferred enticing the winning faction into the peace process in Somalia. In March 1992, a diplomatic delegation was put in place to broker a ceasefire that Aidid signed in Mogadishu with the United Nations playing a monitoring role.[51] The United Nations Operation in Somali (UNOSOM I) was authorized to deal with the initially publicized humanitarian crisis and rapid deployment of a peacekeeping force.[52] UNOSOM I was initially a small peacekeeping operation of 50 troops monitoring the March 1992 ceasefire.[53] The United Nations increased its troops to 3,500 forces in April 1992. The United Nations wanted to develop nation-building in Somali, and the United States deployed troops to enhance security for the safe delivery of humanitarian assistance.[54] The United States desired to test its victorious Cold War liberalist ideals of the new world order and advocate realist geopolitical interests in the Horn of Africa.

[50] Malito, "Neutral in Favor of Whom?" p. 288.

[51] Agreement on the Implementation of the Ceasefire signed by Farah Aidid, S/23693, March 3, 1992, p. 25.

[52] United Nations Security Council Resolution 767, "On the Humanitarian Situation in Somalia," UN Doc. S/RES/767, July 27, 1992, adopted 3,101st meeting, paras. 4–5.

[53] United Nations Security Council Resolution 751, "Agreements for the Implementation of Measures Aimed at Stabilizing the Ceasefire through a United Nations Monitoring Mission," UN Doc. S/RES/751, April 24, 1992, adopted 3,069th meeting.

[54] Malito, "Neutral in Favor of Whom?" p. 289.

The United States and UN top-down approach in Somalia failed to create secure conditions for ceasing fighting and protracted peace.[55] Community and reconciliation approaches did work, however, in Somaliland (northwest Somalia). When Somalia collapsed as a state, it was only the clan institution that was functional and thus the elders, as grassroots leaders, rebuilt confidence and cemented justice at the community level.[56] Somaliland and the peacebuilding strategy conforming with top-, middle-, and low-level leaders, better social harmony, and communal relationships—that are integral for Afro-communitarian ethics—commenced. For instance, middle-level *aaqils* representing local chiefs promoted meetings and created compensations to deter violence.[57] Moreover, women groups were empowered to provide communication operations between different clans that created enhanced community engagement.[58] The right to self-determination for the Republic of Somaliland was supported by SNM and elders of clans based in northern areas of Somalia.

Aidid perceived the United Nations as non-neutral when Mohamed Sahnoun, the United Nations Special Representative for Somalia, negotiated with Aidid for a lengthy time, forcibly resigned to signify international efforts to corner Aidid.[59] Ali Mahdi kept negotiating with the United Nations to do more and increase troops. The United Nations abused its principle of impartiality, and it legitimized the factional wings of the United Somali Congress by attempting to transform warlords (Ali Mahdi and Aidid) into advocates of peace.[60]

In November 1992, the United States headed the United Task Force (UNITAF) to establish a secure environment so that humanitarian

[55] Malito, "Neutral in Favor of Whom?" p. 280.

[56] Malito, "Neutral in Favor of Whom?" p. 292.

[57] Michael Walls, "The Emergence of a Somali State: Building Peace from Civil War in Somaliland," *African Affairs*, Vol. 108, No. 432 (July 2009), pp. 374–375.

[58] Michael Walls, Koss Mohammed and Mohamud Omar Ali, *Peace in Somaliland: An Indigenous Approach to Statebuilding* (Nairobi: Interpeace/Academy for Peace and Development, 2008); Walls, "The Emergence of a Somali State," p. 384.

[59] Mohamed M. Sahnoun, *Somalia: The Missed Opportunities* (Washington, DC: United States Institute of Peace Press, 1994).

[60] Ken Mankaus, "International Peacebuilding and the Dynamics of Local and National Reconciliation in Somalia," in *Learning from Somalia: The Lessons of Armed Humanitarian Intervention*, edited by Walter Sheldon Clarke and Jeffrey Herbst (Boulder, CO: Westview Press, 1997), pp. 42–63, p. 53.

operations could commence in the southern part of Somalia.[61] The United States then wanted UNITAF to function under the Command of America with UNOSOM II that included nation-building duties. The military force of UNITAF then lost its military objectives when it was absorbed into more nation-building duties with UNOSOM II. UN and American troops clashed with Aidid's SNA forces in June 1993. SNA belligerents did not want foreign armed intervention anymore due to the questionability of impartiality. UNOSOM II troops inspected Radio Mogadishu, and 24 of its Pakistani forces were murdered in an ambush on June 5, 1993, so the United Nations authorized the use of force by all necessary means (with UNITAF headed by the United States).[62] The United States deployed the Ranger Task Force, but on October 3, 1993, two American Black Hawk Down helicopters were shot at the Battle of Mogadishu, resulting in 18 troops dead. The United States then withdrew from Somalia that left UNOSOM II with a lack of military strategy to also withdraw in March 1995. UNITAF engaged with the military objective and wanted to withdraw rapidly so UNOSOM II could deal with nation-building, but this formed poor coordination and foreign armed forces became combatants in the Somali conflict that increased and legitimized both USC factional wings to continue fighting.[63]

From March 2007 to March 2022, the African Union Mission to Somalia (AMISOM) with IGAD deployed an excess of a 20,000-strong regional peacekeeping operation in Somalia.[64] However, the African Union started with a light mandate but later agreed to the use of force preemptively against al-Shabaab. Kenya has been heavily involved. Nairobi has not focused on a political solution to terrorism in Somalia, but instead linearly opted for military intervention. Kenya has headed contributing soldiers to the mandate of AMISOM that supported transitional Somali governments from 2004 to 2007.[65] Kenya has previously acted as a main

[61] United Nations Security Council Resolution 794, "Gravely Alarmed by the Deterioration of the Humanitarian Situation in Somalia," UN Doc. S/RES/794, December 3, 1992, adopted 3,145th meeting.

[62] United Nations Security Council Resolution 837, "Gravely Alarmed at the Premeditated Armed Attacks," UN Doc. S/RES/837, June 6, 1993, adopted 3,229th meeting.

[63] Malito, "Neutral in Favor of Whom?" p. 291.

[64] Malte Brosig, *Cooperative Peacekeeping in Africa: Exploring Regime Complexity* (London: Routledge, 2015), p. 73.

[65] Joseph Makanda, "Fighting Terrorism in the Horn of Africa: The Role of Ordinary Kenyans in Kenya's Military Intervention in Somalia and the Fight against al-Shabaab," *Journal of African Union Studies*, Vol. 8, No. 1 (April 2019), p. 38.

partner with the African Union, UN, and IGAD.[66] Kenya has led IGAD on counterterrorism with coordination of its member states, training, disseminating information, bolstering border control, and enhancing the capacity of the judicial sector.[67]

Kenya adopted a conventional state-centric foreign armed intervention in Somalia to help combat al-Shabaab, which has contributed to instability. This is similar to the initial intervention of South Africa in Sudan prior to the proper installation of AMIS. Kenya has focused on senior leaders and not engaged with a grassroots approach to empower lower-level leaders. Al-Shabaab are financed by al-Qaeda and are also active in Kenya, which is why Operation Linda Nchi entailed the deployment of the Kenya Defense Forces (KDF) intervened in Somalia on October 16, 2011, with an estimated 2,000 troops and increased forces to 4,600 a few months later to protect Kenyan national security.[68] In March 2012, Kenya agreed to conduct its operations under AMISOM and would deploy 5,000 forces for the AU regional peacekeeping mission.[69] In the south of Somali, 4,000 Kenyan soldiers were integrated into more than 17,000 armed forces with UN partnership with the mandate to protect the transitional government of Somalia.[70] Kenya created a buffer zone in the lower and middle Juba area and Gedo to replicate the stability established with the Somaliland and Puntland models (that have functional governments).[71] This strategy also attempted to debatably reduce the influx and burden of Somali

[66] IGAD has attempted to enhance Somalia's national capacity to foster good governance, peace and security, basic welfare and social services, public administration, and economic development. IGAD actively assisted the African Union to fight terrorism and regional organized crime (Paul D. Williams, "AMISOM under Review," *The RUSI Journal*, Vol. 161, No. 1 (January 2006), pp. 40–49. The African Union worked with the United Nations for AMISOM to receive additional funding.

[67] Makanda, "Fighting Terrorism in the Horn of Africa," p. 39.

[68] Gorm Rye Olsen, "The October 2011 Kenyan Invasion of Somalia: Fighting al-Shabaab or Defending Institutional Interests?" *Journal of Contemporary African Studies*, Vol. 36, No. 1 (2018), p. 39.

[69] China Daily, "Kenya Agrees to Join AMISOM," *China Daily*, December 7, 2011.

[70] Daniel E. Agbiboa, "Terrorism without Borders: Somalia's al-Shabaab and the Global Jihad Network," *Journal of Terrorism Research*, Vol. 5, No. 1 (February 2014), p. 27.

[71] Katy Long, "Kenya, Jubaland and Somali's Refugees: No Quick Fixes," *London School of Economics and Political Science* (October 24, 2011), pp. 1–2; Olsen, "The October 21011 Kenyan Invasion of Somalia: Fighting al-Shabaab or Defending Institutional Interests?" pp. 40, 44.

refugees.[72] Kenya opted to engage with top-level leaders, but did not include respected oppositional leaders, religious figures, and clan leaders on Somalia.[73] Therefore, Kenya did not initially include local clan leaders when creating Jubaland (Azania) in south Somalia.[74] However, the Kenyan government later adopted community grassroots approaches with the "ten household neighborhood" (Nyumba Kumi) initiate to partner with civilians to fight criminality and terrorism.[75] This prescribes a communitarian approach by requesting Kenyans to approach ten households in their community and report suspicious crime and terrorism to their communal leaders. Despite the communitarian initiative to promote social harmony, KDF troops have detained and tortured those who report activities to gather additional information of al-Shabaab.[76] Civilians thus tend to keep silent.

There was speculation that Kenya merely attempted to secure its borders, especially its eastern border with Somalia, rather than promote peace and security in Somali. Kenya and Somalia have been under threat from further al-Shabaab suicide attacks against AMISOM forces under the leadership of the late Emir Ahmed Abdi Godane that has also killed many civilians.[77] Consequently, Kenyan civilians avoid going to shopping malls in certain areas, including the capital, Nairobi. Al-Shabaab have targeted Christian moderates, who are both Christian and Islamic, so Christians are reluctant to attend church on Sundays.[78] A Christian moderate, even if Muslim, is deemed a foe by al-Shabaab.

Due to Kenya displaying their national security interests by interfering in Somalia, active terrorist organizations have fought against such foreign armed intervention. The Somali-based Islamist militancy, al-Shabaab, has attacked Kenya after their intervention also, which includes attacks from

[72] Leslie Anne Warner, "In Somalia, Kenya Risks Death by a Thousand Cuts," *PRISM: A Journal of the Center for Complex Operations*, Vol. 3, No. 3 (2012), pp. 106–107.

[73] This strategy failed to adopt middle and grassroots leaders to undertake key peacebuilding initiatives, which did not comply with Lederach's pyramid of building peace (John Paul Lederach, *Building Peace: Sustainable Reconciliation in Divided Societies* (Washington, DC: United States Institute of Peace Press, 1997), pp. 39–41.

[74] Makanda, "Fighting Terrorism in the Horn of Africa," p. 39.

[75] Makanda, "Fighting Terrorism in the Horn of Africa," p. 44.

[76] Nancy Muchangi, *The Effectiveness of the Nyumba Kumi Initiative as a Police Reform Strategy in Nairobi* County (Nairobi: Strathmore University, 2016).

[77] Isaac Kfir, "Al-Shabaab, Social Identity Group, Human (In)Security and Counterterrorism," *Studies in Conflict & Terrorism*, Vol. 40, No. 9 (2017), p. 777.

[78] Gordon L. Heath and David K. Tarus, *Christian Responses to Terrorism: The Kenyan Experience* (Eugene, OR: Pickwick, 2017).

2013 to 2018. Civilians, students, beheadings, police officers, and bases have been targeted in the Westgate Mall (September 2013), Garissa University College (April 2015), Lamu (July 2017), Mandera Town (January 2018), and Lamu-Malindi Highway (July 2018) respectively.[79] Al-Shabaab have also targeted KDF bases in Somalia that has included Kenya's AMISOM base in El-Adde on January 15, 2016, resulting in a firefight with KDF and the latter recapturing the region.[80] Therefore, in terms of violence, al-Shabaab have engaged with sabotage, guerrilla warfare, and terrorism—yet *Ubuntu* ethics would not justify the attacks because they have not attempted to reach a more harmonious state of affairs.

The United Nations Security Council sanctioned the African Mission to support the Somali government combat the al-Shabaab insurgency, which was supported by al-Qaeda, attempting to conquer the fragile administration.[81] Moreover, the mandate included the adoption of a National Security Plan with the objectives of training the national security forces and providing a safe passage for humanitarian aid in principally central and southern Somalia. The United Nations mission was replaced by another AU mission, instead of or remaining to the United Nations, with the aim to transition and help the Somali National Armed Forces, with dissolution of the mission scheduled for late 2024.[82]

The African Union and ECOWAS in Mali

In March 2012, Captain Amadou Sanogo militarily overthrew President Amadou Toumani Touré.[83] This left a void in northern Mali for extremist Islamist militias to expand their functionality.[84] The military leaders

[79] Makanda, "Fighting Terrorism in the Horn of Africa," p. 34.

[80] Jeffrey Gettleman, "Kenya Rattled as Shabaab Turns Sights on Somalia Military Targets," *The New York Times*, January 20, 2016.

[81] United Nations, "UN Security Council Votes for New Somalia Peacekeeping Force," *France 24*, March 31, 2022.

[82] Meressa K. Dessu, "Is the AU Mission in Somalia Changing in Name Only?" *Institute for Security Studies*, March 29, 2022.

[83] Bambara is the most widely spoken language in Mali, and it is heavily influenced, and similar, with French and France colonized Mali in 1892. Touré was militarily trained in France and the former Soviet Union.

[84] Dario Christiani and Riccardo Fabiani, *From Disfunctionality to Disaggregation and Back? The Malian Crisis, Local Players and European Interests*, Istituto Affari Internazionali Working Papers 13-08, pp. 1–20 (Rome: Istituto Affari Internazionali, March 2013), p. 5.

orchestrating the coup claimed that the government failed to eradicate minority Tuareg rebels. The regime change in Libya in 2011 created further fighting in northern Mali. Many returned to fight for the secular Tuareg group and strengthen "the Movement for the National Liberation of Azawad."[85] This liberation army grew in strength that encouraged the entry of the Movement for Unity and Jihad in West Africa, Ansar Dine, and the al-Qaeda in the Islamic Maghreb.[86] These groups seized and controlled northern Mali to impose strict adherence of Shari'a Law and looted the wealthy artifacts from Timbuktu. This created a humanitarian and refugee crisis.

ECOWAS responded swiftly that was followed by the African Union. ECOWAS condemned the military coup and called for the leaders to surrender power to the former government and for rebels to relinquish their arms. Moreover, ECOWAS wanted to engage with the military reform of the Malian armed forces that was followed by the March 2012 diplomatic and economic sanctions to hit Mali.[87] Mali's neighboring states shut their borders and naval ports. This allowed ECOWAS to pursue ousting the military junta from ruling Mali. In April 2012, the National Movement for the Liberation of Azawad (NMLA) controlled the area and proclaimed an independent homeland for the Tuareg ethnic group from Mali.[88] Yet, a variety of Islamist groups (Ansar Dine, al-Qaeda in the Islamic Maghreb, the Movement for Oneness and Jihad in West Africa, and Boko Haram) became more involved than the NMLA in northern Mali and enacted Shari'a Law in the area.[89] The Economic Community of West African

[85] Kwesi Aning and Fifi Edu-Afful, "African Agency in R2P: Interventions by African Union and ECOWAS in Mali, Côte d'Ivoire, and Libya," *International Studies Review*, Vol. 18, No. 1 (March 2016), p. 128.

[86] Hussein Solomon, "Mali: West Africa's Afghanistan," *The RUSI Journal*, Vol. 158, No. 1 (March 2013), p. 12.

[87] Aning and Fifi Edu-Afful, "African Agency in R2P," p. 128.

[88] Tchioffo Kodjo, *Mali Conflict of 2012–2013: A Critical Assessment – Patterns of Local, Regional and Global Conflict and Resolution Dynamics in Post-colonial and Post-cold war Africa* (Chisinau: Lambert, 2015), p. 52; Lyal S. Sunga, "Has the ICC Unfairly Targeted or Has Africa Unfairly Targeted the ICC?" in *The International Criminal Court in Search of its Purpose and Identity*, edited by Triestino Marinello (London: Routledge, 2015), p. 170.

[89] Catherine Gegout, *Why Europe Intervenes in Africa: Security, Prestige and the Legacy of Colonialism* (Oxford: Oxford University Press, 2017), p. 185.

States Mission in Mali (MICEMA) recommended a 3,000-strong force, but ECOWAS preferred diplomatic efforts.[90]

On December 20, 2012, the UN Security Council authorized an organized ECOWAS mission in northern Mali to fight Islamist extremists for an initial period of one year.[91] ECOWAS deployed this continental peace mission named the African-led International Support Mission to Mali (AFISMA). The African Union assisted ECOWAS by broadening sanctions, such as prohibiting travel and freezing the financial assets of ruling rebels. AFISMA was headed by African contingents and mandated by the United Nations. The mission comprised nearly 7,500 troops from 21 African states, including 1,800 personnel arriving from Chad and 1,200 deployed from Nigeria.

The rebels pressed to seize Bamako, the capital, resulting in French intervention. On January 11, 2013, French armed forces intervened with the deployment of Opération Serval and ECOWAS promptly deployed aerial and ground forces to Mali.[92] On January 17, 2013, Nigeria deployed troops for air attacks and on the ground and 160 men arrived from neighboring Burkina Faso. At the end of January 2013, AFISMA comprised an estimated 1,400 forces from Nigeria, and Chad, Burkina Faso, Gabon, Togo, Senegal, Niger, Côte d'Ivoire, Guinea, Gambia, Ghana, and others contributed troops to make AFISMA to 7,464 forces.[93]

Most of northern Mali was recaptured by Malian soldiers, and in mid-2013, a peace accord was signed between the government and oppositional Tuareg rebels. At this time, the United Nations-led Multidimensional Integrated Stabilization Mission in Mali had taken over AFISMA with French troops remaining.[94] The ceasefire terminated when Malian armed forces shot unarmed protestors.

[90] Economic Community of West African States, "ECOWAS Defense Chiefs Call for International Support on Mali," *ECOWAS*, July 28, 2012.

[91] United Nations Security Council Resolution 2085, "Concerning the Deployment of the African-led International Support Mission to Mali," UN Doc. S/RES/2085, December 20, 2012, adopted 6,898th meeting.

[92] United Nations Security Council Resolution 2085, "Concerning the Deployment of the African-led International Support Mission to Mali;" Yinka Olomojobi, *Frontiers of Jihad: Radical Islam in Africa* (Ibadan: Safari Books, 2015), p. 218.

[93] United Nations Security Council Resolution 2085, "Concerning the Deployment of the African-led International Support Mission to Mali."

[94] Matteo Tondini, "Coalitions of the Willing," in *The Practice of Shared Responsibility in International Law*, edited by André Nollkaemper and Ilias Plakokefalos (Cambridge: Cambridge University Press, 2017), p. 702.

Opération Serval lasted until July 15, 2014, which resulted in French and Malian armed forces restoring order in Mali's major cities. It deployed an estimated 4,000 French soldiers expanding to over 5,000 and 2,900 allied with AFISMA to eradicate Islamic militant groups from northern Mali that were pressing toward central Mali.[95] French fighter jets were used with the French Air Force, Army, Navy, Special Forces, National Gendarmerie, and their Allied Nations. Opération Serval managed to kill several Islamist chiefs. This included Adelhamid Abou Zeid (al-Qaeda commander),[96] Omar Ould Hamah (affiliations with Ansar Dine, al-Qaeda in the Islamic Maghreb, and Movement for Oneness and Jihad in West Africa),[97] and Iyad Ag Ghaly (the founder of Ansar Dine) went in exile to Algeria and Mokhtar Belmokhtar (military commander of al-Qaeda of the in the Islamic Maghreb) fled to Libya.

Opération Serval was replaced by Opération Barkhane on August 1, 2014, which engaged with France's counterinsurgency operations of 3,000 forces deployed in the Sahel area, and principally stationed in N'Djamena, Chad.[98] French troops and their partners killed the head of the al-Qaeda in the Islamic Maghreb, Abdelmalek Droukdel.[99]

In February 2015, another peace agreement was signed between the Azawad movements and Malian administration, but Malian politicians denied their autonomy while corresponding on their local devolution powers. This is now regarded as a low-level conflict. The attempts to reach peace was admirable to form a more harmonious state of affairs between the NMLA and Malian government, but opening fire on unarmed protestors and excluding Islamist groups (that have now either moved, disbanded, or merged within another insurgency) from all peace processes has not inevitably attained a less discordant state of affairs. Democracy has failed in adjacent Burkina Faso with two military coups beginning between January and September 2022 that has caused insecurity in the country, and also in Mali, with fighting enduring with Azawad- and

[95] Hugh Schofield, "Mali and France 'Push Back Islamists'," *BBC News*, January 12, 2013. https://www.bbc.co.uk/news/world-africa-20991723.

[96] Lionel Laurent and Elizabeth Pineau, "France Confirms Death of al-Qaeda's Abou Zeid in Mali," *Reuters*, March 23, 2013.

[97] Al Jazeera, "French Strike 'Kills Mali Rebel Commander'," *Al Jazeera*, March 14, 2014.

[98] The Economist, "François Hollande's African Adventures," *The Economist*, July 21, 2014.

[99] Frank Gardner, "Al-Qaeda Chief in North Africa Abdelmalek Droukdel Killed – France," *BBC News*, June 5, 2020.

al-Qaeda-related insurgencies.[100] Hence, Mali is in a less discordant state of affairs, especially in the north and south.

ECOWAS and the United Nations in Liberia

After Charles Taylor's party named the National Patriotic Front of Liberia (NPFL) launched a Gaddafi-funded coup from Côte d'Ivoire to besiege Monrovia and overthrow Samuel Kanyon Doe, the transitional government collapsed.[101] A few hundred guerrillas (named the Gio tribesmen) entered the north of Liberia, and these rebels were perceived by neighbors as an easy job for the Liberian armed forces to oust. Yet, the army failed to deal with the rebels that made President Doe in Monrovia look weak. The United States and Nigeria provided arms and military advisors to support Doe, but it was later discovered that tribesmen were an oppositional coordinated militia (NPFL). NPFL forces then seized two-thirds of Liberia and civilians fled. Charles Taylor made it clear that peace could not proceed without Doe relinquishing presidential office.

The United Nations and Organization of African Unity (OAU) afterward endeavored to end the war, but factions persistently fought until a democratic process was pursued. The Organization of African Unity became prominent, but it was cemented on the rule of non-intervention and maintaining respect for member state's internal affairs. OAU officials consulted Nigeria and ECOWAS. The Economic Community of West African States Monitoring Group (ECOMOG) would monitor elections in Liberia and observe an arms embargo, a transitional government while planning elections, a peace plan, with the deployment of the Economic Community of West African States Ceasefire Monitoring Group for an instant ceasefire for all warring factions.[102] Taylor did not agree and instructed NPFL combatants to take up weapons and oust Doe that

[100] Aminata Diaby and Nicolas Klingelschmitt, "De Facto Sovereignty and Multilateral Sanctions for a Return to Constitutional Order in a Context of Regional Armed Conflict: The Case of Mali," in *War, State and Sovereignty: Interdisciplinary Challenges and Perspectives for the Social Sciences*, edited by Grégory Daho and Yann Richard (Cham: Palgrave Macmillan, 2023), p. 189.

[101] Alex J. Bellamy and Paul D. Williams, *Understanding Peacekeeping*, 2nd ed. (Cambridge: Polity Press, 2010), pp. 313–314.

[102] Economic Community of West African States, "ECOWAS Decision A/DEC.1/8/90" (Lagos: ECOWAS, 1990).

resulted in the takeover of over 95 percent of Liberia.[103] Amos Claudius Sawyer, a Marxist intellectual, was selected to head the transitional government—Interim Government of National Unity—that was further opposed by NPFL forces with allegations of ECOWAS violating Liberia's internal sovereignty.

Despite the failure of diplomatic negotiation, ECOWAS rapidly deployed forces in Liberia. This was arguably because neighboring states had been burdened with refugees and ECOWAS refuted its plan due to the lack of cooperation from the National Patriotic Front of Liberia faction.[104] In Liberia, between 1990 and 1997, ECOWAS stipulated a peacekeeping force to settle the intra-state conflict and attempted to broker peace for a transitional government and transparent, free, and fair democratic elections. In August 1990, ECOWAS met to form a peace agreement, establish an interim government, and create a monitoring group deployed from Freetown to Monrovia comprising "3,000 troops from Nigeria, Ghana, Guinea."[105] This was the first time that the United Nations worked with a regional organization (ECOWAS in Liberia).[106] ECOWAS stepped in because the historical ally of Liberia, the United States, was caught up dealing with the disintegrating former Soviet Union and successionist independent states. The Cold War ceased. The United States only hinted at saving their nationals with evacuations in Liberia, France had no Francophone ties, and thus the West had abandoned Liberia.

The National Patriotic Front of Liberia militia moved in on Monrovia, but ECOMOG forces pressed them back. ECOMOG overly focused on this faction that gave rise to the Independent NPFL, a splinter of NPFL led by Prince Yormie Johnson, to locate and kill Doe in ECOMOG Headquarters on September 9, 1990.[107] Ghana then supplied an army to ECOMOG raising the force size from 3,500 to 7,000 troops by late September 1990.[108] The mission would now engage in more peace

[103] Clement E. Adibe, "The Liberian Conflict and the ECOWAS-UN Partnership," *Third World Quarterly*, Vol. 18, No. 3 (1997), p. 474.

[104] Abeeku Essuman-Johnson, "The Liberian Refugee Problem and Ghana's Response to it," *LECIA Bulletin*, Vol. 2, No. 1 (1992), pp. 34–40.

[105] Bellamy and Williams, *Understanding Peacekeeping*, p. 313. Sierra Leone and Mali soldiers joined a year later.

[106] Adibe, "The Liberian Conflict," p. 471.

[107] Anna Sylvestre-Treiner, "Liberia: Samuel Doe, Death Washed Down with a Budweiser," *The Africa Report*, November 10, 2021.

[108] Adibe, "The Liberian Conflict," p. 476.

enforcement tasks rather than solely fighting the National Patriotic Front of Liberia. Many Liberians opposed to ECOMOG, and the interim government joined NPFL forces by 1992. On October 15, 1992, Taylor deployed Operation Octopus to reclaim Monrovia so ECOMOG increased troops to 11,256 forces.[109] In January 1993, both ECOMOG and NPFL forces became exhausted and agreed to the United Nations to help with a diplomatic solution. The warring factions in Liberia, OAU, ECOWAS, and the United Nations agreed a new peace plan in Cotonou, Benin, to disarm factions, replace Sawyer and the interim government with a Council of State (the Liberian National Transitional Government).[110]

The demobilization of the fighting factions and election of a government were part of the peace plan with the creation of the United Nations Observer Mission in Liberia (UNOMIL) to monitor the functionality of the peace plan while working with an increased ECOMOG presence. The United Nations Mission deployed 303 observers and later was mandated to engineer local elections and engage with reconstruction and DDR.[111] However, disarmament and reintegration—including this process for many child soldiers—failed. By 1995, UNOMIL decreased from 303 observers to 77 personnel, and only Uganda retained forces in Liberia for the United Nations Mission.

Nigeria reduced troops in ECOMOG, and the regional organization was allied to UNOMIL's mandate. The Abuja Agreement signed on August 19, 1995, became more favorable for Taylor and his NPFL and rival factions. Late 1995, one faction targeted Nigerian-ECOMOG troops and shelled its base in Tubmanburg, Bomi County, due to the confusion of diamond mining locations in control by Prince Johnson, the leader of the National Union for Democratic Progress and splinter from the National Patriotic Front of Liberia. US forces, with Operation Assured Response, evacuated their nationals out of Liberia in April 1996, while the number of refugees increased from violence.[112] The Abuja Agreement was

[109] Adibe, "The Liberian Conflict," p. 477.

[110] Gabriel I. H. Williams, *Liberia: The Heart of Darkness* (Victoria, BC: Trafford, 2002), pp. 176–177.

[111] United Nations Security Council Resolution 866, "On the Proposed Establishment of the United Nations Observer Mission in Liberia (UNOMIL)," UN Doc. S/RES/866, September 22, 1993, adopted 3,281st meeting, para. 3.

[112] John Mintz and Thomas W. Lippman, "Evacuation Imminent in Liberia: Embassy is Crowded Refuge After Renewal of Fighting," *The Washington Post*, April 10, 1996.

revised for better demobilization and disarmament of all factional groups, and to implement general elections and create a government by mid-1997.

Finally, in July 1997, the National Patriotic Front of Liberia, one of the predominant warring factions, won the presidential election by a massive margin of over 75 percent of votes.[113] However, approximately 250,000 people were killed (out of Liberia's 2.5 million population) and an excess of 1,000 peacekeepers were slaughtered.[114] ECOWAS and African regional efforts envisioned to obtain a more harmonious state of affairs, but even when the United Nations helped, a second civil war and spillover in neighboring Sierra Leone embarked.

Assessing Afro-communitarian Ethics in the African Contexts

If considering Afro-communitarian ethics and the phases of violence as permitted by *Ubuntu*, diplomacy and conflict resolution were attempted within the five contexts. However, the severity of the civil wars, terrorism, and violence was extremely difficult to thwart without the use of violence, and thus violence was initiated by AU and ECOWAS peacekeeping missions.

In Burundi, the spillover of the refugee crisis and Hutu reprisals against Tutsi dominance from Rwanda was evident. The legacy of discrimination against Hutus resulted in political emancipatory politics and violence against Tutsis because peaceful protests and diplomacy seemed fruitless. This partially relates to *Ubuntu* ethics when permitting violence. However, the violence was not necessary in Burundi. Sabotage was adopted as the initial stage of violence but it was not permissible because many Tutsi civilians were targeted. The violence may have constituted guerrilla warfare because smaller irregular forces were fighting the Tutsi dominated army. FNL hardliners wanted to kill all Tutsis and thus remained distanced with the Ndadaye administration. The state of affairs, at this point, remained very hostile between Hutu and Tutsi ethnic groups, and thus communal relations would not have complied with the Afro-communitarian principles

[113] Thomas Jayne, "ECOWAS and Liberia: Implications for Regional Intervention in Intra-State Conflicts," in *Africa at the Millennium: An Agenda for Mature Development*, edited by Bakut tswah Bakut and Sagarika Dutt (London: Palgrave Macmillan), pp. 155–176.

[114] Patricia Levy, Michael Spilling and Brett Griffin, *Cultures of the World: Liberia* (New York: Cavendish Square, 2018), p. 29.

of caring, sharing, benevolence, and charity. These social relations were thwarted further when Ndadaye was killed and then his replacement, Ntaryamira, also Hutu, was assassinated, which resulted in further Hutu-Tutsi reprisal attacks.

The refugee crisis worsened, and foreign intervention was required to attempt to bring about a diplomatic solution followed by an armed presence to uphold ceasefire arrangements. South African forces were deployed and managed to secure areas but was later absorbed into AMIB to serve the Arusha Agreement. Poor funding deteriorated the role of AMIB, particularly DDR failed and crime increased, and thus the state of affairs remained disharmonious. For these reasons, AMIB had to rely on South Africa, and the African Union mission was replaced by the United Nations. Although the regional African efforts were inadequate to provide a foreign armed intervention justified the permissible use of violence, as a foreign armed intervention, it was inadequate to secure the country and bring about a more harmonious and less discordant state of affairs between Hutus and Tutsis in Burundi.

In the context of Sudan, African regional efforts included the Naivasha peace process to engage the Khartoum government and SLM/A against Islamic elites. The latter were excluding non-Arabs from a variety of resources that like Burundi, resulted in the creation of "have nots" to form young angry rebellious men in Darfur, western Sudan. The limited access orders thus intensified a disharmonious state of affairs, which fails the Afro-communitarian principles of sharing, benevolence, and caring. The African Union wanted to resolve this conflict but heavily respected the non-intervention principle of respecting state sovereignty, which is why it did not intervene in Darfur. AMIS implemented sanctions, but they did not work and Darfur villages were destroyed by Sudanese armed force and the allied Janjaweed militia. The mandate of AMIS was too weak, and IGAD's rules of engagement related to self-defense were unclear. AMIS was replaced by UNMIS because the African Union ran out of funding. Sudan was against UN force, and Western actors were reluctant to proclaim that the atrocities committed in the Darfur region constituted immediate genocide. Therefore, the efforts of the African Union in terms of peacekeeping and UNMIS were very futile to retaliate against the Janjaweed militia and Sudanese armed forces. The foreign armed intervention did not result in a more harmonious state of affairs between elite Arabs and black Africans, and a discordant situation remained.

The situation in Somalia was chaotic due to a failed state that had no central government. After Barre lost the Ogaden War to Ethiopia, SNM forces attacked the Somalian army and USC forces seized Mogadishu. USC split into two factions that engaged in a full-scale armed conflict during a time that hit civilians with prevalent famine, malnutrition, and disease. The state of affairs was disharmonious and foreign intervention was needed to mediate the conflict and provide an armed presence. UNOSOM and US-led UNITAF were deployed to secure Somalia for humanitarian aid and assistance, while Kenya intervened to protect their borders from terrorist attacks conducted by al-Shabaab. AMISOM initially had a light mandate that was stronger when USC factions were still fighting and al-Shabaab terrorism continued. Many foreign peacekeepers were killed and Western powers parted from the country, which left Somalia in a disharmonious state of affairs and debatably protracted the armed conflict due to the failure to endorse and secure a comprehensive ceasefire between both USC factions. Afro-communitarian ethics were thus not successful with the foreign armed intervention from the United Nations, America, and African Union in Somalia. However, on a more positive note, in Somaliland (northwest Somalia), foreign peace initiatives engaged the community, elders, and women to conform with Lederach's pyramid of building peace—that largely conforms to a positive communal state of affairs.

Similar to the conditions of state failure in Somalia that provided a vacuum for terrorism, the 2012 coup in Mali formed a void in northern Mali for Islamists and Tuareg rebels. ECOWAS was authorized by the United Nations to endorse sanctions and fight to bring about a more harmonious state of affairs. However, rebels closed in the capital, but French operations Serval and Barkhane engaged with counterinsurgency strategy within the Sahel region and preservation of Francophone hegemony. French and allied forces killed many Islamist terrorist leaders, but terrorism continued. AFISMA was succeeded by a UN mission, but French forces remained. The foreign armed interventions failed and left Mali with more violence and a more discordant state of affairs.

Liberia was the first instance when ECOWAS was mandated by the United Nations to engage in a robust and rapid peacekeeping operation. NPFL forces overthrew Doe, and ECOMOG/ECOWAS engaged in conflict resolution and the political settlement of an interim government. Unlike the context of Mali, the West held no interests and America only intervened to evacuate their nationals out of the country. ECOMOG and NPFL continued lengthy fighting to leave the country in a more discordant state of affairs so both groups welcomed the United Nations and the proposal of a new transitional government. However, DDR with UNOMIL failed, and many child soldiers did not benefit from the process and were not reintegrated to their communities. This failure would not support Afro-communitarianism. Although peace was sketchy with the 1997 elections that Taylor won, a second civil war and the spillover of a conflict over the border to Sierra Leone resulted in a less disharmonious state of affairs in the West African region.

Conclusion

How should outsiders respond to mass atrocities against civilians? It is estimated that 200,000 well-armed and trained soldiers are required to save endangered civilians from mass killing with a humanitarian intervention.[115] This figure has never been met with a foreign armed intervention and this is more troublesome for the African continent. African states cannot solve African problems alone due to poor resourcing and funding. Some African countries are deemed as failed states that cannot achieve peace in their home countries, and thus it is unrealistic for them to attain peace in regional situations.[116] The North Atlantic Treaty Organization (NATO) have the power to reach some of the large number in the West or if their air and naval bases are nearby.[117] In Africa, humanitarian intervention "is short on means" while the West "are short on [political] will."[118] However, African leaders are also reluctant to deploy their armies to halt mass killing in the African region. With Chap. 7 of the Charter of the United Nations, the United Nations Security Council negotiates what is deemed a threat to international peace and security on a case-by-case basis. For the Security Council, terrorism, military coups, and humanitarian emergencies are notable threats, and thus mass killing and genocide should also constitute a threat to the peace.[119]

[115] Michael O'Hanlon and P.W. Singer, "The Humanitarian Transformation: Expanding Global Intervention Capacity," *Survival*, Vol. 46, No. 1 (2004), pp. 77–100.

[116] Jakkie Cilliers, Gina van Schalkwyk and Henri Boshoff, "African Security Architecture: Developments Regarding Early Warning and the African Standby Force," *Europa World* (2006).

[117] NATO's intervention in Libya provides an example.

[118] David C. Gompert, Courtney Richardson, Richard L. Kugler and Clifford H. Bernath, *Learning from Darfur: Building a Net-Capable African Force to Stop Mass Killing* (Washington, DC: National Defense University, 2005), p. 5.

[119] Williams, "Military Responses to Mass Killing," p. 169.

In Burundi, although AMIB suffered logistical, resources, and funding in its early days, AMIB had to rely on external funding.[120] Yet, AMIB's prompt response did secure most of Burundi to hand over to a UN multidimensional peacekeeping operation. Similarly, in Sudan, AMIS responded to mass killing but failed with its lack of capacity and resources due to the United Nations Security Council deciding that Sudan's sovereignty was more important.[121] China and Russia are prominent permanent five members of the Council that respect the rule of sovereignty and held oil interests with the Khartoum government. In Mali, the French-led Opération Serval thwarted the regional attempts of ECOWAS and the African Union to bring about a diplomatic solution and Security Sector Reform, which was largely due to France's counterinsurgency strategy in the Sahel and Francophone hegemony. In Liberia, the United Nations permitted ECOMOG/ECOWAS to play the main role in peacekeeping to thwart efforts of NPFL forces, but the ceasefires based on an interim government did not materialize because Taylor objected to it, which dragged out the civil war. ECOWAS and the African Union have the tools with the Mechanism Treaty and Constitutive Act respectively to apply the norms of R2P to act swiftly that can prevent atrocity crimes, and notably civilian deaths. These African regional efforts concerned African-led military interventions as foreign armed intervention that attempted to promote peace and conflict resolution by working with the United Nations to broker ceasefires, work toward a political settlement and encourage elections, engage with DDR, and when the conflicts remain, deploy more troops as a resistance to guerrilla groups.

Therefore, the modes of African peacekeeping missions in these four contexts did comply with Afro-communitarian ethics by initially attempting to resolve conflict, atrocity crimes, terrorism, and civil war without the use of force, but then engaged with permissible use of violence to form a more harmonious state of affairs. Even though the latter was not achieved in several of these contexts due to poor funding, a lack of political will, Western hegemony (to favor one side), and underestimating antigovernmental and terrorist forces, African regional peacekeeping can assist UN multidimensional peacekeeping operations in the future.

[120] Badmus, "African Mission in Burundi (AMIB)," pp. 15–16.
[121] Williams, "Military Responses to Mass Killings," p. 168.

References

Aboagye, Festus. "The African Mission in Burundi: Lessons Learned from the First African Union Peacekeeping Operation." *Conflict Trends*, No. 2 (January 2004), pp. 9–15. https://hdl.handle.net/10520/EJC15836.

Adebajo, Adekeye. *UN Peacekeeping in Africa: From the Suez Crisis to the Sudan Conflicts*. Boulder, CO: Lynne Rienner, 2011.

Adibe, Clement E. "The Liberian Conflict and the ECOWAS-UN Partnership." *Third World Quarterly*, Vol. 18, No. 3 (1997), pp. 471–488. https://doi.org/10.1080/01436599714821.

African Charter on Human and Peoples' Rights (Banjul Charter). "Charter of the African Union," adopted June 27, 1981, OAU Doc. CAB/LEG/67/3 rev. 5, 21 I.L.M. 58 (1982).

African Union. "Communiqué." Communication XIII, July 27, 2004.

African Union. *Current Status of the AU Military Deployment in Darfur*. Darfur Integrated Task Force, Information Update No. 02/06, February 1, 2006.

Agbiboa, Daniel E. "Terrorism without Borders: Somalia's al-Shabaab and the Global Jihad Network." *Journal of Terrorism Research*, Vol. 5, No. 1 (February 2014), pp. 27–34. https://research-repository.st-andrews.ac.uk/bitstream/handle/10023/4916/826-1862-1-SM.pdf.

Agreement on the Implementation of the Ceasefire signed by Farah Aidid. S/23693, March 3, 1992. https://www.peaceagreements.org/viewmasterdocument/1713.

Al Jazeera. "French Strike 'Kills Mali Rebel Commander'." *Al Jazeera*, March 14, 2014. https://www.aljazeera.com/news/2014/3/14/french-strike-kills-mali-rebel-commander.

Aning, Kwesi, and Fifi Edu-Afful. "African Agency in R2P: Interventions by African Union and ECOWAS in Mali, Côte d'Ivoire, and Libya." *International Studies Review*, Vol. 18, No. 1 (March 2016), pp. 120–133. https://doi.org/10.1093/isr/viv017.

Article 4 (h) of its Constitutive Act of the African Union. https://au.int/sites/default/files/pages/34873-file-constitutiveact_en.pdf.

Arusha Peace and Reconciliation Agreements for Burundi. "Arusha Agreement." August 28, 2000. https://www.brookings.edu/wp-content/uploads/2016/07/burundi_arusha-peace-and-reconciliation-agreement-for-burundi.pdf.

Badmus, Isiaka Alani. "The African Mission in Burundi (AMIB): A Study of the African Union's Peacekeeping Success and 'Triangular Area of Tension in African Peacekeeping'." *India Quarterly: A Journal of International Affairs*, Vol. 73, No. 1 (March 2017), pp. 1–20. https://doi.org/10.1177/0974928416683038.

Bellamy, Alex J., and Paul D. Williams. "Who's Keeping the Peace? Regionalization and Contemporary Peace Operations." *International Security*, Vol. 29, No. 4 (April 2005), p. 189, pp. 157–195. https://doi.org/10.1162/isec.2005.29.4.157.

Bellamy, Alex J., and Paul D. Williams. *Understanding Peacekeeping*, 2nd ed. Cambridge: Polity Press, 2010.

Boshoff, Henri. "Historical Overview." In *The Burundi Peace Process: From Civil War to Conditional Peace*, edited by Henri Boshoff, Very Waldemar and George Rautenbach, pp. 3–9. Pretoria: Institute for Security Studies, 2010.

Brosig, Malte. *Cooperative Peacekeeping in Africa: Exploring Regime Complexity*. London: Routledge, 2015.

China Daily. "Kenya Agrees to Join AMISOM." *China Daily*, December 7, 2011. https://www.chinadaily.com.cn/world/2011-12/07/content_14225808.htm.

Christiani, Dario, and Riccardo Fabiani. *From Disfunctionality to Disaggregation and Back? The Malian Crisis, Local Players and European Interests*. Istituto Affari Internazionali Working Papers 13-08, pp. 1–20. Rome: Istituto Affari Internazionali, March 2013. https://www.iai.it/sites/default/files/iaiwp1308.pdf.

Cilliers, Jakkie, Gina van Schalkwyk and Henri Boshoff, "African Security Architecture: Developments Regarding Early Warning and the African Standby Force," *Europa World* (2006).

Demers, Eric. "The Burundian Civil War – 10 Years On." *Norwegian Refugee Council*, May 2, 2003. https://reliefweb.int/report/burundi/burundian-civil-war-10-years.

Dessu, Meressa K. "Is the AU Mission in Somalia Changing in Name Only?" *Institute for Security Studies*, March 29, 2022, https://issafrica.org/iss-today/is-the-au-mission-in-somalia-changing-in-name-only.

Diaby, Aminata, and Nicolas Klingelschmitt. "De Facto Sovereignty and Multilateral Sanctions for a Return to Constitutional Order in a Context of Regional Armed Conflict: The Case of Mali." In *War, State and Sovereignty: Interdisciplinary Challenges and Perspectives for the Social Sciences*, edited by Grégory Daho and Yann Richard, pp. 185–208. Cham: Palgrave Macmillan, 2023.

Economic Community of West African States. "ECOWAS Decision A/DEC.1/8/90." Lagos: ECOWAS, 1990.

Economic Community of West African States. "ECOWAS Defense Chiefs Call for International Support on Mali." *ECOWAS*, July 28, 2012. https://reliefweb.int/report/mali/ecowas-defence-chiefs-call-international-support-mali.

Essuman-Johnson, Abeeku. "The Liberian Refugee Problem and Ghana's Response to it." *LECIA Bulletin*, Vol. 2, No. 1 (1992), pp. 34–40. Gompert, David C., Courtney Richardson, Richard L. Kugler, and Clifford H. Bernath.

Learning from Darfur: Building a Net-Capable African Force to Stop Mass Killing. Washington, DC: National Defense University, 2005.

Gardner, Frank. "Al-Qaeda Chief in North Africa Abdelmalek Droukdel Killed – France." *BBC News*, June 5, 2020, https://www.bbc.co.uk/news/world-africa-52943692.

Gegout, Catherine. *Why Europe Intervenes in Africa: Security, Prestige and the Legacy of Colonialism*. Oxford: Oxford University Press, 2017.

Gettleman, Jeffrey. "Kenya Rattled as Shabaab Turns Sights on Somalia Military Targets." *The New York Times*, January 20, 2016. https://www.nytimes.com/2016/01/21/world/africa/shabab-attacks-somalia-kenya.html.

Heath, Gordon L., and David K. Tarus. *Christian Responses to Terrorism: The Kenyan Experience*. Eugene, OR: Pickwick, 2017.

International Criminal Court. "Situation in Darfur, Sudan." *International Criminal Court*, ICC-02/05 Investigation, March 2005. https://www.icc-cpi.int/darfur.

International Crisis Group. *The AU's Mission in Darfur: Bridging the Gaps*, Africa Briefing No. 6. Nairobi: ICG, July 6, 2005.

Jayne, Thomas. "ECOWAS and Liberia: Implications for Regional Intervention in Intra-State Conflicts." In *Africa at the Millennium: An Agenda for Mature Development*, edited by Bakut tswah Bakut and Sagarika Dutt, pp. 155–176. London: Palgrave Macmillan.

Kfir, Isaac. "Al-Shabaab, Social Identity Group, Human (In)Security and Counterterrorism." *Studies in Conflict & Terrorism*, Vol. 40, No. 9 (2017), pp. 772–789. https://doi.org/10.1080/1057610X.2016.1236569.

Kodjo, Tchioffo. *Mali Conflict of 2012–2013: A Critical Assessment – Patterns of Local, Regional and Global Conflict and Resolution Dynamics in Post-colonial and Post-cold war Africa*. Chisinau: Lambert, 2015.

Laurent, Lionel, and Elizabeth Pineau. "France Confirms Death of al-Qaeda's Abou Zeid in Mali." *Reuters*, March 23, 2013. https://www.reuters.com/article/idUSBRE92M05G/.

Lederach, John Paul. *Building Peace: Sustainable Reconciliation in Divided Societies*. Washington, DC: United States Institute of Peace Press, 1997.

Lemarchand, Rene. *Burundi: Ethnic Conflict and Genocide*. Cambridge: Cambridge University Press, 1995.

Levy, Patricia, Michael Spilling and Brett Griffin. *Cultures of the World: Liberia*. New York: Cavendish Square, 2018.

Long, Katy. "Kenya, Jubaland and Somali's Refugees: No Quick Fixes." *London School of Economics and Political Science* (October 24, 2011), pp. 1–2. https://eprints.lse.ac.uk/69447/1/Katy%20Long%20-%20Kenya%20Jubaland%20and%20Somalias%20refugees.pdf.

Makanda, Joseph. "Fighting Terrorism in the Horn of Africa: The Role of Ordinary Kenyans in Kenya's Military Intervention in Somalia and the Fight against al-Shabaab." *Journal of African Union Studies*, Vol. 8, No. 1 (April 2019), pp. 33–49. https://doi.org/10.31920/2050-4306/2019/v8n1a2.

Malito, Debora Valentina. "Neutral in Favor of Whom? The UN Intervention in Somali and the Somaliland Peace Process." *International Peacekeeping*, Vol. 24, No. 2 (2017), pp. 280–303. https://doi.org/10.1080/13533312.2016.1250626.

Manirakiza, Marc. "Nation-building in Burundi: A History and its Impacts on the Future." *Conflict Trends*, 2 (January 2005), pp. 44–48. https://hdl.handle.net/10520/EJC15854.

Mankaus, Ken. "International Peacebuilding and the Dynamics of Local and National Reconciliation in Somalia." In *Learning from Somalia: The Lessons of Armed Humanitarian Intervention*, edited by Walter Sheldon Clarke and Jeffrey Herbst, pp. 42–63. Boulder, CO: Westview Press, 1997.

Mintz, John, and Thomas W. Lippman. "Evacuation Imminent in Liberia: Embassy is Crowded Refuge After Renewal of Fighting." *The Washington Post*, April 10, 1996. https://www.washingtonpost.com/archive/politics/1996/04/10/evacuation-imminent-in-liberia/4b3daa26-4167-440f-83af-4d40165a2fbd/.

Mtimkulu, Bereng. "The African Union and Peace Support Operations," *Conflict Trends: Focus on Peacekeeping*, No. 4 (January 2005), p. 36. https://hdl.handle.net/10520/EJC15885.

Muchangi, Nancy. *The Effectiveness of the Nyumba Kumi Initiative as a Police Reform Strategy in Nairobi* County. Nairobi: Strathmore University, 2016.

O'Hanlon, Michael, and P.W. Singer. "The Humanitarian Transformation: Expanding Global Intervention Capacity." *Survival*, Vol. 46, No. 1 (2004), pp. 77–100. https://doi.org/10.1080/00396330412331343673.

Okocha, Victor O. *Leadership and Development Crises in Africa: A New Approach to an Old Challenge*. Pittsburgh, PA: Dorrance Publishing, 2018.

Olomojobi, Yinka. *Frontiers of Jihad: Radical Islam in Africa*. Ibadan: Safari Books, 2015.

Olsen, Gorm Rye. "The October 2011 Kenyan Invasion of Somalia: Fighting al-Shabaab or Defending Institutional Interests?" *Journal of Contemporary African Studies*, Vol. 36, No. 1 (2018), pp. 39–53. https://doi.org/10.1080/02589001.2017.1408953.

Report of the Independent Commission of Inquiry on Darfur to the Secretary-General. "Pursuant to Security Council Resolution 1564 (2004) of September 18, 2004." February 1, 2005, S/2005/60, E. 226. https://www.securitycouncilreport.org/atf/cf/%7b65BFCF9B-6D27-4E9C-8CD3-CF6E4FF96FF9%7d/WPS%20S%202005%2060.pdf.

Sahnoun, Mohamed M. *Somalia: The Missed Opportunities*. Washington, DC: United States Institute of Peace Press, 1994.

Schofield, Hugh. "Mali and France 'Push Back Islamists'." *BBC News*, January 12, 2013. https://www.bbc.co.uk/news/world-africa-20991723.

Solomon, Hussein. "Mali: West Africa's Afghanistan." *The RUSI Journal*, Vol. 158, No. 1 (March 2013), p. 12, pp. 12–19. https://doi.org/10.1080/03071847.2013.774635.

Sunga, Lyal S. "Has the ICC Unfairly Targeted or Has Africa Unfairly Targeted the ICC?" In *The International Criminal Court in Search of its Purpose and Identity*, edited by Triestino Marinello. London: Routledge, 2015.

Sylvestre-Treiner, Anna. "Liberia: Samuel Doe, Death Washed Down with a Budweiser." *The Africa Report*, November 10, 2021. https://www.theafricareport.com/144562/pt-5-liberia-samuel-doe-death-washed-down-with-budweiser/.

The Economist. "François Hollande's African Adventures," *The Economist*, July 21, 2014. https://www.economist.com/europe/2014/07/21/francois-hollandes-african-adventures.

Tondini, Matteo. "Coalitions of the Willing." In *The Practice of Shared Responsibility in International Law*, edited by André Nollkaemper and Ilias Plakokefalos, pp. 701–732. Cambridge: Cambridge University Press, 2017.

Totten, Samuel, and Erik Markusen. "Research Note: The US Government Darfur Genocide Investigation." *Journal of Genocide Research*, Vol. 7, No. 2 (June 2005), pp. 279–290. https://doi.org/10.1080/14623520500127571.

United Nations. *Charter of the United Nations.* 1 United Nations Treaty Series XVI, October 24, 1945.

United Nations. "UN Security Council Votes for New Somalia Peacekeeping Force." *France 24*, March 31, 2022. https://www.france24.com/en/live-news/20220331-un-security-council-votes-for-new-somalia-peacekeeping-force.

United Nations. "Explainer: How Darfur Became a 'Humanitarian Calamity and Catastrophic Human Rights Crisis'." *United Nations*, December 14, 2023. https://www.un.org/africarenewal/magazine/december-2023/explainer-how-darfur-became-%E2%80%98humanitarian-calamity-and-catastrophic-human.

United Nations Security Council Resolution 751. "Agreements for the Implementation of Measures Aimed at Stabilizing the Ceasefire through a United Nations Monitoring Mission." UN Doc. S/RES/751, April 24, 1992, adopted 3,069th meeting.

United Nations Security Council Resolution 767. "On the Humanitarian Situation in Somalia." UN Doc. S/RES/767, July 27, 1992, adopted 3,101st meeting.

United Nations Security Council Resolution 794. "Gravely Alarmed by the Deterioration of the Humanitarian Situation in Somalia." UN Doc. S/RES/794, December 3, 1992, adopted 3,145th meeting.

United Nations Security Council Resolution 837. "Gravely Alarmed at the Premeditated Armed Attacks." UN Doc. S/RES/837, June 6, 1993, adopted 3,229th meeting.

United Nations Security Council Resolution 866. "On the Proposed Establishment of the United Nations Observer Mission in Liberia (UNOMIL)." UN Doc. S/RES/866, September 22, 1993, adopted 3,281st meeting.

United Nations Security Council Resolution 1545. "On the Situation in Burundi." UN Doc. S/RES/1545, May 21, 2004, adopted 4,975th meeting.

United Nations Security Council Resolution 1564. "Report of the Secretary-General on the Sudan." UN Doc. S/RES/1564, September 18, 2004, adopted 5,040th meeting.

United Nations Security Council Resolution 1590. "Establishment of UMMIS." UN Doc. S/RES/1590, March 24, 2005, adopted 5,151st meeting.

United Nations Security Council Resolution 1719. "The Situation in Burundi." UN Doc. S/RES/1719, October 25, 2006, adopted 5,554th meeting.

United Nations Security Council Resolution 2085. "Concerning the Deployment of the African-led International Support Mission to Mali." UN Doc. S/RES/2085, December 20, 2012, adopted 6,898th meeting.

Walls, Michael. "The Emergence of a Somali State: Building Peace from Civil War in Somaliland." *African Affairs*, Vol. 108, No. 432 (July 2009), pp. 371–389. https://doi.org/10.1093/afraf/adp019.

Walls, Michael, Koss Mohammed and Mohamud Omar Ali. *Peace in Somaliland: An Indigenous Approach to Statebuilding*. Nairobi: Interpeace/Academy for Peace and Development, 2008.

Warner, Leslie Anne. "In Somalia, Kenya Risks Death by a Thousand Cuts," *PRISM: A Journal of the Center for Complex Operations*, Vol. 3, No. 3 (2012), pp. 105–118. https://ciaotest.cc.columbia.edu/journals/prism%20/v3i3/f_0025980_21271.pdf.

Wheeler, Nicholas J. *Saving Strangers: Humanitarian Intervention in International Society*. Oxford: Oxford University Press, 2000.

Williams, Gabriel I. H. *Liberia: The Heart of Darkness*. Victoria, BC: Trafford, 2002.

Williams, Paul D. "AMISOM under Review." *The RUSI Journal*, Vol. 161, No. 1 (January 2006a), pp. 40–49. https://www.rusi.org/explore-our-research/publications/rusi-journal/amisom-under-review.

Williams, Paul D. "Military Responses to Mass Killing: The African Union Mission in Sudan." *International Peacekeeping*, Vol. 13, No. 2 (2006b), pp. 168–183. https://doi.org/10.1080/13533310500436565.

Williams, Paul D. "The African Union: Prospects for Regional Peacekeeping after Burundi and Sudan." *Review of African Political Economy*, Vol. 33, No. 108 (June 2006c), pp. 352–357. https://www.jstor.org/stable/4007175.

CHAPTER 8

Implications of Non-Interventions in Nigeria, the Niger Delta, Niger, and Syria

Introduction

This penultimate chapter makes a case for promoting and implementing African communitarian ethics in situations where foreign armed interventions may be justified to oppose violence and bring about a more harmonious state of affairs. It could be argued that internationally led interventions are driven by either state or collective interests or utilitarian objectives (or at least in rhetoric). In the context of African conflicts, Western states proceed with selectivity of intervention and weigh up potential relative gains from engagement with an incursion, even if for humanitarian means.[1] Martii Koskiennieni stressed that "selectivity" cannot be avoided because aggression has responses resulting in "some members" obtaining "more protection than others."[2] This has been displayed with the weak intervention to counter the Rwandan civil war and resulting genocide and the exploitation of diamonds by the West in Sierra Leone respectively.

[1] Danny Singh, "Undertaking Critical Legal Theory to Examine Just War Intervention: A Smokescreen for Political Ambitions," in *Comparative Just War Theory: An Introduction to International Perspectives*, edited by Luís Cordeiro-Rodrigues and Danny Singh (Lanham, MD: Rowman & Littlefield, 2000), pp. 75–76.

[2] Martti Koskiennieni, "The Place of Law in Collective Security," *Michigan Journal of International Law*, Vol. 17, No. 2 (1996), p. 464.

D. Singh, *Applied Afro-Communitarian Ethics and Foreign Armed Intervention*, https://doi.org/10.1007/978-3-031-64110-7_8

This chapter engages with a variety of contexts that, for humanitarian reasons, and principally from an applied Afro-communitarian perspective, warrant foreign armed intervention. These scenarios include northern Nigeria, neighboring Niger, and Syria in the Middle East. The context of Nigeria engages with protracted banditry, terrorism from Boko Haram in the northeast fighting for Islamist governance, and militancy in the Niger Delta region challenging environmental degradation and an unequal distribution of oil revenues from the Nigerian federal government. It will be contended that domestic attempts to oppose enemies (Boko Haram in the northeast and ethnic insurgencies in the southern Niger Delta region) with preliminary enmity-like violence and succeeding amnesty and deradicalization programs to reach a harmonious state of affairs are deteriorating. The discordant state of affairs features high insecurity and civilian casualty rates, prevalent property damage, and economic consequences that warrant foreign military intervention to bring about a more harmonious state of affairs.

The context of Niger concerning a recent coup and military junta establishing rule has resulted in the Economic Community of West African States (ECOWAS) debating whether to undertake a foreign armed regional intervention to restore democracy. ECOWAS is also wary of other nearby military regimes in Mali and Burkina Faso; the regional organization is losing members and these states are being supported by Russia and the Wagner Group to retain illiberal regimes and bolster a client relationship with the Kremlin. The Niger military junta may continue to be supported by civilians, but if not, then ECOWAS might undertake action with further sanctions and potential intervention to restore friendly relations with contemporary ECOWAS members in the West African region.

Subsequently, the context of Syria is provided that engages with the civil war that continues today. The Syrian totalitarian regime is largely supported by Russia diplomatically and militarily and the regime has engaged in several chemical weapons attacks against civilians in rebel areas. The United Nations has attempted to vote on a political settlement concerning a transitional government to promote elections and deploy a peacekeeping operation, but Russia and sometimes China veto such Security Council draft resolutions. Western powers have retaliated with military airstrikes on Syrian military and weapons compounds. Despite the North Atlantic Treaty Organization (NATO) engaging in Libya to respond to atrocities perpetrated by Gaddafi and the Libyan armed forces against rebels and civilians as a fulfilment of the Responsibility to Protect doctrine, the Alliance has not been considered for military intervention in Syria.

Boko Haram Terrorism in Nigeria

Nigeria has undergone a few waves of conflict that have resulted in Islamic extremism. Nigeria suffered with a civil war in 1967 that ended in 1970. The Biafran Republic of mainly Igbo ethnicity was supported by China and Italy but lost the civil war to Nigeria. Nigeria was backed by Egypt and East Germany and the assistance of Soviet weapons after NATO refused arms supply. The Nigerian government imposed a naval blockade against the Biafran region in southeast Nigeria that caused mass famine. It is estimated that between half a million and two million Biafrans died from starvation, disease, and fighting.[3]

In 1980, religious and ethnic opposition intensified with Maitatsine in both Maiduguri and Kono. The Maitatsine movement radicalized and recruited poor youth to rebel against the state that wanted to cleanse Islam as a religion in northern Nigeria. After a few more religious skirmishes throughout the 1980s and 1990s, military rulership ceased from the 1999 election won by Olusegun Obasanjo. However, religious riots in northern Nigeria continued, which included the Shari'a, Jos, Miss World, and Muhammad cartoonist riots in the 2000s.[4] Nigeria still has myriad problems, with prolonged banditry, the terrorist activity of Boko Haram in the northeast region, and ethnic militancy in the Niger Delta region. Nigerian terrorism has brought about one of the deadliest conflicts and there have been several staged kidnappings.[5] Boko Haram and armed bandits and herdsmen have caused mass violence, namely, guerrilla warfare and terrorism against the Nigerian security forces and civilians, respectively.

Boko Haram has denounced Western education, which is forbidden. Initially, Boko Haram was a religious group that rejected Western education, influence, and ideas with the aim of instilling strict adherence to Shari'a Law, but did not resort to violence. The ideology was established

[3] Fidelis Mbah, "Nigerians Mark 50 Years of End of Bloody Civil War," Al Jazeera, January 15, 2020.

[4] Emelda Undiandeye Ejeh and Ebunoluwa Popoola, "Amnesty as a Tool in the Deradicalization of Boko Haram Terrorists in Nigeria: A Threat to National Security," *The International Journal of Human Rights* (December 2023), p. 7.

[5] Global Terrorism Index, *Measuring the Impact of Terrorism* (Sydney, NSW: Institute for Economics & Peace, 2019), p. 13.

in 1995 and became radicalized by Abubakar Lavan, but later it was claimed by Ustaz Mohammad Yusuf in 2002 that Boko Haram would replace the Shabaab group and properly interpret the Qur'an.[6] This ideology challenged the Nigerian state secular education system and democracy and it moved to Kanamma (within Yobe State). The three northeastern states of Adamawa, Borno, and Yobe are the most affected by Boko Haram extremism and their rural areas suffer from insecurity, poverty, and lack of access to basic services, as well as interruption of livestock and farming.

In 2004, Boko Haram attacked police outposts, killing officers and looting their arms to form their own arsenal. The insurgency sought its territorial space to practice their interpretation of political-religious ideology, and have committed most attacks in the Borno State. Boko Haram challenged the Nigerian government due to most of its population living in poverty and under 10 percent of the population controlling the wealth of the state.[7] Poverty, unemployment, and children who could not afford state schooling played into the enticement of Boko Haram for many disenfranchised youth resenting greedy, rich, and corrupt Nigerian politicians in northeast Nigeria, resulting in sabotage and Almajiri Islamic education.[8] Yusuf appealed to the rich and prosperous to donate money to fight for Allah's will and cause to rescue Islam from Western spheres of domination and influence. The insurgency also gained followers from Nigeria's neighboring states, Chad, Cameroon, and Niger. The phases of violence from peaceful religious measures and then sabotage are permissible for Afro-communitarians, but the reasons proclaimed by Boko Haram were not to achieve a more harmonious state of affairs, but rather to Islamize the northeast of Nigeria with the use of lethal force. This does not qualify as *Ubuntu* desiring the improvement of communal relations.

Efforts have been made by the Jonathan and Buhari administrations to combat terrorism with robust security responses, the Civilian Joint Task Force (CJTF) assisting the military, and the use of South African

[6] Adetayo Olamide Sowale and Ayodeji Anthony Aduloju, "Deradicalization of Repentant Boko Haram Militants: Institutional Dilemma Between the Victims and Villains in Northeast Nigeria," *Jadavpur Journal of International Relations*, Vol. 27, No. 2 (October 2023), pp. 171–172.

[7] Ebere R. Adigbuo, "Boko Haram: A Race between Amnesty and Criminal Tribunal," *Historical Research Letter*, Vol. 13 (2014), p. 32.

[8] Sowale and Aduloju, "Deradicalization of Repentant Boko Haram Militants," p. 172.

mercenaries.[9] After the July 2009 Boko Haram Uprising resulting in over 1000 deaths, the leader, Yusuf, was killed by the Nigerian police force on July 30, 2009 while in custody in Maidaguri, Borno State, signifying protracted police brutality.[10] In 2010, Abubakar Shekau led Boko Haram with much more forms of violence and transformed the insurgency into a global jihadist movement that was anti-American. Shekau supported jihadism in the Sahel area, such as Somalia, Algeria, Yemen, and Iraq.

Attacks in Nigeria greatly increased, leading to more than 38,600 fatalities, 2.5 million internally displaced persons (IDPs), almost 244,000 refugees, and almost one million children dropping out of school.[11] Consequently, Boko Haram primarily targeted the Nigerian police, army, and then politicians and civilians with assassinations, bombings, and kidnappings.[12] For instance, the April 2014 Chibok kidnapping of 276 schoolgirls aged 16–18 received widespread international attention.[13] Abduction usually entails a ransom for money from the Nigerian government to fund the insurgency. In addition, Boko Haram have forced women and girls into marriage and sexual slavery and have forced boys to be child soldiers.[14] In relation to human security, Boko Haram impacts basic access to food, water resources, finance, and health care in rural households in northeast Nigeria.[15] Therefore, Boko Haram became deadlier, indicating that a further disharmonious state of affairs was the outcome.

As part of counterterrorism, Nigeria has attempted to grant amnesty to repentant Boko Haram terrorists as part of a reintegration and

[9] Tarela Juliet Ike, Danny Singh, Dung Ezekiel Jidong, Sean Murphy, and Evangelyn Ebi Ayobi, "Rethinking Reintegration in Nigeria: Community Perceptions of Former Boko Haram Combatants," *Third World Quarterly*, Vol. 42, No. 4 (January 2021), p. 666; Teniola Tayo, "Soldiers for Rent in the Boko Haram Crisis," *Institute for Security Studies*, February 8, 2021.

[10] Tarela Juliet Ike, Georgios A. Antonopoulos, and Danny Singh, "Community Perspectives of Terrorism and the Nigerian Government's Counterterrorism Strategies: A Systematic Review," *Criminology & Criminal Justice* (July 2022), p. 6.

[11] Ahmadu Abubakar Tafida, Abdullahi Liman Tukur, Elizabeth F. Adebayo, Augustine Anthony Ndaghu, J. I. Onu, and Jude A. Momodu, "Boko Haram Insurgency and Livelihood Vulnerability of Rural Households in Northern Adamawa State, Nigeria," *Research in Globalization*, Vol. 6 (January 2003), p. 2.

[12] Global Terrorism Index, *Measuring the Impact of Terrorism*, pp. 3, 15.

[13] Helon Habila, *The Chibok Girls* (London: Penguin, 2017).

[14] United States Department of State, "2023 Trafficking in Persons Report: Nigeria," *US Department of State*, 2023.

[15] Tafida et al., "Boko Haram Insurgency and Livelihood Vulnerability of Rural Households in Northern Adamawa State, Nigeria," *Research in Globalization*, Vol. 6 (January 2003), p. 1.

deradicalization strategy. This replicated the intentions of the 2009 amnesty program that was relatively successful in the Niger Delta, region and thus the Nigerian federal government wanted to pacify Boko Haram. In April 2016, Nigeria prescribed the amnesty program targeted for low-risk terrorists that would be willing to repent for their previous atrocities. This program included women who married Boko Haram members. A facility was established for repentant combatants to surrender weapons and undergo a deradicalization and reintegration program prior to being reintegrated into society. The participants were promised vocational training as part of deradicalization, rehabilitation, and reintegration of Boko Haram atoners.[16] On February 19, 2020, Nigeria and the governor of Yobe State introduced the National Agency for Education, Rehabilitation, Deradicalization and Integration of Repentant *Insurgents* in Nigeria that officially granted amnesty and deradicalization camps to repentant Boko Haram extremists.[17] There are three programs. First, the Prison Program focuses on Islamic teachers conveying non-violent approaches to Islam that are coupled with vocational training.[18] Second, the Yellow Ribbon Initiative provides "psychological therapy," and young women and children are supported with education-based reintegration to prevent terrorism and undermine radicalization in northeast Nigeria.[19] The Neem Foundation, which is a civil society organization, supports the Initiative. Third, Operation Safe Corridor (OSC) was launched in 2015 by the Nigerian armed forces. OSC includes counseling and training on socially moral and acceptable behavior for deradicalization. An estimated 2000 Boko Haram and Islamic State–West Africa Province members have entered the OSC program.

In the aftermath of the deradicalization program, Boko Haram recipients are released from a rehabilitation center with declarations proving their normal psychological behavior. Once this is confirmed by the government, the repentant individual is reintegrated into a community. The intention of the Nigerian government is to provide deradicalization

[16] Ejeh and Ebunoluwa, "Amnesty as a Tool in the Deradicalization of Boko Haram Terrorists in Nigeria," p. 14.

[17] Ejeh and Ebunoluwa, "Amnesty as a Tool in the Deradicalization of Boko Haram Terrorists in Nigeria," p. 2.

[18] Yomi Kazeem, "Nigeria Keeps Saying It Has Defeated Boko Haram Against All the Evidence," *Quartz Africa*, July 10, 2017.

[19] Sowale and Aduloju, "Deradicalization of Repentant Boko Haram Militants," pp. 174–175.

programs to cease the conflict, and thus the purpose is to create a less discordant state of affairs.

The national laws of Nigeria have also included rules of amnesty. The Nigerian President holds legal powers to pardon any person of a crime, impose a less severe penalty, or remove all punishment.[20] To exercise any of these measures, the President must consult the Council of State and if offenses were committed against the armed forces, air force, or naval fleet, then a court martial is to convict and sentence.[21] These provisions of pardoning do not correlate to amnesty.

After this domestic bill of amnesty with the content of the program remaining concealed and secretive, terrorist activities have still not decreased. Hence, the amnesty program risks impunity and the rule of law that can be undermined. Victims' families, injured soldiers, human rights campaigners, and non-governmental organizations have heavily criticized the program.[22] Those who have committed human rights abuses are not easily pardoned or desired to be reintegrated as civilians into their previous communities in Nigeria.[23] Civilians have been critical of the amnesty program because those who joined Boko Haram reap benefits of assistance, but those who did not join are left with no opportunities or necessities.[24] It is felt by the public that victims of atrocities are neglected while perpetrators of serious human rights violations are rewarded. There have been cases in Borno State when authorities have forcibly retaken released ex-insurgents "to the rehabilitation center after being attacked by" community members "who had suffered under Boko Haram."[25]

Alongside Nigerian civilians pitted against the deradicalization program, IDPs and the armed forces are also hostile toward the process. IDPs from northeast Nigeria resented insurgents attaining a better benefits

[20] Constitution of the Federal Republic of Nigeria, 1999 (Fifth Alteration) (No. 5) Act, 2023, Section 175 (1) (a–d).

[21] Constitution of the Federal Republic of Nigeria, 1999, Section 175 (2–3).

[22] Azimazi Momoh Jimoh, Segun Olaniyi, Olawunmi Ojo, Seye Olumide, and Chido Okafor, "Crisis as Stakeholders Reject Amnesty for 'Repentant' Boko Haram Terrorists," *The Guardian Nigeria*, February 21, 2020.

[23] Ike et al., "Rethinking Reintegration in Nigeria."

[24] Vanda Felbab-Brown, "In Nigeria, We Don't Want Them Back: Amnesty, Defectors' Programs, Leniency Measures, Informal Reconciliation, and Punitive Responses to Boko Haram," *The Brookings Institution*, May 2018.

[25] Sowale and Aduloju, "Deradicalization of Repentant Boko Haram Militants," p. 178.

package than IDP camps.[26] The Nigerian soldiers are confused and angry with the surrendered Boko Haram members entering treatment and deradicalization in rehabilitation centers. Boko Haram members are treated and mediated for the benefit of their well-being. It is only wounded Nigerian soldiers that receive the same treatment. It is perplexing for the soldiers as to why the terrorists who they fight receive the same privileges as they do, if not more. Civilians and the military in northeast Nigeria have not been consulted about the secretive deradicalization program.[27]

Many Boko Haram extremists were forcibly conscripted so amnesty may seem fair, but once radicalized, the social identity is too strong to denounce allegiance to the extremist group.[28] Despite amnesty efforts, Boko Haram has made it clear that it will keep fighting for an Islamic Emirate in Nigeria. This means that the insurgency does not recognize the legitimacy of the Nigerian government and negotiation is difficult to accomplish. In response, in September 2015, Nigeria's National Security Council urged the Boko Haram group to surrender their arms and violence and engage with peace.[29]

The principles of *Ubuntu* do not necessarily analyze law but focus on how to preserve, promote, and restore communal relations, which requires the absence of violence as the final outcome. Based on this notion, the Truth and Reconciliation Commission in South Africa granted amnesty and promoted a more harmonious, and less discordant, state of affairs. However, unlike the Commission in South Africa, the amnesty program in Nigeria failed to consult the public to gain their consent and trust. This largely explains why Nigerian communities are skeptical of the program and hostile toward repentant Boko Haram extremists who are reintegrated into civilian communities after serving their time in a deradicalization camp. The amnesty program is only available for low-risk terrorists, but there is no truth-telling or Truth and Reconciliation Commission established. Forgiveness is a main segment of *Ubuntu* principles and thus a more inclusive and evaluative approach to offering amnesty for repentant Boko Haram extremists must be encouraged to engage with civic leaders

[26] Amnesty International, *Nigeria: Stars on Their Shoulders: Blood on Their Hands: War Crimes Committed by the Nigerian Military* (London: Amnesty International, 2015).

[27] Sowale and Aduloju, "Deradicalization of Repentant Boko Haram Militants," p. 180.

[28] Daniel Egiegba Agbiboa, "The Social Dynamics of the Nigerian Taliban: Fresh Insight from the Social Identity Theory," *Social Dynamics: A Journal of African Studies*, Vol. 41, No. 3 (November 2015), pp. 415–437.

[29] Sowale and Aduloju, "Deradicalization of Repentant Boko Haram Militants," p. 170.

and the communities that may be willing to accept them back into society to restore a harmonious state of affairs.[30] It can be argued that the amnesty program has not been inclusive for middle and community actors, and thus reintegrated Boko Haram extremists lack social capital and revert to banditry and loyalty that retains strong social identity with the insurgency. Despite these efforts to restore communal relations and counter terrorist violence, religion and ethnicity have continued to divide Nigeria, resulting in a discordant state of affairs.

Niger Delta Militancy, Oil Exploitation, and Environmental Degradation

In southern Nigeria, the Niger Delta region (comprising Akwa, Bayelsa, Cross Rivers, Delta, Edo, and Rivers States) contains high wildlife and biodiversity resources. The area holds 33.6 billion barrels of crude oil and 163 billion cubic feet of natural gas.[31] From solely oil, between 1970 and 2000, Nigeria gained an estimated US $300 billion that equated to 96 percent of its international revenue.[32] However, due to weak transparency and endemic corruption, Nigeria may have earned much more from oil based in the Niger Delta region. For instance, former President Obasanjo (1999–2007) also acted as Minister of Petroleum because a minister was not recruited.[33] Despite lucrative earnings in the area, the Niger Delta remains one of the least developed regions in Nigeria. This can be explained from the 'resource curse' analogy that has intensified income inequality

[30] Lederach similarly contends that peace and conflict resolution have a better chance of success if top, middle, and community levels are consulted (John Paul Lederach, "Of Nets, Nails, and Problems: The Folk Language of Conflict Resolution in a Central American Setting," in *Conflict Resolution: Cross-cultural Perspectives*, edited by Kevin Avruch, Peter Black and Joseph A. Scimecca) (New York: Greenwood Press, 1991), pp. 165–186, p. 171).

[31] Christopher Bankole Ndubisi Ogbogbo, "The Niger Delta People and the Resource Control Conflict, 1966–1995: An Assessment of Conflict Handling Style," in *Perspectives on Peace and Conflict in Africa: Essays in Honor of General (Dr.) Absulsalami A. Abubakar*, edited by Isaac O. Albert (Ibadan: University of Ibadan, 2005), p. 169, pp. 169–180.

[32] Ngozi Okonjo-Iweala, Charles C. Soludo, and Mansur Muhtar, "Introduction," in *The Debt Trap in Nigeria: Towards a Sustainable Debt Strategy*, edited by Ngozi Okonjo-Iweala, Charles C. Soludo and Mansur Muhtar (Trenton, NJ: Africa World Press, 2003), p. 1, pp. 1–20.

[33] Jeremiah Shola Omotola, "Liberation Movements and Rising Violence in the Niger Delta: The New Contentious Site of Oil and Environmental Politics," *Studies in Conflict & Terrorism*, Vol. 33, No. 1 (May 2009), p. 37.

from oil discovery and its exploitation resulting in environmental degradation. The fishery and farming occupations have been hampered from such ecological damage and almost uninhabitable areas that have increased poverty due to the negative impact on local livelihoods.[34] An estimated 30–35 million "tons of carbon dioxide" and approximately "12 million tons/year of methane" entered the atmosphere.[35] It is the Nigerian state, oil-gaining communities, and oil multinational corporations that benefit at the expense of the local Niger Delta population. Therefore, oil resources and the exportation of oil have created conflict in the Niger Delta area.

Since Nigeria's return to civilian rule in 1999, the Niger Delta has generated ethnic militia groups to engage in sabotage against exploitative oil production and its threat to local environmental life. The Niger Delta militants (called the 'Niger Delta Avengers') are also referred to as insurgents and are fighting the exploitation of foreign oil corporations by attacking underwater pipelines, and the scuffle for oil wealth has resulted in further regional insecurity and Nigeria's energy supply crisis.[36] These militias have been grouped into the Movement for the Emancipation of the Niger Delta (MEND) and the Niger Delta People's Volunteer Force (NDPVF). The militants have been engaged in sabotage, kidnapping, oil bunkering (crude oil theft), and petro-criminality to control resources and restore polluted land due to oil exploration that has not benefitted the region economically.[37] Equitable and environmental rights to oil are the main objectives of the militants, which is why they have engaged in sabotage of oil pipelines. The relative deprivation and frustration-aggression hypothesis can explain the rising violence from militias in the Niger Delta region.

The loss of livelihoods due to environmental degradation, such as by fishermen, antagonized the militants to vandalize oil pipelines that resulted in rigorous militarization and amnesty from the Obasanjo and Yar'adua administrations, respectively.[38] During Obasanjo's presidency, a

[34] Omotola, "Liberation Movements and Rising Violence in the Niger Delta," pp. 37, 41.

[35] Omotola, "Liberation Movements and Rising Violence in the Niger Delta," p. 42.

[36] BBC News, "Nigeria Arrests 'Avengers' Oil Militants," *BBC News*, May 16, 2016, https://www.bbc.co.uk/news/world-africa-36301835.

[37] Tarela Juliet Ike, Danny Singh, Sean Murphy, Dung Ezekiel Jidong, Fran Porritt, and Evangelyn Ebi Ayobi, "Community Perspectives of Former Terrorist Combatants, Militants and Reintegration Programmes in Nigeria: A Systematic Review," *Behavioral Sciences of Terrorism and Political Aggression*, Vol. 14, No. 2 (2022), p. 143.

[38] Ike et al., "Community Perspectives of Former Terrorist Combatants," pp. 143–144.

heavy-handed approach was preferred to deal with sabotage of oil production activity, which included sentencing for treason, capital punishment, and environmental activists being detained and tortured. Obasanjo also hired private military contractors to intimidate activists and the Nigerian armed forces killed 2000 out of 15,000 civilians in the Bayelsa State, but oil companies have tried to restore their credibility by paying low reparations and implementing community development projects, such as rebuilding roads and schools and implementing vocational training.[39] Therefore, Nigeria has attempted to oppose the Niger Delta region with militarization to control ethnic militia groups. Yet, violence, piracy, and kidnappings persist.

In 2000, the Niger Delta Development Commission was created to identify and discuss environmental and developmental issues in the area, with 3 percent of the overall annual budget of oil- and gas-producing companies going to the Commission. Yet, group and class interests made this mechanism difficult. Violence continued that is demonstrated with MEND responding to the arrest and detention of their leader, Asari Dokubo, with continual sabotage targeting oil installations and kidnapping of foreign oil workers in late 2005 and early 2006, which plummeted oil production.[40] On June 25, 2009, the late Nigerian President, Umara Musa Yar'Adua, implemented an amnesty program for Niger Delta militants who had engaged in sabotage and attacks due to grievances against the Nigerian federal government.

The Post-Amnesty Program (PAP) engaged with the deradicalization and reintegration of militants, with the militants promising to renounce their groups within 60 days to attain eligibility for a US $250 million deradicalization program that included training and four years of monthly allowances.[41] Residents of the Niger Delta area have been denied managerial and ownership rights to oil reserves located in the south of Nigeria and next to the Gulf of Guinea. Oil is exploited in this area and Niger Delta people are deemed a minority to Nigeria's federalism. The Land Use Act of 1978 ensures that Niger Delta civilians do not receive commensurate

[39] Omotola, "Liberation Movements and Rising Violence in the Niger Delta," p. 44.

[40] Omotola, "Liberation Movements and Rising Violence in the Niger Delta," p. 46.

[41] Markus Schultze-Kraft, "Understanding Organized Violence and Crime in Political Settlements: Oil Wars, Petro-criminality and Amnesty in the Niger Delta," *Journal of International Development*, Vol. 29, No. 5 (July 2017), p. 620.

benefits.[42] To voice this discontent, Niger Delta communities protested peacefully, but then moved to violence. The oil industry has been represented by the Nigerian federal government and multinational oil corporations, such as Shell, Chevron Texaco, Exxon Mobil, Total, Elf, and Eni-Agip. The young population in the Niger Delta operate as organized armed groups and have engaged in guerilla warfare by attacking Nigerian security forces and engaging in sabotage by damaging oil installations. As a solution, the Nigerian government extended its hand for amnesty and forgiveness for all Niger Delta militants willing to accept these terms to receive monthly payments and training opportunities in exchange for relinquishing arms and non-fighting. Throughout the rehabilitation process, disarmed militants would receive 65,000 Nigerian naira (US $841) monthly.[43] Over 26,000 militants from the groups reluctantly proceeded to the camps due to the heavy Nigerian military force that came with it and received a monthly stipend and vocational training.[44]

Although militancy and violence has decreased since the amnesty program in the Niger Delta region, criminal violence persists due to continual oil exploitation, spillages, and environmental damage. For example, from 2006 to 2020, an estimated 110,000 oil barrels spilled into rivers, forests, and swamps, with 90 percent of incidences due to negligence from multinational corporations.[45] Over 23 years, another study reported that the Niger Delta region suffered from 7940 oil spillages, with 67 percent of them occurring onshore, and out of the 5320 onshore oil spillages, 81 percent were due to sabotage.[46] From 2011, Shell claimed 1010 oil spillages, comprising 110,535 barrels within its operations, and from 2014, Eni claimed 820 oil spillages, including 26,286 barrels within its

[42] Rhuks Temitope Ako, "Nigeria's Land Use Act: An Anti-Thesis to Environmental Justice," *Journal of African* Law, Vol. 53, No. 2 (2009), pp. 289–304.

[43] Ejeh and Ebunoluwa, "Amnesty as a Tool in the Deradicalization of Boko Haram Terrorists in Nigeria," p. 13.

[44] Schultze-Kraft, "Understanding Organized Violence and Crime in Political Settlements," p. 621.

[45] Ashoka Mukpo, "As Shell, Eni Quit Niger Delta, State-backed Report Describes Legacy of Carnage," *Mongabay*, May 16, 2023.

[46] Akinola S. Akinwumiju, Adedeji A. Adelodun, and Seyi E. Ogundeji, "Geospatial Assessment of Oil Spill Pollution in the Niger Delta of Nigeria: An Evidence-based Evaluation of Causes and Potential Remedies," *Environmental Pollution*, Vol. 267 (December 2020), p. 1.

pipelines.[47] Furthermore, the higher ranks of the militants were paid off with contract work to protect oil pipelines, and security surveillance and ex-militia leaders acted as Goodluck Jonathan's clients to support his 2015 re-election.[48]

Due to this patrimonial system that included criminality to bolster clientelism and political survival, in the mid-2000s, hundreds of thousands of crude oil barrels were stolen.[49] Niger Delta militants have engaged in sabotage of oil facilities that placed Nigeria in a recession in 2015.[50] Oil multinational corporations are also slow to resolve oil spills related to their pipelines. To provide one of many examples, in 2016, it took Shell 10 days to start resolving its oil spill caused by equipment failure resulting in 50 barrels contaminating a swamp that damaged fish nets belonging to the local community.[51] The Nigerian legal rules stipulate that an oil spill must be reported within 24 hours and action should be undertaken within 24 hours.[52]

The insurgency continues to fight for the Niger Delta's emancipation from Nigeria, but after a 2009 agreement, sabotage of oil installations remains. Although amnesty has reduced Niger Delta militancy violence, the deradicalization programs for Boko Haram insurgents have been undermined by the CJTF and communal members attacking repentant Boko Haram insurgents, namely women and girls, due to sexual violence stigma and poor confidence in sincere repentance.[53]

[47] Amnesty International, *Negligence in the Niger Delta: Decoding Shell and Eni's Poor Record on Oil Spills* (London: Amnesty International, 2018), pp. 5, 7.

[48] Schultze-Kraft, "Understanding Organized Violence and Crime in Political Settlements," p. 622.

[49] Peter Lewis and Michael Watts, *Nigeria: The Political Economy of Governance – Discussion Paper, Doing Development Differently Program* (Washington, DC: World Bank, 2015), p. 19.

[50] Akinwumiju, Adelodun and Ogundeji, "Geospatial Assessment of Oil Spill Pollution in the Niger Delta of Nigeria," p. 2.

[51] Amnesty International, *Negligence in the Niger Delta*, p. 9.

[52] National Oil Spill Detection and Response Agency, *Oil Spill Recovery, Clean-up, Remediation and Damage Assessment Regulations*, 2011, Part VII (102), p. 76 (cited in Amnesty International, *Negligence in the Niger Delta*, p. 13).

[53] Ike et al., "Community Perspectives of Terrorism," p. 15; Ike et al., "Rethinking Reintegration in Nigeria," 667; Ike et al., "Community Perspectives of Former Terrorist Combatants," p. 153.

ECOWAS and the Military Junta in Niger

In the context of Niger, on July 26, 2023, the Presidential Guard overthrew President Mohamed Bazoum, which was condemned by ECOWAS and the African Union. Bazoum was released from detention, but the National Council for the Safeguard of the Homeland, a military junta, seized power. Therefore, General Abdourahamane Tchiani is ruling the country as the *de facto* president of the military junta. Nigerian President and ECOWAS chair Bola Ahmed Tinubu has indicated that ECOWAS should conduct sanctions and intervene with its fellow countries comprising ECOWAS standby forces to restore the democratically elected Bazoum.[54] ECOWAS immediately authorized closing borders, installing a no-fly zone for all commercial flights in and out of Niger, and Nigeria cut Niger's power supply "on the 80 megawatt Birnin-Kebbi line and ECOWAS Central Bank froze Nigerien state assets and enterprises, which cancelled US $51 million (CFA Francs 30 billion) bond distribution."[55] Despite these sanctions and potential ECOWAS military intervention, Tchiani's military and allies boast an estimated 30,000 soldiers that would trump the 7000 standby forces from ECOWAS. If other countries join Tinubu, then ECOWAS could gain better support. Similarly, the United Nations Security Council has condemned the coup d'état and vowed support for ECOWAS and the African Union.[56]

Niger, which is north of Nigeria, and the military juntas in Burkina Faso and Mali have interests in determining if ECOWAS would collectively intervene with military action. Burkina Faso and Mali would be against a military intervention in Niger because both have leaders of military juntas—Captain Ibrahim Traoré (Burkina Faso)[57] and Colonel Assimi Goïta (Mali)—ruling their countries. Instability in Niger could spread to Nigeria.

A discordant state of affairs, however, is not evident in Niger, Burkina Faso, and Mali because many civilians have demonstrated their public

[54] Oluwatimilehin Sotubo, "ECOWAS: In Need of Help in Niger?" *RAND Corporation*, August 25, 2023.

[55] Bate Felix and Anait Miridzhanian, "What Sanctions Have Been Imposed on Niger since the Coup?" *Reuters*, August 8, 2023.

[56] United Nations, "Niger: Security Council Strongly Condemns 'Efforts to Unconstitutionally Change' Government," *United Nations News*, July 29, 2023.

[57] It will be difficult for Traoré to fill Thomas Sankara's legacy of deposing the French-backed government to challenge poverty, famine, and hunger in Western Africa.

support for military rulership. The desire of ECOWAS to restore democratic governance in Niger from a collective military intervention could challenge military authoritarianism within the region, but it is debatable as to whether it will bring about strong democracies for a more harmonious state of affairs.

Niger, like Burkina Faso, has good relations with Russia and may have the Wagner Group deployed to save their military junta regimes.[58] The military juntas of Mali, Burkina Faso, and Niger have declared their intentions to leave ECOWAS due to sanctions imposed upon them for deposing democratically elected presidents, and the alleged failure of the alliance to help them fight terrorism and insecurity.[59] The withdrawal of these three West African states from ECOWAS would create a further regional discordant state of affairs because the security strategy would deviate from consulting and utilizing the services of ECOWAS, the African Union, and the UN (including their wider peacekeeping mandates).

The Syrian Civil War

The Syrian case may warrant open revolution. Since 2011, the Bashar Hafez al-Assad regime has engaged in a slow mass-homicide campaign against protestors with the support of Alawites, Christians, and the large Sunni merchant class and businesses positioned in urban cities, namely Damascus and Aleppo.[60] In a recent report, there have been 230,224 recorded civilian deaths, 154,871 people have been arrested, and about 14 million Syrians have been displaced.[61]

After the failure of protests, the remaining forms of Afro-communitarian permissible commenced. These comprised attempted sabotage, guerrilla warfare, and terrorism from a variety of groups fighting for different reasons. To provide one example, in northern Syria, Kurdish combatants located in Rojava have aligned with the Syrian Defense Forces and Kurdistan Workers' Party in Turkey and Iraqi Kurds were initially

[58] Gilles Yabi, "The Niger Coup's Outsized Global Impact," *Carnegie Endowment for International Peace*, August 31, 2023.

[59] Olayinka Ajala, "Mali, Burkina Faso and Niger Want to Leave ECOWAS. A Political Scientist Explains the Fallout," *The Conversation*, February 5, 2024.

[60] Robert A. Pape, "When Duty Calls: A Pragmatic Standard of Humanitarian Intervention," *International Security*, Vol. 37, No. 1 (Summer 2012), p. 71.

[61] Syrian Network for Human Rights, "On the 12th Anniversary of the Popular Uprising," *Syrian Network for Human Rights*, March 15, 2023, pp. 1, 6, 11.

supported by the United States in their territorial struggle against the al-Assad regime.[62] In addition, Islamic State are fighting for a regional caliphate. The group are fighting the Syrian administration. During this process, Islamic State are engaged in mass atrocities, including beheadings when apostasy is proven, and being beaten for shaving, voting and not being Sunni.[63] In retaliation, Syrian-led illegal chemical weapons have targeted civilians, property, and hospitals in rebel-based areas, resulting in widespread international condemnation.[64]

Investigations conducted by the United Nations corroborate that chlorine gas was dropped at least two times in rebel-based strongholds in 2014, 2015, and 2017, but Russia and China vetoed suggested sanctions against the Syrian regime.[65] The United States does focus on fighting Islamic State, but it has not committed to large ground forces or engaging with aerial war in Syria that has failed to circumvent al-Assad's decisive support from Russia, Iran, Hezbollah, and Turkey.[66] Based on the notion of implementing collective security law, the concept of "selectivity" depends "on whether the aggressor" can "invoke the support of a permanent member" of the United Nations Security Council.[67] This is evident in the context of Syria, particularly Russia vetoing several draft UN Security Council Resolutions against condemnation of the suppression of protestors and a cessation of military flights over Aleppo.[68]

Even if UN Security Council condemnation of chemical attacks is vetoed, multilateral intervention can be undertaken because diplomacy has proved fruitless. This form of foreign armed intervention commenced

[62] Anthony H. Cordesman and Aram Nerguizan, "The Case for and against a 'Realist' Strategy in Syria," *Center for Strategic & International Studies*, January 24, 2017, p. 3.

[63] Jeff McMahan, "Syria is a Modern-day Holocaust. We Must Act," *The Washington Post*, November 30, 2015, https://www.washingtonpost.com/news/in-theory/wp/2015/11/30/syria-is-a-modern-day-holocaust-we-must-act/.

[64] United Nations Security Council Resolution 2118, "In Regard to the Framework for Elimination of Syrian Chemical Weapons during the Syrian Civil War," UN Doc. S/RES/2118, September 27, 2013, adopted 7038th meeting, 4–6, Annex I.

[65] BBC News, "Syria War: Russia and China Veto Sanctions," *BBC News*, February 28, 2017.

[66] Cordesman and Nerguizan, "The Case for and Against a 'Realist' Strategy in Syria," p. 1.

[67] Koskiennieni, "The Place of Law in Collective Security."

[68] UN Security Council, "France, Germany, Portugal and United Kingdom of Great Britain and Northern Ireland: draft resolution 612," UN Doc. S/2011/612, October 4, 2011; UN Security Council, "Indiscriminate aerial bombings in Aleppo: draft resolution 846," UN Doc. S/2016/846, October 8, 2016.

in April 2018 by Western powers (the United States, the United Kingdom, and France) that dropped over 100 aircraft and naval missiles targeting a variety of the Syrian regime's chemical weapons storage and research units.[69]

Assessing Afro-communitarian Ethics in the Non-Interventions

In Nigeria, internal governmental efforts to fight enemies (Boko Haram and ethnic insurgencies in the Niger Delta region) with initial enmity-like violence and subsequent amnesty and deradicalization programs to bring about a harmonious state of affairs are failing with the former terrorist group. The amnesty program in Nigeria for repentant Boko Haram extremists has attempted reintegration and forgiveness, which would comply with *Ubuntu* and the Truth and Reconciliation Commission in South Africa, but it may be considered as a 'buyout' for engaging in terrorist activity, and thus the Nigerian amnesty program merely professes leniency. As for Niger Delta militants, the payments for disarmament and demobilization worked but environmental degradation and sabotage of oil constellations remain. The situation of high insecurity, high civilian casualties, property damage, and economic repercussions warrants foreign military intervention.

ECOWAS has problems with Niger, Burkina Faso, and Mali that are threatening democracy in West Africa. If the military juntas continue to be supported by their communities and foster good relations with one another, then, under the ethics of Afro-communitarianism, an intervention advocating stages of violence to restore democratically elected leaders would not be required. The restoration of democracies is not a significant burden for Afro-communitarian moral philosophy, unless the current regimes are undertaking conditions of a less discordant situation and less harmonious state of affairs.

In Syria, without international military assistance to halt civilian casualties, a less discordant state of affairs can only be reached if a foreign armed intervention engages with sabotage and works toward an open revolution by potentially supporting rebels to do so. This potentially proposed hazardous solution does not advocate diplomacy or third-party mediation because these avenues have been exhausted alongside multiple Moscow and Beijing vetoes to safeguard the respect for Syrian sovereign territorial

[69] Julian Borger, "Syria: US, UK and France Launch Strikes in Response to Chemical Attack," *The Guardian*, April 14, 2018.

integrity in response to al-Assad utilizing chemical weapons against innocent civilians in rebel-based areas. If applying Metz's reformation of *Ubuntu* ethics, violence can be used in self-defense due to the failure of friendly alternatives, and a discordant state of affairs can be countered with comparable violence and a more harmonious state of affairs can be reached that ends discord once a settlement has been attained. Perhaps this reformation is true for the destiny of Syria from the Arab Spring Movement and rise of rebels and terrorists. However, these belligerent groups are spread, not united and fight for different reasons. The groups aim to conquer regions that have great powers backing different sides, which prolongs the war and disharmonious state of affairs.

Conclusion

Nigeria commenced its deradicalization strategy with robust military means, but this approach was met with more violence from Boko Haram, resulting in further collateral damage, obliteration of properties, and gross human rights violations. This military strategy from Obasanjo resulted in increased resentment of the government from the public and thus Yar'Adua attempted a softer civilian amnesty strategy.[70] However, the Nigerian public have not embraced the *Ubuntu* concept of forgiveness as with amnesty in South Africa.

In the Niger Delta region, the militants are an increasing youth movement fighting for liberation against colonial Nigerian federalism and international oil companies exploiting resources and keeping the revenue, which has left the region one of the least developed in Nigeria. The civilian population in the Niger Delta region are generally supportive of the efforts of the militias engaging in sabotage, oil bunkering, and kidnappings. The militant groups have undertaken PAP due to lethal force of the national army, but patron–client relations with politicians have resulted in further violence to protect oil installations and oil bunkering has increased. After PAP, criminal alliances have risen with the militant groups due to grievances and a means to fund the liberation of armed struggle (guerilla warfare) for political representation and fairness in the distribution of oil rents. Dealing with the Niger Delta militants with military force to complement PAP alongside all local, state, federal, private, and oil multinational corporation actors has perpetuated and protracted (organized) violence in the

[70] Sowale and Aduloju, "Deradicalization of Repentant Boko Haram Militants," p. 172.

Niger Delta region. Therefore, oil-bearing communities in the Niger Delta region are debatably in a less harmonious state of affairs. Perhaps, the Nigerian federal government could properly invest in human development and capital in the Niger Delta region rather than solely relying on the relatively successful amnesty program to foster a more protracted harmonious state of affairs.

In Niger, an ECOWAS intervention with potential backing from the African Union and/or United Nations would serve as a deterrent for those planning coups and success could transition democracies in Burkina Faso and Mali from military rule once more.[71] However, Nigerians would not support an ECOWAS-based military intervention if the costs are higher than the benefits, and Nigeria is plagued with internal conflict problems of its own. In addition, the Wagner Group has reached out to military juntas in Mali and Burkina Faso and has pledged to support Niger to enhance Russian foreign policy on undermining democracies, selling weapons, and deploying security forces to develop client states in West Africa. Similarly, Burkina Faso and Mali have pledged to deploy their armed forces to support Niger's junta.

The context of Syria demonstrates the lethal use of violence from the totalitarian regime that has been protected by Russia with numerous vetoes in the United Nations Security Council to warrant intervention. Due to NATO intervening in Libya that created cynicism about promoting regime change, the same is feared with the Responsibility to Protect doctrine in Syria.

It can thus be argued that the West African region, particularly Nigeria and its neighbors, is in a disharmonious state of affairs that foreign-led diplomacy from the African Union, ECOWAS, and potentially the United Nations could resolve. For the Syrian civil war, a diplomatic solution is unlikely, and thus a foreign armed intervention, potentially within the United Nations, is needed to bring a halt to atrocities and work on forming a more harmonious state of affairs. If diplomacy fails and hostilities rise, then the phases of permissible Afro-communitarian violence can be undertaken with a foreign armed intervention from a combination of these mentioned regional and international organizations.

[71] Sotubo, "ECOWAS: In Need of Help in Niger?"

References

Agbiboa, Daniel Egiegba. "The Social Dynamics of the Nigerian Taliban: Fresh Insight from the Social Identity Theory." *Social Dynamics: A Journal of African Studies*, Vol. 41, No. 3 (November 2015), pp. 415–437. https://doi.org/10.1080/02533952.2015.1100364.

Adigbuo, Ebere R. "Boko Haram: A Race between Amnesty and Criminal Tribunal." *Historical Research Letter*, Vol. 13 (2014), pp. 29–40. https://www.iiste.org/Journals/index.php/HRL/article/view/15481.

Ajala, Olayinka. "Mali, Burkina Faso and Niger Want to Leave ECOWAS. A Political Scientist Explains the Fallout." *The Conversation*, February 5, 2024. https://theconversation.com/mali-burkina-faso-and-niger-want-to-leave-ecowas-a-political-scientist-explains-the-fallout-222388.

Akinwumiju, Akinola S., Adedeji A. Adelodun, and Seyi E. Ogundeji. "Geospatial Assessment of Oil Spill Pollution in the Niger Delta of Nigeria: An Evidence-based Evaluation of Causes and Potential Remedies." *Environmental Pollution*, Vol. 267 (December 2020), pp. 1–13. https://doi.org/10.1016/j.envpol.2020.115545.

Ako, Rhuks Temitope. "Nigeria's Land Use Act: An Anti-Thesis to Environmental Justice." *Journal of African Law*, Vol. 53, No. 2 (2009), pp. 289–304. https://doi.org/10.1017/S0021855309990076.

Amnesty International. *Nigeria: Stars on Their Shoulders: Blood on Their Hands: War Crimes Committed by the Nigerian Military.* London: Amnesty International, 2015. https://www.amnesty.org/en/wp-content/uploads/2021/05/AFR4416572015ENGLISH.pdf.

Amnesty International. *Negligence in the Niger Delta: Decoding Shell and Eni's Poor Record on Oil Spills.* London: Amnesty International, 2018. https://www.amnesty.org/en/documents/afr44/7970/2018/en/.

BBC News. "Nigeria Arrests 'Avengers' Oil Militants." *BBC News*, May 16, 2016. https://www.bbc.co.uk/news/world-africa-36301835.

BBC News. "Syria War: Russia and China Veto Sanctions." *BBC News*, February 28, 2017. https://www.bbc.co.uk/news/world-middle-east-39116854.

Borger, Julian. "Syria: US, UK and France Launch Strikes in Response to Chemical Attack." *The Guardian*, April 14, 2018. https://www.theguardian.com/world/2018/apr/14/syria-air-strikes-us-uk-and-france-launch-attack-on-assad-regime.

Constitution of the Federal Republic of Nigeria, 1999 (Fifth Alteration) (No. 5) Act, 2023, Section 175 (1) (a–d).

Cordesman, Anthony H., and Aram Nerguizan. "The Case for and against a 'Realist' Strategy in Syria." *Center for Strategic & International Studies*, January 24, 2017. https://www.csis.org/analysis/case-and-against-realist-strategy-syria.

Ejeh, Emelda Undiandeye, and Ebunoluwa Popoola. "Amnesty as a Tool in the Deradicalization of Boko Haram Terrorists in Nigeria: A Threat to National Security." *The International Journal of Human Rights* (December 2023), pp. 1–24. https://doi.org/10.1080/13642987.2023.2297313.

Felbab-Brown, Vanda. "In Nigeria, We Don't Want Them Back: Amnesty, Defectors' Programs, Leniency Measures, Informal Reconciliation, and Punitive Responses to Boko Haram." *The Brookings Institution*, May 2018. https://www.brookings.edu/articles/in-nigeria-we-dont-want-them-back/.

Felix, Bate, and Anait Miridzhanian. "What Sanctions Have Been Imposed on Niger since the Coup?" *Reuters*, August 8, 2023. https://www.reuters.com/world/africa/what-sanctions-have-been-imposed-niger-since-coup-2023-08-08/.

Global Terrorism Index. *Measuring the Impact of Terrorism*. Sydney, NSW: Institute for Economics & Peace, 2019.

Habila, Helon. *The Chibok Girls*. London: Penguin, 2017.

Ike, Tarela Juliet, Danny Singh, Dung Ezekiel Jidong, Sean Murphy, and Evangelyn Ebi Ayobi. "Rethinking Reintegration in Nigeria: Community Perceptions of Former Boko Haram Combatants." *Third World Quarterly*, Vol. 42, No. 4 (January 2021), pp. 661–678. https://doi.org/10.1080/01436597.2021.1872376.

Ike, Tarela Juliet, Georgios A. Antonopoulos, and Danny Singh. "Community Perspectives of Terrorism and the Nigerian Government's Counterterrorism Strategies: A Systematic Review." *Criminology & Criminal Justice* (July 2022a), pp. 1–30. https://doi.org/10.1177/17488958221110009.

Ike, Tarela Juliet, Danny Singh, Sean Murphy, Dung Ezekiel Jidong, Fran Porritt, and Evangelyn Ebi Ayobi. "Community Perspectives of Former Terrorist Combatants, Militants and Reintegration Programmes in Nigeria: A Systematic Review." *Behavioral Sciences of Terrorism and Political Aggression*, Vol. 14, No. 2 (2022b), pp. 142–168. https://doi.org/10.1080/19434472.2020.1834431.

Jimoh, Azimazi Momoh, Segun Olaniyi, Olawunmi Ojo, Seye Olumide, and Chido Okafor. "Crisis as Stakeholders Reject Amnesty for 'Repentant' Boko Haram Terrorists." *The Guardian Nigeria*, February 21, 2020. https://guardian.ng/news/crisis-as-stakeholders-reject-amnesty-for-repentant-boko-haram-terrorists/.

Kazeem, Yomi. "Nigeria Keeps Saying It Has Defeated Boko Haram Against All the Evidence." *Quartz Africa*, July 10, 2017. https://qz.com/africa/1024655/boko-haram-remains-active-in-nigeria-despite-the-governments-claims-of-victory.

Koskiennieni, Martti. "The Place of Law in Collective Security." *Michigan Journal of International Law*, Vol. 17, No. 2 (1996), pp. 455–490. https://repository.law.umich.edu/cgi/viewcontent.cgi?article=1497&context=mjil.

Lederach, John Paul. "Of Nets, Nails, and Problems: The Folk Language of Conflict Resolution in a Central American Setting." In *Conflict Resolution: Cross-cultural Perspectives*, edited by Kevin Avruch, Peter Black and Joseph A. Scimecca, pp. 165–186. New York: Greenwood Press, 1991.

Lewis, Peter, and Michael Watts. *Nigeria: The Political Economy of Governance – Discussion Paper, Doing Development Differently Program*. Washington, DC: World Bank, 2015.

Mbah, Fidelis. "Nigerians Mark 50 Years of End of Bloody Civil War." *Al Jazeera*, January 15, 2020. https://www.aljazeera.com/features/2020/1/15/nigerians-mark-50-years-of-end-of-bloody-civil-war.

McMahan, Jeff. "Syria is a Modern-day Holocaust. We Must Act." *The Washington Post*, November 30, 2015. https://www.washingtonpost.com/news/in-theory/wp/2015/11/30/syria-is-a-modern-day-holocaust-we-must-act/.

Mukpo, Ashoka. "As Shell, Eni Quit Niger Delta, State-backed Report Describes Legacy of Carnage." *Mongabay*, May 16, 2023. https://news.mongabay.com/2023/05/as-shell-eni-quit-niger-delta-state-backed-report-describes-legacy-of-carnage/.

National Oil Spill Detection and Response Agency, *Oil Spill Recovery, Clean-up, Remediation and Damage Assessment Regulations*, 2011, Part VII (102), p. 76 (cited in Amnesty International. *Negligence in the Niger Delta: Decoding Shell and Eni's Poor Record on Oil Spills*. London: Amnesty International, 2018, p. 13).

Ogbogbo, Christopher Bankole Ndubisi. "The Niger Delta People and the Resource Control Conflict, 1966–1995: An Assessment of Conflict Handling Style." In *Perspectives on Peace and Conflict in Africa: Essays in Honor of General (Dr.) Absulsalami A. Abubakar*, edited by Isaac O. Albert, pp. 169–180. Ibadan: University of Ibadan, 2005.

Okonjo-Iweala, Ngozi, Charles C. Soludo, and Mansur Muhtar. "Introduction." In *The Debt Trap in Nigeria: Towards a Sustainable Debt Strategy*, edited by Ngozi Okonjo-Iweala, Charles C. Soludo and Mansur Muhtar, pp. 1–20. Trenton, NJ: Africa World Press, 2003.

Omotola, Jeremiah Shola. "Liberation Movements and Rising Violence in the Niger Delta: The New Contentious Site of Oil and Environmental Politics." *Studies in Conflict & Terrorism*, Vol. 33, No. 1 (May 2009), pp. 36–54. https://doi.org/10.1080/10576100903400597.

Pape, Robert A. "When Duty Calls: A Pragmatic Standard of Humanitarian Intervention." *International Security*, Vol. 37, No. 1 (Summer 2012), pp. 41–80. https://doi.org/10.1162/ISEC_a_00088.

Schultze-Kraft, Markus. "Understanding Organized Violence and Crime in Political Settlements: Oil Wars, Petro-criminality and Amnesty in the Niger Delta." *Journal of International Development*, Vol. 29, No. 5 (July 2017), pp. 613–627. https://doi.org/10.1002/jid.3287.

Singh, Danny. "Undertaking Critical Legal Theory to Examine Just War Intervention: A Smokescreen for Political Ambitions." In *Comparative Just War Theory: An Introduction to International Perspectives*, edited by Luís Cordeiro-Rodrigues and Danny Singh, pp. 61–79. Lanham, MD: Rowman & Littlefield, 2000.

Sotubo, Oluwatimilehin. "ECOWAS: In Need of Help in Niger?" *RAND Corporation*, August 25, 2023. https://www.rand.org/pubs/commentary/2023/08/ecowas-in-need-of-help-in-niger.html.

Sowale, Adetayo Olamide, and Ayodeji Anthony Aduloju. "Deradicalization of Repentant Boko Haram Militants: Institutional Dilemma Between the Victims and Villains in Northeast Nigeria." *Jadavpur Journal of International Relations*, Vol. 27, No. 2 (October 2023), pp. 169–183. https://doi.org/10.1177/09735984231184005.

Syrian Network for Human Rights. "On the 12th Anniversary of the Popular Uprising." *Syrian Network for Human Rights*, March 15, 2023. https://reliefweb.int/report/syrian-arab-republic/12th-anniversary-popular-uprising-total-230224-civilians-documented-dead-including-15275-who-died-due-torture-154871-arrested-andor-forcibly-disappeared-and-roughly-14-million-syrians-displaced.

Tafida, Ahmadu Abubakar, Abdullahi Liman Tukur, Elizabeth F. Adebayo, Augustine Anthony Ndaghu, J. I. Onu, and Jude A. Momodu. "Boko Haram Insurgency and Livelihood Vulnerability of Rural Households in Northern Adamawa State, Nigeria." *Research in Globalization*, Vol. 6 (January 2003), pp. 1–9. https://doi.org/10.1016/j.resglo.2023.100116.

Tayo, Teniola. "Soldiers for Rent in the Boko Haram Crisis." *Institute for Security Studies*, February 8, 2021. https://issafrica.org/iss-today/soldiers-for-rent-in-the-boko-haram-crisis.

United Nations. "Niger: Security Council Strongly Condemns 'Efforts to Unconstitutionally Change' Government." *United Nations News*, July 29, 2023. https://news.un.org/en/story/2023/07/1139272.

United Nations Security Council. "France, Germany, Portugal and United Kingdom of Great Britain and Northern Ireland: draft resolution 612." UN Doc. S/2011/612, October 4, 2011.

United Nations Security Council. "Indiscriminate aerial bombings in Aleppo: draft resolution 846." UN Doc. S/2016/846, October 8, 2016.

United Nations Security Council Resolution 2118. "In Regard to the Framework for Elimination of Syrian Chemical Weapons during the Syrian Civil War." UN Doc. S/RES/2118, September 27, 2013, adopted 7,038th meeting.

United States Department of State. "2023 Trafficking in Persons Report: Nigeria." *US Department of State*, 2023. https://www.state.gov/reports/2023-trafficking-in-persons-report/nigeria.

Yabi, Gilles. "The Niger Coup's Outsized Global Impact." *Carnegie Endowment for International Peace*, August 31, 2023. https://carnegieendowment.org/2023/08/31/niger-coup-s-outsized-global-impact-pub-90463.

CHAPTER 9

Conclusions

Introduction

This final chapter concludes on the application of Afro-communitarian ethics to foreign armed intervention. It is important to summarize the core morals and values of Afro-communitarianism, which includes direct interpretations of the way of *Ubuntu*. Efforts to maintain and restore communal relations with the notion of humans co-existing with one another are the bedrock of Afro-communitarianism. With this thought, violence is avoided and under its consequentialist version should only be used if mediation, unarmed peaceful protests, and dialogue have been exhausted or would be fruitless if attempted. If communal relations are still damaged and the only way to halt a disharmonious state of affairs is through violence and fighting will be stopped once a settlement was commenced, then violence can be permissible. It can undertake hierarchized forms from sabotage, guerrilla warfare, terrorism, and open revolution. These processes of *Ubuntu* were undertaken by Nelson Rolihlahla Mandela and the uMkhonto we Sizwe (Spear of the Nation (MK)) in South Africa to end the discriminative apartheid regime, resulting in negotiations with Frederik Willem de Klerk of the National Party and there are a variety of anti-colonial movements that have followed similar means. This includes movements against European colonialization in Guinea-Bissau, Mozambique, Angola, and India. The burden thus rests on rebutting a

D. Singh, *Applied Afro-Communitarian Ethics and Foreign Armed Intervention*, https://doi.org/10.1007/978-3-031-64110-7_9

discordant state of affairs and forming a more harmonious situation for communal relations to bring about peace.

These communal ethics can avert a conflict relapsing. This is similar to the objectives of peacebuilding, which can be defined as the action, identification, and support of structures to bolster peace to avert the potential relapse into conflict.[1] Peace can be sustainable if efforts are made to resolve violence by transforming war (and the system that advocated it) into a structured system promoting peace. Lederach focused on leadership to ensure the sustainability of peacebuilding with top, middle, and grassroots leveled leadership.[2] At the top level, senior politicians and military leaders are brought into the mediation process and peace negotiations. This is the common approach. Yet, middle leaders comprising civil society organizations and leaders in the health business, educational sectors, and respected individual and religious leaders are highly respected to undertake these peacebuilding initiatives. The grassroots approach is based on most of the people that can be included with community controls, peace commissions, and healing trauma. These initiatives that the United Nations advocate also engage with the growing role of promoting peace at the grassroots level by engaging local-level communities that are affected by conflict and insecurity.

Although Afro-communitarian ethics would not be too concerned with the role of the United Nations (UN) or their definitions on peacebuilding, other Western regional organizations such as the North Atlantic Treaty Organization (NATO) and the US in multilateral and unilateral interventions, when considering foreign armed intervention on the global scale, including the African continent, they are highly relevant or even unavoidable. The role of the world organization, NATO, or America as the global hegemonic police to respond to atrocity crimes or other injustice—that *Ubuntu* ethics aims to rebut crimes against the people if peaceful means are flawed—is inevitable when discussing foreign armed intervention. Therefore, the role of the United Nations and US will be summarized to provide its relationship with foreign armed intervention. After coverage of these Western-based organizations, the role of the African Union and

[1] Boutros Boutros-Ghali, "An Agenda for Peace: Preventive Diplomacy, Peacemaking and Peacekeeping," Report of the Secretary-General Pursuant to the Statement Adopted by the Summit Meeting of the Security Council (New York: United Nations, January 31, 1992), p. 11.

[2] John Paul Lederach, *Building Peace: Sustainable Reconciliation in Divided Societies* (Washington, DC: United States Institute of Peace Press, 1997), pp. 39, 41.

Economic Community of West African States (ECOWAS) will be evaluated in relation to foreign armed intervention, which is specifically related to conflict and humanitarian emergencies within the African continent. Subsequently, the similarities and differences of conflict resolution and just war theory with Afro-communitarianism are provided. Finally, a pragmatic approach on foreign armed interventions is provided that provides scope for Afro-communitarianism that can endorse contexts where *Ubuntu* ethics would justify violence to restore a harmonious state of affairs by rebutting violence.

The Role of the United Nations in Foreign Armed Intervention

During the Cold War, mass killings were halted singularly by states without UN Security Council authorization. This included interventions by India in the east of Pakistan to save Bengalis against Pakistani military annexation in December 1971, Vietnam in Cambodia against the Pol Pot regime in December 1978, and the Kagera War of Tanzania fighting back against Uganda's invasion headed by Idi Amin Dada Oumee in 1978–1979.[3] Therefore, permission for a humanitarian intervention of a host state can be avoided by a single state or even a coalition such as Western states with Operation Desert Storm encouraging no-fly zones and safe havens in the north of Iraq and NATO bombing Serbia with Operation Allied Force to save the Kosovar Albanian population from ethnic cleansing.

The United Nations is the highest actor honoring international legality, especially with the use of force, but prefers to avoid using armed force if a sovereign state does not want interference.[4] Due to this respect for state sovereignty and/or weak political will, the United Nations Security Council failed to prevent mass killings from the Khmer Rouge totalitarian regime led by Pol Pot in Cambodia, the civil war in Bosnia after its 1992 referendum, the 1994 Rwandan genocide and atrocities committed by the Sudanese armed forces, and Janjaweed militia in Darfur.

[3] Paul D. Williams, "The African Union: Prospects for Regional Peacekeeping after Burundi and Sudan," *Review of African Political Economy*, Vol. 33, No. 108 (June 2006), p. 172.

[4] Article 2 (4) of the Charter of the United Nations.

In the early 1990s, the United Nations Security Council did authorize military force, based on humanitarian measures, in Somalia without governmental consent due to the absence of a functioning state authority.[5] It is the inherent right of states as enshrined under traditional international law versus victim's rights that remains ambiguous within the world organization. The rule of non-intervention has, however, been challenged by the norms of the Responsibility to Protect (R2P) doctrine. Military force for humanitarian purposes is pursued by international organizations, states and coalitions of willing states and the powerful states within these entities usually have stronger political will if their *realist* geopolitical interests are at stake. If there are interests, the protection of civilians will be stronger,[6] but when interests are lacking, then the prioritization of saving human lives are circumvented.[7] NATO does not necessarily only use force against a state attacking one of its members (as collective defense) because it can use force beyond its borders (and debatably outside the 1949 Washington Treaty).[8] It did so with UN Security Council consent in Bosnia, but circumvented UN Security consent in Serbia/Kosovo.[9]

Therefore, using military coalitions require UN Security Council permission, such as Opération Turquoise led by the French in Rwanda in 1994, International Force led by Australia in East Timor in 1999, and International Security Assistance Force led by the British in Afghanistan in 2001. Yet, like NATO in Serbia/Kosovo, Australia did not consult the United Nations Security Council in the Solomon Islands Regional Assistance Mission in 2003.[10] Yet, NATO's intervention in Serbia/Kosovo rebutted ethnic cleansing that intensified during the bombing, and it resulted in a better harmonious state of affairs with the independence of

[5] Paul D. Williams, "Military Responses to Mass Killing: The African Union Mission in Sudan," *International Peacekeeping*, Vol. 13, No. 2 (2006), pp. 170–171.

[6] Michael Wesley, "Toward a Realist Ethics of Intervention," *Ethics & International Affairs*, Vol. 19, No. 2 (September 2005), p. 70.

[7] "For all the money governments spend on their militaries, it would appear that international society is still not prepared to conduct effective responses to mass killing that prioritize the needs of the victims" (Williams, "Military Responses to Mass Killing," p. 181).

[8] North Atlantic Treaty Organization, "The North Atlantic Treaty," April 4, 1949, Washington, DC.

[9] Williams, "Military Responses to Mass Killing," p. 171.

[10] Alex J. Bellamy and Paul D. Williams, "Who's Keeping the Peace? Regionalization and Contemporary Peace Operations," *International Security*, Vol. 29, No. 4 (April 2005), pp. 184–189.

Kosovo, but ethnic tensions remain between Kosovar Albanians and Serbs within Kosovo.

For liberal peace theorists, external forces intervene and engage in peace processes, but are distanced from parties fighting. This strategy is to retain neutrality and impartiality to avoid favoring one side, but it caused passivity of the United Nations in Rwanda.[11] Quite often, the United Nations deal with activity of insurgents during civil wars.[12] This challenges the preexisting state's legitimacy on its use of violence to weaken state power structures. The aim of an insurgency is ultimately to derail and overthrow a government with the use of organized armed conflict. Insurgents thus perceive their goals to govern as legitimate actors to challenge a government, and terrorist groups tend to get marginalized and fade over time.[13] This is why terrorists sometimes adapt to an insurgency for more of a following based on their ideals of legitimacy, social justice, political struggle, and self-determination to overthrow a constitutional government, e.g., as evident with the Revolutionary United Front in Sierra Leone.

When considering Afro-communitarian ethics in Rwanda, the United Nations engaged to monitor the Arusha Accords, but the foreign armed intervention was marred by a weak mandate and the withdrawal of troops during the early phases of the genocide. The United Nations thus failed to rebut violence and the genocide, and the intervention did not result in a more harmonious, and less discordant, state of affairs. In Sierra Leone, UNAMSIL attempted to rebut violence, but a hostage crisis and killing of peacekeepers required support from British forces and thus the United Nations intervention did not entirely result in a less disharmonious state of affairs.

[11] Debora Valentina Malito, "Neutral in Favor of Whom? The UN Intervention in Somali and the Somaliland Peace Process," *International Peacekeeping*, Vol. 24, No. 2 (2017), p. 281.

[12] An insurgency can be defined as a non-governmental armed and organized resistance group that attempts to amalgamate asymmetric warfare as part of tactical "political opposition" with violent means for social and/or political change (Emelda Undiandeye Ejeh and Ebunoluwa Popoola, "Amnesty as a Tool in the Deradicalization of Boko Haram Terrorists in Nigeria: A Threat to National Security," *The International Journal of Human Rights*, (December 2023), p. 6.)

[13] Mustafa Coşar Ünal, "Terrorism Versus Insurgency: A Conceptual Analysis." *Crime, Law and Social Change*, Vol. 66 (January 2016), pp. 52–54.

American Unilateralism

The chapter on Iraq exhibited that America and its allied coalition forces engaged with gradual increases of violence during two interventions from sanctions in August 1990 (argued as a form of violence because it impacted on civilians), aerial strikes, military occupation, and the Surge targeting terrorism. These forms of violence intended to rebut alleged enmity violence from Saddam Hussein. Sabotage was conducted with the destruction of Iraqi governmental and military infrastructure. The Iraqi army and Presidential Guard allied to the Ba'ath political party were attacked. Moreover, the Baghdad Presidential Palace was targeted. Debatably, an open revolution of uncontrolled violence to defeat terrorism (as the main Western goal) driving the Surge in 2007 also materialized. However, sanctions do not qualify as the initial friendly alternative of violence and thus the only friendly alternative processed by the United States was with the deployment of UN weapons inspectors and the later Duelfer Report to search for active weapons of mass destruction (WMD), weapons stockpiles and a blueprint for a future WMD program. Yet, nothing concrete was discovered but the Republican hawks of the Bush administration still presented the one percent doctrine because they wanted the invasion of Iraq and forced regime change.

There was no early exit strategy. When the United States armed forces left Iraq in December 2011, terrorism peaked once more and the region was engulfed with dispersed chapters of Islamic State. Moreover, the neocolonialist liberal statebuilding, reconstruction, Security Sector Reform (SSR), and democratization were tainted by grand corruption, which included dishonest UN officials. The United States–led intervention in Iraq did not rebut violence because Saddam Hussein was not hostile toward America, did not possess WMD, and did not have amicable relations with al-Qaeda. Iraq is in a worse state of affairs after the United States–led foreign armed intervention and the second invasion were not supported by the United Nations Security Council as the legitimate authority. Based on this postulation, the foreign armed intervention contravened both Afro-communitarianism and traditionalist ethics of war. It is only the levels of violence that had a similar structure devised by Afro-communitarianism (and Mandela with the African National Congress against the National Party's apartheid regime), but friendly alternatives were not exhausted by the United States.

Although one could argue that the United States conducted brief strikes in Iraq in 1990 as a humanitarian intervention to protect the

invasion of Kuwait and atrocities committed against the Kurdish community, Saddam Hussein did not impose a direct threat to the United States in 2003. The latter invasion was to promote American foreign policy and deceit of supposed WMD that was disproved by two reports, so the war was not justified under Afro-communitarianism because the aim was not to promote a harmonious state of affairs.

The Role of the African Union and Economic Community of West African States

After eras of slavery, colonialism, imperial exploitation, conflict, and repression, Afro-communitarianism has attempted to change the philosophy of Africa, and its ethics, to focus on togetherness, and social and communal harmony for a better state of affairs. The Organization of African Unity (OAU) respected non-intervention, which is why it remained passive with the international community in Rwanda, the Democratic Republic of Congo, and Burundi. In international relations studies, Pan-Africanism was, however, reinvigorated by the African Union replacing the Organization of African Unity in 2002. The Union became far more responsive toward African conflicts with its Peace and Security Council. This was because the African Union engaged with the philosophy of an entire inclusivity of African renaissance.[14] Norms of solidarity and the culture of African people and communities brought political rulers and elites with support and togetherness for continental political unity and concerns of external economic over-dependency, even if opposed against other Africans.[15] African political elites are thus encouraged to work together as part of harmony so African states conform with ethics and expectations of norms.[16] These ideals of collectivism on decision-making share some traits with *Ubuntu* and Afro-communitarianism.

The African Union has not directly been involved with regional intervention to deal with terrorism so states with the problems are faced to

[14] Fantu Cheru, *African Renaissance: Roadmaps to the Challenge of Globalization* (London: Zed Books, 2002).

[15] Sabelo J. Ndlovu-Gatsheni, "Pan-Africanism and the International System," in *Handbook of Africa's International Relations*, edited by Tim Murithi (New York: Routledge, 2014), pp. 26–27, pp. 21–29.

[16] Thomas Kwasi Tieku, "Theoretical Approaches to Africa's International Relations," in *Handbook of Africa's International Relations*, edited by Tim Murithi (New York: Routledge, 2014), p. 16, pp. 11–20.

challenge it themselves.[17] This has included states like Nigeria with Boko Haram and Kenya with al-Shabaab due to little practical AU continental support. Kenya perceived that the main hub of al-Shabaab's base was in Somalia, so Kenya intervened to protect and pursue their realist national security interests. Terrorists tend to take up bases in failed states because there is a less chance of foreign armed intervention.[18]

Like the Charter of the United Nations that supported the principle of non-intervention and respect for state sovereignty, the Responsibility to Protect (R2P) doctrine provided conditions for state to respect by virtue of retaining their sovereign rights of non-interference; the African Union did the same. The Union has stressed that intervention may be warranted in a fellow Member State to deter serious human rights abuses (that includes war crimes, crimes against humanity, ethnic cleansing, and genocide).[19] These atrocity crimes are also mentioned in the third pillar of R2P that can invoke a response from the United Nations Security Council.[20] The Economic Community of West African States (ECOWAS) has similarly indicated that sovereignty constitutes responsibility.[21] Like the African Union's Constitutive Act, ECOWAS revised its Treaty in 1993 to pursue peace and security for more rapid resolution and prevention of internal and international armed conflicts.[22] ECOWAS held the legitimacy to intervene within a timely manner as demonstrated in Liberia and subsequently in neighboring Sierra Leone. Therefore, the African Union and ECOWAS share norms and values with the Responsibility to Protect

[17] Kelechi Ani and Victor Ojakorotu, "Terrorism in Africa: A Comparative Evaluation of al-Shabaab and Boko Haram," *Affrika Journal of Politics, Economics and Society*, Vol. 7, No. 1 (June 2017), pp. 11–28.

[18] Joseph Makanda, "Fighting Terrorism in the Horn of Africa: The Role of Ordinary Kenyans in Kenya's Military Intervention in Somalia and the Fight against al-Shabaab," *Journal of African Union Studies*, Vol. 8, No. 1 (April 2019), p. 38.

[19] Organization of African Unity, "Constitutive Act of the African Union," July 11, 2000, Article 4 (h).

[20] United Nations Summit Outcome Document, "2005 World Summit Outcome," *United Nations General Assembly Doc.* A/RES/60/1, 60th session, October 24, 2005, paras. 138–139.

[21] Kwesi Aning and Fifi Edu-Afful, "African Agency in R2P: Interventions by African Union and ECOWAS in Mali, Côte d'Ivoire, and Libya," *International Studies Review*, Vol. 18, No. 1 (March 2016), p. 120.

[22] Economic Community of West African States, "Revised Treaty of the Economic Community of West African States," Vol. 2373, No. I-42835, July 24, 1993, Article 58 (2).

doctrine. This was evident of the African Union and ECOWAS regarding intervention in Mali.

The Relationship Between Conflict Resolution and Afro-communitarianism

Lederach contends that local ownership and agency must be part of conflict mediation to avoid the top-down externally driven liberal peace thesis only working with political and military leaders.[23] This all-inclusive community approach shares some traits and values with Afro-communitarian ethics due to the importance of humanness and the idea that humans are humans via other humans/people. Based on this postulation, when negotiating peace and attempting for a settlement to a conflict, foreign actors can encourage all levels to participate and increase public and civic confidence to the entire process. Consideration of communal needs can support working toward restoring a communal harmonious state of affairs and eliminate a discordant situation.

Differences Between Just War Theory and Afro-communitarianism

According to Aquinas, a Christian theologist, war may be initiated if it is based on a just cause, has a right intention, has support from a legitimate authority, contains a reasonable chance of victory, and avoids disproportionate civilian casualties and private property damage of the military objectives.[24] Traditionalist just war theorists, Walzer, attempts to separate the justification of waging war (*ad bellum*) with the conduct in war (*in bello*) so the war waged may be impermissible, but may be fought in battle justly.[25] However, from an Afro-communitarian perspective, such a distinction between *ad bellum* and *in bello* is not helpful because war cannot

[23] John Paul Lederach, "Of Nets, Nails, and Problems: The Folk Language of Conflict Resolution in a Central American Setting," in *Conflict Resolution: Cross-cultural Perspectives*, edited by Kevin Avruch, Peter Black and Joseph A. Scimecca (New York: Greenwood Press, 1991), p. 171.

[24] Rory Cox, "The Ethics of War up to Thomas Aquinas," in *The Oxford Handbook of Ethics of War*, edited by Seth Lazar and Helen Frowe (Oxford: Oxford University Press, 2018), p. 114.

[25] Michael Walzer, *Just and Unjust Wars: A Moral Argument with Historical Illustrations* (New York: Basic Books, 1977).

be fought justly if it is not initiated justly and vice versa. Rather than debating a legitimate authority (usually UN Security Council permission) for self-defense or protection as the just cause, Afro-communitarianism is more concerned with countering enemy violence with enmity-like violence in an attempt to reach a less discordant situation, so promoting a more harmonious state of affairs.

For Afro-communitarians, the methods of conduct in war (four stages) are aimed at rebutting violence with violence to seek a peaceful situation. From the Aquinas approach, legitimate authority is needed for *ad bellum*, and this was stressed by traditionalists supporting international law authorization from the United Nations Security Council, *e.g.* in self-defense.[26] However, Afro-communitarianism does not affirm this position because the importance does not rest on the legitimate authority and of violence advocated by the state or rebellion group (just cause). Instead, Afro-communitarians would not conform with states and human rights framed within Western stipulations of social justice (as traditionalist search for), because these factors do not permit violence to rebut hostile actions and thus seek a better harmonious state of affairs. Afro-communitarianism is concerned with going to war against an alleged wrong or evil side and punishing that side.[27]

Afro-communitarians would only comply with Aquinas and traditionalists that a war waged must contain a just cause and should be sought as a final resort. Yet, the just cause would differ for Afro-communitarians because it is to promote friendly-like relations, shared identity, and social harmony (*Ubuntu*) that traditionalists omit. War as a last resort is shared by both traditionalists and Afro-communitarians to promote non-violent alternatives but Afro-communitarians focus on what constitutes friendly or enmity means, which is undervalued by traditionalist just war theorists.

The Pragmatism of Afro-communitarianism

Quite often, foreign armed intervention holds international interests and even if they promote good and rights with sanctions and military means, they seek immediate peace (ceasefire) and externally driven statebuilding initiatives. Restoring broken community relations by considering *Ubuntu* ethics is not understood by international actors, which is the bedrock of

[26] Charter of the United Nations, 1945, Article 51.

[27] This was evident with the International Criminal Tribunal for Rwanda.

collective community values, solidarity, compassion, forgiveness, and dialogue, and thus these forms of social justice break down to fail forming a less discordant state of affairs. The situation may even be worse after foreign armed intervention, as evident in Rwanda (spreading to Burundi and the Democratic Republic of Congo) and Iraq (forming further sectarian violence and leaving a vacuum for the emergence of Islamic State after full American troop withdrawal).

It is tempting to promote the use of NATO and the United States to engage in humanitarian interventions to save lives because they have the aerial power to engage in sabotage that mirrors military necessity, but this approach has proved too robust in the contexts of Serbia/Kosovo and Iraq, respectively, resulting in high civilian casualties. For these reasons, international, regional, and unilateral foreign armed interventions can learn from Afro-communitarianism to focus more on restoring communal relations and only engaging in the necessary forms of phased violence and ceasing it once a more harmonious, and less discordant, state of affairs has been reached. This African moral philosophy would also benefit the geopolitical interests of intervening states because it would avoid protracted incursions that cost a lot of financial and military resources. It would also result in rethinking top-down externally driven statebuilding and post-conflict reconstruction initiatives so that middle and community actors can also be consulted in peace and security crises. If taking these interests into consideration, Afro-communitarian ethics can help international interventionist efforts in political stalemates (namely, Syria) and contexts that deserve a foreign armed intervention (such as northeast Nigeria) to rebut enmity behavior with permissible violence as a last resort to foster a better harmonious state of affairs to rid of terrorism that is plaguing the Middle East and West Africa.

Although Afro-communitarianism would be against the interests of individual states or international organizations and instead prefer working on repairing severed communal relations, any form of intervention to rebut violence cannot rid of geopolitical realities in contemporary society. A pragmatic argument exhibits that compliance with Afro-communitarianism can be reached with interim interests based on external geopolitical quest. This was evident with the United States national security and counterinsurgency strategy in both Afghanistan and Iraq branded as the war on terror.[28] Moreover, NATO's intervention in Kosovo contained geopolitical ambitions for stability and European Union Enlargement Policy.[29] Hence, realist interests are part of subordinate Afro-communitarian interests resting on a less discordant state of affairs by rebutting enmity-behavior with violence. An intervention may not always be permissible under authorization of the United Nations Security Council to comply with international law (as in Serbia/Kosovo and Iraq).[30] There are thus notable faults with international law and just war theory (permission from a legitimate authority *jus ad bellum* to comply with this example here).

However, Afro-communitarianism can be tried as ethics globally as an alternative consequentialist measure of armed force (because as history has presented, hegemons will always engage in armed interventions to pursue their geopolitical interests as the ends—even if for alleged humanitarian means). Unlike traditional just war theory, the *Ubuntu* ethics resting on humanness, belonging, and presenting the community as the utmost good can promote a better state of harmonious affairs within an intervened state. As shown in the African contexts, the African Union and ECOWAS can monitor and support ceasefire and peacekeeping processes to assist a host government or situation of civil war by supporting national armed forces fight factional militias and violent extremists to work toward a more harmonious state of affairs. It will be noted that in most of these contexts concerning African conflicts that are initially regionally supported, the legitimate authority is often the United Nations that takes over African missions. Despite this arrangement, the intervening states can take *jus ad bellum* seriously with conflict transformation, by avoiding victor's justice (as in the former Yugoslavia, Rwanda, and Sierra Leone) and rapid exclusionary democratization in war-torn states (namely, Iraq).

The lessons learned of failed intervention in Iraq can promote applied Afro-communitarian ethics in future foreign armed intervention. Efforts from US unilateralism in Iraq and their withdrawal in late 2011 have been

[28] Tom Lansford, *9/11 and the Wars in Afghanistan and Iraq: A Chronology and Reference Guide* (Santa Barbara, CA: ABC-CLIO, 2012), p. xi.

[29] Zoltan Barany and Robert Rauchhaus, "Explaining NATO's Resilience: Is International Relations Theory Useful?" *Contemporary Security Policy*, 32, no. 2 (2011), pp. 286, 289, 293–294.

[30] David M. Malone and Karin Wermester, "Boom and Bust? The Changing Nature of UN Peacekeeping," *International Peacekeeping*, Vol. 7, No. 4 (2000), p. 48; Peterson, "Did Iraq Ever Become a Just War?"

undermined by the emergence of terrorist groups and retaliatory fighting. Yet, peaceful means should have been exhausted with the Saddam Hussein regime to promote a less discordant state of affairs to comply with the initial Afro-communitarian deontological perspective. Notwithstanding robust intervention as part of the war on terror to rebut terrorism and contain Iran with enmity-like violence, it has intensified transnational terrorism, namely fragments of Islamic State, and many insurgents in sub-Saharan Africa have retained their relationships with al-Qaeda. Afro-communitarian ethics can thus better interrogate efforts to foster peaceful relationships between once warring parties and bring about a better harmonious state of affairs that can warrant phased enmity-like violence once diplomacy, monitoring, and peace agreements have been exhausted.

References

Ani, Kelechi, and Victor Ojakorotu. "Terrorism in Africa: A Comparative Evaluation of al-Shabaab and Boko Haram." *Affrika Journal of Politics, Economics and Society*, Vol. 7, No. 1 (June 2017), pp. 11–28.

Aning, Kwesi, and Fifi Edu-Afful. "African Agency in R2P: Interventions by African Union and ECOWAS in Mali, Côte d'Ivoire, and Libya." *International Studies Review*, Vol. 18, No. 1 (March 2016), pp. 120–133. https://doi.org/10.1093/isr/viv017.

Barany, Zoltan, and Robert Rauchhaus. "Explaining NATO's Resilience: Is International Relations Theory Useful?" *Contemporary Security Policy*, Vol. 32, No. 2 (August 2011), pp. 286–307. https://doi.org/10.1080/13523260.2011.590355.

Bellamy, Alex J., and Paul D. Williams. "Who's Keeping the Peace? Regionalization and Contemporary Peace Operations." *International Security*, Vol. 29, No. 4 (April 2005), pp. 184–189. https://doi.org/10.1162/isec.2005.29.4.157.

Boutros-Ghali, Boutros. "An Agenda for Peace: Preventive Diplomacy, Peacemaking and Peacekeeping." Report of the Secretary-General Pursuant to the Statement Adopted by the Summit Meeting of the Security Council. New York: United Nations, January 31, 1992.

Cheru, Fantu. *African Renaissance: Roadmaps to the Challenge of Globalization*. London: Zed Books, 2002.

Cox, Rory. "The Ethics of War up to Thomas Aquinas." In *The Oxford Handbook of Ethics of War*, edited by Seth Lazar and Helen Frowe, pp. 99–121. Oxford: Oxford University Press, 2018.

Economic Community of West African States. "Revised Treaty of the Economic Community of West African States." Vol. 2373, No. I-42835, July 24, 1993, Article 58 (2).

Ejeh, Emelda Undiandeye, and Ebunoluwa Popoola. "Amnesty as a Tool in the Deradicalization of Boko Haram Terrorists in Nigeria: A Threat to National Security." *The International Journal of Human Rights* (December 2023), pp. 1–24. https://doi.org/10.1080/13642987.2023.2297313.

Lansford, Tom. *9/11 and the Wars in Afghanistan and Iraq: A Chronology and Reference Guide*. Santa Barbara, CA: ABC-CLIO, 2012.

Lederach, John Paul. "Of Nets, Nails, and Problems: The Folk Language of Conflict Resolution in a Central American Setting." In *Conflict Resolution: Cross-cultural Perspectives*, edited by Kevin Avruch, Peter Black and Joseph A. Scimecca, pp. 165–186. New York: Greenwood Press, 1991.

Lederach, John Paul. *Building Peace: Sustainable Reconciliation in Divided Societies*. Washington, DC: United States Institute of Peace Press, 1997.

Makanda, Joseph. "Fighting Terrorism in the Horn of Africa: The Role of Ordinary Kenyans in Kenya's Military Intervention in Somalia and the Fight against al-Shabaab." *Journal of African Union Studies*, Vol. 8, No. 1 (April 2019), pp. 33–49. https://doi.org/10.31920/2050-4306/2019/v8n1a2.

Malone, David M., and Karin Wermester. "Boom and Bust? The Changing Nature of UN Peacekeeping." *International Peacekeeping*, Vol. 7, No. 4 (2000), pp. 37–54. https://doi.org/10.1080/13533310008413862.

Malito, Debora Valentina. "Neutral in Favor of Whom? The UN Intervention in Somali and the Somaliland Peace Process." *International Peacekeeping*, Vol. 24, No. 2 (2017), pp. 280–303. https://doi.org/10.1080/13533312.2016.1250626.

Ndlovu-Gatsheni, Sabelo J. "Pan-Africanism and the International System." In *Handbook of Africa's International Relations*, edited by Tim Murithi, pp. 21–29. New York: Routledge, 2014.

North Atlantic Treaty Organization. "The North Atlantic Treaty." April 4, 1949, Washington, DC: NATO. https://www.nato.int/cps/en/natohq/official_texts_17120.htm.

Organization of African Unity. "Constitutive Act of the African Union." July 11, 2000, Article 4 (h). https://au.int/sites/default/files/pages/34873-file-constitutiveact_en.pdf.

Peterson, Matt. "Did Iraq Ever Become a Just War? As Contours Evolved, the Morality of Fighting Did Too." *The Atlantic*, March 24, 2018. https://www.theatlantic.com/international/archive/2018/03/iraq-war-ethics/556448/.

Tieku, Thomas Kwasi. "Theoretical Approaches to Africa's International Relations." In *Handbook of Africa's International Relations*, edited by Tim Murithi, pp. 11–20. New York: Routledge, 2014.

Ünal, Mustafa Coşar. "Terrorism Versus Insurgency: A Conceptual Analysis." *Crime, Law and Social Change*, Vol. 66 (January 2016), pp. 21–57. https://doi.org/10.1007/s10611-015-9601-7.

United Nations. *Charter of the United Nations.* 1 United Nations Treaty Series XVI, October 24, 1945.

United Nations Summit Outcome Document. "2005 World Summit Outcome." *United Nations General Assembly Doc.* A/RES/60/1, 60th session, October 24, 2005.

Walzer, Michael. *Just and Unjust Wars: A Moral Argument with Historical Illustrations.* New York: Basic Books, 1977.

Wesley, Michael. "Toward a Realist Ethics of Intervention." *Ethics & International Affairs*, Vol. 19, No. 2 (September 2005), pp. 55–72. https://doi.org/10.1111/j.1747-7093.2005.tb00500.x.

Williams, Paul D. "Military Responses to Mass Killing: The African Union Mission in Sudan." *International Peacekeeping*, Vol. 13, No. 2 (2006), pp. 168–183. https://doi.org/10.1080/13533310500436565.

Index[1]

[1] Note: Page numbers followed by 'n' refer to notes.

D. Singh, *Applied Afro-Communitarian Ethics and Foreign Armed Intervention*, https://doi.org/10.1007/978-3-031-64110-7

GPSR Compliance
The European Union's (EU) General Product Safety Regulation (GPSR) is a set of rules that requires consumer products to be safe and our obligations to ensure this.

If you have any concerns about our products, you can contact us on

ProductSafety@springernature.com

In case Publisher is established outside the EU, the EU authorized representative is:

Springer Nature Customer Service Center GmbH
Europaplatz 3
69115 Heidelberg, Germany

www.ingramcontent.com/pod-product-compliance
Lightning Source LLC
Chambersburg PA
CBHW071321230926
51849CB00002B/281

* 9 7 8 3 0 3 1 6 4 1 0 9 1 *